Cumulative Childhood Harm in Family Law and Criminal Justice Systems

India Bryce
https://orcid.org/0000-0002-3616-8003
University of Southern Queensland, Australia

Simone Collier
https://orcid.org/0009-0008-3658-8535
University of Southern Queensland, Australia

IGI Global
Scientific Publishing
Publishing Tomorrow's Research Today

Vice President of Editorial Melissa Wagner
Director of Acquisitions Mikaela Felty
Director of Book Development Jocelynn Hessler
Production Manager Mike Brehm
Cover Design Jose Rosado

Published in the United States of America by
IGI Global Scientific Publishing
701 East Chocolate Avenue
Hershey, PA, 17033, USA
Tel: 717-533-8845 | Fax: 717-533-7115
Website: https://www.igi-global.com E-mail: cust@igi-global.com

Library of Congress Cataloging-in-Publication Data

Names: Bryce, India editor | Collier, Simone, 1971- editor
Title: Cumulative childhood harm in family law and criminal justice systems / edited by India Bryce and Simone Collier.
Description: Hershey : IGI Global Scientific Publishing, 2026. | Includes bibliographical references and index. | Summary: "This book explores how repeated adverse experiences in childhood are shaped by interactions with family law and criminal justice systems. It examines whether legal responses protect children from harm or contribute to ongoing trauma, disadvantage, and system involvement"-- Provided by publisher.
Identifiers: LCCN 2026026462 (print) | LCCN 2026026463 (ebook) | ISBN 9798337395241 hardcover | ISBN 9798337395258 paperback | ISBN 9798337395265 ebook
Subjects: LCSH: Abused children--Legal status, laws, etc. | Abused children--Services for--Law and legislation | Child abuse--Law and legislation | Child sexual abuse--Law and legislation | Child sex offenders--Psychological aspects | Juvenile delinquency | Juvenile justice, Administration of | Parent and child (Law) | Domestic relations
Classification: LCC K1965 .C86 2026 (print) | LCC K1965 (ebook)
LC record available at https://lccn.loc.gov/2026026462
LC ebook record available at https://lccn.loc.gov/2026026463

British Cataloguing in Publication Data
A Cataloguing in Publication record for this book is available from the British Library.

Table of Contents

Detailed Table of Contents

This chapter discusses the lives of justice-involved youth and contrasts that with the ways in which offending youth are portrayed in the media and by politicians. The chapter then examines the impact of the accumulation of ACEs, and their impact on violent and repeat offending, followed by a discussion about ways in which Attachment Theory can explain this behaviour. The chapter concludes with policy and practice implications for youth justice agencies, based on an examination of three key questions, which identify what governments could do to address populist narratives, the actions needed by youth justice agencies needed to focus on ACEs, and concl;udes with addressing ACEs through a Trauma-Informed Care (TIC) approach.

This chapter examines Adverse Childhood Experiences (ACEs) within Singapore's correctional system, focussing specifically on youth and women offenders, who are two distinct populations with a higher number of ACEs as compared to the general population. These populations demonstrate trauma profiles and rehabilitation needs that align with findings in international literature, warranting targeted intervention approaches. Understanding the needs of the two specialised populations, Singapore Prison Service adopts a tailored approach to address the responsivity factor in rehabilitation. Through analysis of international research and local evidence, including the implementation of the T-care framework by SPS, we explore how trauma-informed practices can enhance rehabilitation outcomes for these vulnerable populations.

The disadvantage and adversity that predisposes a child to abuse and neglect may in fact be just as damaging to lifespan development and wellbeing as the abuse itself. Essentially, risk factors, victimization experiences and victimization types are significantly more predictive and more valuable, in research and in practice, when considered cumulatively. With regard to pathways to coercive recruitment, particularly into criminal activity (Gangs, violent extremism, smuggling and drug-muling), the research regarding 'cross over kids' highlights the importance of cumulative harm in explaining the outcomes observed among crossover children (Bromfield & Miller, 2012). These experiences, in turn, can result in young people turning to gangs and crime as a means of gaining love, respect and power.

This chapter will discuss the incidence of adverse childhood experiences amongst adult serial killers and how the cycle of violence impacts on future violent criminal behaviour. By considering the Trauma-Control Model (Hickey, 1997), issues relating to the ability to cope with the accumulation of adverse childhood trauma and the response undertaken through serial homicide, can help to identify potential triggers in individuals at higher risk of engaging in this behaviour and develop effective interventions to prevent the incidence of serial homicide.

Individuals who experience homicide often have backgrounds marked by extensive childhood adversity—such as abuse, neglect, and household dysfunction—which undermines psychological resilience and support. The CDC-Kaiser ACE Scale provides a tool for quantifying such early trauma, yet research more frequently explores its links to offending than to victimisation. This chapter addresses the gap by reviewing evidence that higher ACE scores elevate the risk of homicide victimisation, examining how overlapping adversities foster psychological vulnerabilities and risky behaviours. Highlighting gradient effects and the conditional vulnerability model, the chapter offers insights into pathways from childhood trauma to fatal outcomes, identifying high-risk populations and discussing crucial implications for prevention, intervention, and policy.

Cumulative harm refers to the impact of several adverse experiences, on an individual's well-being. Within the family law system in Australia, although the impact of high conflict separation has attracted research, cumulative harm in circumstances where

Preface

INTRODUCTION

Since its public recognition in 1962, following the seminal work of Kempe and colleagues, child maltreatment has been acknowledged in both research and practice as occurring not only in isolated incidents, but more commonly as repeated and enduring experiences across childhood. Subsequent research has made clear that for many children, maltreatment is not a singular event, but part of a prolonged pattern of adversity. As Bromfield and Higgins observed, the majority of children who experience maltreatment endure multiple incidents over extended periods of time. This recognition has fundamentally reshaped how harm to children is understood, assessed, and addressed within family law and criminal justice systems.

The landmark Adverse Childhood Experiences (ACEs) Study further transformed the field by demonstrating strong correlations between adverse childhood experiences and later medical, psychological, and behavioral difficulties. Critically, the study showed that the impact of adversity is dose-related: the greater the number of adverse experiences a child endures, the more profound the consequences in adulthood. This accumulating impact has come to be known as *cumulative harm*, a concept that captures not only the presence of multiple harms, but their compounding and interrelated effects over time.

Cumulative harm has been defined as a series or pattern of harmful events and experiences—historical, ongoing, or both—in which risk factors are often multiple, interconnected, and co-existing during critical developmental periods. Gilmore's comparison of cumulative harm to global warming is particularly apt: it is a complex, often incremental process, driven by human and environmental factors, and one that can be difficult to detect until its effects are profound and entrenched.

This edited volume traces the intellectual and practice-based journey from early understandings of child maltreatment to contemporary conceptualizations of cumulative harm, chronic maltreatment, and re-victimization. The chapters collectively examine how accumulated adversity shapes individuals across the lifespan—behaviorally, physically, and psychologically—while also attending to the ways in which gender, culture, family law conflict, and domestic violence intersect with and exacerbate harm. Contributors explore how systems intended to protect children may, at times, struggle to adequately recognize or respond to chronic and cumulative patterns of victimization, particularly within legal and justice contexts.

Importantly, this book does not stop at description or critique. It also outlines trauma-informed prevention and intervention approaches that offer pathways toward more effective, compassionate, and developmentally informed responses to cumulative harm. These approaches are essential for practitioners, policymakers, and researchers seeking to disrupt cycles of adversity and promote healing and resilience.

This volume is unique in its explicit and comprehensive focus on the chronicity of maltreatment and victimization, drawing on a diverse range of international and multidisciplinary perspectives. It brings together theoretical frameworks and the latest empirical research to deepen understanding of accumulated adversity and its implications for best practice in child protection, family law, and criminal justice systems. Written for professionals and researchers alike, this book aims to advance both knowledge and practice, fostering more nuanced, systemic, and humane responses to cumulative childhood harm.

ORGANIZATION OF THE BOOK

Chapter 1, introduces the field of Developmental and Life-Course Victimology, which studies victimization as a dynamic process shaped by ecological and transactional dimensions. It explores the "Cycle of Violence" and intergenerational transmission, emphasizing the need to distinguish between findings of general effects versus subtype-specific mechanisms of continuity. The Chapter identifies key components such as victimization propensity, developmental cascades, and post-traumatic growth, which explain why some trajectories persist while others break the cycle. It calls for prospective longitudinal studies to better understand the permutation from victim to perpetrator and to develop more effective de-victimization interventions.

In **Chapter 2,** Authors focus on the impact of parental incarceration on children, who are often considered the "forgotten victims" of crime. It details how parental imprisonment compounds existing adversities like poverty and abuse, acting as a criminogenic risk factor that fuels intergenerational cycles of criminalization. The Chapter examines sentencing practices in South Australia, noting that while judicial officers have considerable discretion, the human rights of children are rarely explicitly considered in court. It advocates for trauma-informed, child-centric sentencing responses to break intergenerational cycles and mitigate the long-term developmental trauma experienced by these children.

Chapter 3 explores the cumulative impact of Adverse Childhood Experiences (ACEs) on justice-involved youth, highlighting that over half of these individuals experience more than one ACE. It contrasts the reality of structural disadvantage—such as poverty and single-parent households—with the punitive populist narratives often promoted by media and politicians. The Chapter details how trauma disrupts brain development, leading to hypervigilance and impaired decision-making that often manifests as violent or repeat offending. It suggests that youth-justice agencies should adopt Trauma-Informed Care (TIC) and developmental crime prevention strategies rather than relying on short-term, punitive "tough-on-crime" measures.

In **Chapter 4**, Authors from Singapore Prison Service document the high prevalence of ACEs in Singapore's correctional populations, particularly among youth and women offenders, where rates exceed 90% and 80% respectively. The Chapter highlights how cumulative childhood adversity increases recidivism risks and serves as a significant barrier to rehabilitation by affecting emotional regulation and the agency to desist. It details the adoption of the "T-care" framework by the Singapore Prison Service, a structured trauma-informed engagement model designed for non-clinical staff to manage stress reactions. Results from T-care pilots indicate improvements in self-regulation for offenders and enhanced empathy and understanding among correctional officers.

In **Chapter 5**, the author explores the disadvantage and adversity that predisposes a child to abuse and neglect may in fact be just as damaging to lifespan development and wellbeing as the abuse itself. Essentially, risk factors, victimization experiences and victimization types are significantly more predictive and more valuable, in research and in practice, when considered cumulatively. With regard to pathways to coercive recruitment, particularly into criminal activity (Gangs, violent extremism, smuggling and drug-muling), the research regarding 'cross over kids' highlights the importance of cumulative harm in explaining the outcomes observed among crossover children (Bromfield & Miller, 2012). These experiences, in turn, can result in young people turning to gangs and crime as a means of gaining love, respect and power.

Chapter 6 examines the link between profound childhood adversity and the development of serial homicide offenders, utilizing Hickey's Trauma-Control Model. It reports that serial killers exhibit significantly higher rates of physical, sexual, and psychological abuse compared to the general population. Unresolved trauma acts as a catalyst for violent fantasies, which serve as a maladaptive coping mechanism to exert a sense of control that is absent in real life.

In **Chapter 7**, the Author shifts the focus from perpetrators to victims, using conditional vulnerability theory to explain how cumulative childhood adversity increases the risk of homicide victimization. It argues that repeated exposure to violence in childhood disrupts neurodevelopment and attachment, leading to impaired risk assessment and involvement in high-risk social networks. The Chapter notes intersectional disparities, with women and people of colour experiencing the most complex patterns of trauma and higher rates of lethal victimization. It advocates for multidisciplinary prevention that integrates public health and law enforcement to bolster protective factors like supportive adult relationship.

Chapter 8 introduces cumulative harm as a critical construct in family law, moving beyond the "event model" of isolated incidents. It identifies various "harm touch points" children face during high-conflict separations, including parental alienation, substance misuse, and exposure to forensic processes. The Chapter critiques the adversarial nature of the legal system, which often pits parents against each other and leaves children "in the middle" for years. It advocates for better integration of social science knowledge to measure the lifelong consequences of cumulative harm and for therapeutically supported interventions like reunification therapy.

In **Chapter 9** the Author analyses the legal concept of "unacceptable risk" in Australian family law, arguing it should be understood as an assessment of cumulative risk. It discusses the shift toward "promoting safety" as a pivotal factor under recent legislative amendments, emphasizing that safety is a fluid, context-dependent concept. The Chapter points out that while the law traditionally focuses on "big harms" like sexual abuse, it often struggles to account for the accumulation of "little risks" like chronic conflict or emotional neglect. It suggests that a multidisciplinary approach involving court experts is necessary to identify patterns of concern that collectively become intolerable for a child's wellbeing.

ACKNOWLEDGMENT

There is no book without authors, so we acknowledge first and foremost the contributions of our authors, it takes a significant effort to contribute to a book such as this and their expertise, insight, creativity, and generosity is so very appreciated, and we thank them most sincerely. We thank our publisher, IGI Global for their support, guidance patience, and for taking a chance on this passion project. They may never know the impact they have had at a grassroots level, for vulnerable families but enabling us to create this work, for practitioners to read and consume, in order to improve their service delivery.

We thank our families and loved ones who have taken this journey alongside us, and our colleagues, which have reviewed, proofread and given their insights to this book and to the perspectives contained within.

Finally, we thank you, our readers. Without those who are willing to read our words and consider our thoughts and perspectives, the important research, theory and lived experiences contained in this volume cannot continue to grow, to be implemented, to be challenged, and to continue to gain the momentum needed to truly service our vulnerable children and families in child protection practice.

CONCLUSION

As editors of this volume, we return to the central premise that has guided its development: cumulative childhood harm is not an aberration at the margins of family law and criminal justice systems, but a pervasive and enduring reality for many children and families who come into contact with them. The chapters in this book collectively demonstrate that harm is most often experienced not as a single, discrete event, but as an accumulation of adversities that intersect, compound, and reverberate across development and into adulthood. Recognising this reality requires a fundamental shift in how professionals conceptualise risk, responsibility, and response.

Across diverse jurisdictions and disciplines, the contributors have shown how cumulative harm is shaped by chronic maltreatment, repeated exposure to violence, systemic inequities, and, at times, institutional responses that are ill-equipped to address complexity over time. The impact of these experiences is evident in physical health, mental health, behaviour, relationships, and life trajectories. Importantly, this volume highlights that cumulative harm does not affect all children in the same way; gender, culture, socio-economic context, family law conflict, and domestic violence profoundly influence both exposure to harm and access to protection and healing.

A consistent theme throughout the book is the need for systems to move beyond episodic, incident-based decision-making. Family law and criminal justice responses that focus narrowly on isolated events risk obscuring the broader patterns of adversity that place children at ongoing risk. Contributors call for greater integration of trauma-informed, developmentally attuned, and culturally responsive frameworks that can better capture the lived realities of children experiencing chronic harm. Such approaches demand collaboration across disciplines and systems, as well as a willingness to challenge entrenched practices and assumptions.

At the same time, this volume underscores the importance of hope and possibility. By deepening our understanding of cumulative harm, we are better positioned to intervene earlier, respond more effectively, and prevent the escalation of adversity across the lifespan. The research, theory, and practice insights presented here offer a foundation for more nuanced assessment, more humane decision-making, and more effective prevention and intervention strategies.

In bringing this book to completion, our intention has been to provide a resource that advances scholarship while remaining grounded in the realities of practice.

We hope it will inform policy, guide practitioners, and inspire further research that continues to refine how cumulative childhood harm is understood and addressed. Ultimately, the challenge before us is not simply to recognise cumulative harm, but to ensure that our systems respond in ways that protect children, promote healing, and interrupt the intergenerational transmission of adversity.

Chapter 1
Beyond the Cycle and the Intergenerational Transmission of Violence:
A Developmental and Life-Course Victimology to Understand Trajectories in Victimization and Offending

Oscar Ivan Cortes-Perez
https://orcid.org/0000-0002-2439-8266
Autonomous University of San Luis Potosi, Mexico

ABSTRACT

The purpose of this chapter is to formally introduce the field of Developmental and Life Course Victimology and its areas of application, understood as a trans-disciplinary area within Victimology to study and conceive, in the first instance, victimization as an active and dynamic process with ecological, intersectional, and transactional dimensions that allows us to account for the mechanisms of continuity and persistance (polyvictimization and/or revictimization), alternative trajectories to victimization cycles (e.g., transition to perpetration of violence), but also points of change (growth and devictimization).

INTRODUCTION

> *"But what if we could better understand stability and change in victimization and its consequences over time? If we could, perhaps we would be in a better place*

DOI: 10.4018/979-8-3373-9524-1.ch001

to develop and guide effective policies and support interventions for victims. Yet such an understanding would first require organizing the knowledge about what we know about the nature of victimization as we live our lives through time. In essence, what it seems we might need is a life-course theory of victimization."
-Jillian J. Turanovic, 2018-

Over the years, areas such as criminology (developmental and life-course) have made it possible to identify the dynamics between risk factors and strengthening factors (both promotive and protective) that contribute to the perpetration of violence through the study of people's life contexts at different stages of their lives. In this way, it has been possible to demonstrate how particular Adverse Childhood Experiences (ACEs), more specifically, the experience of direct violence (as a victim or perpetrator) or indirect violence (as a witness) produce cumulative and progressive effects that include the perception of the violence experienced and the motivation, ideation, and perpetration of violence in later stages throughout life.

Hence, the emergence of concepts such as the Cycle of Violence and Intergenerational Transmission of Violence has enabled a diachronic understanding of violence, which even extends to subsequent generations. However, the literature itself has recognized the need to understand violence not only from the mechanisms (of development) that directly lead to the perpetration of violence itself, but also from the mechanisms of victimization (including polyvictimization) and the cumulative and sequential effects and impacts in order to account for those trajectories that are not limited exclusively to the identification and explanation of mechanisms of perpetration, but also to prolonged and chronic forms of victimization (revictimization and polyvictimization), transitions and/or permutations from experiences of victimization to subsequent experiences of perpetration, but also importantly, the turning points of change such as devictimization and growth as a social agency.

The purpose of this chapter is to formally introduce the field of Developmental and Life Course Victimology and its areas of application, understood as a transdisciplinary area within Victimology to study and conceive, in the first instance, victimization as an active and dynamic process with ecological, intersectional, and transactional dimensions that allows us to account for the mechanisms of continuity and persistence (polyvictimization and/or revictimization), alternative trajectories to victimization cycles (e.g., transition to perpetration of violence), but also points of change (growth and devictimization).

This chapter, therefore, represents an exploratory conceptual review that allows us to identify theoretical and integrative relationships for a better understanding, study, and analysis of victimization processes in a more dynamic and continuous approach, as well as the role of conceptual models on developmental trajectories that allow us to identify relevant areas for future research on processes of continuity, change, or even the overlap from victim to perpetrator. This review therefore considers theoretical contributions from areas of knowledge within criminology, victimology, sociology, and psychology related to research on victimization processes, intergenerational transmission of violence, as well as developmental and life course perspectives. This chapter will begin by providing a description of one of the areas that gave rise to the study of violence in a more dynamic and continuous sense: the intergenerational processes of violence perpetration.

THE CYCLE OF VIOLENCE AND THE INTERGENERATIONAL TRANSMISSION OF VIOLENCE: SCOPE AND LIMITATIONS

In the mid-20th century, the contexts of violence experienced from an early age were seen in the imaginary collective as a 'seed' that would eventually germinate and produce future offenders, in other words, those who experienced some form of abuse (usually physical or sexual) during childhood would eventually become offenders in subsequent stages of development (mainly during adolescence and early adulthood) (Turanovic & Pratt, 2024; Widom & Osborn, 2021; Widom, 2017; Widom & Wilson, 2015). Although there was insufficient empirical research on such causal claims, it was in the late 1980s, with the seminal work of Cathy Spatz Widom, that evidence began to emerge demonstrating the existence, albeit not in a predestinating and inescapable manner, of the links between childhood victimization and the perpetration of violence in later stages, thus referring to the *Cycle of Violence* (Turanovic & Pratt, 2024; Widom & Osborn, 2021; Widom, 2017) and the *Intergenerational Transmission of Violence* (Widom, 2017; Widom & Wilson, 2015).

The Cycle of Violence

The *Cycle of Violence* was initially referred to as the process by which an infant who experiences physical abuse predicts subsequent involvement in perpetrating violence in adolescence or adulthood (Turanovic & Pratt, 2024; Widom & Osborn, 2021; Widom, 2017). However, to date, any form of violence (including neglect) has been considered both individually and cumulatively and multiply (e.g., polyvictimization) within conceptualization and research, showing correlational evidence of victimization in early stages of development as a risk factor for the ideation, motivation, and eventual perpetration of violence (see Pereda & Guerra, 2025; Bryce, 2025; Berzenski & Yates, 2022; Eisner et al., 2021; Widom & Osborn, 2021; Papalia et al., 2020; Farrington & Malvaso, 2019; Widom, 2017).

Some of the theoretical perspectives that have helped provide an understanding of the phenomenon can be found within approaches to social cognition, social learning, and differential association (see Boxall, 2025; Bryce & Schaffer, 2024b;

Cortes-Perez, 2024a; Bartol & Bartol, 2021; Lyon & Welsh, 2017; Widom & Wilson, 2015), as well as those extensions that include constructs such as coercion as a form of interaction and transmission of violence (Cortes-Perez, 2024a; Bartol & Bartol, 2021; Lyon & Welsh, 2017; Patterson, 2016; Vander Ven & Colvin, 2012), and other more critical theories (Boxall, 2025; Bryce & Schaffer, 2024b). Nevertheless, the reality is that the mechanisms by which these elements interact and their sequence within post-victimization contexts that ultimately produce possible trajectories toward perpetration are not yet fully understood.

The Intergenerational Transmission of Violence

On the other hand, other approaches have emerged that are not limited to the individualizing processes of perpetrating violence addressed by the Cycle of Violence, but also to future social interactions in an intergenerational or transgenerational way. For example, do some people who are victimized at an early age grow up and end up perpetrating violence against their children later in life? This is one of the questions that led to the idea of how experiences of victimization could be replicated from one generation to another, mainly in contexts of child abuse.

Although the concepts of the Cycle of Violence and Intergenerational Transmission are used in conjunction and sometimes interchangeably in research, the author of this chapter considers both phenomena to be processes usually interconnected by two elements, which in turn can be differentiated from each other. On the one hand, there is the process of permutation or overlap from victim to perpetrator of violence (Cycle of Violence). On the other hand, there is the transmission of definitions of violence (general or specific, supportive or rejecting, as well as those definitions of moral neutralization) from one generation to another, usually within the family environment. However, a conceptual expansion that could include intergenerational and transgenerational transmission within a specific subculture or community environment (school, neighborhood, subcultures, etc.) is considered opportune.

Notwithstanding that current research has identified evidence of the transmission of violence from one generation to the next, there are variations in terms of frequency, modality, and the population that perpetrates it (Boxall et al., 2025; Berzenski & Yates, 2022; Widom & Osborn, 2021; Farrington & Malvaso, 2019; Widom, 2017; Widom & Wilson, 2015). Therefore, intergenerational transmission involves more complex mechanisms than was previously believed (Widom, 2017; Widom & Wilson, 2015), and there is still a lack of clarity regarding its characteristics and interaction processes. As such, some questions that remain unanswered concern how the cycle of violence and the intergenerational transmission of violence are affected by the duration, intensity, victim-perpetrator relationship, the specific form(s) of abuse, the age or stage of development at which victimization occurs, and how the social context in which childhood abuse occurs can lead to or mitigate subsequent negative consequences (Turanovic & Pratt, 2024; Berzenski & Yates, 2022; Widom, 2022; Olomi et al., 2020; Papalia et al., 2020).

Consequently, when discussing Intergenerational Transmission of Violence, specifically child abuse, authors such as Berzenski and Yates (2022) have emphasized the need to differentiate between findings and mechanisms of continuity with general effects and those with specific effects, depending on the type of violence under analysis, rather than a single, generic, one-dimensional category.

We must distinguish research studies that represent findings specific to one maltreatment subtype (usually CPA [Child Physical Abuse]) from those that can be generalized across multiple maltreatment subtypes, just as it is equally important to integrate research on individual maltreatment subtypes beyond CPA and CSA [Child Sexual Abuse] into this corpus of work.

Second, greater specificity regarding the specific types of maltreatment under study may help to interpret extant variability in published rates of IGTM [Intergenerational Transmission of Maltreatment] across studies and samples. Confounding single and multiple maltreatment experiences may contribute to confusion when trying to compare IGTM rates [...]

Third, type-specific investigation may reveal important information about mechanisms by which specific maltreatment experiences are transmitted. Certain types of maltreatment may be more vulnerable to particular mechanisms of transmission than others and/or specific mechanisms may operate differently in the context of particular maltreatment subtypes. (Berzenski & Yates, 2022, p. 355)

We propose that focusing on subtype specificity in patterns of IGTM will reveal that, just as subtypes of maltreatment have different correlates and consequences, the continuity of these experiences varies across generations as well [...] We advocate for a more nuanced focus on subtype-specific versus subtype-general processes to achieve a multidimensional model of IGTM that accounts for both continuity and discontinuity in form and function across generations. (Berzenski & Yates, 2022, p. 354).

In order to provide a multidimensional and in-depth approach to the processes of continuity and change, Berzenski and Yates (2022) incorporate the concept of *Homotypic Continuity* (a form of abuse is perpetrated and subsequently replicated in the same way towards the subsequent generation), *Heterotypic Continuity* (a form of abuse is exercised but changes its form of transmission to another form of abuse; e.g., a context of neglect that predicts psychological abuse in the subsequent generation), and *Undifferentiated Continuity* (some forms of abuse are more likely to be transmitted in general than others; e.g., a context of child neglect that produces multiple forms of abuse in the subsequent generation).

Whereas the Cycle of Violence and the Intergenerational Transmission of Violence may be two different concepts, they are never opposed or antagonistic, and although current empirical studies show variations derived from the type of violence transmitted in question as well as their methodological designs (Berzenski & Yates, 2022), the fundamental aspect that this paradigm seeks to address lies in the study of two key but sometimes overlooked phenomena: firstly, intergenerational continuity and discontinuity (Inter- and Transgenerational Transmission of Violence), and secondly, permutation (overlap) and its processes of persistence and/or change throughout the life-course (Cycle of Violence) and their respective correlational and causal mechanisms.

Unfortunately, some literature has provided generalized explanations, while other literature has omitted some fundamental points, such as whether it is possible to transition from victim to perpetrator without transmitting violence in later stages of life to other generations, whether the transmission of violence can occur not only from the perspective of perpetration but also from victimization itself (the experience of harm and injustice and perceptions of it) through negative definitions of violence (e.g., negative impacts on fundamental beliefs that are transmitted from one generation to another, the transmission of trauma from generation to generation, or the transmission of identity stereotypes or discourses of power that perpetuate and normalize violence from generation to generation), thus evidencing a transmission of violence without perpetrating it; another question would be, of course, the influence of extra-familial victimization (e.g., testifying or suffering victimization at school, in institutions, or in the community) on the Cycle of violence or inter- and transgenerational transmission; whether there is a risk that a single context of victimization could trigger a possible trajectory toward perpetration (ideas or motivations); the differential extent to which a condition of re-victimization, recurrent victimization, or polyvictimization may influence the presence of Cycle(s) of Violence and/or Intergenerational Transmission of Violence and their subsequent effects (intergenerational perpetration or victimization and throughout the life-course).

Therefore, in order to address these gaps, experiences of victimization and perpetration (overlap) respectively need to be studied within an area that allows for a more dynamic approach to developmental trajectories and their ramifications throughout the life-course and under an ecological (Bryce, 2025; Turanovic, 2023; Widom, 2022; Olomi et al., 2020; Widom & Wilson, 2015), intersectional (Bryce & Schaffer, 2024a, 2024b; Widom & Osborn, 2021; Widom, 2017; Widom & Wilson, 2015), transactional (Bryce, 2025; Bryce & Schaffer, 2024a, 2024b; Widom, 2022; Olomi et al., 2020), and multidimensional approach(Boxall, 2025; Berzenski & Yates, 2022) that is not limited exclusively to understanding perpetration and previous experiences as simple factors or personal and/or environmental predispositions, but instead takes as its primary focus an in-depth understanding of the contexts of victimization and their subsequent effects on the life-course. Therefore, a *Developmental and Life-Course Victimology* is necessary.

DEVELOPMENTAL AND LIFE-COURSE VICTIMOLOGY: A CONCEPTUAL EXPANSION

For a long time, talking about an experience of victimization was conceived as a specific event that occurred at a particular time, viewed in an abstract and isolated manner, with victimization being recognized only as that interaction where victim and offender, at a particular time, place, and manner, had an exchange or encounter, leaving aside the multifaceted conditions that previously shaped the contexts of victimization, and more importantly, the subsequent impacts and effects, not only immediate, but also those that were direct or indirect in the medium and long term in the life course of individuals. As a result, little attention was paid to the phenomena of violence experienced from even very early stages of development, until the late 1990s, when a differentiated and evidence-based approach began to be proposed that allowed development to be taken into consideration as a functional element for understanding the qualities, characteristics, forms, and prevalence of violence throughout the different stages of life, from childhood and adolescence to adulthood, thus giving rise to *Developmental Victimology*.

Developmental Victimology

Developmental Victimology is an area of Victimology that focuses on studying victimization, its impacts, and the needs of victims in a dynamic and differentiated way from different stages of life to identify the variability and evolution of experiences throughout the stages of development, primarily those related to childhood and adolescence (Bryce, 2025, 2019; Pereda, 2024; Bryce & Schaffer, 2024a; Finkelhor, 2008a, 2008b).

This field possesses two key elements that dominate its studies: the role that the stage of development plays in contexts of vulnerability and risk, and the impact of victimization during childhood and adolescence into adulthood (Bryce, 2025, 2019). Hence, Developmental Victimology provides a paradigm shift where the experiences and impacts of victimization are interconnected, thus informing a context of victimization as a process or condition, sometimes prolonged/chronic or cumulative, rather than a single fragmented event (Bryce, 2025, 2019; Pereda, 2024; Finkelhor, 2008b), which implies that people will rarely experience a single victimization process during their lifespan, being violence a constant throughout the stages of a person's development (Bryce, 2025; Pereda, 2024; Contreras-Taibo,

2024; Finkelhor, 2008b), thereby creating continuous, multiple, prolonged, and/or chronic cycles of victimization (Bryce, 2025; Contreras-Taibo, 2024; Widom, 2022; Benedini et al., 2016).

> *"Violence against children and adolescents is a historical constant that occurs in all cultures and societies. It is a universal and complex problem, resulting from the interaction of individual, family, social, and cultural factors that must be unravelled". (Pereda, 2024, pp. 86-87)*

Therefore, studying the co-occurrence of different forms of victimization, based on the concept that they are connected, constitutes an approach that is more in line with the reality of Victimology and responds to a real problem faced by many children that needs to be studied. (Pereda, 2024, p. 89)

Development Victimology is an important field that allows us to identify and understand both risks and impacts, in order to recognize how people find themselves in a context of vulnerability and/or differential exposure to victimization, Revictimization, or Polyvictimization (Pereda, 2024; Bryce, 2019). "We see the ramifications for adulthood, the intergenerational, cyclical transition of abuse, neglect, and dysfunction" (Bryce, 2019, p. 167).

Given that Developmental Victimology emerged at a historical moment when experiences of victimization in childhood and adolescence were minimized, ignored, or conceived under adult-centric frameworks, and despite the fact that over the past 20 years Developmental Victimology has been gaining ground and international recognition in research on child and youth victimization (e.g., revictimization and polyvictimization) and its short-, medium-, and long-term effects (Bryce, 2025; Turanovic, 2023; Widom, 2022), the truth is that there are still specific questions that remain unstudied in an exhaustive, prolonged, or continuous long-term manner, mainly regarding how early experiences of victimization vary individually throughout the course of life (which is not limited to the transition to early adulthood), how these variations occur, and the most appropriate mechanisms for intervention with victims (Turanovic, 2018, 2023) and survivors based on their context and assessments of victimization experiences lived throughout a continuum called the Life-Course.

Thus, it is important to remember that a person's development does not end with the transition to early adulthood, but rather continues into later stages, as development is a dynamic process that interacts with microsocial and macrosocial variables (Olomi et al., 2020; Papalia et al., 2020). However, it also contains a historical component, as these micro and macro variables show intergenerational changes. Therefore, not only does it matter where and how a person developed, but also what socio-historical moment the person belongs to and their transitions throughout life (Neil & Sampson, 2021). For example, it is not the same to have been a child in a predominant social context during the 1980s in a region of the global north versus the global south and how they have grown up throughout their lives, or the social realities experienced by children during the 2000s or even during an armed conflict or a pandemic and how they have developed in later stages (see Sampson & Neil, 2024, and Neil & Sampson, 2021, as examples of generational and social-historical analysis of racism throughout the life course).

Life-Course Perspective in Victimology

The Life Course perspective refers to the differential study of socially constructed roles and phases in all stages of life (e.g., early childhood, puberty, adolescence, early adulthood, older adulthood, etc.) that affect how people engage in specific social practices and systems, the cognitive appraisals of such experiences, and thus the agency responses provided to life events (Turanovic, 2018).

One of the first reflections on the life course perspective applied to the field of victimology can be found in Turanovic (2018, and later Turanovic, 2023), who outlines some key elements that must be considered in victimological (longitudinal) research, some of which show links to other theories already developed within victimology (e.g., Lifestyle-Routine Activities Theory, Risk Dependence and Heterogeneity, Code of the Street, etc.) that need to be incorporated longitudinally and intersectionally, and not just transversally or focused on a single differential category (e.g., sex, age, ethnicity, colour, etc.) in isolation (Figure 1).

Figure 1.

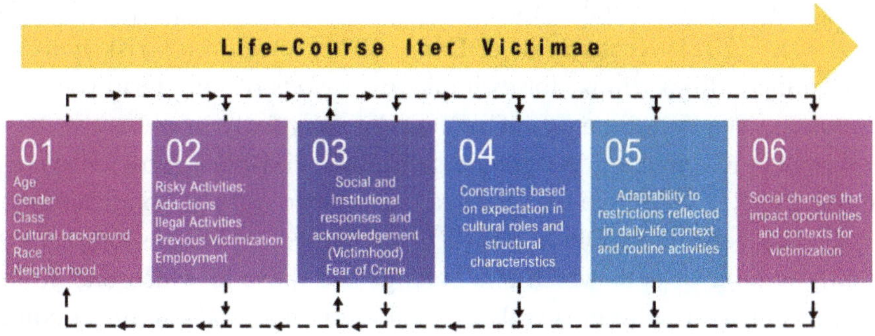

Source: Own creation.

The following are reflections inspired by the initial work of Turanovic (2018, 2023) through the following points on a Life Course Victimology, which shows affinity with some key points of Developmental Victimology:

1. The contexts of victimization show dynamism throughout the life course. They can be studied and explained from an ecological approach to understand the

contexts, characteristics, and patterns of exposure and differential vulnerability in their life context.

2. Some contexts and characteristics of victimization exhibit greater patterns and risk of occurrence at certain stages of development throughout the life course.
3. Victimization does not occur in isolation or spontaneously, nor does it result from a personal decision. In reality, the risk of victimization is shaped by the social contexts that are prevalent or predominant within people's life courses.
4. The agency capacities (choice and autonomy) of victims can modify the risks of victimization; however, these agency capacities change throughout life, differing at each stage of development and depending on the social-historical context.
5. The consequences and impacts of victimization vary not only individually at a specific point in time, but also throughout a person's life course and across stages of development.
6. The social bonds that are formed throughout life can shape responses to victimization. However, victimization can also modify how bonds develop, strengthen, or dissolve over the life-course, thus influencing subsequent impacts.
7. Victimization can produce negative turning points that lead to continuity or persistence (cumulative impact and eventual revictimization/multiple victimization), or positive turning points (e.g., post-traumatic growth and the eventual breaking of the victimization cycle).

Differential exposure, which does not always result exclusively from a personal decision but rather from social and structural components (Turanovic & Pratt, 2024; Kubrin & Osey, 2021; Kruttschnitt & Kang, 2021) toward high-risk individuals, places, or temporalities (think, for example, of periods of long-term social, civil, armed, community, or military conflict) can exponentially increase the presence of a context of victimization. As people grow, their lifestyles experience changes (Turanovic, 2023, 2018; Bryce, 2019) that are intrapersonal (e.g., appraisals, perceptions, decisions, behaviors) (Olomi et al., 2020), interpersonal (e.g., social networks), community (e.g., groups to which one belongs and those to which one no longer belongs), as well as structural (social, political, economic, and cultural conditions), and, of course, situational mechanisms. In other words, people and the circumstances of their lives and the contexts in which they are part change throughout their lives (Bryce, 2025; Wikström et al., 2024; Papalia et al., 2020; Olomi et al., 2020).

Although not all risky lifestyles are exclusively defined by the stage of development in which they occur, some contexts of victimization risk may be more prevalent or predominant at certain stages of development (e.g., neglect or abandonment, coercive control, economic or property violence, etc.). Therefore, from a Life Course victimological perspective, these distinctions must be recognized in their examinations (Turanovic, 2023, 2018) and how they are being perpetrated at each stage of development. For example, how does coercive control vary when exercised among the youth population, the adult population, vs. from an adult to an infant? How does coercive control against children vary from one generation to another? What is the variability of victimization through bullying throughout the stages of development? Among others.

Socio-structural and cultural conditions shape the way social interactions occur, the differential exposure to certain lifestyles, but also forms of adaptation, accessibility, and response to one's social context (Kubrin & Osey, 2021), producing impacts on attitudes and perceptions towards victimization and violence, and thus, the social reaction to violence is modified. These conditions vary as individuals grow and society advances. Therefore, when considering structural conditions and their cultural adaptations, it is necessary to emphasize that Life-Course Victimology recognizes the importance of the social and historical context of victimization (Turanovic, 2018).

Developmental and Life-Course Victimology: Aims and Scope

In light of the above, it has been deemed an opportune and relevant historical moment to provide an integration similar to that which occurred with criminology in order to identify, describe, and explain in a more dynamic, comprehensive, and in-depth manner, in this case, the developmental trajectories toward victimization, but also those victimization cycles that repeat and persist in order to answer how, why, and under which circumstances some people culminate in contexts of recurrent victimization, others in trajectories of polyvictimization, or even some in more chronic and prolonged conditions such as revictimization throughout their lives.

Furthermore, to identify, describe, and explain how some victims succeed in breaking the cycles of victimization without going through processes of continuity and/or persistence, but also how some victims who have experienced multiple contexts of victimization have broken the cycle of victimization, and the role of post-traumatic growth in breaking these cycles and eventual de-victimization.

Similarly, understanding the mechanisms of those trajectories that end up involving subsequent generations within the contexts and impacts of victimization, that is, how inter- and intragenerational cycles of victimization are transmitted and, of course, how (previous) victimizations can help us understand why some victims are involved in violent trajectories as perpetrators.

Although the study of this last point on criminal trajectories is of interest and relevance to Developmental and Life Course Criminology, the author of this chapter considers that the permutation or overlap from victim to perpetrator cannot be adequately investigated and explained without considering victimization in the sense that has been emphasized throughout this chapter. Therefore, with all the progress that has been made in Victimology research, it is time to talk about *Developmental and Life Course Victimology* (Figure 2).

Figure 2.

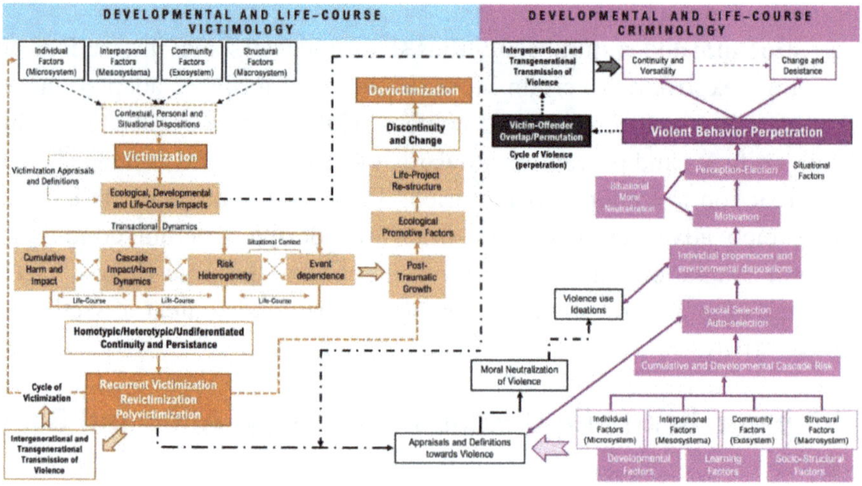

Source: Own creation.

As such, this author defines Developmental and Life-Course Victimology as a field of Victimology that studies victimization from ecological, intersectional, and transactional perspectives, the mechanisms of continuity and persistence that lead to Recurrent Victimization, Polyvictimization or Revictimization, its characteristics and impacts, both individual and inter- and transgenerational, the cycles of overlapping towards perpetration, as well as the study and promotion of processes of change and the breaking of cycles of victimization that explain Devictimization at different stages of development within a victim's life course. Similarly, but with different objects of study than Developmental and Life-Course Criminology[1] (see Wiktröm et al., 2024), Developmental and Life-Course Victimology recognizes that:

1. People are different and change (they have propensities and risks that are differential and change throughout life).
2. The environments in which people develop and function are different and change (they influence their development and agency mechanisms in different and changing ways).
3. The contexts of victimization and their subsequent effects or impacts must be investigated in a continuum, considering individual dynamics (differential propensities, exposures, or vulnerabilities), environmental dynamics (the spaces and environments in which one is part of), the prevailing social and structural

conditions, and the specific situational conditions of victimization in order to identify, describe, and explain the developmental trajectories that involve processes of continuity, change, and permutations.

From the perspective of Developmental and Life-Course Victimology, social agency is recognized as an active mechanism that can shape the experiences and degree of vulnerability experienced by victims and survivors. However, these agency capacities depend not only on the degree of effectiveness of specific developmental competencies, but also on age (autonomy vs. degree of dependence) and the socio-historical conditions within the stages of development. For example, a young child cannot make absolute decisions about where to study, where to live, or with whom to interact, as adults make decisions on behalf of the child (Turanovic, 2018). As soon as the infant grows up, they gain autonomy and social recognition of it. However, once they transition into old age, they may lose some autonomy, increasing their vulnerability to other forms of victimization that would not occur in other stages of development (adapted from Turanovic, 2018). Therefore, the capacity for choice and autonomy is studied in an intersectional manner, taking into account at all times the individual's life course and the social and structural context in which they are immersed.

Finally, from a Developmental and Life-Course Victimology perspective, victimization constitutes a process or even a set of complex interconnected, cumulative, and/or progressive processes that can inform a condition of victimization rather than just an event. Thus, Developmental and Life Course Victimology is an area that avoids fragmented analysis and responses to experiences of victimization throughout the developmental stages across the life course.

...fragmentation promotes a partial and isolated understanding of the problems that may get in the way of devising enduring solutions [...] Second, there is a considerable evidence that common risk factors co-occur and create vulnerability for a wide variety of victimizations[...] Third, the fragmented responses may lead to misunderstandings about what is most damaging and deserving of priority treatment [...] Fourth, the fragmented response may fail to get practitioners targeted on the problem that most needs to be addressed [...] Fifth, fragmentation results in considerable inefficiency, duplication of effort, and unnecessary competition [...] Finally, fragmentation may contribute to a dilution of impact (Finkelhor, 2008a, pp. 19-20).

Hence, Developmental and Lifecourse Victimology focuses its research and study on three key components of victimization and violence: Victimization Continuity/Persistence, Permutation/Overlap, and Change/Devictimization.

In order to provide greater clarity and understanding in this text, the following section compiles and describes the findings of the literature review conducted on processes of continuity, permutation, and change across in victimology. Subsequently, in the discussion section, a reflective analysis will be carried out on ways of addressing, studying, and explaining these contexts under ecological, intersectional, and interdisciplinary paradigms.

CONTINUITY AND PERSISTENCE OF VICTIMIZATION: RECURRENT VICTIMIZATION, POLYVICTIMIZATION, AND REVICTIMIZATION

Not only does victimization have an impact on psychosocial, physical, economic, and even community spheres, but it also increases the risk of a second victimization experience, regardless of whether the perpetrator is the same person or not (Bryce, 2025; Contreras-Taibo, 2024; Olomi et al., 2020; Contreras-Taibo et al., 2019). It is therefore possible to affirm that previous victimization constitutes a mechanism that provides correlational or causal evidence in the production of various cycles and trajectories of victimization, highlighting the presence of a process of continuity and persistence in the life history of those who suffer it.

Throughout the literature, mainly victimological, multiple conceptualizations have emerged about persistent and continuous forms of victimization, including Recurrent Victimization (Contreras-Taibo, 2024; Daigle, 2021), Polyvictimization (Bryce, 2025, 2019; Contreras-Taibo, 2024; Pereda, 2024; Daigle, 2021; Finkelhor, 2008), Revictimization (Bryce, 2025, 2019; Olomi et al., 2020), and, from an environmental perspective, Near-Repeat Victimization (Andresen, 2024). For this chapter, we will focus on the first three, which are more closely associated with developmental and life course perspectives, as they are direct dynamics of ongoing interpersonal violence rather than geographically based victimization, as Near-Repeat Victimization does.

Recurrent Victimization has been referred to as a general concept to highlight exposure to and experience of more than one instance of victimization throughout the life-course at any stage of development and any violence affecting the same person (Contreras-Taibo, 2024; Daigle, 2021). This concept may also involve forms of repeated victimization (Contreras-Taibo, 2024), which implies experiencing more than one context of victimization of the same type (Daigle, 2021). Recurrent victimization varies depending on the violent acts studied; however, interpersonal violence tends to be the subject of recurrent victimization processes to a greater extent than other forms of violence (e.g., property crimes) (Contreras-Taibo, 2024).

On the other hand, *Polyvictimization* is used exclusively in the contexts of childhood and adolescence and refers to the set of multiple experiences of victimization (usually four or more during 12 months) that children and adolescents experience within the same stage of development (Pereda, 2024; Bryce, 2019; Finkelhor, 2008b). This concept encompasses forms of interpersonal violence that are not limited exclusively to child abuse, including, for example, witnessing violence, bullying, and other forms of conventional violence (e.g., robbery, assault, etc.). Polyvictimization conceives victimization as a continuous and chronic condition within a stage of development (Bryce, 2025; Pereda, 2024; Finkelhor, 2008b).

Likewise, Revictimization from Developmental and Life-Course Victimology refers to the accumulation of multiple experiences of victimization throughout any stage of development in an individual's life course (as opposed to the concept of Polyvictimization, which focuses on one stage of development, mainly childhood and adolescence) (Bryce, 2025, 2019). "Revictimisation (or persisting poly-victimisation) is also a broader model, exploring the same adversities as poly-victimisation, although from a 'whole of lifespan' perspective" (Bryce, 2025, p. 160). Some research has shown that people who experience some form of victimization are more likely to be exposed to and vulnerable to other forms of violence, not only during the same stage of development, but also in later stages (e.g., adulthood) (Bryce, 2025, 2019; Olomi et al., 2020).

Both Polyvictimization and Revictimization focus on differential vulnerability and the role of environmental conditions in the accumulation of victimization experiences that account for persistence and continuity (Bryce, 2019).

> *Persistence is a pathway in which child maltreatment, domestic violence, family conflict, and disruption propel children into an intensively and generalized victimized condiction that in turn generates general anger/aggression, which, by fuelling and sustaining defiant, challenging, rule-violating behaviour, tends to lock them into an even more persistent victimized condition (Bryce, 2019, p. 157).*

In addition, as referred in previous work (Cortes-Perez, 2024b) when speaking of prior victimization processes, reference is made not only to those officially reported, but also to any process of violation of fundamental human rights by the use and perpetration of violence interpersonally (individual or collective) or even institutionally (e.g., abuse of power, institutional sexual abuse, harassment, threats, coercion, etc.). Likewise, the analysis of victimization should include not only those completed behaviours but also those that are attempted (Cortes-Perez, 2024b) as part of persistent victimization trajectories analysis.

Some specific models that have been used in the cross-sectional study of persistence and continuity processes involve perspectives of heterogeneity and dependence. In contrast, those of a more longitudinal nature involve models of cumulative risk and developmental cascades under ecological-transactional approaches, which are described below.

Heterogeneity and Dependence

Much of the research on repeated victimization has been framed by two predominant theoretical models: "Risk Heterogeneity" and "State Dependence" (Contreras-Taibo, 2024; Andresen, 2024; Daigle, 2021; Contreras-Taibo et al., 2019; Turanovic, 2018; Turanovic & Ogle, 2018), which have sometimes been referred to as antagonistic models (Turanovic & Ogle, 2018) due to their conceptual construction. However, both theories show a good capacity for conceptual integration.

According to Turanovic (2018), researchers approached the study of victimization by trying to determine whether it was the result of "population heterogeneity" or "state-dependent" processes. Population heterogeneity factors refer to those stable differences between individuals that make some people more prone to victimization than others, and state-dependent processes refer to changes, events, and actions within individuals that can alter a person's future risk of victimization (Turanovic, 2018).

Although these proposals were initially conceived to explain mechanisms of continuity in the perpetration of violence (Turanovic & Ogle, 2018), today they constitute models that have been applied par excellence in research on processes of continuity or persistence at the situational level of victimization.

The *Risk Heterogeneity* perspective suggests that processes of continuity and persistence such as Recurrent Victimization, Revictimization, or Polyvictimization can be explained by the stable risk factors that produced the first victimizing event (Contreras-Taibo, 2024; Turanovic & Ogle, 2018), since it is the persistence of these factors or dispositions within the context of life that do not show variation, thus producing new victimizations even at the hands of different perpetrators (Contreras-Taibo, 2024; Contreras-Taibo et al., 2019). Therefore, if exposure and/or vulnerability continue and remain stable, the predisposition and/or occurrence of other victimization experiences will be more likely.

The Dependence perspective assumes that initial victimization can produce mechanisms and processes that exacerbate the future risk of victimization (Contreras-Taibo, 2024; Contreras-Taibo et al., 2019; Turanovic & Ogle, 2018), depending on the dynamics that occur in the victimization process and the conditions of vulnerability that the perpetrator may now be aware of and "boost" to control the victim and produce new victimizing events (Contreras-Taibo, 2024; Contreras-Taibo et al., 2019; Turanovic & Ogle, 2018) with even greater versatility. Unlike the Heterogeneity model, the Dependency State perspective assumes continuity processes as a direct consequence of previous victimization (Contreras-Taibo, 2024; Turanovic & Ogle, 2018). In these types of conditions, "subsequent victimization is usually carried out by the original perpetrator, with [new victimization] generally occurring very soon after" (Contreras-Taibo, 2024, p. 107), see, for example, cases of school violence, family violence, or intimate partner violence.

Thus, continuity or persistence "may be due to the perpetrator's knowledge of the victim and their environment acquired during the original victimization process, which will allow them to access the victim more easily at a later time" (Contreras-Taibo, 2024, pp. 107-108). Previous victimization reinforces exposure, vulnerability, and a sense of helplessness, negatively impacting the capacity for agency and choice to confront, escape, or even avoid a new violent event (Contreras-Taibo, 2024; Contreras-Taibo et al., 2019).

Today, far from being competing dichotomous models, both perspectives have been proposed for comprehensive use, recognizing that both conditions (Heterogeneity and Dependence) can coexist and explain processes of continuity throughout the life-course (Turanovic, 2018; Turanovic & Ogle, 2018).

Victimization Propensity

Similar to the propositions of the Lifestyle and Routine Activities Theory, *Victimization Propensity* refers to the set of dispositions in a person's life context that exacerbate exposure to new victimization processes based on environmental, geographical, structural, occupational, and situational characteristics in the person's lifestyle (Contreras-Taibo, 2024; Fattah, 2019):

1. *Spatial Conditions*: Residential conditions in the city, ecological proximity to violence, social disorganization, segregation, crime, etc.
2. *Structural Conditions*: Sociodemographic variables such as age, gender, colour, sexual orientation, race, social class, etc.
3. *Conditions linked to illicit or deviant activities*: Substance abuse, risky behaviours and/or situations, violent behaviour, criminality, mass or macrosocial violence.
4. *Occupational Conditions*: Characteristics and contexts of the profession or occupation that increase exposure or differential risk to particular contexts of violence.
5. *Situational Conditions*: Transitory conditions that increase risk (social conflict, health conditions, social pressure, migration, mobility, etc.)

In addition to identifying the time lapse between each victimization experienced, the concept of Victimization Propensity has been an area of interest within Victimology and its processes of continuity and persistence (Daigle, 2021). However, these approaches are often used transversally, requiring a shift to a more dynamic ecological-transactional approach.

The Ecological-Transactional Model: Cumulative Harm/Risk and Developmental Cascades

Within the perspectives of development and the life-course, there has been interest in studying how functioning and impacts in one domain or competence of development throughout life subsequently influence another and, therefore, its respective functioning (Masten & Cicchetti, 2010), creating the need to incorporate paradigms that make it possible to visualize how these impacts end up producing causal chains. This type of approach has been referred to as the Ecological-Transactional Model.

The Ecological-Transactional approach considers two important elements of analysis: the accumulation of risks and impacts and their additive examination, and how these risks and impacts are continuous, progressive, and interactive, producing these causal chains throughout a person's life, referred to as the developmental cascade effect (Bartol & Bartol, 2021; Masten & Cicchetti, 2010), which allow for a more dynamic study of the trajectories of continuity and persistence.

The concept of Cumulative Harm has been referred to as an Australian term that incorporates the construct of Complex Trauma into research on adverse experiences of child and youth victimization (primarily abuse) to highlight the set of patterns and sequences of harmful events, whether historical or ongoing, that make the factors multiple, interconnected, and coexisting elements in the stages of development (Bryce, 2025, 2019), recognizing that recurrent and/or continuous victimization produces profound and exponential impacts and effects (Bryce, 2019).

Thus, this construct allows us to encapsulate the implications of the accumulation of adverse experiences during childhood throughout life (Bryce, 2025), meaning that trauma caused at a very early age by violent contexts has the potential to have long-lasting and even irreversible adverse effects and impacts on areas related to social and personal functioning (Bryce, 2025, 2019; Widom, 2022; Bartol & Bartol, 2021; Masten & Cicchetti, 2010) throughout life. In this way, the elements that shape cumulative harm are characterized by the presence of prolonged and persistent elements of dysfunction, dysregulation, disadvantage, and disconnection (Bryce, 2025).

However, although the terms Cumulative Risk and Cumulative Harm are used interchangeably in the literature, the reality is that they are not mutually exclusive concepts and represent a reciprocal and interactive relationship (Bryce, 2025).

> *A cumulative risk model assumes that the accumulation of risk factors has a higher predictive power for negative outcomes than any single risk factor, in isolation. The cumulative risk model is empirically supported across social, medical, and psychological domains and a cumulative ecological transactional model provides enhanced predictive capability for repeated maltreatment (Bryce, 2025, pp. 158-159).*

Damage and Cumulative Risk have provided research resources to understand better the frequency, manifestations, and impacts of repeated victimization cycles, allowing us to understand how a person is affected, and how harm shapes differential vulnerability and effects throughout a person's development, identifying how dependency and autonomy status can even exacerbate the risk of persistent victimization trajectories (Bryce, 2025).

On the other hand, the set of cumulative, progressive, and interactive consequences or impacts on the domains or competencies of development that ultimately produce transactional effects on other domains of the same order, but eventually also impact other systems or competencies of a different order, has been referred to as Developmental Cascades (Masten & Cicchetti, 2010). Thus, cascading effects explain why some problems in early stages of development can predict difficulties in adulthood that do not influence later stages of development (Masten & Cicchetti, 2010).

> *Cascade effects encompass a broad array of phenomena studied in developmental science within and across multiple levels of function, from the molecular level to the macrolevel. Cascade models may account for the pathways by which gene-environment interplay unfolds over time in epigenesis to shape development, linking genes to neural levels of function to behaviour to social experience, through processes of multilevel dynamics. These cascades may flow downward across levels, upward, or across domains of function in a developing system and its interactions with other systems as development proceeds (Masten & Cicchetti, 2010, p. 492).*

Thus, as the Developmental Cascade model is interactive, it focuses not only on negative impacts (risk and causal factors) but also on protective factors (Bartol & Bartol, 2021), and the production of positive development cascades (promotive factors) that can inform processes of change or variation in particular developmental trajectories across the lifespan. The presence of protective and promotive factors leads to the development of positive cascades that produce new protective and promotive factors in new domains, systems, and stages of development throughout the life-course (Bartol & Bartol, 2021; Masten & Cicchetti, 2010).

> *Developmental cascade research has the potential to inform, test, and refine theories of change that are integral to understanding pathways of adaptation, maladaptation, psychopathology, and resilience. Such knowledge is central to the goal of designing preventive interventions with strategic timing and targets (Masten & Cicchetti, 2010, p. 494).*

Therefore, transactional models integrate individual, family, social, and political contexts into their examinations and analyses, which interact and relate to each other to influence the person's experience (Bryce, 2025; Olomi et al., 2020)..

> *Given that development is a dynamic, iterative process that occurs across the lifespan, is important to consider risk factors in three ways: (1) how an individ-*

ual's responses and context differ depending on developmental stage (e.g., early childhood vs adolescence), (2) how responses and context interact and evolve over time, and (3) how responses and contexts can be targeted with intervention at particular developmental stages [...]
While many studies of RV [Revictimization] assert a mediational relationship for a single mechanistic factor [Child Sexual Abuse Mediator Variable Revictimization] we assert that RV will be better understood by a model that accounts for the complex interplay of individual (internal states and behaviours) and ecological mediators, as well a the developmental timing of the emergence of or exposure to such factors (Olomi et al., 2020, p. 272, see Figure 3).

Figure 3.

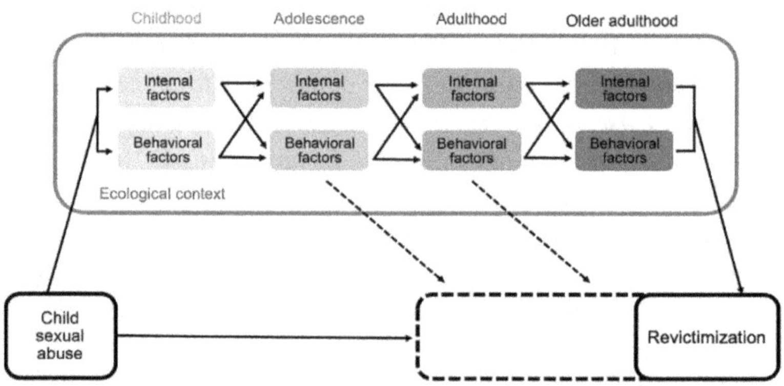

Source: Olomi et al., 2020

Therefore, transactional models integrate individual, family, social, and political contexts into their examinations and analyses, which interact and relate to each other to influence the person's experience (Bryce, 2025; Olomi et al., 2020).

Hence, inspired by the work of Olomi et al. (2020) and derived from all of the above-illustrated in this chapter, the Ecological-Transactional Model within Developmental and Life-Course Victimology, which forms a basis for research into the mechanisms of continuity and persistence, but also the possible process of change, can be illustrated in Figure 4 below. Nevertheless, it is important to reiterate that both protective/promotive factors and risk factors interact within an entire ecosystem that is not limited to the interpersonal (mesosystem) but also includes higher-order systems such as culture, politics, economics, history, and the dominant ideologies in a specific social-historical context. As such, there is no single trajectory or path regarding the victimization mechanisms of continuity and/or change for each person (adapted from Berzenski & Yates, 2022).

Figure 4.

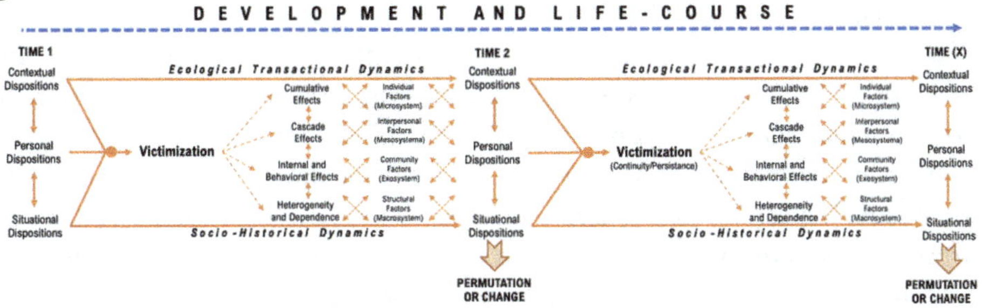

Source: Own creation

CHANGE AND TRANSFORMATION: POST-TRAUMATIC GROWTH AND DEVICTIMIZATION

How victims and survivors cope with the impacts or consequences of victimization and/or revictimization/polyvictimization is closely related to coping mechanisms and social support networks (Echeburúa-Odriozola, 2021; Turanovic, 2018; Widom, 2017; Finkelhor & Kendall-Tackett, 2008), which shape their views of the world, from themselves, and of others. One of the current fields of research that has begun to gain interest, and further study is how some victims have been able to overcome the adverse contexts that victimization has caused in their life histories, which has been referred to as Post-traumatic Growth.

Post-traumatic growth was defined initially by Tedeschi and Calhoun in the mid-1990s to refer to the set of positive psychosocial changes that victims may experience after traumatic or highly challenging events (e.g., victimization) (Contreras-Taibo et al., 2025; Sicilia, 2024). These changes may involve modifications in values, appreciations, meanings, sense of life, socialization mechanisms, among others (Contreras-Taibo et al., 2025; Sicilia, 2024), thus being transformations with positive impacts on various cognitive, attitudinal, and behavioural spheres, and can be perceived both as a process and as a result (Sicilia, 2024).

> *The result is a complex combination of cognitive, emotional, and social processes that lead to lasting, positive change in the individual. While the result is reflected and defined in specific dimensions (relationships with others, personal strength, new possibilities, spiritual change, and appreciation of life), the process is reflected in a set of components that refer to the moments, phases, and paths that people go through from just before the trauma to the beginning or end of the change (Sicilia, 2024, p. 120).*

However, it is important not to confuse Post-traumatic Growth with resilience mechanisms, which, although interrelated, show key conceptual differences:

> *While resilience is a holistic capacity of individuals, groups, and communities to adapt psychologically and socially to adversity with the least possible impact, post-traumatic growth is a process and/or result of profound transformation that stems from dealing with certain challenging and traumatic circumstances and their aftermath. When there is resilience, there is less trauma, less disruption, and more preservation of a system of values and beliefs, which may even have constituted a protective factor; consequently, there is also less suffering, challenge, need for effort to overcome, reworking, and personal change (Sicilia, 2024, p. 129).*

When Post-Traumatic Growth is studied as an outcome, it is comprised of at least five key elements or basic dimensions (Sicilia, 2024) (Sicilia, 2024):

1. *Relationships with others*: Experiences of positive changes in social relationships. Although social bonds are the product of transactional interactions between individuals and their support networks (Turanovic, 2018), it is important to recognize that these bonds develop differently depending on the individual's stage of development, varying in strength and sustainability over the life course.
2. *Personal strength*: Growth is experienced through self-confidence, self-esteem, a sense of emotional strength, and how the victim's identity is defined and constructed.
3. *Openness to new possibilities*: The presence and changes in the face of new possibilities, paths, or opportunities toward activities that produce greater satisfaction, thus involving the creation of new interests or the reinforcement of positive ones; activities and habits that were not previously considered (e.g., the creation of official support networks groups, activism, etc.).
4. *Spiritual changes*: Previous religious beliefs are not only a valuable way of coping with adversity, but also allow giving meaning to lived experiences (Contreras-Taibo et al., 2025).
5. *Appreciation of life*: This involves the degree of appreciation that each person assigns by changing their sense of priorities and valuing what they have (Contreras-Taibo et al., 2025).

In addition, when post-traumatic growth has been examined and analyzed as a process, there are dynamic mechanisms that comprise it, and these mechanisms are key elements to consider within the processes of change from a developmental and life course perspective (Sicilia, 2024, pp. 123-124):

a. The person's circumstances prior to the trauma: Moderate well-being, a complex, active, open, and hopeful cognitive style are characteristics that contribute to growth.
b. The critical traumatic event: What is traumatic is changeable and dynamic depending on personal circumstances and is marked by the experience of the trauma, not the event itself.
c. The breakdown of the person's fundamental and core beliefs and the vital challenge of rebuilding them: Higher-order goals and beliefs, as well as the ability to manage emotional distress, define what is "critical" for an individual.
d. Intrusive rumination: Recurring, unwanted, and difficult-to-avoid thoughts derived from trauma-related anxiety and related to the experience, which do not lead to a valid or satisfactory response, are part of the process, for example, asking oneself, "What did I do to deserve this?"
e. Emotional management and coping: Redefining personal goals or beliefs that are no longer sustainable for the person, redirecting intrusive thoughts, and finally, reducing distress through emotional regulation.
f. Intentional rumination: The development of conscious and introspective thoughts allows us to elaborate and reformulate the experience, reconstruct the meaning of what happened, and find meaning in the present.
g. Self-analysis and self-disclosure: Through reflection, writing, or other forms of expression, such as talking about or recounting the growth experience, will influence the transition from one type of rumination to another and emotional management.
h. Sociocultural influences: Social support, the presence of resources for comfort and containment, and references for the construction of new cognitive frameworks and ways of seeing the world can help generate adaptive coping behaviours.
i. Post-traumatic growth: Relationships with others, personal strength, new possibilities, spiritual change, and appreciation of life.
j. Narrative development and wisdom, increased resilience, and compassion.

Recovery involves self-determination and self-management, as well as making important decisions about one's own life. Recovery is influenced by the individual's needs, preferences, strengths, goals, culture, and personal history, with non-linear growth and possible setbacks, in a context of social support and reciprocal relationships (Sicilia, 2024, p. 126).

These elements (both growth as a result and as a process) have been found even in high proportions in contexts of revictimization (mainly of a sexual nature), in which it has been possible to show that persistent trajectories can also change (see Contreras-Taibo et al., 2025).

In summary, if adversity is capable of becoming a catalyst for growth, various sources can have a multiplier effect, leading to greater post-traumatic growth. Previous studies have obtained similar results, finding that the accumulation of adversities correlates positively with post-traumatic growth (Contreras-Taibo et al., 2025, p. 84).

In this way, the challenge facing Developmental and Life-Course Victimology concerning Post-Traumatic Growth will be to determine the mechanisms by which growth occurs and, of course, how this growth contributes to the processes of Devictimization, understood as a process of comprehensive transformation that involves overcoming and reframing the trauma, restructuring one's life project, and the transformation of the conditions that made the harm and injustices experienced possible, the latter argument being a component of what in the Global South has been referred to as Transformative Justice towards a guarantee of non-repetition.

FROM VICTIMIZATION TO PERPETRATION: THE ROLE OF DEVELOPMENTAL AND LIFE-COURSE VICTIMOLOGY IN THE UNDERSTANDING OF VICTIM-OFFENDER PERMUTATION AND OVERLAP

Victimization has not always been a topic of great discussion or interest among the criminological community (Turanovic, 2018, 2023), even within undergraduate and graduate criminology programs globally. If we look at how much is taught about victimology, victims, victimization, and victimhood, the proportion is minimal (including researcher clusters).

Throughout the international literature, emphasis has been placed on the impacts on the social cognition of victims and survivors (e.g., belief systems about oneself, other people, and the world in general); those impacts on self-cognitions may include feelings of low self-esteem, a sense of loss of control over one's own life, (self-) blame, shame, anxiety or distress, rumination, suicidal ideation, and depressive symptoms. In contrast, cognitions about others may involve, to name a few, perceptions of injustice, hypervigilance or suspicion, hostile attributions, anger, resentment, or even vengeful thoughts, among others (Pereda, 2024; Eisner et al., 2021; Echeburúa-Odriozola, 2021; Bryce, 2019), which, as mentioned in previous sections, demonstrate the cumulative impact and, therefore, a greater propensity toward revictimization or polyvictimization.

However, although some authors have referred to the importance of considering the contexts of Polyvictimization within the subsequent dynamics in the perpetration of violence (Turanovic & Pratt, 2024; Widom, 2017; Finkelhor & Kendall-Tackett, 2008) and in agreement with Eisner et al., (2021), little research has been done on the developmental contexts through which multiple experiences of victimization (e.g., Polyvictimization or Revictimization) could not only shape the mechanisms of perpetration, but also the earliest stages prior to perpetration per se, such as the ideation of using violence as a coping mechanism, motivations for using violence (e.g., revenge, power, generalized anger, etc.), fantasies, moral neutralizations toward the use of violence, or perception-choice mechanisms (Wikström et al., 2024), which shape decisions about whether or not to engage in some form of violence. So, the frequency and duration of the victimizing event or series of events, as well as the multiple types of those experienced, are elements of interest in understanding how people who have experienced victimization can perpetrate violence at later stages.

In this regard, a relevant and recent study was conducted through the Zurich longitudinal project on Social Development from Childhood to Adulthood, known as z-proso, in which Eisner et al. (2021) conducted a study with a youth population in Switzerland to examine whether the accumulation of multiple experiences of interpersonal victimization (e.g., polyvictimization) was associated with an increase in the generation of violent ideations in late adolescence (17 years) and early adulthood (20 years). The study also sought to assess whether violent ideation was directly affected by experiences of victimization or by adverse situations in a broader sense, as well as to investigate whether violent ideation decreased as the person grew older (psychosocial maturity) and to determine whether there were significant differences between men and women (Eisner et al., 2021). Some of the relevant conclusions of the study include the following:

- Exposure to multiple contexts of victimization is closely associated with the frequency of ideations such as killing, attacking, or humiliating another person based on controlled prospective risk factors (Eisner et al., 2021), so the greater the number of victimization experiences (e.g., Recurrent Victimization, Revictimization, or Polyvictimization), the greater the likelihood of presenting ideations about the use of violence, the frequency of which, of course, could be mediated by environmental, developmental, and situational risk factors, allowing for insight into intragroup individual variability.
- Unlike experiences of victimization (polyvictimization), experiencing multiple adversities in life (e.g., parental divorce, school exclusion, leaving home, severe illness, death of a loved one or close relative, financial problems, or unemployment of a parent) does not increase the likelihood of violent ideation in the adolescent population and has a minimal effect on the young adult population (Eisner et al., 2021). "These findings are consistent with the notion that ideations of attacking and killing others tend to be triggered specifically by experiences of interpersonal harm-doing rather than by noxious stimuli more generally" (Eisner et al., 2021, p. 479).

- The impact of victimization can have negative effects on cognitive and emotional processes, such as anger or hostile attribution, and reduced moral control over one's violent behaviour (Eisner et al., 2021). "They may be indicative of a set of motivations that have evolved and are activated when someone feels intentionally threatened, and which are based on responses related to revenge and retaliation (Eisner et al., 2021, p. 479). This is consistent with theoretical proposals about motivation within development and the life course:

The conditions experienced during development shape how perceptions of other people and the world are established, and therefore how motivational mechanisms in a person's development and life course are established (Bryce & Schaffer, 2024b; Sinnamon, 2017; Petherick, 2015; Petherick & Sinnamon, 2014); these in turn produce cognitive mechanisms (e.g., perception-election and decision-making) toward a specific action or inaction (Wikström et al., 2024). Thus, in a dynamic and changing way, the characteristics, experiences, and conditions during a person's development and life course "motivate behaviour in an often unconscious way, so that deficiencies, delays, and difficulties influence decision-making when we try to satisfy our needs" (Bryce & Schaffer, 2024b, p. 170).

- There are other mechanisms involved in the dynamics of the development of violent ideation. Specifically, violent ideation in late adolescence and early adulthood can be predicted in circumstances where there is a history of hostile or aggressive thoughts, internalized symptoms, and moral neutralization of violence (Eisner et al., 2021).

Our finding that internalizing symptoms at an earlier age uniquely predict violent ideations both in late adolescence and early adulthood is consistent with previous research that finds that anxiety and depression are associated with an increased tendency to experience ruminative thought processes generally, and anger ruminations in particular (Eisner et al., 2021, p. 479)

- There is no evidence to support differences between men and women regarding the association between experiences of victimization and violent ideation. However, it is necessary to identify whether particular forms of victimization (e.g., physical, psychological, or sexual violence, assaults in public places, property crimes) explain the variability between sexes in the literature (Eisner et al., 2021).
- There is no substantial evidence to support the hypothesis that the effects of polyvictimization on violent ideation decrease during the transition from

adolescence to early adulthood (Eisner et al., 2021). Therefore, change does not naturally occur as a result of psychosocial maturity.

- The study found that cognitive processes such as moral neutralization of violence are a predictor of violent ideation.
- The research allows us to focus attention and importance on victim support and victimization prevention processes, as it is the impact of victimization, particularly violent ideation, that in turn can contribute to greater negative impacts on victims and survivors of violence (Eisner et al., 2021).

DISCUSSION AND FUTURE DIRECTIONS FOR A DEVELOPMENTAL AND LIFE-COURSE VICTIMOLOGY AGENDA

In the opinion of the author of this chapter, this last point referred to by Eisner and colleagues (2021) is highly relevant, since the ideation of violence as a coping mechanism produces cumulative and long-lasting effects that can inform not only subsequent victimization or permutation processes, but also mechanisms of permutation and overlap on more than one occasion between victimization and perpetration of violence in a continuous and/or repeated manner, thus evidencing an additional trajectory involving mechanisms of continuous permutation, that is, entries and exits between being a victim and perpetrating violence across the lifespan, which would even allow for a better understanding of the assertion that life contexts associated with criminality constitute a risk factor for future victimization (Fattah, 2019; Turanovic, 2018).

Irrespective of the findings identified in the study, Eisner and colleagues (2021) emphasize the need to consider and study variations in violent ideation depending on the society being investigated (e.g., environments and/or subcultures of violence and how they are perpetuated) as well as within the stage(s) of development. Similarly, Widom and Osborn (2021) have suggested studying the perpetration and intergenerational transmission of violence not only in males but also in females. Therefore, the best way to answer questions about the role of victimization (any form of violence) and the underlying mechanisms in the development of criminal and/or violent behavior is through prospective longitudinal studies that allow for the monitoring of these infants and adolescents in their other stages of development (Widom & Osborn, 2021; Farrington & Malvaso, 2019).

According to Eisner et al. (2021) studies that can provide the best evidence for the hypothetical effects of victimization on violent ideation in real-life circumstances require longitudinal data with a clear temporal order between the experience of victimization and the hypothetical outcome. They also require data on dispositional characteristics, behaviours, and life circumstances that are likely to explain differences among individuals in their tendency to experience violent ideation (Eisner et al., 2021, p. 473).

Furthermore, while there has been research on how victimization can be perpetuated from one generation to the next (e.g., in the context of collective victimization and macro-victimization; see the psychosocial concept of intergenerational trauma), little research has been undertaken on the extent to which and how the transition from victim to perpetrator is perpetuated from generation to another, namely, whether a generation whose trajectory of having suffered forms of victimization and engaging in violent behaviour (e.g., abuse, neglect, or other forms of interpersonal violence) will be replicated in subsequent generations (see the case of corporal punishment in Farrington & Malvaso, 2019).

> *Little is known about the similarities or differences in risk factors from one generation to the next [...] However, to our knowledge, the extent to which the association between abuse and perpetration is perpetuated intergenerationally is unknown (Farrington & Malvaso, 2019, p. 203).*

The above therefore reveals a gap not only in research-action, but also epistemically, showing an emerging field of study where Developmental and Life Course Victimology can contribute interdisciplinarily, alongside Developmental and Life Course Criminology, where experiences of victimization can be studied first from the perspective of Developmental and Life Course Victimology, and subsequently in an interdisciplinary manner through Developmental and Life Course Criminology in ecological transactional terms to explain eventual perpetration and its mechanisms of change or desistance, which criminology has already enabled to be developed within its longitudinal studies. This will provide a more comprehensive and comparative understanding of the multiplicity of developmental trajectories ranging from devictimization, revictimization/ polyvictimization, the permutation of victimization-perpetration, and their mechanisms of change over the life course of individuals.

CONCLUSION

Throughout this chapter, it has been recognized that, although not all forms of violence or experiences of victimization arise from isolated contexts and factors and/ or spontaneously, nor are the contexts and subsequent responses unrelated to previous experiences, studies using developmental and life course approaches to understand violence should not be based exclusively on criminology as the sole approach, as it is necessary to study and incorporate the contributions of victimology using intersectional and longitudinal approaches that allow us to establish, in a broader sense, how violence can produce multiple ramifications or trajectories (multifinality and equifinality) throughout the life cycle of individuals and in different ways at different stages of development, from the pregnancy stage to older adulthood.

> *There is no singular explanation for why it happens, how it changes over the life course, or how it impacts people's lives. A focus on victimization and its consequences over the life span requires using a highly integrative and interdisciplinary approach—one that unifies seemingly divergent conceptions of stability and change in human development (Turanovic, 2018, pp. 20-21).*

It is necessary to begin providing or using victimological approaches in longitudinal research when considering how processes of continuity (revictimization and poly-victimization), change (devictimization), and/or permutation/overlap (perpetration of violence) occur in a person's lifespan, especially when seeking to identify how, when, and in which manner the processes of initial victimization shape the violence experienced as new forms of victimization, future perpetration, or even processes of change toward devictimization. Nevertheless, more importantly, how appropriate victim-oriented prevention can even prevent the creation of violent trajectories in later stages, which, when they occur, require not only victimological interventions, but also criminological, psychosocial, and trauma-focused interventions.

REFERENCES

Andresen, M. A. (2024). (Near-) Repeat Victimization. In: M. A. Andresen, *Environmental Criminology: Evolution, Theory, and Practice* (3rd Ed., pp. 294-314). Routledge.

Bartol, C. R., & Bartol, A. M. (2021). *Criminal Behavior: A Psychological Approach* (12th ed.). Pearson Education.

Benedini, K. M., Fagan, A. A., & Gibson, C. L. (2016). The cycle of victimization: The relationship between childhood maltreatment and adolescent peer victimization. *Child Abuse & Neglect*, *59*, 111–121. DOI: 10.1016/j.chiabu.2016.08.003 PMID: 27568065

Berzenski, S. R., & Yates, T. M. (2022). Revisiting a Multidimensional Model of Intergenerational Transmission of Child Maltreatment. In: Krugman, R. D., Korbin, and J. E. (Eds.), *Handbook of Child Maltreatment* (2nd Ed., pp. 351-370) Springer. https://doi.org/DOI: 10.1007/978-3-030-82479-2_17

Boxall, H. (2025). From Home to Heart: Adolescent Violence in the Home as a Turning Point in Intimate Partner Violence Trajectories. In Cortes-Perez, O. I. (Ed.), *Ecologies of Violence: A Comparative Perspective in Contemporary Victimology and Criminology* (pp. 121–138). Springer., DOI: 10.1007/978-3-031-91957-2_7

Bryce, I. (2019). Cumulative harm: Chronicity, revictimisation, and developmental victimology. In: I. Bryce, Y. Robinson, & W. Petherick (Eds.), *Child abuse and neglect forensic issues in evidence, impact and management* (pp. 151–173). Academic Press. https://doi.org/DOI: 10.1016/B978-0-12-815344-4.00009-X

Bryce, I. (2025). The Accumulation of Childhood Maltreatment, Developmental Trauma and Victimology. In Cortes-Perez, O. I. (Ed.), *Ecologies of Violence: A Comparative Perspective in Contemporary Victimology and Criminology* (pp. 155–171). Springer., DOI: 10.1007/978-3-031-91957-2_9

Bryce, I., & Schaffer, K. (2024a). Child Femicide. In Cortes-Perez, O. I. (Ed.), *Forensic Victimology and Femi(ni)cide: A Transdisciplinary Approach on Forensic Evidence and its Contexts* (Vol. I, pp. 99–116). Springer., DOI: 10.1007/978-3-031-72512-8_3

Bryce, I., & Schaffer, K. (2024b). Motivations for Juvenile Offending Behaviour and Femicide. In Cortes-Perez, O. I. (Ed.), *Forensic Victimology and Femi(ni)cide: A Transdisciplinary Approach on Forensic Evidence and its Contexts* (Vol. II, pp. 165–188). Springer., DOI: 10.1007/978-3-031-72516-6_5

Contreras-Taibo, L. (2024). Victimización Reiterada. In Contreras-Taibo, L., & García-López, E. (Eds.), *Victimología Forense. Perspectivas Iberoamericanas* (pp. 101–116). Manual Moderno.

Contreras-Taibo, L., Huepe-Artigas, D. & Navarrete-García, G. (2019). Magnitude and characteristics of revictimization through child sexual abuse in Chile. *Legal and Criminological Psychology*. 01-14 https://doi.org/DOI: 10.1111/lcrp.12158

Contreras-Taibo, L., Navarrete, G., Pereda, N., & Pinto-Cortez, C. (2025). Transformación tras la adversidad: Crecimiento postraumático en sobrevivientes de violencia sexual infantil. *Anuario de Psicología Jurídica, 35*(1), 79–87. DOI: 10.5093/apj2025a10

Cortes-Perez, O. I. (2024a). Forensic Discussion and Formulation: Ecological-Intersectional Perspectives in Victimology and Criminology to Understand Feminicide. In Cortes-Perez, O. I. (Ed.), *Forensic Victimology and Femi(ni)cide: A Transdisciplinary Approach on Forensic Evidence and its Contexts* (Vol. II, pp. 29–85). Springer., DOI: 10.1007/978-3-031-72516-6_2

Cortes-Perez, O. I. (2024b). Forensic victimology and context analysis: The ecological-intersectional dimensions model on the victimization context. In Cortes-Perez, O. I. (Ed.), *Forensic Victimology and Femi(ni)cide: A Transdisciplinary Approach on Forensic Evidence and its Contexts* (Vol. II, pp. 245–283). Springer., DOI: 10.1007/978-3-031-72516-6_8

Daigle, L. (2021). Recurring Victimization. In: L. Daigle (Eds.), *Victimology. The Essentials* (3° Ed., pp. 58-72). SAGE.

Echeburúa-Odriozola, E. (2021). De la macrovictimización a la microvictimización. Vulnerabilidad, resiliencia, y estrategias de afrontamiento en las víctimas de sucesos traumáticos. En: G. Varona-Martínez, *Macrovictimización, Abuso de Poder y Victimología: impactos intergeneracionales* (pp. 551-567). Aranzadi.

Eisner, M., Averdijk, M., Kaiser, D., Murray, A. L., Nivette, A., Shanahan, L., van Gelder, J., & Ribeaud, D. (2021). The association of polyvictimization with violent ideations in late adolescence and early adulthood: A longitudinal study. *Aggressive Behavior, 47*, 472–482. DOI: 10.1002/ab.21965 PMID: 33908056

Farrington, D. P., & Malvaso, C. G. (2019). Physical Punishment and Offending in Two Successive Generations of Males. In I. Bryce, Y. Robinson, W. Petherick (Eds.), *Child Abuse and Neglect: Forensic Issues in Evidence, Impact and Management* (pp. 203–224). Academic Press. https://doi.org/DOI: 10.1016/B978-0-12-815344-4.00011-8

Fattah, E. A. (2019). *Victimology: A Discipline in Transition*. Canadian Scholar Press.

Finkelhor, D. (2008a). Child Victims: An Introduction. In Finkelhor, D. (Ed.), *Childhood Victimization. Violence, Crime, and Abuse in the Lives of Young People, (pp. 03–21)*. Oxford University Press.

Finkelhor, D. (2008b). Developmental Victimology. In D. Finkelhor, Childhood Victimization. Violence, Crime, and Abuse in the Lives of Young People, (pp. 22–46). Oxford University Press.

Finkelhor, D., & Kendall-Tackett, K. (2008). Developmental Impact. In: D. Finkelhor, Childhood Victimization: Violence, Crime, and Abuse in the Lives of Young People (pp. 65–91). Oxford University Press.

Jollife, D., & Auty, K. M. (2023). Developmental and Life-Course Criminology: An Overview. In A. Liebling, S. Maruna & L. McAra, The Oxford Handbook of Criminology (7th Ed., pp. 121-145). Oxford University Press.

Kazemian, L., Farrington, D. P., & Piquero, A. R. (2019). Developmental and Life-Course Criminology. In Farrington, D. P., Kazemian, L., & Piquero, A. R. (Eds.), *The Oxford Handbook of Developmental and Life-Course Criminology (pp. 03-10)*. Oxford University Press., DOI: 10.1093/oxfordhb/9780190201371.013.1

Kruttschnitt, C., & Kang, T. (2021). Theoretical Perspectives on the Victimization of Women. In Pratt, T. C., & Turanovic, J. J. (Eds.), *Revitalizing Victimization Theory: Revisions, Applications, and New Directions* (pp. 163–184). Routledge.

Kubrin, C. E., & Ousey, G. C. (2021). Understanding Victimization: The Role of Cultural Theories. In Pratt, T. C., & Turanovic, J. J. (Eds.), *Revitalizing Victimization Theory: Revisions, Applications, and New Directions* (pp. 77–103). Routledge.

Lyon, D. R., & Welsh, A. (2017). *The psychology of criminal and violent behaviour*. Oxford University Press.

Masten, A. S., & Cicchetti, D. (2010). Developmental Cascades. *Development and Psychopathology*, *22*(3), 491–495. DOI: 10.1017/S0954579410000222 PMID: 20576173

Neil, R., & Sampson, R. J. (2021). The Birth Lottery of History: Arrest over the Life Course of Multiple Cohorts Coming of Age, 1995-2018. *American Journal of Sociology*, *126*, 1127–1178. DOI: 10.1086/714062

Olomi, J., Wright, N., & DePrince, A. (2020). Revictimisation of sexually abused children. In I. Bryce & W. Petherick, Child Sexual Abuse: Forensic Issues in Evidence, Impact, and Management, (pp. 267-291). Academic Press. https://doi.org/ DOI: 10.1016/B978-0-12-819434-8.00013-1

Papalia, N., Luebbers, S., & Ogloff, J. (2020). A developmental life course approach to the study of offending and victimisation following child sexual abuse. In Bryce, I., & Petherick, W. (Eds.), *Child sexual abuse: Forensic issues in evidence, impact and management* (pp. 293–323). Academic Press., DOI: 10.1016/B978-0-12-819434-8.00014-3

Patterson, G. R. (2016). Coercion theory: The study of change. In Dishion, T. J., & Snyder, J. J. (Eds.), *The Oxford handbook of coercive relationship dynamics (pp. 07–22)*. Oxford University Press.

Pereda, N. (2024). La perspectiva de la Victimología del Desarrollo y el Concepto de Polivictimización. In Contreras-Taibo, L., & García-López, E. (Eds.), *Victimología Forense. Perspectivas Iberoamericanas* (pp. 86–100). Manual Moderno.

Pereda, N., & Guerra, C. (2025). Exploring the Intersection of Self-Reported Victimization and Offending: Risk Profiles Among a Representative Sample of Spanish Adolescents. *Victims & Offenders*, •••, 1–20. DOI: 10.1080/15564886.2025.2515091

Petherick, W. (2015). Motivations. In Petherick, W. (Ed.), *Applied Crime Analysis: A Social Science Approach to Understanding Crime, Criminals, and Victims* (pp. 148–171). Academic Press., DOI: 10.1016/B978-0-323-29460-7.00008-9

Petherick, W., & Sinnamon, G. (2014). Motivations: Offender and Victim Perspectives. In Petherick, W. (Ed.), *Profiling and Serial Crime: Theoretical and Practical Issues* (3rd ed., pp. 393–430). Academic Press., DOI: 10.1016/B978-1-4557-3174-9.00018-5

Sampson, R. J., & Neil, R. (2024). The social foundations of racial inequalities in arrest overthe life course and in changing times. *Criminology*, *62*(2), 177–204. DOI: 10.1111/1745-9125.12374

Sicilia, L. (2024). El crecimiento postraumático en sobrevivientes de abuso sexual infantil. En L. Contreras-Taibo y E. García-López, Victimología Forense. Perspectivas Iberoamericanas (pp. 117-147). Manual Moderno.

Sinnamon, G. (2017). Psychopathology as a Mediator of Antisocial and Criminal Behavior. In Petherick, W., & Sinnamon, G. (Eds.), *The Psychology of Criminal and Antisocial Behavior: Victim and Offender Perspectives* (pp. 1–50). Academic Press., DOI: 10.1016/B978-0-12-809287-3.00001-8

Turanovic, J. J. (2018). Towards a Life Course Theory of Victimization. In Decker, S. H., & Wright, K. A. (Eds.), *Criminology and Public Policy: Putting Theory to Work* (2nd ed., pp. 85–103). Temple University Press.

Turanovic, J. J. (2023). Victimization and its consequences over the life course. *Crime and Justice, 52*(1), 265–342. DOI: 10.1086/727029

Turanovic, J. J., & Ogle, M. R. (2018). State Dependence and Population Heterogeneity in Theories of Victimization. In Huebner, B. M. (Ed.), *Oxford Bibliographies.* Oxford University Press., DOI: 10.1093/obo/9780195396607-0232

Turanovic, J. J., & Pratt, T. C. (2024). *Thinking About Victimization. Context and Consequences* (2nd ed.). Routledge., DOI: 10.4324/9781003269557

Vander Ven, T., & Colvin, M. (2012). Coercion and Crime. In Cullen, F., & Wilcox, P. (Eds.), *The Oxford Handbook of Criminological Theory* (pp. 607–624). Oxford University Press., DOI: 10.1093/oxfordhb/9780199747238.013.0031

Widom, C. S. (2017). Long-term impact of childhood abuse and neglect on crime and violence. *Clinical Psychology : a Publication of the Division of Clinical Psychology of the American Psychological Association, 24*(2), 186–202. DOI: 10.1037/h0101743

Widom, C. S. (2022). Long-term Consequences of Childhood Maltreatment. In Krugman, R. D., & Korbin, J. E. (Eds.), *Handbook of Child Maltreatment* (2nd ed., pp. 371–395). Springer., DOI: 10.1007/978-3-030-82479-2_18

Widom, C. S., & Osborn, M. (2021). The cycle of violence: Abused and neglected girls to adult female offenders. *Feminist Criminology, 16*(3), 266–285. DOI: 10.1177/1557085120987628

Widom, C. S., & Wilson, H. W. (2015). Intergenerational Transmission of Violence. In Lindert, J., & Levav, I. (Eds.), *Violence and Mental Health.* Springer., DOI: 10.1007/978-94-017-8999-8_2

Wikström, P. H. Treiber, k., & Roman, G. (2024). *Character, Circumstances, and Criminal Careers: Towards a Dynamic Developmental and Life-Course Criminology.* Oxford University Press.

ENDNOTES

1 Developmental and Life-Course Criminology is an area of criminology that focuses on the study of developmental processes and their trajectories toward the perpetration of violence, as well as the mechanisms of persistence and/or

change that occur throughout a person's lifespan through longitudinal research on risk, protective, and promotive factors across an entire social ecosystem (Wikström et al., 2024; Jollife & Auty, 2023; Cullen et al., 2021; Kazemian et al., 2019). Therefore, this area focuses more attention on the person who produces or perpetrates the violent act, compared to victimology, which studies those who suffer it.

Chapter 2
Trauma-Informed, Child-Centric Sentencing to Reduce the Intergenerational Harm

Katherine J. McLachlan
https://orcid.org/0000-0001-7171-2089
Flinders University, Australia

ABSTRACT

A significant adverse life event is the incarceration of a parent. Children of prisoners often experience multiple challenges in addition to parental incarceration, including child abuse and neglect, social exclusion and poverty, as well as household dysfunction. These adverse events increase the risk of contact with the youth and adult justice systems. Some children may also become second-generation incarcerated parents themselves. Trauma-informed responses may assist in breaking the cycle of intergenerational criminalisation and incarceration. To examine trauma-informed sentencing responses to parents, first, this chapter discusses the impact of parental incarceration and cumulative adversity on the life trajectories of children. Second, a sample of current sentencing remarks of adults is then analysed to determine how judges acknowledge and respond to the potential impact of intergenerational incarceration. Finally, trauma-informed criminal justice strategies for courts are discussed to mitigate the trauma and criminality associated with sentencing parents to incarceration.

DOI: 10.4018/979-8-3373-9524-1.ch002

INTRODUCTION

When parents are incarcerated, their children are the forgotten victims of crime. Parental incarceration often compounds multiple existing challenges and adversities, including child abuse and neglect, social exclusion and poverty, as well as household dysfunction. Adversity and the resulting trauma are considered criminogenic risk factors, increasing the risk of contact with the criminal justice system. This chapter examines how sentencing courts consider the impact of parental incarceration on children and proposes how trauma-informed court responses may assist in breaking the cycle of intergenerational criminalisation and incarceration, given that some children may grow up to become incarcerated parents themselves.

HOW MANY CHILDREN HAVE INCARCERATED PARENTS?

There is an unexpected dearth of information about children of prisoners. The exact number of dependent children (i.e., under 18 years of age) affected by parental incarceration at any point in time in Australia is unknown. It has been estimated that five per cent of all Australian children are affected by parental imprisonment each year (Legislative Council Legal and Social Issues Committee, 2022; Quilty, 2005), with First Nations Australian[1] children about four times more likely to experience parental imprisonment (Dennison et al., 2013; Dowell et al., 2017; Legislative Council Legal and Social Issues Committee, 2022). The AIHW (2023a) reported that 40 per cent of people entering prison identify as having one or more dependent children, with 68 per cent having two or more children. First Nations people entering prison are more likely (47%) than non-Indigenous people (34%) to have dependent children (AIHW, 2023a). Similar patterns have been observed overseas, with approximately half of men and two-thirds of women in prison having dependent children (Hagan, 1996).

SECTION ONE: ADVERSITY, TRAUMA AND PARENTAL INCARCERATION

While having an incarcerated parent does not cause a child themselves to be incarcerated, children of prisoners often experience chronic adversity, sometimes referred to as Adverse Childhood Experiences (ACEs), associated with criminality (Wolff et al., 2025). ACEs include physical, sexual and emotional child abuse, neglect and household dysfunction, including parental incarceration, domestic abuse, parental mental health issues or parental substance abuse issues (Felitti et al., 1998).

Children may experience multiple ACEs concurrently, such that when a parent is incarcerated, they may also be dealing with the impact of additional adversity. In addition to individual and familial adversity, children may also be distressed and disadvantaged by broader factors such as crime victimisation, exposure to community violence, socioeconomic status, and social isolation, which also impact children's life course trajectories (Finkelhor et al., 2013). Indeed, it has been argued that ACEs focusing on individual factors underestimate and "decontextualise experiences of adversity and obscure the broader societal forces that create and maintain disadvantage" (Cunningham, 2025, p. 57; see also Finkelhor et al., 2013).

Exposure to adversity can be thought of as occurring in doses. The more adversity a child experiences, the greater the "trauma load". As the trauma load increases, especially during childhood, which is perceived to be a "stress-sensitive" period (Khoury et al, 2010), there is a greater likelihood that adversity will result in further adversity and trauma (Wolff et al., 2025). Developmental trauma is the negative impact of adversity on a child's functioning and well-being across various functional domains (such as emotional, psychological, neurophysiological, social, etc). People involved in the criminal justice system tend to have high trauma loads (Ford et al., 2024). The trauma load of having an incarcerated parent depends on a range of factors, including the gender and role of the parent, the age of the child at separation, the length and degree of disruptiveness this is for the child, with separation generally more harmful when the child is young (Sheehan & Levine, 2006; Sherman, 2005).

Exposure to adversity may also lead to post-traumatic growth. Children of prisoners are not homogeneous, and parental incarceration may not be inherently traumatic for all children. This may be true, for example, if the child remains in the care of a protective and loving parent, and/or if the removal and incarceration of a parent makes the child's household physically and emotionally safer. There is certainly evidence that some children "cope with the challenges of parental incarceration in positive, resourceful, and multifaceted ways" (Johnson & Arditti, 2022, p. 29; see also Shine for Kids, 2024). However, in most cases, parental incarceration is perceived as likely to negatively impact a child's development and life course trajectory.

The Impact of Parental Incarceration on the Life Trajectories of Children

There is not a direct relationship between parents and their children being incarcerated, but rather "parental incarceration may exacerbate existing adversities and set into motion new chains of events or cascades of adversity" (Johnson & Arditti, 2022, p. 32). An almost 20-year-old study from Victoria found that children of prisoners faced complex adversity in addition to parental incarceration, with most experiencing "[p]roblems with family violence, drug and alcohol abuse… physical and emotional abuse and neglect of children… parental mental health and… transience" (Sheehan & Levine, 2006, p. 36). The study used Magistrate court file data of 156 children to examine the care arrangements and factors that brought the children of prisoners to the attention of the child welfare and justice systems. More than half of the children were aged five years or younger. There was often missing data about the status of fathers (e.g., 31 children did not have fathers identified as family members in their files). This was likely because the mothers were primary (or indeed sole) carers and their criminalisation led to the child protection concerns (Sheehan & Levine, 2006, p. 79). The study found that children's living arrangements were often described as "ones of considerable chaos, neglect and transience" (Sheehan & Levine, 2006, p. 29).

Cumulative adversity, including but not limited to parental incarceration, may result in complex trauma for many children. Complex trauma refers to "the cumulative or compounded impact of multiple or prolonged traumatic stressors, leading to 'underlying' dysfunction across a person's life (McLachlan, 2024, p. 18). Condry and Smith (2018) acknowledge the many ways that parental incarceration impacts children's well-being: weaker family relationships, poor health and behavioural changes, disengagement in schooling and education, as well as entrenching social exclusion and widening inequality and poverty. Parental incarceration may be made more distressing due to broader issues of poverty and survival (Cunningham, 2025).

In some cases, the incarceration of a violent parent may have a positive impact on the social and emotional well-being of a child. This may be true, for example, where that parent is the source of pain or suffering, such as by perpetrating domestic/family violence or child abuse (Condry & Smith, 2018). However, while removing a parent from the family home might be a protective factor for some children, the incarceration of a violent father may result in additional criminogenic risks of entrenched poverty, domestic abuse perpetrated by other "step-fathers" and mothers' boyfriends, and additional ACEs. Indeed, Hagan (1996, p. 25) has proposed that:

> *incarceration of negligent, violent, and abusive parents where the imprisonment of the parents [is often thought to benefit] children by removing serious risks of current and future harm. Yet I do not know how often this is the case. My suspicion is that imprisonment of parents is more often a traumatic life event that initiates or intensifies rather than reduces the problems of the involved children.*

Cunningham (2025) refers to the case of 13-year-old Jax, who became the "informal primary caregiver" to their siblings after their father's incarceration, relying on the sales of cannabis and shoplifting to feed their family when the absence of their father "thrust Jax and their four siblings from subsistence living into abject poverty" (Cunningham, 2025, p.142).

Parental Incarceration, Development, Identity and Belonging

Adolescence (i.e., between the ages of 10 and 17) is a time of significant biological, neurological, and physical development for children. The incarceration of a parent may result in social and emotional trauma in the short term, manifesting as behavioural issues, educational challenges, poor mental health, aggression and emotional dysregulation (Shine for Kids, 2024). In the longer term, parental incarceration may also lead to developmental trauma, impacting children's cognitive and psychosocial development (Johnson & Arditti, 2022).

Parental incarceration is also associated with social stigma, isolation, and emotional trauma (such as grief and loss, shame and depression), which may also have long-term effects on a child's functioning and behaviour (Flynn et al., 2015; Murray et al., 2012; Paynter et al., 2022; Sheehan & Levine, 2006; Shine for Kids, 2024). Parental incarceration can undermine a sense of identity and belonging for children. This is especially true for adolescents, whose identity development is closely tied to their social, cultural, and historical experiences (Johnson & Arditti, 2022). Sheehan & Levine (2006) highlighted that incarceration meant that, for many children:

> *family connections that are already tentative for these children can break down completely, and the children move into foster care. Changes in schools, in place of residence, in access to friendships, leisure and community activities create significant instability for these children, which may have life-long consequences, making the children vulnerable to mental health and relationship problems, to poor education and employment outcomes. (Sheehan & Levine, 2006, p. 5)*

This negative impact on a child's ability to engage with school as well as how they spend their leisure time and with whom they associate, all increase the risk of criminalisation (Connolly, 2022; Oldrup & Frederiksen, 2018). Without parents to monitor and supervise children's behaviour and provide love, support and care (Johnson & Arditti, 2022), children may be more likely to be influenced by the behaviour and support provided by antisocial associates, increasing the likelihood of disengagement from education and prosocial leisure activities (Johnson & Arditti, 2022). These are all risk factors for offending, both as a child and as an adult (see the Risk-Need-Responsivity model, Bonta & Andrews, 2017).

The Impact of Having an Incarcerated Mother

Mothers are often the primary caregivers for dependent children, and the impact of maternal incarceration is significant (Epstein, 2014; Hagan, 1996). Children of sole parents are effectively orphaned when their parents are incarcerated. While women represent about eight per cent of people who are incarcerated in Australia (Australian Bureau of Statistics, 2024), women in prisons are a growing population, in Australia and internationally (Australian Institute of Health and Welfare, 2020). Most women in custody are under the age of 40 years (Australian Institute of Health and Welfare, 2020), increasing the likelihood of being mothers of dependent children. Globally, approximately two-thirds of incarcerated women identify as mothers to at least one dependent child (Epstein, 2014; Lovell et al., 2020). As noted by Lovell et al. (2020):

> *Women experiencing incarceration have commonly endured complex histories that often include child abuse, sexual abuse, neglect, domestic violence, and drug and alcohol addiction, leading to a high incidence of children being removed by child protection services. These life events can result in complex trauma often exhibited by low self-esteem, inability to display emotions, physical or psychological agitation, self-injury, and suicide attempts. Further, this... may create issues with parenting, alcohol, and substance abuse, as well as affecting mental health. These factors, combined with a lack of nurturing and inappropriate parental role modeling in childhood, can make parenting their children challenging... (p. 2)*

When mothers are incarcerated, they often receive short sentences of less than six months (Epstein, 2014), which can undermine multiple protective factors for both the mother and child(ren). Having an incarcerated mother increases the risk of contact with child protection agencies due to the presence of additional adversity in their household, commonly relating to parental mental health issues, substance abuse and domestic abuse (Sheehan & Levine, 2006). Contact with child protection agencies is a predictor of future criminalisation and engagement in the youth justice and adult correctional service systems. Out-of-home care is associated with parental incarceration as well as offending as a child and an adult (Rémond et al., 2023).

Intergenerational Trauma and Incarceration

In Australia in 2022, one in four adult prison entrants reported one or more parents or carers had been in prison when they were a child (Australian Institute of Health and Welfare, 2023a; see also Rémond et al., 2023). Australian First Nations people in prison are 2.5 to three times more likely to have had a parent incarcerated during childhood than their non-Indigenous counterparts (Rémond et al., 2023). South Australian research found that 240 adults in custody had 1,138 family members ever incarcerated, with 100 respondents (42% of the sample) reporting that the history of familial incarceration had had a "major effect" on or "totally determined" their lives (Halsey & de Vel-Palumbo, 2020).

Adult children of incarcerated parents are more likely to commit more serious, violent offences (Rémond et al., 2023) and have poorer behaviour in prison, especially those who reported incarceration of their mother (see Novero et al., 2011). Arguably, this may be due to how developmental trauma manifests, increasing the likelihood that incarcerated children of prisoners will be more reactive and less able to regulate their emotions under stress.

Parental incarceration increases the likelihood of children being criminalised (Farrington et al., 2015). A systematic review and meta-analysis of almost 3.5 million children across 25 publications found that children with criminalised parents were more than twice as likely to perpetrate criminal behaviour as those without parents who offended (Besemer et al., 2017). The reasons for this are complex (Auty et al., 2017), for "[c]riminal parents tend to live in the most economically and socially disadvantaged circumstances, which increases the likelihood of their children becoming criminally involved too" (Auty et al., 2017, p. 217).

Thus, intergenerational incarceration may be an outcome of pre-existing disadvantage rather than the result of parental imprisonment per se (King, 2019). A recent Welsh study has found evidence to support the "intergenerational continuity of ACEs", where fathers who had experienced a high number of ACEs as children themselves had children who experienced a high ACEs load (Ford et al, 2024). Specifically, children "of fathers with four or more [ACEs] were almost three times more likely to have been exposed to 2–3 ACEs and six times more likely to have been exposed to four or more ACEs" (Ford et al., 2024, p. 6). However, the association between intergenerational adversity and intergenerational incarceration is not linear. Intergenerational exposure to compounded ACEs may relate to the impact of ACEs on the well-being and functioning of fathers (and their ability to parent), as well as additional socioeconomic and intrafamilial factors. Conversely, recent research using longitudinal data from Chicago concluded that, for White families at least, parental contact with the criminal justice system predicts children's contact with the justice system, independent of the familial adversity they experience (Wildeman et al., 2024).

Although the impact of maternal incarceration is significant, there is also a clear intergenerational impact of paternal incarceration. Many adults in prison grew up without a birth father in their lives, often due to paternal violence, criminality and incarceration. A systematic review and meta-analysis of the impact of parental (most often paternal) incarceration on later life trajectory by Murray et al. (2012) found that parental incarceration predicted an increased risk for children's antisocial behaviour (p. 190). Separation per se was not the reason for this increased risk. The longitudinal Cambridge Study in Delinquent Development found that 63 per cent of sons who were convicted of offences had fathers also with criminal convictions (Farrington et al., 1996). A Danish study found that intergenerational criminality could be reduced for boys if a father received a community-based sentence rather than a custodial sentence (Wildeman & Andersen, 2017). In addition to avoiding the criminogenic impact of prison, community-based sanctions for fathers led to the reduction in other risk factors for future criminality, such as placement in out-of-home care, and a loss of familial employment/income (Wildeman & Andersen, 2017).

SECTION TWO: HOW DO JUDGES SENTENCE PARENTS AND ADULT CHILDREN OF INCARCERATED PARENTS?

So far, this chapter has examined the prevalence of parental incarceration and its traumatic impact on dependent children. Parental incarceration tends to occur in families already experiencing multiple adversities, and the direct and indirect impacts of parental incarceration change children's life course trajectories in some cases, resulting in second-generation incarceration. This section examines the extent to which sentencing judges consider the impacts of parental incarceration when sentencing an adult who has been found guilty of an offence.

Sentencing is "the process of determining an appropriate sanction in response to proven criminal behaviour based on the law, the context, and the surrounding circumstances of the offence" (McLachlan, 2024, p. 172). Sentencing judges and magistrates are bound by the sentencing calculus, which includes sentencing purposes, principles and factors. Given that the primary purpose of sentencing in South Australia (the jurisdiction from which the data are taken) is to protect the safety of the community (per *Sentencing Act 2017* (SA), s 3), it makes sense that judicial officers might consider the criminogenic impacts of incarceration on members of society, including on the dependent children of defendants. There are 11 legislated sentencing factors, including the defendant's general background and offending history, their remorse and their prospects for rehabilitation (*Sentencing Act 2017* (SA), s. 11). Previously, the *Criminal Law (Sentencing) Act 1988* (SA) included as sentencing factor "the probable effect any sentence under consideration would have on dependants of the defendant" (s 10(1)(n)), but this was removed with the introduction of the *Sentencing Act 2017* (SA). Nevertheless, judicial officers retain considerable discretion in sentencing; they may choose whether (or not) dependent children are a relevant sentencing factor for consideration (Flynn et al., 2015).

Under common law (and legislation in some Australian jurisdictions), family hardship may be regarded as exceptional circumstances that reduce or amend a sentencing sanction. "Exceptional" is rarely defined in legislation or case law but is generally accepted to mean "quite out of the ordinary" (*Hodder v The Queen* (1995) 81 A Crim R 88 at p. 111). "Exceptional circumstances" are determined by a judge and enable a less significant penalty to be imposed for serious offences by "outweigh[ing] the paramount consideration of protecting the safety of the community (whether as individuals or in general) and personal and general deterrence" (e.g., *Sentencing Act 2017* (SA) ss 51(2), 54(2)). A defendant's lawyer must provide evidence to show that exceptional circumstances exist. Judges may avoid exceptional family hardship by imposing alternatives to imprisonment (such as a suspended sentence or court-ordered home detention) or reducing time in custody through shorter-than-usual sentences, thereby enabling defendants to remain with their families and dependents and continue to provide familial, social, and financial support.

Walsh and Douglas (2016) examined Australian sentencing appeals heard between January 2000 and June 2014 in which defendants appealed their sentences, arguing family hardship. From 85 cases (involving 51 mothers and 34 fathers) across all Australian jurisdictions where family hardship was considered, they concluded that:

> *the human rights of children are rarely (explicitly) considered by judicial officers. We suggest that the consideration of the human rights of the child and, relatedly, the family should play a more important role in the consideration of the appropriate sentence in Australian jurisdictions. (Walsh & Douglas, 2016, p. 160)*

Walsh and Douglas (2016) identified that the presence of no alternative carer for a child qualified as "exceptional" in some cases (see *R v Edwards* [2011] QCA 331).

South Australian Snapshot Study: Sentencing Parents and Adult Children

In this snapshot study, the published sentencing remarks from March to May 2025 in South Australia were reviewed to identify a sample of 21 adult defendants who were parents and/or children of previously incarcerated parents. Sentencing remarks are the published judicial statement that summarises the offending behaviour, various aspects of the sentencing calculus upon which the judicial officer has relied, and the sanction itself (McLachlan, 2024, p. 172). In South Australia, sentencing remarks are published online by the Courts Administration Authority for 28 days before being removed from public access. All sentencing remarks involving parental incarceration were downloaded.

The analysis aimed to examine:

- How did sentencing judges recognise the relevance of dependent children in sentencing? Did having dependent children influence the sanction imposed on a parent?
- When sentencing adult children of prisoners, did sentencing judges use information about intergenerational incarceration to inform their decision-making?

Sentencing remarks were analysed using content analysis. Content analysis aims to identify patterns, trends, meaning, and significance in qualitative data by categorising, quantifying, and examining key themes in that data (Vaismoradi et al., 2013). The sentencing remarks were manually coded, given the small sample size (for more information about the analysis, refer to McLachlan, 2022). All defendants and judges were de-identified.

The Defendants

Seventeen adults were parents of one or more dependent children: four were mothers and 13 were fathers. Eight adults (four of whom were also parents) were previously dependent children of incarcerated parents. Three First Nations men and one non-Indigenous man were second-generation prisoners who did not have children, as per Table 1.

Table 1. Parental status and Indigeneity of the defendants in the sample (n=21)

Mothers	Fathers	Second-generation Incarcerated Parents	Sons
3, non-Indigenous	7, non-Indigenous	2, non-Indigenous men	1, non-Indigenous
	3, Indigenous	2, Indigenous (one man, one woman)	3, Indigenous

The most serious offence types for which the defendants were convicted were interpersonal offences of violence (n=13), six drug trafficking offences, one driving offence, and one theft offence. As illustrated in Table 2, nine of the 17 parents (52.9%) received non-custodial sentences.

- Two mothers received suspended sentences (for non-violent offences), and two were incarcerated (for interpersonal offences). The mother who identified as Aboriginal was incarcerated for robbery.
- Seven of the 13 identified fathers were incarcerated.
- Of the nine non-Indigenous fathers, three were incarcerated (two for drug trafficking, one for assault), one received a sentence of home detention (for drug trafficking), and five received suspended sentences (four for domestic violence offences and one for drug trafficking offences).
- Finally, all four First Nations fathers were incarcerated (three for assault and one for theft).
- Two of the three First Nations sons were incarcerated (for interpersonal offences), with one receiving a suspended sentence (for assault).

Table 2. The sentence imposed on the parents in the sample (n=17)

Offence Type	Incarceration	Suspended Sentence	Home detention
Offences against the person	6	4	
Drug offences	2	3	1
Traffic/driving offence		1	
Theft offence	1		

The decision to incarcerate the defendants would have been influenced by "... a number of factors... including parenting considerations, but also considerations such as the seriousness of the offence, the part the offender played in the commission of the offence and the nature of the offender's criminal history" (Walsh & Douglas, 2016, p. 145). Nevertheless, it is clear from the data that half the parents received custodial sentences.

How Did Sentencing Judges Recognise the Relevance of Dependent Children in Sentencing?

The judicial officers recognised the relevance of dependent children when sentencing adults in a range of ways, specifically:

- As a protective factor or disincentive to offend in the future (BKL, CVK)
- As a reason to impose a community-based sanction, where the parent was a sole or significant carer of dependent children (RCD, WCD)
- As a reason to impose a sentence of incarceration, to specifically keep the defendant's child(ren) safe (LSK).

In some cases, although the judge acknowledged that the defendants were parents, they were either not providing care at the time of sentencing (or were not the primary caregiver), or no evidence was presented regarding their parenting role. Therefore, in the absence of active parenting duties, their children were not a significant sentencing factor (e.g., AKG, FMP, JRG, KVH; NSF; SKR, SRH).

For example, in the case of a mother, KVH, the Judge said:

You have seven children, aged between five and 18 years of age. Your youngest four children, aged five, six, seven and 10, were removed from your care in 2022, because of the ongoing domestic violence that you were subjected to and consequently, the children were in an unacceptably unsafe environment. Your eldest three, aged 11, 16 and 18, live with your former partner and father of six of your seven children. (R v KVH)

In this case, the judge identified that KVH was a victim of domestic abuse, that her children had been removed because of the domestic abuse, yet they were then placed in the care of the abusive partner. The judge then imposed a sentence of incarceration.

Similarly, in sentencing ABP, Judge A acknowledged that ABP was a mother:

> *Your partner was an alcoholic and drug user and you were subject to physical, mental and financial abuse. You had two children in that relationship, a daughter born in 2015 and a son in 2017. Your partner walked out of that relationship with your son, and you retained full time custody of your daughter until mid-2023, when you were arrested in relation to alleged drug trafficking, and the Department for Child Protection removed your daughter from your care. Both children now live with your [abusive] former partner and you have fortnightly access visits. (R v ABP)*

There is no indication in either case that the court acknowledged the complexity of the adversity experienced by these mothers, the value of mother-child reunification, or the importance of children having contact with their mothers, which would be more easily facilitated through a community-based sanction.

The Risk to Children is Perceived as a Reason Not to Offend

Judges often identified children as strong reasons for defendants not to offend in the future. For example, Judge S stated that "I consider it is likely that the needs of your son and your health problems **would motivate you to comply**." (R v CVK, emphasis added). Similarly, in sentencing BKL, Judge B said:

> *You have a seven-year-old daughter and a 10-year-old son. You live in your own home... You have a mortgage on the property, which is primarily serviced through your income. I am confident, given the jeopardy to your liberty that these offences have caused, and the effect that this court case has had on you and your family, that [will not reoffend]... your prospects of rehabilitation are fair to good for a variety of reasons... your family, whose security you have placed in jeopardy, is a powerful motivating factor for you to remain offence free. (R v BKL)*

The Parent is the Sole or Significant Carer

In sentencing WCD for assaulting the mother of his children, Judge W discussed the impact of the sentence on the children shared by the defendant and victim in detail. He determined that the safety of the community would be best served by suspending the defendant's sentence of incarceration, allowing him to remain in the community. Judge W said:

... You have two children of that marriage, a son aged 12 and a daughter aged nine... [you have] custody of your children every second week. Thankfully, you and the victim, your ex-wife, are allowed to go to school and club activities of your children so they may have the comfort of seeing both their parents there, which is usually very important for children... Both [of your children] seem very well supported by you and your ex-wife together with [your son sometimes becoming] overwhelmed and, therefore, los[ing] control of his emotional responses. He and you have a good relationship. You must continue to help him... so that he thrives. He needs to be able to rely on a predictable and comfortable routine of life when he is with you.

Your daughter... also has a positive relationship with you... [but] at times she becomes overly emotional... Your children, understandably, miss their old life and home. They will need a lot of care and love from you to continue to adjust from their old life.

... [The mother of your children] wants for you to 'experience the weight of guilt for your actions and that it will be a catalyst for growth and change'. Her powerful comments resonate with the Court... For the reasons that have been said on your behalf, your apology, your children's need for your parenting and, in particular, your ex-wife's desire to see you grow, I will fully suspend the period of imprisonment if you enter into a bond in the following terms: that you be of good behaviour for 18 months, the bond is in the sum of $500 and, thirdly, the mandatory firearm conditions. (R v WCD)

Where the defendant was the sole carer for dependent children, in one case, the judge put significant weight on the well-being of the children when imposing a community-based sentence for their father, stating that:

you are now the sole carer of your children [under the age of eight] and it will be important for their sake that you are able to properly function and properly care for them. I agree their wellbeing is an important consideration. (R v RCD)

Finally, in sentencing DJV, Judge U converted his sentence for drug trafficking to one of home detention, acknowledging that:

When you were 17, your first daughter was born. She is now 10. You also have a daughter who is five and a daughter who is just six months old. All of your daughters have been under the care of the Department of Child Protection, and I was told the two oldest still are... I was told that your youngest daughter has now very recently been returned to your sole care. If you are to be incarcerated, I was told your youngest daughter would go to your sister... On balance, I have decided to order you serve your sentence on home detention. I consider, in all the circumstances, it is in the best interests of both you and the community that you continue your rehabilitation outside of a custodial setting and working and caring for your youngest daughter. (R v DJV)

Keeping Children Safe Through Incarceration

Conversely, in another matter involving domestic violence, the judge quoted a victim impact statement from the child of the defendant, where they said, "Daddy makes me sad. Daddy makes me worried" (*R v DTW*). In imposing a suspended sentence, Judge K said to the defendant, "make sure that [your children's mother] and your children are safe, ...by staying away" (*R v DTW*). In a further case where the victim was the mother and a 13-month-old child, the judge acknowledged that the defendant's father had been incarcerated but focused on the incarceration of the defendant as a tool to keep the victims safe (*R v LSK*).

The Adverse Impact of Incarceration on a Child Was Identified Then Explicitly Disregarded

In the notable case of CVK, a 55-year-old father was convicted of drug trafficking and money laundering offences. He was sentenced to three years, nine months and 28 days of incarceration, with a non-parole period of one year and 11 months. CVK is the sole parent of a 17-year-old boy, halfway through his final year of school. Judge S acknowledged "the hardship that will be suffered by your son", and stated:

> *Your imprisonment will likely disrupt his schooling. He works part time, but his income is unlikely to cover the rent for the property where you both currently live. There is no-one that he can live with, apart from your elderly mother who has a terminal illness and has been given a life expectancy of some months. (R v CVK)*

Nevertheless, she concluded that "[t]he circumstances evoke sympathy, but these circumstances are of your own making. There is no evidence that that hardship is out of the ordinary, special or uncommon, such that it should have a material effect on sentence..." (R v CVK). This contradicts the findings of Walsh and Douglas (2016) that the incarceration of a sole parent may well qualify as an exceptional circumstance (i.e., "hardship out of the ordinary"). Arguably, in this case, the Judge's decision may pose a risk of greater harm to the community over the long term, by increasing the risk of intergenerational disadvantage and criminality.

In the case of JRS, a 24-year-old Aboriginal father, Judge H noted:

> *You grew up in very difficult circumstances... your father, with whom you had no meaningful relationship, was extremely violent towards your mother throughout your childhood. He would often beat her in your presence, exposing to you to the horrific aftermath of such awful violence on a regular basis. You felt unsafe and frightened in the family home growing up... You have two children together with your partner, now aged around four and one. Prior to your remand in custody, you say you had a close and loving relationship with your children. Your time*

in custody away from them, and your partner, has proved very challenging for you and, I suspect, has been a source of ongoing distress and regret. (R v JRS)

While acknowledging the defendant's childhood adversity and the likely distress that incarcerating him would cause his children, Judge H then imposed a sentence of incarceration for the defendant's non-violent offending.

When Sentencing Adult Children of Prisoners, did Sentencing Judges use Information about Intergenerational Incarceration to Inform their Decision-Making?

In the very small sample of eight adult children of prisoners (seven sons and one daughter, four of whom were also parents, as per Table 1), the judge identified that the defendants' fathers had been incarcerated; however, the role of second-generation incarceration was only a relevant sentencing factor in one case. In three cases, where judges recognised that an Aboriginal defendant was a second-generation prisoner, they acknowledged the fathers' incarceration (NJK, MIL and AJM). In sentencing a 28-year-old First Nations man, Judge M stated that:

You informed me that your father was always incarcerated and that you grew up without any role models. You have only seen your father two or three times and you informed me that he is still in custody at this time... You told me that your brothers and uncles were all in gaol... (R v NJK)

In sentencing MIL, a 20-year-old Aboriginal man, Judge S stated:

You are rebuilding a relationship with your father, who for some of your childhood was in prison... as a child you were frequently exposed to domestic violence and regularly assaulted by both your parents... and after being assaulted by your dad you used to take out your anger on other people. (R v MIL)

The risk of second-generation incarceration appeared to have no bearing on the sanction imposed (imprisonment in all cases).

In the case of a mother whose father had been incarcerated, Judge B summarised the woman's childhood adversity in detail:

... Your father committed a criminal offence [when you were about five] and was sentenced to prison... You were socially disadvantaged at a young age with your father being incarcerated. ... When you were 15 years of age your mother... commenced using methamphetamine and you in turn became introduced to the substance... Your mother... left [you] in Adelaide with your siblings. There were bad influences all around you. You became homeless and started couch surfing, all the while, using drugs... You have a three-year-old daughter whom your mother is currently looking after. (R v SAM)

The judge acknowledged her role as a mother, stating, "... you have a supportive family and a young daughter. Hopefully, your daughter will keep you on the right track upon your release." The judge also recognised the steps she had taken to rehabilitate, noting "I accept that you are doing everything you can to try and turn your life around." However, the judge then identified no exceptional circumstances existed and imposed a sentence of incarceration on SAM, a 23-year-old Aboriginal mother, for three years, one month and 2 days, with a non-parole period of one year and five months imprisonment.

Conversely, in the case of JAP, Judge D did acknowledge the relevance of parental incarceration. She said:

> *... Your parents were both heavy drug users and described as extremely neglectful parents. Your father spent a significant amount of time in custody. Your mother would often leave you in the care of others. You had what might be described as an extremely dysfunctional childhood. (R v JAP)*

In imposing a sanction for drug trafficking for JAP, a non-Indigenous 31-year-old man, Judge D said:

> *... In taking all of these features into account,* **including your deprived and dysfunctional childhood** *and the efforts that you have made towards your rehabilitation, I consider that* **there are good reasons** *to suspend the term of imprisonment that I have imposed. (R v JAP, emphasis added)*

In considering how best to achieve community safety, arguably, courts should reflect carefully and regularly on the impact of their decisions to incarcerate a parent. Three recent meta-analyses all reported a stable relationship between exposure to ACEs and the risk of recidivism in children (cited in Wolff et al., 2025).

Instinctive synthesis (i.e. an unstructured and individualised approach to sentencing based on judicial discretion, McLachlan, 2024, p. 173) is a cornerstone of sentencing in Australia. Arguably, in achieving the principal purpose of sentencing to promote community safety, parental incarceration and dysfunctional childhoods should be consistently regarded as relevant sentencing factors, albeit not always meeting the threshold of "exceptional circumstances". As early as 2005, the Australian Law Reform Commission argued that family hardship should be a general sentencing factor in all cases, not just those arising in the context of "exceptional circumstances". Indeed, Walsh and Douglas (2016) argue that it "should be a significant factor that is weighed with other factors in the process of 'instinctive synthesis'... [such that] **the best interests of the child** should always be considered" (p. 161, emphasis added).

SECTION THREE: THE VALUE OF TRAUMA-INFORMED SENTENCING RESPONSES

The Convention of the Rights of the Child (UN, 1989), to which Australia is a signatory, states that "in all actions concerning children, whether undertaken by public or private social welfare institutions, courts of law, administrative authorities or legislative bodies, the **best interests of the child** shall be a primary consideration" (article 3.1, emphasis added). While this is compelling, it is not binding in South Australia. Nevertheless, such an approach has been advocated for at the state and territory level (see, e.g., *Michael v The Queen* [2004] WASCA 4 (22 January 2004) [57]). It is being applied in other jurisdictions, such as Denmark and Finland (Oldrup & Frederiksen, 2018), as well as the UK (Epstein, 2014).

In 2011, the United Nations Committee on the Rights of the Child (UNCRC) considered children of incarcerated parents and stated that:

> *Children dependent on a parent in prison* ***should be taken into account whenever decisions are made about the parent,*** *from the point of arrest onwards, including by the judges dealing with the case. The impact of any proposed sentence on the children should be taken into consideration at point of sentencing (p. 4-5 [22], emphasis added).*

Trauma-informed approaches are being integrated into prevention and intervention strategies across child protection, policing, youth justice, courts, adult corrections, and mental health services (McLachlan, 2024). While there are studies of trauma-informed youth justice (e.g., Day et al., 2023), there are few to no publications on the value of trauma-informed practices when sentencing parents of dependent children. Trauma-informed practice requires that service providers understand and recognise adversity and its traumatic impacts, respond in an evidence-informed way that focuses on the individual and prevent further trauma (Substance Abuse and Mental Health Services Administration, 2014). To be trauma-informed, a service or sector must work to apply four key steps to:

1. Realise what trauma is and the potential impacts of adversity,
2. Recognise trauma symptoms experienced by the individual accessing the service,
3. Respond appropriately to the individual's unique trauma, and
4. Resist re-traumatisation by avoiding insensitive or inappropriate responses when providing services (Substance Abuse and Mental Health Services Administration, 2014).

This chapter began in Section One by *realising* the potentially traumatic impact of parental incarceration on the functioning, well-being and life course trajectory of children of prisoners. Section Two then explored how sentencing courts *recognise* the relevance of hardship on the children of defendants. Finally, this section examines how sentencing courts could *respond* using a trauma-informed approach to *resist re-traumatisation*.

Trauma-informed responses are characterised by the establishment and maintenance of safety, trust, collaboration, voice, and choice, as well as empowerment, alongside recognition of the significance of gender, culture, and historical factors (Substance Abuse and Mental Health Services Administration, 2014). As is clear in the scenario of "Andrew" that follows (from Connolly, 2022), safety, trust and control over children's own lives are quickly lost when parents are incarcerated.

The case of "Andrew"

The South Australian Commissioner for Children and Young People considered the impact of parental incarceration on children, consulting with 66 children and 74 parents (Connolly, 2022). In her report, Connolly cited the case of "Andrew", a 15-year-old boy, who:

> *... lived with his dad, a single parent. He doesn't really know his mum with whom he never really had much contact. The day Andrew's Dad was arrested by police at the family home is the day his life changed. He describes being in a state of 'absolute confusion', and how 'everything felt unreal'. 'Everything did a flip that day' and he says that he 'lost his* **sense of security'** *in his life.*
>
> *Andrew explained that he had no idea what was going on, or what was going to happen to him from that day forward. He didn't really have any other family he could call upon and he didn't know who or how to reach out for help... He explained that not knowing where to go for help was one of the biggest issues he faced.*
>
> *... He also spoke about how being young for him meant he had* **no control***; how he couldn't decide what he wanted to do, or where he wanted to be.*
>
> *Not having somewhere to live was just one part of Andrew's situation. Andrew also talked about having no money to buy food and getting so used to eating very little that 'you started to view not eating as a way to save money'. He talked about the impact this had on his mental health; how 'it feels as though you are living in a world that no one else would understand' and where 'you lose your dignity as well as any hopes you had for the future'.*
>
> *Andrew said some of his most vivid memories from the day his Dad got arrested included wondering where his stuff would go; even the toys he'd had since he was a kid. He said, 'you eventually get used to not having any possessions – after something like this happens you don't get attached to things anymore'.*
>
> *Andrew also talked about how he 'got told nothing'... He also said he* **lost the ability to trust** *on that day, and that this is something he is still working on changing, but feels he has a way to go yet... (Connolly, 2022, p. 13, emphasis added)*

This case demonstrates the importance of trauma-informed responses, which promote the *safety* of children. It ensures that they can *trust* the government and other agencies to have their best interests at the centre of policy and practice, and that they will be kept informed, with their interests being paramount.

Maintaining Safety: The Best Interests of Children

Trauma-informed responses aim to achieve safety, prioritising the well-being of children as well as the safety of the community when sentencing parents. Like the UK, in Australia it should be:

> *a legal requirement that in every case where a mother [or father] with a dependent child is at risk of a custodial sentence, the sentencer must acquire information about the dependent children, and must then weigh the... rights of the children [to a family life without interference by a public authority except where necessary] against the seriousness of the offence. (Epstein, 2014, p. 16)*

To promote safety for the children of defendants, this study suggests that many judges do reflect on the social and emotional wellbeing of defendants' children, and if it is appropriate, impose community-based sanctions (or indeed no-contact conditions) on parents. However, there is no legislative requirement that judges give regard to the best interests of children or even consider doing so. Arguably, such sanctions would have been appropriate in cases such as those of CVK and "Andrew" (above).

Establishing Trust

As previously stated, judges have considerable discretion when determining whether parental incarceration and dysfunctional childhoods are "good reasons" or "exceptional circumstances" that influence the imposed sanction. Ideally, defendants and their children should be able to trust that the courts will give regard to the welfare and best interests of dependent children in every case as part of their deliberations relating to the safety of the community. Children of prisoners are members of the community, and their future well-being should be part of the deliberations, such that incarceration is truly reserved for the most serious cases of interpersonal violence. Indeed, the law states that imprisonment should be an option of last resort (see e.g., *Sentencing Act 2017* (SA), s. 10(2)), and the public should trust that this is genuinely true in all cases, especially if the impact on children is disproportionately negative compared to the reduction in future offending that incarceration is likely to cause (See, e.g. the UK High Court case of *R (on the application of Stokes) v Gwent Magistrates Court* [2001] All ER (D) 125, cited by Epstein, 2014, p. 5).

To give regard to defendants' children is not synonymous with no custodial sentences (and, as shown in the case of DTW, it may be that a custodial sentence is explicitly imposed to promote the safety of the children). Nevertheless, to establish trust, the legislation (and sentencing judges) should clearly articulate the well-being of dependent children as a specified and relevant sentencing factor to be incorporated into the sentencing calculus, in the same way other sentencing factors, such as impact on victims and the nature, circumstances and seriousness of the offence, are considered.

Voice & Choice

Connolly (2022) and others have spoken with children about the impacts of parental incarceration, with children's perspectives providing "a more complete and nuanced picture of risk, competence, and resilience" (Johnson & Arditti, 2022, p. 33). Children's voice and choice can be elevated by encouraging greater participation and visibility within the sentencing process. The Victorian Legislative Council Legal and Social Issues Committee (Legislative Council Legal and Social Issues Committee, 2022) identified a need for more child-centric processes where children are more visible at the sentencing stage, with opportunities to communicate their preferences and needs. Children's best interests should include their self-identified preferences, in terms of where and with whom they would like to live, as well as access to their mothers and fathers. In cases where parents are incarcerated, corrective services and child protection agencies should (but rarely do) work together to enable children to have access to their parents (if that reflects their wishes and interests).

Collaboration (Between Agencies)

In addition to collaborating with children to act in their best interests, there is a need for collaboration between justice and social service agencies. The absence of any discussion of children's welfare in the snapshot study highlighted the siloed nature of government responses to families at risk of entrenched and intergenerational ACEs. At the time a parent is taken into custody, dependent children are not automatically the statutory responsibility of child protection authorities (with exceptions, such as when a single mother of a baby or infant is imprisoned). Twenty years ago, a Victorian study found that:

> *there was no co-ordinated response by the child protection and justice systems ... no formal case-planning process that brought together the key stakeholders in decisions about, for example, children and their care. It was clear that it is essential for all agencies and organisations who work with the children of prisoners,* ***collaborate*** *to identify the needs of these children... to ensure a comprehensive approach. (Sheehan & Levine, 2006, p. 6, emphasis added)*

There is no dedicated government agency in (South) Australia responsible for ensuring the well-being of children of adults in custody. Internationally, and certainly in South Australia, there has been a systemic failure for decades for any agency to identify children of prisoners as their core business, or to develop a coordinated government response to support the children of incarcerated parents (Flynn et al.,

2015; Legislative Council Legal and Social Issues Committee, 2022, p. xii; Sheehan & Levine, 2006).

Further, the UNCRC emphasise:

The need for proper recording of the existence and number of children of incarcerated parents... This should be done early in the criminal justice process and information shared appropriately to enable appropriate support for the children, with due regard to the children's right to privacy and mindful of the need to avoid discrimination or stigma towards children identified as having incarcerated parents. (UNCRC, 2011, p. 4 [20])

Recent research undertaken in the Adelaide Women's Prison (AWP) found that the Department for Correctional Services (DCS) was unsure how many incarcerated mothers were housed in AWP and, therefore, how many dependent children were within the community without their mothers (Brew-Bevan, 2023). In 2024, 168 women in custody at the AWP self-identified as having 303 children, with DCS data suggesting the actual number of children was closer to 450 (Brew-Bevan, 2023). This lack of certainty is unacceptable.

Empowerment

A key strategy to empower children of incarcerated parents is to develop child-centric policies for courts. Flynn et al. (2015) refer to parental mental illness as being parallel to parental incarceration. They demonstrate that in the case of parental mental illness, there is often a systemic, coordinated case management approach applied that encompasses both the parent and the child(ren) affected. Such an approach aims to empower the affected family to build capacity and promote (re)unification through family care plan meetings with professional stakeholders as well as family members, including children. Flynn et al. (2015) ask why such an approach cannot be used when parents are incarcerated.

Gender, Culture and Historical Factors

The snapshot study, unlike previous research (e.g., McLachlan, 2022; O'Hear & Wheelock, 2025), found that non-Indigenous mothers and fathers were both likely to receive community-based sentences (at 66.7%). Previous research found that judges may be influenced by gender stereotypes (O'Hear & Wheelock, 2025) and tend to be more sympathetic towards non-Indigenous mothers than Aboriginal mothers or fathers, or non-Indigenous fathers (McLachlan, 2022). Children of prisoners have been found to report always feeling loved by their mothers, more so than their fathers, and significantly more so than children in the general population (Oldrup & Frederiksen, 2018). Maintaining a connection between children and incarcerated mothers is an important, protective factor in reducing future offending. However, this snapshot study goes further, suggesting two key things:

- First, the sanction imposed on a sole parent and its impact on the safety of a child should be a significant sentencing consideration, regardless of the parent's gender; and
- Second, parental incarceration may be more likely to result in intergenerational incarceration of sons but is likely to have a notable adverse impact on daughters.

The gender of children has previously been found to be a relevant moderator of the risk of parental incarceration, with more sons than daughters likely to be second-generation prisoners (Johnson & Arditti, 2022).

First Nations defendants were more likely to receive custodial sentences than their non-Indigenous counterparts (87.5% vs 30.8%). This could, in part, be attributed to the seriousness of their offending: Aboriginal defendants in the sample were convicted of more violent, interpersonal offences. Nevertheless, the snapshot study shows that even when judges identified defendants as Aboriginal, they overlooked or paid minimal attention to cultural factors or intergenerational trauma known to be associated with Aboriginality.

Aboriginal and Torres Strait Islander children are more likely to have a parent incarcerated than non-Indigenous children (Dennison et al., 2013; Dowell et al., 2017; Legislative Council Legal and Social Issues Committee, 2022). Judicial education and policies could encourage the use of culture and trauma reports where it is apparent that intergenerational trauma associated with Indigeneity is relevant (McLachlan, 2023). Australia could (and should) draw from the Canadian model, where there is national legislation that specifically refers to Aboriginality as a sentencing factor. Section 718.2(e) of the Canadian *Criminal Code* states:

> *all available sanctions, other than imprisonment, that are reasonable in the circumstances and consistent with the harm done to victims or to the community should be considered for all offenders, with particular attention to the circumstances of Aboriginal offenders.*

Courts should always consider the long-term impacts on community safety when sentencing Aboriginal defendants to custody, aiming to avoid creating another Stolen Generation through the removal of parents from Aboriginal families, wherever possible. For First Nations peoples, community safety is best achieved by promoting connection to Country, culture, family and identity (Australian Institute of Health and Welfare, 2023b)—none of which is achievable in prison.

Resisting Re-Traumatisation

This chapter has outlined that the incarceration of parents can result in the compounding of other childhood adversities such as poverty, social exclusion, abuse and neglect, and ultimately increase the risk of a child having contact with child protection systems, out-of-home care, youth justice and adult corrections. Given that the fundamental purpose of sentencing is to ensure community safety, the longer-term impacts on children should be a key consideration when sentencing parents, in terms of ensuring the safety of the community for future generations, not just for the present. Breaking the cycle of intergenerational incarceration should be a good reason for ensuring that incarceration is reserved only for those who present an imminent risk of harm to the community.

CONCLUSION

It is estimated that five per cent of children in Australia are affected by parental incarceration. This chapter began by examining the impact of parental incarceration and cumulative adversity on the life trajectories of children. Children of prisoners experience multiple challenges that are compounded by parental incarceration. This adversity includes child abuse and neglect, social exclusion and poverty, as well as household dysfunction, resulting in complex trauma and an increased risk of second-generation criminalisation and incarceration. Second, a snapshot sample of 21 current sentencing remarks of adults was analysed to determine how judges acknowledge and respond to the impact of intergenerational incarceration. The evidence suggested that judicial discretion influenced the degree to which children's interests were taken into consideration.

Finally, trauma-informed strategies for courts are discussed to mitigate the intergenerational trauma and criminality associated with parental incarceration. There is currently no government agency responsible for ensuring the well-being of children of adults in custody, allowing children's best interests to be overlooked. Given that the criminal justice system's fundamental purpose is to protect the community's safety, not just for this generation but for future generations, it makes sense that justice and social welfare agencies work together to break the cycle of intergenerational criminalisation by establishing practices and reforms to reduce re-traumatisation.

REFERENCES

Australian Bureau of Statistics. (2024). *Prisoners in Australia.* https://www.abs.gov.au/statistics/people/crime-and-justice/prisoners-australia/latest-release

Australian Institute of Health & Welfare. (2023a). *The Health of People in Australian Prisons 2022.* https://www.aihw.gov.au/reports/prisoners/the-health-of-people-in-australias-prisons-2022/

Australian Institute of Health and Welfare. (2020). *The health and welfare of women in Australia's prisons.*

Australian Institute of Health and Welfare. (2023b). *Community Safety for First Nations People.*

Australian Law Reform Commission. (2005). *Sentencing of Federal Offenders, Discussion Paper No 70.*

Auty, K. M., Farrington, D. P., & Coid, J. W. (2017). The Intergenerational transmission of criminal offending: Exploring Gender-Specific Mechanisms. *British Journal of Criminology, 57*, 215–237. DOI: 10.1093/bjc/azv115

Besemer, S., Ahmad, S. I., Hinshaw, S. P., & Farrington, D. P. (2017). A systematic review and meta-analysis of the intergenerational transmission of criminal behavior. *Aggression and Violent Behavior, 37*, 161–178. DOI: 10.1016/j.avb.2017.10.004

Bonta, J., & Andrews, D. A. (2017). *The Psychology of Criminal Conduct* (6th ed.). Routledge.

Brew-Bevan, E. (2023). *Parental Needs of Incarcerated Mothers – Hidden figures in need of a voice.* [Honours thesis, Flinders University].

Condry, R., & Smith, P. S. (2018). The Sociology of Punishment and the Effects of Imprisonment on Families. In Condry, R., & Smith, P. S. (Eds.), *Prisons, Punishment and Family: Towards a New Sociology of Punishment* (pp. 1–24). Oxford University Press.

Connolly, H. (2022). *Join the Dots: considering the impact of parental incarceration on children and young people*. Commissioner for Children and Young People.

Cunningham, T. (2025). *Criminalised young people and the worlds we create for them: An exploration of discourse, power and subjectivity.* [PhD thesis, Flinders University].

Day, A., Malvaso, C., Boyd, C., Hawkins, K., & Pilkington, R. (2023). The effectiveness of trauma-informed youth justice: A discussion and review. *Frontiers in Psychology*, *14*, 1157695. DOI: 10.3389/fpsyg.2023.1157695

Dennison, S., Stewart, A., & Freiberg, K. (2013). A prevalence study of children with imprisoned fathers: Annual and lifetime estimates. *The Australian Journal of Social Issues*, *48*(3), 339–362. DOI: 10.1002/j.1839-4655.2013.tb00286.x

Dowell, C. M., Preen, D. B., & Segal, L. (2017). Quantifying maternal incarceration: A whole-population linked data study of Western Australian children born 1985–2011. *Australian and New Zealand Journal of Public Health*, *41*(2), 151–157. DOI: 10.1111/1753-6405.12613

Epstein, R. (2014). *Mothers in prison: The sentencing of mothers and the rights of the child. Howard League What is Justice? Working Papers 3/2014.* The Howard League for Penal Reform.

Farrington, D. P., Barnes, G., & Lambert, S. (1996). The concentration of offending in families. *Legal and Criminological Psychology*, *1*(1), 47–63.

Farrington, D. P., Ttofi, M. M., Crago, R. V., & Coid, J. W. (2015). Intergenerational similarities in risk factors for offending. *Journal of Developmental and Life-Course Criminology*, *1*(1), 48–62. DOI: 10.1007/s40865-015-0005-2

Felitti, V. J., Anda, R. F., Nordenberg, D., Williamson, D. F., Spitz, A. M., Edwards, V., Koss, M. P., & Marks, J. S. (1998). Relationship of Childhood Abuse and Household Dysfunction to Many of the Leading Causes of Death in Adults: The Adverse Childhood Experiences (ACE) Study. *American Journal of Preventive Medicine*, *14*(4), 245–258. DOI: 10.1016/s0749-3797(98)00017-8

Finkelhor, D., Shattuck, A., Turner, H., & Hamby, S. (2013). Improving the Adverse Childhood Experiences Study scale. *JAMA Pediatrics*, *167*(1), 70–75. DOI: 10.1001/jamapediatrics.2013.420

Flynn, C., Bartlett, T., Arias, P. F., Evans, P., & Burgess, A. (2015). Responding to children when their parents are incarcerated: Exploring the responses in Victoria and New South Wales, Australia. *Law in Context (Bundoora, Vic.)*, *32*, 4–27. DOI: 10.3316/informit.040884869356222

Ford, K., Bellis, M. A., Hughes, K., Judd, N., & Barton, E. R. (2024). Exploring the intergenerational continuity of ACEs amongst a sample of Welsh male prisoners: A retrospective cross-sectional study. *Child Protection and Practice*, *3*, 100053. DOI: 10.1016/j.chipro.2024.100053

Hagan, J. (1996). The Next Generation: Children of Prisoners. In: *The Unintended Consequences of Incarceration: Papers from a conference organized by the Vera Institute of Justice* (pp. 21 – 40). Vera Institute of Justice.

Halsey, M., & De Vel-Palumbo, M. (2020). *Generations through prison: Experiences of intergenerational incarceration.* Routledge.

Johnson, E. I., & Arditti, J. A. (2022). Adolescents with Incarcerated Parents: Toward Developmentally Informed Research and Practice. In Krysik, J., & Rodriguez, N. (Eds.), *Children of Incarcerated Parents: From Understanding to Impact* (pp. 23–40). Springer Nature., DOI: 10.1007/978-3-030-84713-5_2

Khoury, L., Tang, Y. L., Bradley, B., Cubells, J. F., & Ressler, K. J. (2010). Substance use, childhood traumatic experience, and posttraumatic stress disorder in an urban civilian population. *Depression and Anxiety, 27*, 1077–1086. DOI: 10.1002/da.20751

King, S. (2019). Sentencing Parents – Sentencing their Children? *EuroVista, 1*(3), 137–146.

Legislative Council Legal and Social Issues Committee. (2022). *Inquiry into children affected by parental incarceration.* Parliament of Victoria.

Lovell, B., Steen, M., Esterman, A., & Brown, A. (2020). The Parenting Education Needs of Women Experiencing Incarceration in South Australia: Proposal for a Mixed Methods Study. *JMIR Research Protocols, 9*(8), e18992. DOI: 10.2196/18992

McLachlan, K.J. (2022). *'I cannot dismiss from my mind your traumatic and tragic upbringing': Trauma-informed sentencing in South Australia* [PhD Thesis, University of South Australia].

McLachlan, K. J. (2023). Trauma-informed sentencing of adults who are life-course persistent offenders. In Malvaso, C., McGee, T. R., & Homel, R. (Eds.), *Frontiers in Developmental and Life-Course Criminology: Methodological Innovation and Social Benefit* (pp. 115–124). Routledge., DOI: 10.4324/9781003294740-11

McLachlan, K. J. (2024). *Trauma-Informed Criminal Justice: Towards a More Compassionate Criminal Justice System.* Palgrave Macmillan/Springer Nature. https://link.springer.com/book/10.1007/978-3-031-59290-4

Murray, J., Farrington, D. P., & Sekol, I. (2012). Children's Antisocial Behavior, Mental Health, Drug Use, and Educational Performance After Parental Incarceration: A Systematic Review and Meta-Analysis. *Psychological Bulletin, 138*(2), 175–210. DOI: 10.1037/a0026407

Novero, C. M., Booker Loper, A., & Warren, J. I. (2011). Second-Generation Prisoners. *Criminal Justice and Behavior, 38*(8), 761–778. DOI: 10.1177/0093854811406637

O'Hear, M., & Wheelock, D. (2025). The sentencing advantage of female defendants in homicide cases. *Drake Law Review, 72*(1), 37–72.

Oldrup, H., & Frederiksen, S. (2018). Are the Children of Prisoners Socially Excluded? A Child- Centred Perspective. In Condry, R., & Smith, P. S. (Eds.), *Prisons, Punishment and Family: Towards a New Sociology of Punishment?* (pp. 102–116). Oxford University Press.

Paynter, M., Heggie, C., Matheson, L., Rillie, C., Beals, D., & Bray, M. (2022). Maternal incarceration in a provincial prison in Canada: A qualitative study. *Journal of Advanced Nursing, 78*(7), 2123–2138. DOI: 10.1111/jan.15154

Quilty, S. (2005). The magnitude of experience of parental incarceration in Australia. *Psychiatry, Psychology, and Law : an Interdisciplinary Journal of the Australian and New Zealand Association of Psychiatry, Psychology and Law, 12*(1), 256–257.

R v ABP (District Court of SA, Judge E, 25 March 2025)

R v AJM (District Court of SA, Judge M, 31 March 2025)

R v AKG (District Court of SA, Judge B, 16 May 2025)

R v BKL (District Court of SA, Judge B, 28 March 2025)

R v CVK (District Court of SA, Judge S, 15 April 2025)

R v DJV (District Court of SA, Judge U, 14 April 2025)

R v DTW (District Court of SA, Judge K, 16 April 2025)

R v FMP (District Court of SA, Judge M, 24 April 2025)

R v JAP (District Court of SA, Judge D, 27 March 2025)

R v JRG (District Court of SA, Judge T, 17 March 2025)

R v JRS (District Court of SA, Judge H, 30 April 2025)

R v KVH (District Court of SA, Judge B, 6 May 2025)

R v LSK (District Court of SA, Judge A, 28 March 2025)

R v MIL (District Court of SA, Judge S, 26 March 2025)

R v NJK (District Court of SA, Judge M, 31 March 2025)

R v NSF (District Court of SA, Judge B, 11 April 2025)

R v RCD (District Court of SA, Judge P, 14 May 2025)

R v SAM (District Court of SA, Judge B, 13 March 2025)

R v SKR (District Court of SA, Judge W, 23 April 2025)

R v SRH (District Court of SA, Judge A, 5 March 2025)

R v WCD (District Court of SA, Judge W, 24 April 2025)

Rémond, M., Zeki, R., Austin, K., Bowman, J., Galouzis, J., Stewart, K., & Sullivan, E. (2023). *Intergenerational incarceration in New South Wales: Characteristics of people in prison experiencing parental imprisonment. Trends & issues in crime and criminal justice no. 663*. Australian Institute of Criminology., DOI: 10.52922/ti78863

Sheehan, R., & Levine, G. (2006). *Parents as Prisoners: Maintaining the Parent-Child Relationship. Report for the Criminology Research Council Project Grant CRC 39/05-06*. Australian Institute of Criminology.

Sherman, A. (2005). Children of Prisoners: Background Briefing Report. The Center for Research on Children in the U.S. (CROCUS) & Georgetown Public Policy Institute.

Shine for Kids. (2024). *Case Worker & Foster Carer Guidebook*. https://shineforkids.org.au/wp-content/uploads/2024/08/Case-Worker-and-Foster-Carer-guidebook-FINAL.pdf

Substance Abuse and Mental Health Services Administration. (2014). *SAMHSA's Concept of Trauma and Guidance for a Trauma-Informed Approach*. US Department of Health and Human Services.

United Nations. (1989, November 20) *Convention on the Rights of the Child*. General Assembly resolution 44/25. https://www.ohchr.org/sites/default/files/crc.pdf

United Nations Committee on the Rights of the Child (UNCRC). (2011, September 30) Report and Recommendations of the Day of General Discussion on 'Children of Incarcerated Parents'. https://www.ohchr.org/sites/default/files/Documents/HRBodies/CRC/Discussions/2011/DGD2011ReportAndRecommendations.pdf

Vaismoradi, M., Turunen, H., & Bondas, T. (2013). Content analysis and thematic analysis: Implications for conducting a qualitative descriptive study. *Nursing & Health Sciences, 15*, 398–405. https://doi.org/doi:10.1111/nhs.12048

Walsh, T., & Douglas, H. (2016). Sentencing Parents: The Consideration of Dependent Children. *Adelaide Law Review, 37*, 135–161.

Wildeman, C., & Andersen, S. H. (2017). Paternal incarceration and children's risk of being charged by early adulthood: Evidence from a Danish policy shock. *Criminology*, *55*(1), 32–58. DOI: 10.1111/1745-9125.12124

Wildeman, C., Sampson, R. J., & Baker, G. (2024). Adult Children of the Prison Boom: Family Troubles and the Intergenerational Transmission of Criminal Justice Contact. *Demography*, *61*(1), 141–164. DOI: 10.1215/00703370-11153107

Wolff, K. T., Craig, J. M., Baglivio, M. T., & Papalia, N. (2025). Are More ACEs Always Worse? Exploring Nonlinear Associations with Youth Behavior. *Journal of Youth and Adolescence*. Advance online publication. DOI: 10.1007/s10964-025-02225-5

ADDITIONAL READING

Day, A., Malvaso, C. G., Butcher, L., O'Connor, J., & McLachlan, K. (2023). Co-producing trauma-informed Youth Justice in Australia? *Safer Communities.*, *22*(2), 106–120. DOI: 10.1108/SC-08-2022-0030

McLachlan, K. J. (2023). Using a trauma-informed practice framework to operationalise the #raisetheage campaign. *Current Issues in Criminal Justice*, *36*(4), 433–450. DOI: 10.1080/10345329.2023.2196099

McLachlan, K. J. (2024). *Trauma-Informed Criminal Justice: Towards a More Compassionate Criminal Justice System.* Palgrave Macmillan/Springer Nature. https://link.springer.com/book/10.1007/978-3-031-59290-4

KEY TERMS AND DEFINITIONS

Adverse Childhood Experiences: Adversity experienced during childhood, including abuse and neglect, household dysfunction (e.g., domestic abuse, familial mental health, substance abuse issues, incarcerated parent), or social challenges such as poverty and racism.

Adversity: Experiences and events that have the potential to harm an individual's functioning and well-being and may result in trauma.

Children of prisoners: children of fathers and/or mothers who are or have been incarcerated, whether the children are dependent (under 18 years) or adults

Dependent Children: people under 18 years of age

Sentencing: the process of determining an appropriate sanction in response to proven criminal behaviour based on the law, the offending context, and the surrounding circumstances of the offence.

Trauma: the negative impact of adverse events and experiences across the life course, which may manifest in different ways (e.g., psychological trauma, emotional trauma, neurophysiological trauma)

Trauma-informed practice: ways of working that realise and recognise adversity and its potential to cause trauma, and acts to respond to people who may have trauma in a way that is informed by scientific evidence and principles of practice (namely, safety; trust; collaboration; voice, choice and empowerment; peer support; and recognition of gender, culture and historical factors).

ENDNOTE

1 This chapter refers to First Nations Australians but also uses the terms Indigenous (and non-Indigenous) as well as Aboriginal and Torres Strait Islander peoples. No offence is intended with the use of any term.

Chapter 3
The Accumulation of ACEs and the Impact on Offending for Incarcerated Youth

Anthony Mark Jamieson
https://orcid.org/0009-0009-1966-6105
University of Sunshine Coast, Australia

ABSTRACT

This chapter discusses the lives of justice-involved youth and contrasts that with the ways in which offending youth are portrayed in the media and by politicians. The chapter then examines the impact of the accumulation of ACEs, and their impact on violent and repeat offending, followed by a discussion about ways in which Attachment Theory can explain this behaviour. The chapter concludes with policy and practice implications for youth justice agencies, based on an examination of three key questions, which identify what governments could do to address populist narratives, the actions needed by youth justice agencies needed to focus on ACEs, and concl;udes with addressing ACEs through a Trauma-Informed Care (TIC) approach.

INTRODUCTION

Adverse Childhood Experiences (ACEs) are maltreatment, abuse and family dysfunction events endured by children, which are well known for having a long-lasting impact on the lives of young people (Van Wyk, 2023, p. 74). Research evidence suggests that enduring ACEs leads to a range of negative life outcomes, including

DOI: 10.4018/979-8-3373-9524-1.ch003

poor academic achievement, homelessness, difficulty in maintaining employment, and offending behaviour (Ogilvie et al., 2022).

Research suggests that all 10 of the ACEs identified in the initial study by Felitti et al., (1998) have a negative impact on the development of young people (Perry et al., 2018). Moreover Craig et al. (2023) find that all ACEs can lead to chronic offending behaviour, suggesting they all have a similar likelihood of contributing in some way to a career in crime. However, research also suggests that it is the cumulative effect of ACEs that has a greater negative effect on life outcomes (Yannon et al., 2024).

Most often, youths in custody experience multiple ACEs (Malvaso et al., 2019). The prevalence varies depending on the research context but most research suggests that well over half will experience more than one ACE (Malvaso et al., 2022a). However, it appears to be the cumulative effect of adversities faced that has the strongest impact on both the seriousness of youth offending and its chronicity (DeLisi et al., 2021; Yannon et al., 2024).

The source of the accumulation of ACEs is the burden of structural disadvantage that many justice-involved youth have to survive during their childhood and adolescent years (Stathis et al., 2008), over which they have virtually no control (Phoenix, 2016). For example, many live in lower socioeconomic areas, where there is high unemployment and poverty, and come from large, single-parent families (Thomsen & Homel, 2024). When this is combined with the burden of ACEs, the result is often a lack of support for the young person, a subsequent lack of resilience towards navigating challenging events, and ultimately a particular vulnerability towards offending behaviour (Thomsen & Homel, 2024). This reality contrasts sharply with the manner in which offending youth are portrayed in the Australian media and by politicians, who have targeted these young people for the purpose of political gain and ratings (Riddle et al., 2024).

This chapter begins with a discussion about the lives of justice-involved youth and contrasts that with the ways in which offending youth are portrayed in the Australian media and by politicians. It then examines the impact of the accumulation of ACEs, and their impact on violent and repeat offending, followed by a discussion about ways in which Attachment Theory can explain this behaviour. The chapter concludes with policy and practice implications for youth-justice agencies, based on an examination of three key questions.

TRAUMA FOR JUSTICE-INVOLVED YOUTH

Whether young people learn to behave in a criminalised manner (Bandura, 1978), drift into delinquency (Matza, 1990), or live according to stigmatising labels (Becker, 1963), there is substantial evidence that young people who have suffered abuse, neglect and harm are more likely to engage in offending behaviour than young people who have not experienced maltreatment (Stewart et al., 2008). Due to prolonged exposure to traumatic events, some young people respond by acting aggressively and rebelliously, making dangerous choices, harming others and breaking rules and laws in an attempt to survive psychologically and defend themselves (Kelley et al., 2014). Therefore, it is not surprising that young people with a history of trauma are frequently arrested, including for serious crimes, such as sex offences, assaults and murder (Zettler et al., 2017).

It is useful to provide a definition of trauma at this point. There are many definitions, but most of them have common themes about highly stressful events that damage human functioning and coping mechanisms, and are a natural reaction to the experience of distressing or harrowing events (Evans et al., 2018). For example, Perry (2008) describes trauma from a neurobiological perspective and notes it is an experience or repetition of experiences which trigger the body's stress response systems in such excessive and extended ways as to instigate changes to the manner in which the neural system works. The Diagnostic and Statistical Manual of Mental Disorders (DSM–V) (American Psychiatric Association, 2013) has a more detailed definition, which includes the physical and mental impact on people of being directly or indirectly exposed to wars, violence of any kind, disasters, accidents or medical emergencies. A more straightforward definition is that it is an experience of real or perceived threat to life, bodily integrity and/or sense of self, to which the victim(s) are repeatedly exposed over a period of time (Bateman et al., Bateman, 2013).

Understanding the trauma of justice-involved youth is important because exposure to trauma is an antecedent to their offending (Benekos & Merlo, 2016; Yoder et al., 2018). Quinn et al., (2017) argue that there is a mutual relationship between trauma and offending behaviour, which is that trauma exposure leads to a young person displaying antisocial and illegal behaviour, which in turn increases the risk of re-traumatisation and further exposure to violence (Charak et al., 2019). Van der Kolk (2007) states that people with childhood histories of trauma make up almost all criminal justice populations, both youth and adult.

Trauma negatively impacts brain development because the higher-order parts of the brain – the cortical and limbic systems – depend on healthy development of the lower parts of the brain i.e. the brainstem and midbrain. If development of these parts is compromised due to complex trauma, then the state of fear induced by trauma will regularly shut down the cortical system in favour of the survival part of the brain, the brainstem. This compromises the long-term cognitive and memory abilities of children (Perry, 2008).

Significant early trauma often leads to poorly regulated stress responses, due to over-activated neurological functions which inaccurately assess danger and tend to identify threats when there are none in a particular situation (Van Der Kolk et al.,

1996). This means that the nervous system is constantly in a state of arousal, resulting in young people often being on high alert, which in turn interferes with higher-order functioning skills that suppress impulsive behaviours and aid concentration and sound decision-making. The overall effect of this is inaccurate processing of information and inappropriate responses, such as violent assaults, to neutral stimuli (Pickens, 2016).

OFFENDING YOUTH AS PORTRAYED BY THE AUSTRALIAN MEDIA AND POLITICIANS

Youth crime in Australia is regarded as an important social issue and one that is often the subject of political debate (Cunneen et al., 2015). Young people are expected to behave in law-abiding ways as part of a natural progression towards adulthood (Hay et al., 2024) and to assist in making this a reality, there are some restrictions placed upon their behaviour and movement within society by lawmakers and police (Cunneen et al., 2015): for instance with regard to consumption of alcohol (S53A) and loitering in public spaces (S47) (Police Powers and Responsibilities Act 2000 Qld) (Austl.). When a young person ignores these restrictions and behaves in ways that transgress the accepted social views of acceptable lawful conduct (Case et al., 2021), the broadly-held view is that the young person needs to be held responsible for their behaviour in some way (Cunneen et al., 2015).

The justice view of youth offending, which is the dominant view propounded by Australian politicians and the Australian media, says just because they are legally children, does not excuse them from their crimes and they need to be held accountable as would an adult (Cavadino & Dignan, 2006). This view is characterised by the public expectation that young people will be punished for their crimes and tends to focus on high-profile offences as examples of what happens when youth crime laws are not strict (Knight, 2024). This expectation is supported by contemporary political and Australian media discourse, which focuses on a tough-on-crime approach and holds a view that young offenders, by virtue of their criminality, have surrendered their rights as a citizen, and that victims of crime are fully deserving of legal and criminal protection (Drake & Henley, 2014). This view overlooks the fact that many young offenders are also victims of crime themselves, i.e. they are both offender and victim (Armytage & Ogloff, 2017), and that many apparently innocent citizens are themselves known to the police for the commission of, mostly minor, offences (Drake & Henley, 2014).

When the Australian media reports the persistent law-breaking behaviour of young people, this can lead to concern from adults that there is a youth-crime problem. This concern may stem from Australian media images of young people acting in ways that are perceived as irresponsible, rebellious or dangerous and beliefs that they lack discipline and respect for others (Muncie, 2015). At these times there are often calls for punitive action because of a view that this is necessary for young people to understand that their actions will not be tolerated (Riddle et al., 2024). Lynch et al., (2022), and Riddle et al., (2024), state that more lenient diversionary practices, e.g., restorative justice conferencing, are only tolerated because of the existence of punitive options. The use of incarceration has continued to increase for youth offenders in most Australian states and territories due to the increasing presumption against bail in response to community-based concerns, meaning that diversionary options are often bypassed (Cunneen, 2008).

Governments have publicly acknowledged that youth offending is strongly associated with disadvantage, particularly for Indigenous youth (Vardon, 2021) and that these adversities are often traumatic for young people and increase the risk of them behaving unlawfully (Department of Child Safety Youth and Women, 2018). Yet governments appear reticent to implement initiatives that address these adversities (McLachlan, 2024b), which may be the case because both sides of Australian politics want to demonstrate that their "tough-on-crime" credentials are stronger than their political opponent's (Cunneen & White, 2011). This reticence extends to executive leaders within the youth justice system (Hales et al., 2016), who as public servants report to the Minister of the day and are required to give effect to "official public sector priorities, policies and decisions professionally and impartially" (Public Sector Ethics Act, 1994, s9). Should those priorities change, then executives must change theirs accordingly so that they can serve the priorities of the government of the day (Queensland Government, 2023).

However, claims that youth crime is out of control are not borne out by the statistics over the past decade. In the period between 1 July 2014 and 30 June 2024:

- The daily Australian national average number of young people under community-based youth-justice supervision actually decreased. In 2014-15 there were 5,629 young people being supervised by Australian youth-justice agencies per day (Australian Institute of Health and Welfare, 2016) but by 2023/24 that figure had decreased by 33 per cent to 4,227 (Australian Institute of Health and Welfare, 2025).
- The annual numbers tell the same story. In 2014/15 there were 11,360 youth supervised by Australian youth-justice agencies (Australian Institute of Health and Welfare, 2016), a figure that decreased by 23 per cent, to 9,224 over the next decade (Australian Institute of Health and Welfare, 2025).
- From the national population of those aged 10-17, the rate per 10,000 has decreased from 21 young people per day in 2014/15 (Australian Institute of

Health and Welfare, 2016) to 12 in 2023/24 (Australian Institute of Health and Welfare, 2025).

- Moreover, there has been an 8 per cent decrease in overall national youth offences per person in the last 10 years, from 50,714 in 2014/15 (Australian Bureau of Statistics, 2017), to 46,798 in 2023/24 (Australian Bureau of Statistics, 2025).
- Indigenous over-representation has increased though, from 43 per cent in 2014/15 to approximately 54 per cent in 2023/24 (Australian Institute of Health and Welfare, 2025).
- The total number of young people in youth detention has decreased slightly from 4,721 in 2014/15, to 4,578 in 2023/24 (Australian Institute of Health and Welfare, 2016, 2025).

The offending trend seems to be driven by decreases in illicit drug offences and theft (Australian Bureau of Statistics, 2025). However, the source of public concern appears to be clearer when one looks at the statistics across the most prevalent offence types. In 2014/15 the most common offence type was theft (35 per cent), followed by acts intended to cause injury (15 per cent) and illicit drug offences (11 per cent) (Australian Bureau of Statistics, 2017). In 2023/24 these were still the three most prevalent offence types, however, acts intended to cause injury had increased to 25 per cent, while theft (12 per cent) and illicit drug offences (6 per cent) had decreased (Australian Bureau of Statistics, 2025). The increase in acts intended to cause injury may be the issue to which the Australian media and politicians are referring. That is, youth crime, while reducing overall, appears to have become more violent (Atkinson, 2022). These violent offences are often the most impactful for victims, and thus the most newsworthy, which may be fuelling public concern (Antolak-Saper, 2020).

IMPACT OF THE ACCUMULATION OF ACES

The above statistics do not mention that youth offenders are more likely than their non-offending peers to have endured ongoing maltreatment and neglect and to have been negatively impacted by violent and dysfunctional upbringings (Astridge et al., 2023; Baglivio et al., 2014). They are also more likely to come from socioeconomically disadvantaged communities and to have had contact with child-protection agencies, including being placed in out-of-home care (Baidawi & Sheehan, 2019). These combined experiences often have a range of negative impacts on a young person, including below-average school achievement, physical illnesses, poor mental health and justice involvement (Kurlychek & Johnson, 2019).

In Australia these negative impacts are more conspicuous in the lives of many Aboriginal and Torres Strait Islander young people (Peters & Mika, 2017). Researchers suggest that this disadvantage is the result of intergenerational trauma, along with entrenched systemic and structural inequalities (Atkinson et al., 2014) which have resulted in the over-representation of Indigenous youth in the justice system. Scholars argue this is the result of the intersecting impacts of colonisation, socioeconomic disadvantage, institutional racism, and the practices of the criminal justice system (Cunneen, 2006). Despite Indigenous people comprising only 3.8 per cent of the Australian population in the latest census (Australian Institute of Health & Welfare, 2023), Indigenous youth comprised 53.3 per cent of total offenders as at 30 June 2023 (Australian Institute of Health and Welfare, 2024). In Queensland Indigenous youth are 27 times more likely to be incarcerated than their non-Indigenous peers (Department of Youth Justice, 2024).

These negative impacts have been studied extensively in recent years by scholars, seeking to determine the link with offending. A key topic of such research has been adverse childhood experiences (ACEs). These are instances of childhood maltreatment and family dysfunction that are usually inflicted upon the child by an adult who is in a position of trust, and as such represent a fundamental breach of that trust that has deleterious long-term impacts for the child (Felitti et al., 1998). The term was coined after a landmark study in 1998, which studied 10 types of adverse events, although the authors identified that there were more types of adversities than those listed (Felitti et al., 1998). The 10 types of adverse events include: (1) emotional abuse; (2) physical abuse; (3) sexual abuse; (4) emotional neglect; (5) physical neglect; (6) witnessing domestic violence; (7) carers who abuse alcohol and/or drugs; (8) carers who have mental health challenges; (9) carers who been incarcerated; and (10) carer loss through separation, divorce or death. An ACE score from 0-10 is determined by whether a child has endured any or all of these events (Anda et al., 2010).

King (2020) says that the ACE score is based on the straightforward idea that ACEs have a harmful impact on child development and that they seem to work in an additive way, meaning that the type and seriousness of each ACE is less important than their number. Duron et al., (2021) suggest that multiple ACE exposures have worse impacts for youth than single exposures. Thus, if ACE scores are viewed as a "cumulative risk model, higher ACE scores denote higher levels of adversity" (Duron et al., 2021, p. 2). This means that each additional ACE increases the likelihood of negative impacts. Moreover, ACEs are accumulated across life-course development, which means that ACEs that occur earlier in the child's life are related to those that occur later and increase the risk of even more ACEs (Duron et al., 2021). Kahn et al., (2020) take this further and suggest that each additional ACE not only has an additive impact, but a multiplicative one as well. ACEs have long been recognised for negatively influencing individual outcomes such that each additional ACE exposure increases the risk for negative health and behavioural outcomes (Duron et al., 2021). Greater exposure to ACEs early in life is associated with greater risk of mortality, many forms of morbidity, mental health difficulties, and behavioural health problems over the life course (Duron et al., 2021).

Craig et al., (2021) note that the ACEs identified in the original study are more likely to occur in offending populations than in other groups within a community. Moreover DeLisi et al., (2021) suggest that those with more and varied ACEs tend to start offending earlier and for longer: i.e. they say that each ACE increases the likelihood of "… serious, violent, and chronic delinquency by 35 per cent suggesting that the most abused youth have 350 per cent higher odds of career criminality than youth without abuse experiences" (DeLisi et al., DeLisi, 2021, p. 2). Not only are those with a higher ACE score more likely to engage in criminality; that criminal behaviour is more likely to involve dangerous offences over longer time frames (Malvaso et al., 2021). Indeed Baglivio et al., (2020) state that with each ACE comes an increased risk of criminal behaviour by a factor of 35 times. Four ACEs seems to be regarded as the tipping point in the literature, for not only justice involvement (Kahn et al., 2020). Craig et al., (2021) state that for youth involved with youth justice, 73-75 per cent of those who reported at least one ACE also reporting three or more ACEs.

Prevalence statistics from a meta-analysis conducted by Malvaso et al. (2021) identify that offending youth are more likely to endure all of those 10 ACEs. Specifically, physical and sexual abuse, household substance abuse, household mental illness, and parental offending are twice as common in offending youth. Domestic violence and parental separation/divorce is three times higher than among non-offending youth, while emotional abuse, emotional neglect, and physical neglect, are eight times higher than for non-offending youth (Malvaso et al., 2021).

Lacey et al., (2020) found that ACEs tend to cluster into particular groups, which means that when ACEs occur, they are unlikely to occur singly i.e. those that report one ACE are likely to report multiple ACEs. For example, Lacey et al., (2020) found that the primary caregiver's mental health issues was a key ACE, as it was significantly linked with four other ACEs, namely: parental separation and divorce; criminal history of parents; verbal abuse; and physical abuse. The original ACE study (Felitti et al., 1998) found that at least 81 per cent of participants who admitted to experiencing one ACE also admitted to at least one other (Lacey et al., 2020). Such youth are sometimes referred to as polyvictims and they reportedly are more likely to have higher levels of PTSD than youth with one ACE (Malvaso et al., 2021).

Wolff et al., (2018) and Baglivio et al., (2016) note that having four or more ACEs is strongly predictive of early onset offending and chronic recidivism due to the interrelatedness and cumulative impact of ACEs. Having four or more ACEs in childhood leaves a person 11 times more likely to be incarcerated during their lifetime (Allen & Donkin, 2015). Bellis et al. (2016) note that there is a dose-response relationship between the number of ACEs and longer-term negative outcomes. The more ACEs, the worse the longer-term life outcomes are likely to be. Justice-involved youth are 13 times less likely than the general population to have experienced no ACEs at all (Wolff et al., 2018).

It should be noted that the ACE literature often talks about ACEs and trauma as being interchangeable terms: Wolff et al. (2022), Zettler and Craig (2024). The two concepts are similar but not the same (Malvaso et al., 2021). Just because a person has experienced highly negative events such as ACEs, it does not automatically follow that they will be traumatised by those events (Sirhan et al., 2024; Swedo et al., 2024). The Centers for Disease Control and Prevention (CDC) has described ACEs as "potentially traumatic" events (CDC, 2024, p. 1), in recognition of this point. However, it does seem true that ACEs often have a highly deleterious, long-term impact on most people, that is similar to trauma (CDC, 2024) and for many youths this manifests itself in the form of offending behaviour (Malvaso et al., 2023). This does not happen to every young person though. There are many children and young people who are abused or neglected who do not engage in law-breaking behaviour (McLachlan, 2024b). It is more accurate to say that most justice-involved youth have experienced some form of maltreatment and an ACE score provides an indicator of the level of that maltreatment (McGuire et al., 2024). Thus this chapter has talked about ACEs but with an awareness that the impact of ACEs is regarded as being similar to trauma (CDC, 2024).

IMPACT OF ACES ON VIOLENT AND REPEAT OFFENDING

Given the ongoing focus of the Australian media and politicians on youth offending, and the concern that offending is becoming more violent and repeated, it is worth looking at the links between that type of offending and ACEs. There are several reasons why ACEs are significantly correlated with violent and repeat offending.

One explanation is that a chaotic household characterised by violence, abuse and neglect creates poor attachment between parent and child (Amarante, 2024). This in turn leads to inadequate coping skills for dealing with conflict and differences of opinion and creates the conditions for poor interpersonal functioning later in life (Bowlby, 1969; Thomas et al., 2021). Moreover, as indicated in Social Learning Theory (Bandura, 1978), a young person who experiences physical and/or sexual abuse, or witnesses domestic violence, has an increased chance of using violence themselves in future because such acts of violence are considered normal ways of behaving in relationships (Krushas et al., 2025).

Second, ACEs may also lead to the development of problematic behaviours, which are a precursor to violent offending. Such behaviours include copying the offending behaviour of delinquent peers, challenges with school attendance and performance, mental health challenges, acting without thinking, and misusing drugs and/or alcohol (Perez et al., 2018). These are important because they are indicators that the presence of ACEs has led some young people to fail to mature as expected and develop the resilience to adapt to life's challenges. These problematic behaviours can lead to others, such as having difficulty managing emotions like anger and frustration, difficulties in making friends, and poor academic performance (McLachlan, 2024a; Perez et al., 2018).

Third, youth with a history of abuse and/or neglect often have a decreased ability to accurately identify emotions. As such, they are likely to adopt a hypervigilant default position of identifying facial cues as being angry, so as not to miss any danger (Lujan & Fanniff, 2018). This may lead to frequent misperceptions about the intent of others and increase the likelihood of responding impulsively with aggression or violence to a misperceived threat (Lujan & Fanniff, 2018). As Fox et al., (2015, p. 164) note, "individuals who were abused or neglected during childhood are far more likely to commit a violent act than those who did not experience abuse and neglect."

Fourth, ACEs directly influence violent offending through the pathway of anger and poor impulse control. Li et al. found that physical abuse had the greatest influence in this regard (Li et al., 2025), while (Van Wyk, 2023) found that the combination of anger, poor self-control and ACEs was present in people who committed violent acts (Van Wyk, 2023). Craig et al. (2023), and Baglivio and Wolff (2023) also note that ACEs often lead to mental health issues, which in turn may lead to violent behaviour under some circumstances such as when a young person is incarcerated.

In terms of repeat offending, Wolff et al. (2022) and Li et al. (2025) found a higher prevalence of ACEs led to more frequent youth offending than their peers with lower ACEs, regardless of race or gender. Research suggests that a repeat youth offender whose developmental history features extensive and interconnected maltreatment and family dysfunction often develop antisocial personality traits (Baglivio & Wolff, 2023; Moffitt, 1993). Such youth often experience repeated negative reactions with parents and carers, which heightens their antisocial personality attributes and narrows the range of behavioural responses, with a bias towards counterproductive actions (Novak, 2022). Moreover Craig (2019) suggests that cumulative ACEs reduce the ability of a young person to focus positively on the future and increases their likelihood of repeat offending because they are less likely to put effort into tasks that are helpful but boring, and focus more on experiences that are counterproductive but exciting.

A potential reason for this is that when young people endure multiple ACEs, the intensifying and collective effects of these experiences are likely to result in substantial difficulties in areas such as wellbeing, money management and displaying appropriate social skills, along with mental health challenges, unemployment and welfare dependence (Leiting et al., 2024). It must be remembered that many justice-involved youth also have to survive their adolescent years with the burden of structural disadvantage (Stathis et al., 2008), over which they have virtually no control (Phoenix, 2016). Many live in lower socioeconomic areas where there is high unemployment and poverty, and come from large, single-parent families (Thomsen & Homel, 2024). Combined with the burden of ACEs, the result is often a lack of support for the young person, a subsequent lack of resilience for navigating challenging events, and ultimately a particular vulnerability towards offending behaviour (Thomsen & Homel, 2024).

ATTACHMENT THEORY LINK TO THE ACCUMULATION OF ACES

Attachment Theory was developed by Bowlby (1969) and the term "attachment" refers to the powerful bonds of love and affection that usually exist between a child and their carers, due to the ways for which the child is cared (Berk, 2003). Attachment can also denote a person's emotional link to others, referring to the extent to which we like and admire others, and are seeking their good opinion of us (Costello & Laub, 2020). The relationship between the child and carers develops through series of inherent signs that commence from birth and when attachment is secure the child will use the carers as a secure base and is happy to see them after a time separation (Berk, 2003).

Attachment Theory suggests that both nature and nurture are important, as early life experiences set a pattern for behaviour in childhood and adolescence. Both continuity and discontinuity of development are relevant here, in that children develop continually but there are also sensitive developmental periods. There is also one universal developmental course relevant to all people (Berk, 2003). Attachment has a long-term influence on the development of a sense of self and others, ability to positively influence their environment, and the ability to self-regulate. Secure early attachments provide the framework for the child to develop skill, confidence and the resilience to appropriately cope with difficult life experiences (Kinniburgh et al., 2005).

Johnson (2003) takes the stance that Attachment Theory is, "... essentially a theory of trauma ..." (p. 9), or a paradigm where traumatic childhood experiences are balanced against the resilience capacity of an individual to manage the impact of that trauma. Sroufe et al. (1999) take a different tack in defining Attachment Theory as being a theory both of psychopathology and of normal development. Those authors suggest attachment could be viewed as a balance between vulnerability and resiliency to the experience of the childhood development process.

Moreover, there are insecure forms of attachment where the child is avoidant (unresponsive) of the carer, resistant (angry, clingy), or disorganised (flat, dazed) upon the carer's return (Berk, 2003). Insecure attachments have been linked to several undesirable life outcomes, including mental health issues and poor relationships with other children. The majority of abused children have insecure attachments and this tends to occur due to the factors (Kinniburgh et al., 2005) that were associated with the original ACE study (Anda et al., 2010), e.g. abuse, unavailability and inconsistency of carers for many reasons (e.g. hospitalisation, imprisonment); harsh and inconsistent discipline; neglect; and being raised by carers who experienced childhood trauma themselves. A child who experiences insecure attachment will often manage overpowering experiences through inappropriate responses such as physical violence, detachment and avoidance. Unless the child is taught more appropriate and socially acceptable skills, it is likely that they will continue to display lower-order survival skills, which may lead to undesirable ways of behaving in many situations (Kinniburgh et al., 2005), including committing offences. There is a clear link between harsh and inconsistent caregiving styles and youth offending (Yoder et al. 2018), which were demonstrated by Hoeve et al. (2009) as resulting from "... rejection, hostility and neglect, and psychological control ..." (p. 765).

Attachment is a key area of difficulty for traumatised young people (Ford & Blaustein, 2013). Such difficulties may also result in challenges with the appropriate expression of emotion, which can lead to the traumatised young person emotionally shutting down, or exploding with rage. Once such powerful emotions start, it is very difficult for the young person to restore their equilibrium and they may remain heightened for long periods and the individual may resort to unhelpful self-management strategies in order to restore their calm, such as drug use, or self-harm (Kinniburgh et al., 2005). When a young person has difficulty with self-regulation, they are more likely to engage in behaviours that are spontaneous, reckless, instinctive and overly emotional, behaviours in short, which are more likely to lead to committing offences (Ford & Blaustein, 2013). Furthermore Creeden (2009) suggests that a young person's trauma and insecure attachments may have a considerable influence on the way that the prefrontal cortex operates, an area of the brain that is closely related to a person's executive cognitive functional level. The overpowering emotions that are caused by a lack of ability to self-regulate might also be the reason for thinking errors, poor memory and lack of detail when questioned by authorities, lack of affect and other behaviours regarded as avoidant (Creeden, 2009).

Self-regulation involves several skills (Ford & Blaustein, 2013) which are challenging when a young person has a higher-than-average level of bodily stimulation, a reduced ability to modify behaviour under stress and a reduced attention span (Australian Childhood Foundation, 2015). Self-regulation includes the ability to: intentionally concentrate their minds; be aware of the surrounds and one's current bodily reactions; marshal their recall ability so they can learn and adjust effectually to events occurring in the present; and reclaim or keep a level of emotion that makes them feel better and to help them calm down and feel motivated. This is difficult for traumatised young people because they need to simultaneously maintain in their minds key themes related to secure attachment, such as trust, familiarity, friendliness, while dealing with the intrusion of insecure attachment themes, such as being neglected, abused, manipulated, deceived, and treated as worthless (Ford & Blaustein, 2013).

POLICY AND PRACTICE IMPLICATIONS

Policy shall be taken here to mean the intention of a particular government, with regard to a particular matter or area, in this case youth justice, delivered through policy instruments such as legislation, or internal policy documents (Australian Public Service Academy, 2024). The broad aim of youth-justice policy is to assist governments to be better informed about matters relating to youth offending in Australia and to inform future policy decisions (Australian Public Service Academy, 2024). Policy questions help stimulate thought and action about various matters of public interest and define a position to be taken by governments on those matters (Hoskins, 2022). Conversely, practice will be taken to mean the hands-on work with youth that assists with discharging the responsibilities of youth-justice agencies (Day & Malvaso, 2024), including delivery of programs, appearing in court, providing care and support in youth detention centres. Practice implications in this context refer to matters that will have a direct impact on reducing youth offending (Department of Youth Justice and Victim Support, 2024a). This chapter poses three broad questions for governments to consider, which have policy and practice implications and which really need to be considered if governments are serious about addressing cumulative ACEs.

Are Governments Willing to Counter the Populist Narrative About Youth Offending?

That is, do they want to have youth offenders viewed as youth who have experienced ACEs, which has led to their offending, and rehabilitation efforts will take their ACEs into account? Or will they promote the populist view that these young people are incorrigible and beyond redemption and the only way to deal with their offending is through punitive measures (Benier et al., 2020; Sparks, 2021). The populist view is being reinforced by a long-standing Australian media narrative which provides daily highlights of youth offending in Australia. It is fair to say that governments around Australia have been unwilling to effectively counter that narrative (Hickey & Wallis, 2023).

A recent report from the Queensland Family and Child Commission (QFCC, 2024) notes that Australia-wide, a key statistic for children who entered the youth-justice system at age 10, was that 94 per cent had contact with child-protection agencies. While this percentage decreases as children age, such that by the time they are 18, the percentage is 37 per cent, the point is that these children have experienced some level of abuse and neglect in the home, which requires the intervention of the state. Moreover, two-thirds of incarcerated youth in the 2022/23 financial year had been placed in out-of-home-care on three or more occasions (QFCC, 2024). Thus, it is clear that there is a strong crossover between justice involvement and child protection (Baidawi et al., 2023), and clear evidence that these youth come from disrupted, abusive and neglectful households that have been a precursor to their offending (QFCC, 2024). Governments around Australia talk about providing support for the victims of youth offending and the damage done by these young people (Productivity Commission, 2024) but rarely mention remind the public that these youth are likely to have been victimised themselves (Joshi & Truong, 2024).

It is arguable though that in some jurisdictions, most notably the Northern Territory (Doel-Mackaway & Williamson, 2023) and Queensland (Riddle et al., 2024), there is a moral panic among the public, which is exacerbated by the aforementioned Australian media coverage (Gerritsen et al., 2023). A moral panic refers to situations when a particular group, in this case adolescents, has been identified as posing a clear danger to public and moral safety, creating a society-wide feeling of alarm about an imminent threat (Cohen, 1972). Arguably the moral panic has strongly contributed to populist approaches being implemented by governments which are counter to all available evidence and do not reduce offending (Australian Human Rights Commission, 2024). There are however, some examples of evidence-informed approaches that have worked elsewhere in the world, which have reduced offending and been comparatively cheaper to implement, from which Australian jurisdictions could learn (Vincent et al., 2024).

These examples include the Diagrama Model in Spain, which has successfully worked with violent youth offenders and focuses on re-educating young people and providing them with key life skills (McGuire, 2019). Extensive work in Scotland to increase the minimum age of criminal responsibility to 12, has worked to protect the rights of incarcerated youth and ceased the use of YDCs for children younger than 18 (Dyer et al., 2024). Other effective approaches include the Missouri Model in the United States, which uses a genuine therapeutic approach (Bjur, 2023) and also the approach of small facilities (maximum of eight beds) in the Netherlands and New York, which are closer to the young person's home (Oostermeijer & Dwyer, 2019). Such approaches are more trauma-informed (Malvaso et al., 2024; Schiraldi et al., 2021) and could be investigated for implementation in Australia. However, they would require significant political will to re-educate criminal justice agencies and the Australian public about evidence-based practice (Wood et al., 2023) and the economic benefits of more effective approaches (Queensland Government Statistician's Office, 2021).

The moral panic (Cohen, 1972) could be addressed by a sustained, balanced campaign (Goodfellow, 2024; Merlo, 2024) that acknowledges the impact and seriousness of youth offending but focuses on reasons for offending and an evidence-based approach to reducing youth offending (Justice Reform Initiative, 2023; Rose et al., 2024). This should involve, and ideally would be led by, governments, who control the funding and legislative power (Productivity Commission, 2024). As part of this campaign, governments could educate the public about the high costs of criminal-justice and crime-prevention approaches (Productivity Commission, 2024; Rose et al., 2024) and generally address the economic costs of youth offending. The following is calculated in 2022/23 dollars by way of illustration. These costs are calculated for Queensland as this is where the author is based, but the costs will vary for each jurisdiction depending on a range of factors and most are higher than in Queensland (Productivity Commission, 2024). The cost to youth justice supporting a young person while living in the community is approximately $111,000 per year but increases to approximately $669,000 per year if they are incarcerated (Productivity Commission, 2024). If addressing ACEs reduces offending, therefore reducing these costs, then governments can showcase not only their ability to reduce youth crime but also their economic management credentials (Productivity Commission, 2024).

The campaign would also educate the public that the use of violence by youth relates to their upbringing and need for support and would emphasise that many justice-involved youth have disabilities, where violence is a mode of communication (Joshi & Truong, 2024). Instead of labelling youth as violent offenders, a better term is "victim-survivor" (Joshi & Truong, 2024, p. 11), as that acknowledges their life experiences to date and brings in a strength-based element of resilience that shows that many justice-involved youth have done well just to survive (Usher et al., 2021).

If successful, the campaign would allow for youth-justice agencies to focus more on strengths-based approaches (Schmidt et al., 2023) that are known to be successful (Upton, 2023), rather than perpetuating the punitive moral panic that is the current reality (Merlo, 2024; Riddle et al., 2024).

What Action Will Youth-Justice Agencies Take to Address the Impact of Cumulative ACEs for Justice-Involved Youth?

As outlined above, the level of ACE prevalence is high (Malvaso et al., 2022a) and research has shown that ACEs predict offending, including violent, repeat offending. This suggests that addressing ACEs may also assist with the reduction of violent, repeat offending (Van Wyk, 2023), which has been the subject of Australian media scrutiny (Riddle et al., 2024). Arguably the prevalence and impact of ACEs is something to which youth-justice agencies may not have paid sufficient attention (Joshi & Truong, 2024). For example, the 2024 Report on Government Services about Youth-justice Services across Australia, to which all jurisdictions contributed, makes no mention of ACEs, suggesting that if any jurisdiction is currently responding to this aspect of the lives of youth offenders, it is not something about which they are willing to report (Productivity Commission, 2024). This suggests that they are either not working on addressing ACEs at all, or if they are, the approach is quite nascent and it is too early to confidently provide meaningful information (Pettus, 2023). The following actions are suggested.

One: If governments do decide to address the impact of cumulative ACEs, then youth-justice agencies would do well to investigate therapeutic approaches and other tertiary crime prevention strategies which enable them to intervene earlier and potentially more intensively (Australian Human Rights Commission, 2024). Therapeutic approaches should be able to address several ACEs, to be focused on addressing violence, flexible enough to meet diverse needs (including disabilities) and must occur in partnership with other organisations, such as child-protection agencies and non-government organisations. This is because young people will probably have contact with multiple organisations. To avoid missed opportunities and minimise duplication, it would greatly assist if all organisations involved shared information and operated using the same principles (Joshi & Truong, 2024; Malvaso et al., 2023).

The decision point about cumulative ACEs is when overall approaches would lead to an effective reduction of offending. The first decision is whether to identify whether a young person has any ACEs, so that youth-justice agencies know what they are dealing with (Hoehn & De Young, 2024), particularly as research suggests that if a young person divulges that they have an ACE, it is possible that they have also endured others (Yannon et al., 2024). This would involve some form of screening and there are advocates who call for youth to be screened for ACEs upon entry to the youth-justice system so that agencies can better understand and respond more effectively and appropriately to their target population (Kerr-Davis et al., 2023; Leiting et al., 2024). Others caution against this, on the basis that it can be expensive, time consuming, misused and potentially retraumatising, particularly if therapeutic support is not provided after screening (Finkelhor (2018) and Folk et al. (2023)). Other authors such as Malvaso et al. (2023) point out that a specific tool would be needed because the ACEs inventory itself (the standard 10 ACEs) was created for research purposes only and was not designed for screening or therapeutic use, a fact reinforced by one of the creators (Anda et al., 2020). There are screening tools and screening approaches available which researchers suggest are effective (Modrowski et al., 2023), although other scholars note it is more appropriate to refer a young person to a mental health provider to be screened for PTSD, as there are existing guidelines available to steer practitioners (Hoehn & De Young, 2024).

There is also a consideration to screen for Positive Childhood Experiences (PCEs), which is an opposite concept to ACEs and represents factors in the lives of youth where there are resilience and strengths, such as school engagement, family supports, other supportive adults and participation in leisure activities (Baglivio & Wolff, 2020). Screening for PCEs alongside ACEs could more fully demonstrate the scope of the young person's life and represent a more strengths-based approach (Hoehn et al., 2024).

Two: Youth-justice agencies could also consider an overall crime prevention approach which enables a focus on cumulative ACEs and addresses violent, repeat offending within a clear framework (Whitten et al., 2018). Of the four major types of crime prevention approaches – Developmental, Situational, Criminal Justice and Community-focused (Tonry & Farrington, 1995) – the Developmental approach may have some applicability for ACEs but that has not been as widely implemented in Australia as other approaches (Justice Reform Initiative, 2023). For example, in Queensland a number of situational crime-prevention strategies have been introduced, such as engine immobilisers in certain areas, and co-responder police patrols (Department of Youth Justice Employment Small Business and Training, 2023), along with some community crime approaches, such as the Cairns Safer Streets approach (Department of the Premier and Cabinet, 2024) and the Townsville Early Action group (Department of Youth Justice and Victim Support, 2024b).

There have also been numerous criminal-justice system approaches, such as building more youth detention centres, electronic monitoring devices, introducing harsher laws and identifying serious, repeat offenders (Department of Youth Justice Employment Small Business and Training, 2023). Given that the Australian media narrative has not diminished despite the existence of these punitive measures, it is arguable that these approaches have not had the desired impact, suggesting different approaches may be needed (Higginson et al., 2017). Arguably, addressing ACEs aligns with a developmental-crime approach, because the aim of that approach is to use data to steer resource allocations to tackle the issues that create the conditions for offending, such as ACEs (Malvaso et al., 2022b). Ideally this would be done before offending behaviour becomes established, which in the case of this cohort would be soon after their first offence, to avoid them becoming violent, repeat offenders (Homel & Thomsen, 2017). This approach would have a focus on "… enlightened support … and certainly not on punishment" (Homel & Thomsen, 2017, p. 3).

Three: Youth-justice agencies could undertake include some internal investigations to collect more research on other ACEs relevant to their jurisdiction, in addition to the standard 10 (Peltonen et al., 2024). The authors of the initial ACE study (Felitti et al., 1998) always maintained that there are more ACEs than those and that group merely represented the top 10 in their research. They mentioned that there are others, such as being assaulted by peers, and sibling violence (Anda et al., 2020), which might be usefully added to more fully understand the life experience of youth and the developmental impact on offending (Peltonen et al., 2024). For example, an Australian study used 14 ACEs, including the usual 10, plus bullying, neighbourhood violence exposure, death of a close friend/family member, and any neglect. That study found that those that had the highest number of ACEs were more likely to have been bullied and to have witnessed neighbourhood violence, suggesting that the usual 10 ACEs do not provide a full picture of the adversities faced by youth offenders (Malvaso et al., 2022b).

Four: Frontline staff could use the RNR framework, given its prominence within youth justice in Australia, as a vehicle to address cumulative ACEs. Crucially the developers of the RNR framework, Bonta and Andrews (2024), say that ACEs predict youth offending and should be addressed because they are a barrier to offending reduction. They recommend that ACEs are addressed as specific responsivity factors rather than as criminogenic risk factors because they are static just like the young person's criminal history. Once they have occurred, they cannot be undone and remain a fixed element of the life history of the youth (Bonta & Andrews, 2024).

To address ACEs in this manner, youth-justice agencies should slow down the process of working with maltreated youth (Moss & Klapdor, 2022). The pace at which these agencies work is dictated by forces such as performance outcomes, public demands and pressure from other criminal justice agencies such as police and courts (Vidal et al., 2019). The reality is that youth who have experienced ACEs have been harmed in various ways, resulting in difficulty trusting others, including service providers (Van Wyk, 2023). Therefore, it behoves youth-justice agencies to spend time in developing a level of trust with the young person, especially when they have been let down repeatedly by adults (Joshi & Truong, 2024). While this takes some time, it is time well spent because processes thereafter are less likely to be as turbulent (Wood et al., 2023). Traditional approaches to working with justice-involved youth create situations where youth are brought into situations over which they have no control and are expected to behave perfectly. Such approaches assume that youth have no internal motivation, when the opposite is demonstrably true. Better results are obtained when frontline staff can tap into that motivation (Brummer & Thorsborne, 2024).

Having established some level of trust, it must be then ascertained whether ACEs have occurred to the young person (Bonta & Andrews, 2024). If the youth-justice agency decides to screen for ACEs, a potential advantage is that more detailed information could be gleaned from that approach. If the policy decision is not to screen (McLennan et al., 2024) and the agency already uses the Youth Level of Service/Case Management Inventory (YLS/CMI, or variant) to risk-assess youth, then the agency could use the YLS/CMI to identify ACEs (Ogilvie et al., 2022) and sensitively ask the young person about their experiences (Andrews et al., 2011). For example, one of the questions in Part III of the YLS/CMI is: Has the youth been a "Witness of Domestic Violence", or a "Victim of Neglect" (Hoge & Andrews, 2021, p. 15). These are both ACEs (National Center for Juvenile Justice, 2010) so the data is available for youth-justice agencies to begin collecting information about them.

The data available in this manner are surface-level but would at least provide the beginning of a conversation with each young person (Noel et al., 2024). If it is suspected by frontline staff that there may be some trauma from the ACEs, the next step would be to arrange for a mental-health assessment, to look for signs of PTSD symptoms, such as "… anxiety, interpersonal distrust and emotional dysregulation …" (Bonta & Andrews, 2024, p. 255). This information would provide a baseline for each young person (Peltonen et al., 2024).

The next step would be to refer the young person to an intervention that addresses ACEs and violent offending and is trauma-informed (Yannon et al., 2024). Youth-justice agencies would need to make available such interventions and there are numerous programs available. The one recommended here is Trauma Focused-Cognitive Behavioural Therapy (Psychology Training and Supervision, 2023). TF-CBT is targeted at youth up to age 21, who have experienced maltreatment, have antisocial thoughts, and/or beliefs, and have behavioural problems, such as violent offending (Psychology Training and Supervision, 2023). This program is recommended because: it specifically acknowledges ACEs as drivers for trauma-related behaviour and attempts to address them in ways that involve the young person's family; it is designed to be flexible and respond to the individual needs of young people (Psychology Training and Supervision, 2023); it is CBT-based, which aligns with the General Personality and Cognitive Social Learning theory behind the RNR framework (Andrews et al., 2011); and it is available in Australia (Psychology Training and Supervision, 2023). Australian youth-justice agencies are familiar with CBT approaches and thus there may be greater buy-in for that approach (Productivity Commission, 2024). However, there are other trauma-related programs that are also well-regarded and could be considered, such as TARGET (Trauma Affect Regulation: Guide for Education and Therapy) (Marrow et al., 2014) or SPARCS (Structured Psychotherapy for Adolescents Responding to Chronic Stress) (National Child Traumatic Stress Network, 2016). The choice of program would need to be carefully considered by the youth-justice agency, to determine which best suits its needs (Malvaso et al., 2024). However, as a minimum it would need to address ACEs and violent offending (Portwood et al., 2023).

Could ACEs be Addressed Through a Trauma-Informed Care (TIC) Approach?

TIC is a framework for working with people who have experienced trauma and has been defined as a:

> *strengths-based framework that is responsive to the impact of trauma, emphasising physical, psychological, and emotional safety for both service providers and survivors, and creates opportunities for survivors to rebuild a sense of control and empowerment. It is grounded in and directed by a thorough understanding of the neurological, biological, psychological and social effects of trauma and interpersonal violence and the prevalence of these experiences … (Bateman et al., 2013, p. 9).*

The primary focus of TIC is on minimising the likelihood of re-experiencing traumatic events and addressing the underlying causes of trauma and posttraumatic distress. TIC is aimed at helping people who have histories of trauma, such that service delivery is organised around the recognition and acknowledgment of trauma, together with a cognisance of and sensitivity to its nuances and effective treatment (Bateman et al., 2013; Hanson & Lang, 2016).

There are several key principles that support a TIC approach including: safety; trustworthiness; transparency; collaboration; empowerment; an awareness of trauma, culture, historical and gender issues; and increasing resilience and competence (Berliner & Kolko, 2016; Donaldson et al., 2018; Urquhart & Jasuira, 2013). TIC should be individualised to the client and be focused on three key areas: the establishment of safety for each person, in both the physical and psychological senses: self-regulation competencies; and providing strengths-based opportunities (Australian Human Rights Commission, 2021; Berliner & Kolko, 2016; Hopper et al., 2009).

As a response to youth offending, TIC is an approach that may have some applicability because research suggests that youth in this system have experienced above-average rates of trauma, and there appears to be a link between offending and trauma (Zettler & Craig, 2022). Many of these youth are ineligible for mental health support as they do not meet the threshold for a Posttraumatic Stress Disorder

(PTSD) diagnosis. Leitch (2017) says that TIC has helped shed some light on the impact of negative life events and how they affect the developing child. TIC has assisted with recognising that the influence of early trauma should be addressed by service providers and policy makers. The link between TIC and ACEs is that TIC is the overall framework that recognises and caters to the experience of maltreatment (Goddard, 2021), and ACEs are the key indicators that the individual has endured and been negatively impacted by during this maltreatment (Malvaso et al., 2019).

Australian youth-justice agencies started implementing TIC several years ago (Malvaso et al., 2024) and there is an expectation that Australian youth-justice agencies will work in trauma-informed ways. The AYJA National Standards state that trauma-informed responses are to be applied in working with youth offenders (AYJA, 2023). However, there is little evidence to suggest that implementation was completed in any jurisdiction (Malvaso et al., 2024). It is perhaps more accurate to state that those agencies are trauma-aware (Urquhart & Jasuira, 2013), which means the full extent of their actions is most likely about including some trauma-related statements in their policies and procedures, and to deliver some kind of trauma-informed training (Williams, 2023).

Given the length of time since implementation commenced, this would suggest that it is difficult to undertake TIC in a youth-justice environment and perhaps efforts to do so have been abandoned in favour of other, more pressing, activities (Malvaso et al., 2024). The reasons for this may include a lack of agreement within agencies about whether this should be an approach that they adopt. As Bonta and Andrews (2024) state, given that youth-justice agencies are the ones administering justice, it is difficult to rationalise how they can also be trauma-informed. Perhaps some staff, including senior executives, who possess punitive attitudes themselves, may not agree with the organisation being trauma-informed, thus stymying TIC implementation (Malvaso et al., 2024). Another reason might be that, by its very nature, the youth-justice experience is likely to re-traumatise youth thus undermining trauma-informed attempts (McLachlan, 2024a). It could also be because, as outlined in Polyvagal Theory (Porges, 2020), there is a fundamental need for TIC to be delivered in safe and protected spaces, which are difficult to find in youth-justice spaces, especially in youth detention centres (Baidawi et al., 2023). Because of this, a trauma/adversity paradox could be said to exist. There is evidence of adversity, with the likelihood of trauma, and healing from the impact of that adversity/trauma requires genuine and safe relationships (Bentzin, 2024), yet the youth-justice system often makes the impact of that adversity/trauma worse. For example, Pickens (2016) claims that youth-justice systems may unwittingly establish ways of relating to young people which neglect to acknowledge and deal with adversity-related behaviours that were an antecedent to their offending behaviour (Morgan, 2017; Pickens, 2016; Robinson, 2016).

TIC could provide youth with a process and environment for dealing with their adversity in youth-justice agencies, ideally leading them to manage their lives in a more constructive manner (Pickens, 2016). A TIC focus has the potential to allow the system to adopt an approach that is safer and more therapeutic than other options that have a more punitive intent, such as isolation rooms in youth detention (Elwyn et al., 2015; Roy et al., 2019). Moreover, justice-involved youth have often experienced the frustration of not having their needs met by various systems (education, health, child protection) resulting in lost opportunities that have paved the way for offending behaviour (McLachlan, 2024a). When this is coupled with the fact that the youth in this dataset are involved for an average of six years with youth justice, this seems like plenty of time to address their adversity/trauma, especially if it shortens their offending duration (White & Gooda, 2017). After all, it is the role of youth justice to address the underlying factors that lead to offending (AYJA, 2023; Department of Youth Justice, 2020).

A commitment to implementing TIC requires organisations to make significant practice adjustments (Bateman et al., 2013; Jankowski et al., 2019). To be effective, all staff of an organisation, no matter their status or pay grade, should fully integrate a TIC approach into the way they operate every day, because every experience that a service user has should reinforce messages of trauma recovery and minimise the possibility of re-traumatisation (Australian Institute of Family Studies, 2016; Dierkhising & Branson, 2016). The practice adjustments include staff training, an examination of the quality of relationships between service users and staff, changes to operating policies, and challenging assumptions about how services are provided. Organisations should build workforce capacity, examine whether changes are needed to the daily supervision of workers, and work to create and sustain organisational cultures that are personal, holistic, creative, open, safe and therapeutic (Bateman et al., 2013; Dierkhising & Branson, 2016). Full implementation is likely to take two-three years, because internal consensus needs to be reached on shared goals, and strong commitment to action and collaboration from leaders is required (Dierkhising & Branson, 2016; Elwyn et al., 2015).

In summary, the issue with TIC is that it is arguably counter to the moral panic surrounding youth justice and has been regarded as a soft option at a time when increasingly punitive approaches are being implemented and quick results are expected (McLachlan, 2024a). Also, implementation of TIC would require youth-justice agencies and governments to promote the view that offending youth are victim-survivors, which is counter to the current zeitgeist and would make governments look "soft on crime" (McAra & McVie, 2023). Thus, it is unlikely in the current environment, particularly as it has not yet been successfully undertaken in any Australian jurisdiction (Malvaso et al., 2024), despite successful implementation in other countries e.g. the Missouri Model (Bjur, 2023; Huebner, 2013) and the Diagrama Model (Bjur, 2023; McGuire, 2019). Thus, TIC is broadly seen as a progressive idea but one that has been too time-consuming to implement, without certainty of results and without universal acceptance that youth-justice agencies should be undertaking this approach (McAra & McVie, 2023).

CONCLUSION

This chapter has discussed the trauma endured by justice-involved youth in the form of ACEs and outlined the links between those ACEs and their offending behaviour. This was then starkly contrasted with the moral panic-driven ways in which offending youth are portrayed in the Australian media and by politicians, which flies in the face of the evidence that shows youth offending has decreased overall. The chapter then examined the impact of cumulative ACEs and their impact on violent and repeat offending, followed by a discussion about ways in which Attachment Theory can explain this behaviour. The chapter concluded with a discussion of three key questions for youth-justice agencies, which examined what governments could do to address populist narratives, the actions needed to focus on ACEs, and addressing ACEs through a Trauma-Informed Care approach.

The question remains about whether governments will continue to focus on short-term punitive approaches that will likely have limited success and may worsen the impact of trauma, but are publicly palatable and election-winning. Or will they adopt a longer-term view that seeks to address the issues that are relevant to their lives of justice-involved youth i.e. ACEs, but in ways that are currently regarded as soft options, despite the possibility of improved results? The way forward is clear, but political courage is required.

REFERENCES

Allen, M., & Donkin, A. (2015). *The impact of adverse experiences in the home on the health of children and young people, and inequalities in prevalence and effects.* University College London Institute of Health Equity. Retrieved 1 March from www .instituteofhealthequity.org

Amarante, J. (2024). *Adverse Childhood Experiences and Adolescent Substance Use: The Roles of Emotion Regulation and Attachment Security.* FORDHAM UNIVERSITY.

American Psychiatric Association. (2013). *Diagnostic and Statistical Manual 5 - Posttraumatic Stress Disorder* (5th ed.). American Psychiatric Publishing.

Anda, R. F., Butchart, A., Felitti, V. J., & Brown, D. W. (2010). Building a framework for global surveillance of the public health implications of adverse childhood experiences. *American Journal of Preventive Medicine*, *39*(1), 93–98. DOI: 10.1016/j. amepre.2010.03.015

Anda, R. F., Porter, L. E., & Brown, D. W. (2020). Inside the Adverse Childhood Experience Score: Strengths, Limitations, and Misapplications. *American Journal of Preventive Medicine*, *59*(2), 293–295. DOI: 10.1016/j.amepre.2020.01.009

Andrews, D. A., Bonta, J., & Wormith, J. S. (2011). The Risk-Need-Responsivity (RNR) Model. *Criminal Justice and Behavior*, *38*(7), 735–755. DOI: 10.1177/0093854811406356

Antolak-Saper, N. (2020). The Adultification of the Youth Justice System: The Victorian Experience. *Law in Context. A Socio-legal Journal, 37*(1), 99-113. https:// doi.org/DOI: 10.26826/law-in-context.v37i1.118

Armytage, P., & Ogloff, J. (2017). *Youth Justice Review and Strategy: Meeting needs and reducing offending - Executive Summary July 2017.* Melbourne, Australia: Victoria State Government Retrieved from www.justice.vic.gov.au

Astridge, B., Li, W. W., McDermott, B., & Longhitano, C. (2023). A systematic review and meta-analysis on adverse childhood experiences: Prevalence in youth offenders and their effects on youth recidivism. *Child Abuse & Neglect*, *140*, 1–14. DOI: 10.1016/j.chiabu.2023.106055

Atkinson, J., Nelson, J., Brooks, R., Atkinson, C., & Ryan, K. (2014). Addressing Individual and Community Transgenerational Trauma. In Dudgeon, P., Milroy, H., & Walker, R. (Eds.), *Working together: Aboriginal and Torres Strait Islander mental health and wellbeing principles and practice.* Kulunga Research Network.

Atkinson, R. (2022). *Youth Justice Reforms Review - Final Report*. Brisbane, Australia: Queensland Government Retrieved from www.youthjustice.qld.gov.au/_Australian media/documents

Australian Bureau of Statistics. (2017). *4519.0 - Recorded Crime - Offenders, 2014-15*. https://www.abs.gov.au/ausstats/abs@.nsf/Lookup/by%20Subject/4519.0~2014-15~Main%20Features~Youth%20Offenders~4

Australian Bureau of Statistics. (2025). *Recorded Crime - Offenders*. www.abs.gov.au/statistics/people/crime-and-justice/recorded-crime-offenders/latest-release#

Australian Childhood Foundation. (2015). *9 Plain English Principles of Trauma Informed Care*. Retrieved 23 April from https://childhoodtrauma.org.au/2015/april/trauma-informed-care

Australian Human Rights Commission. (2021). *Guidelines for Working With a Trauma-informed Approach*. www.humanrights.gov.au/sites/default/files/ahrc_sr_2021_8_trauma-informed_approach_a4_r2_0.pdf

Australian Human Rights Commission. (2024). *'Help way earlier!': How Australia can transform child justice to improve safety and wellbeing*. www.humanrights.gov.au/our-work/childrens-rights/publications/help-way-earlier

Australian Institute of Family Studies. (2016). *Principles of Trauma-informed approaches to child sexual abuse: A discussion paper*. https://aifs.gov.au/cfca/publications/trauma-informed-care-child-family-welfare-services/introduction

Australian Institute of Health & Welfare. (2023). *Profile of Australia's population*. Retrieved 20 August from www.aihw.gov.au/reports/australias-health/profile-of-australias-population#

Australian Institute of Health and Welfare. (2016). *Youth Justice in Australia 2014–15*. https://www.aihw.gov.au/reports/youth-justice/youth-justice-in-australia-2014-15/data

Australian Institute of Health and Welfare. (2024). Youth justice in Australia 2022–23. https://www.aihw.gov.au/reports/youth-justice/youth-justice-in-australia-annual-report-2022-23/contents/numbers-and-rates-of-young-people-under-supervisio

Australian Institute of Health and Welfare. (2025). *Youth justice in Australia 2023-24*. www.aihw.gov.au/reports/youth-justice/youth-justice-in-australia-2023-24/contents/about

Australian Public Service Academy. (2024). *Delivering Great Policy*. www.apsacademy.gov.au/aps-craft/strategy-policy-evaluation/delivering-great-policy

AYJA. (2023). *National Standards for Youth Justice in Australia 2023*. www.ayja.org.au

Baglivio, M. T., Epps, N., Swartz, K., Sayedul Huq, M., Sheer, A., & Hardt, N. S. (2014). The Prevalence of Adverse Childhood Experiences (ACE) in the Lives of Juvenile Offenders. *OJJDP Journal of Juvenile Justice*, *3*(2), 12–34.

Baglivio, M. T., & Wolff, K. T. (2020). Positive Childhood Experiences (PCE): Cumulative Resiliency in the Face of Adverse Childhood Experiences. *Youth Violence and Juvenile Justice*, *19*(2), 1–24. DOI: 10.1177/1541204020972487

Baglivio, M. T., & Wolff, K. T. (2023). Adverse Childhood Experiences (ACEs) and Violent Offending Among Juveniles with Justice System Involvement: Theory, Research, and Implications for Policy. In Portwood, M. J. L. S. G., & Roberts, M. C. (Eds.), *Handbook of Adverse Childhood Experiences: A Framework for Collaborative Health Promotion* (pp. 123–136).

Baglivio, M. T., Wolff, K. T., DeLisi, M., & Jackowski, K. (2020). The Role of Adverse Childhood Experiences (ACEs) and Psychopathic Features on Juvenile Offending Criminal Careers to Age 18. *Youth Violence and Juvenile Justice*, *18*(4), 337–364. DOI: 10.1177/1541204020927075

Baglivio, M. T., Wolff, K. T., Epps, N., & Nelson, R. (2016). Predicting Adverse Childhood Experiences. *Crime and Delinquency*, *63*(2), 166–188. DOI: 10.1177/0011128715570628

Baidawi, S., Ball, R., Newitt, R., Turnbull, L., Kembhavi-Tam, G., Avery, S., & Sheehan, R. (2023). *Research Report – Care Criminalisation of Children with Disability in Child Protection Systems*. Royal Commission into Violence, Abuse, Neglect and Exploitation of People with Disability.

Baidawi, S., & Sheehan, R. (2019, December). 'Crossover kids': Offending by child protection-involved youth. *Trends and Issues in Crime and Criminal Justice*, *582*, 1–23.

Bandura, A. (1978). Social Learning Theory of Aggression. *Journal of Communication*, *28*(1), 12–29.

Bateman, J., Henderson, C., & Kezelman, C. (2013). *Trauma-Informed Care and Practice: Towards a cultural shift in policy reform across mental health and human services in Australia*. www.mhcc.org.au

Becker, H. S. (1963). *Outsiders: studies in the sociology of deviance*. The Free Press.

Bellis, M. A., Ashton, K., Hughes, K., Ford, K., Bishop, J., & Paranjothy, S. (2016). Adverse Childhood Experiences (ACEs) in Wales and their Impact on Health in the Adult Population. *European Journal of Public Health*, *26*, 111–112.

Benekos, P. J., & Merlo, A. V. (2016). A Decade of Change: Roper v. Simmons, Defending Childhood, and Juvenile Justice Policy. *Criminal Justice Policy Review*, *30*(1), 102–127. DOI: 10.1177/0887403416648734

Benier, K., Wickes, R., & Moran, C. (2020). 'African gangs' in Australia: Perceptions of race and crime in urban neighbourhoods. *Australian and New Zealand Journal of Criminology*, *54*(2), 220–238. DOI: 10.1177/0004865820965647

Bentzin, B. (2024). *A conversation about a trauma-informed court*. City of Austin. Retrieved 8 February from www.beingwellwithbianca.com

Berk, L. E. (2003). *Child Development* (6th ed.). Pearson Education.

Berliner, L., & Kolko, D. J. (2016). Trauma Informed Care: A Commentary and Critique. *Child Maltreatment*, *21*(2), 168–172. DOI: 10.1177/1077559516643785

Bjur, K. (2023). *The Donald Mackay Churchill Fellowship to investigate effective responses to youth gangs for use in youth detention centres*. www.churchilltrust.com.au/fellow/kate-bjur-qld-2022/

Bonta, J., & Andrews, D. A. (2024). *The Psychology of Criminal Conduct* (7th ed.). Routledge.

Bowlby, J. (1969). Attachment and Loss Volume 1: Attachment. Hogarth Press.

Brummer, J., & Thorsborne, M. (2024). *Becoming a Trauma-Informed Restorative Educator: Practical skills to change culture and behavior*. Jessica Kingsley Publishers.

Case, S., Lorenzo-Dus, N., & Morton, R. (2021). YOT Talk: Examining the communicative influences on children's engagement with youth justice assessment processes. *European Journal of Criminology*, •••, 1–20. DOI: 10.1177/1477370821996850

Cavadino, M., & Dignan, J. (2006). *Penal Systems: A Comparative Approach*. Sage Publications Ltd.

Centers for Disease Control and Prevention. (2024). *About Adverse Childhood Experiences*. www.cdc.gov/aces/about/index.html

Charak, R., Ford, J. D., Modrowski, C. A., & Kerig, P. K. (2019). Polyvictimization, Emotion Dysregulation, Symptoms of Posttraumatic Stress Disorder, and Behavioral Health Problems among Justice-Involved Youth: A Latent Class Analysis. *Journal of Abnormal Child Psychology*, *47*(2), 287–298. DOI: 10.1007/s10802-018-0431-9

Cohen, S. (1972). *Folk Devils and Moral Panics: The Creation of the Mods and Rockers*. Granada Publishing.

Costello, B. J., & Laub, J. H. (2020). Social Control Theory: The Legacy of Travis Hirschi's Causes of Delinquency. *Annual Review of Criminology*, *3*(1), 21–41. DOI: 10.1146/annurev-criminol-011419-041527

Craig, J. M. (2019). The Potential Australian mediating Impact of Future Orientation on the ACE–Crime Relationship. *Youth Violence and Juvenile Justice*, *17*(2), 111–128. DOI: 10.1177/1541204018756470

Craig, J. M., Malvaso, C., & Farrington, D. P. (2021). All in the Family? Exploring the Intergenerational Transmission of Exposure to Adverse Childhood Experiences and Their Effect on Offending Behavior. *Youth Violence and Juvenile Justice*, *19*(3), 292–307. DOI: 10.1177/15412040211003648

Craig, J. M., Malvaso, C., & Farrington, D.P. (2023). The Association Between Adverse Childhood Experiences and Different Types of Offending Behavior: An Examination Across Two Generations of British Males. *International Journal of Offender Therapy and Comparative Criminology*, 306624X231198808. https://doi.org/DOI: 10.1177/0306624X231198808

Craig, J. M., Zettler, H., & Trulson, C. R. (2023). Trauma and Violent Misconduct Among Incarcerated Juveniles: The Australian mediating Role of Mental Health. *Journal of Developmental and Life-Course Criminology*, *9*(1), 121–140. DOI: 10.1007/s40865-022-00220-z

Creeden, K. (2009). How trauma and attachment can impact neurodevelopment: Informing our understanding and treatment of sexual behaviour problems. *Journal of Sexual Aggression*, *15*(3), 261–273. DOI: 10.1080/13552600903335844

Cunneen, C. (2006). Racism, Discrimination and the Over-Representation of Indigenous People in the Criminal Justice System: Some Conceptual and Explanatory Issues. *Current Issues in Criminal Justice*, *17*(3), 329–346. DOI: 10.1080/10345329.2006.12036363

Cunneen, C. (2008). Changing the Neo-Colonial Impacts of Juvenile Justice. *Current Issues in Criminal Justice*, *20*(1), 43–58.

Cunneen, C., & White, R. D. (2011). *Juvenile Justice: Youth and Crime in Australia* (4th ed.). Oxford University Press.

Cunneen, C., White, R. D., & Richards, K. (2015). *Juvenile Justice: Youth and Crime in Australia* (5th ed.). Oxford University Press ANZ.

Day, A., & Malvaso, C. (2024). 'Back to Basics': A Practice Approach to Reforming Youth Justice. *Child and Youth Services*, •••, 1–25. Advance online publication. DOI: 10.1080/0145935x.2024.2372790

DeLisi, M., Drury, A. J., & Elbert, M. J. (2021). Frequency, chronicity, and severity: New specification of adverse childhood experiences among federal sexual offenders. *Forensic Science International. Mind and Law*, *2*(202111), 1–7. DOI: 10.1016/j.fsiml.2021.100051

Department of Child Safety Youth and Women. (2018). *Working Together Changing the Story: Youth Justice Strategy 2019–2023*. www.youthjustice.qld.gov.au/_Australian media/documents/our-department/strategies-and-reform/changing-the-youth-justice-story/strategy.pdf

Department of the Premier and Cabinet. (2024). *Community Safety Plan for Queensland*. Retrieved 1 May from www.qld.gov.au/communitysafety

Department of Youth Justice. (2020). *Youth Justice Framework for Practice Foundations: Our way of working*. Queensland Government. https://www.youthjustice.qld.gov.au/search?num_ranks=10&collection=qld-gov&query=major&profile=youth-justice

Department of Youth Justice. (2024). *Youth Justice Pocket Stats March 2024*. Retrieved from www.desbt.qld.gov.au/youth-justice/data

Department of Youth Justice and Victim Support. (2024a). *About Youth Justice*. www.youthjustice.qld.gov.au/our-department/who-we-are/about

Department of Youth Justice and Victim Support. (2024b). *Early Action Groups*. www.youthjustice.qld.gov.au

Department of Youth Justice Employment Small Business and Training. (2023). *Youth justice: key information*. https://desbt.qld.gov.au/youth-justice/about

Dierkhising, C. B., & Branson, C. E. (2016). Looking Forward: A Research and Policy Agenda for Creating Trauma-Informed Juvenile Justice Systems. *Journal of Juvenile Justice*, *5*(5), 14–30.

Doel-Mackaway, H., & Williamson, B. (2023). *'Just ask us, come and see us'. Aboriginal young people in the Northern Territory must be listened to, not punished*. https://theconversation.com/just-ask-us-come-and-see-us-aboriginal-young-people-in-the-northernterritory-must-be-listened-to-not-punished-199297

Donaldson, W., Jury, A., & Poole, S. (2018). *Trauma-Informed Care: Literature Scan*. www.tepou.co.nz

Drake, D. H., & Henley, A. J. (2014). 'Victims' Versus 'Offenders' in British Political Discourse: The Construction of a False Dichotomy. *Howard Journal of Criminal Justice, 53*(2), 141–157. DOI: 10.1111/hojo.12057

Duron, J. F., Williams-Butler, A., Liu, F. Y., Nesi, D., Pirozzolo Fay, K., & Kim, B. E. (2021). The Influence of Adverse Childhood Experiences (ACEs) on the Functional Impairment of Justice-Involved Adolescents: A Comparison of Baseline to Follow-Up Reports of Adversity. *Youth Violence and Juvenile Justice*, •••, 1–18. DOI: 10.1177/15412040211016035

Dyer, F., Gibson, R., Morrison, P., & Murphy, C. (2024). *Youth Justice in Scotland: Still fit for the future?* www.cycj.org.uk

Elwyn, L. J., Esaki, N., & Smith, C. A. (2015). Safety at a girls secure juvenile justice facility. *Therapeutic Communities, 36*(4), 209–218. DOI: 10.1108/tc-11-2014-0038

Evans, C., Graves, K., & Antonopoulos, G. (2018). Trauma among children and legal implications. *Cogent Social Sciences, 4*(1), 1–9. DOI: 10.1080/23311886.2018.1546791

Felitti, V. J., Anda, R. F., Nordenberg, D., Williamson, D. F., Spitz, A. M., Edwards, V., Koss, M. P., & Marks, J. S. (1998). Relationship of Childhood Abuse and Household Dysfunction to Many of the Leading Causes of Death in Adults: The Adverse Childhood Experiences (ACE) Study. *American Journal of Preventive Medicine, 14*(4), 245–258. DOI: 10.1016/S0749-3797(98)00017-8

Finkelhor, D. (2018). Screening for adverse childhood experiences (ACEs): Cautions and suggestions. *Child Abuse & Neglect, 85*, 174–179. DOI: 10.1016/j.chiabu.2017.07.016

Folk, J. B., Ramaiya, M., Holloway, E., Ramos, L., Marshall, B. D. L., Kemp, K., Li, Y., Bath, E., Mitchell, D. K., & Tolou-Shams, M. (2023). The Association Between Expanded ACEs and Behavioral Health Outcomes Among Youth at First Time Legal System Contact. *Research on Child and Adolescent Psychopathology, 51*(12), 1857–1870. DOI: 10.1007/s10802-022-01009-w

Ford, J. D., & Blaustein, M. E. (2013). Systemic Self-Regulation: A Framework for Trauma-Informed Services in Residential Juvenile Justice Programs. *Journal of Family Violence, 28*(7), 665–677. DOI: 10.1007/s10896-013-9538-5

Fox, B. H., Perez, N., Cass, E., Baglivio, M. T., & Epps, N. (2015). Trauma changes everything: Examining the relationship between adverse childhood experiences and serious, violent and chronic juvenile offenders. *Child Abuse & Neglect, 46*(1), 163–173. DOI: 10.1016/j.chiabu.2015.01.011

Gerritsen, R., McDonald, T., Anthony, T., & Napaltjari, V. (2023). *Beneath the Alice Springs 'crime wave' are complex issues – and a lot of politics*. The Conversation. Retrieved 29 January from https://theconversation.com/beneath-the-alice-springs-crime-wave-are-complex-issues-and-a-lotof-politics

Goddard, A. (2021). Adverse Childhood Experiences and Trauma-Informed Care. *Journal of Pediatric Health Care, 35*(2), 145–155. DOI: 10.1016/j.pedhc.2020.09.001

Goodfellow, P. (2024). *An Exploration of Factors Influencing the Recent Levels of Incarceration of Girls in England and Wales*. University of Bedfordshire.

Hales, T., Kusmaul, N., & Nochajski, T. (2016). Exploring the Dimensionality of Trauma-Informed Care: Implications for Theory and Practice. *Human Service Organizations, Management, Leadership & Governance, 41*(3), 317–325. DOI: 10.1080/23303131.2016.1268988

Hanson, R. F., & Lang, J. (2016). A Critical Look At Trauma-Informed Care Among Agencies and Systems Serving Maltreated Youth and Their Families. *Child Maltreatment, 21*(2), 95–100. DOI: 10.1177/1077559516635274

Hay, C., Hargrove, E., Davidson, K. M., & Cobb, A. (2024). Knowing and Caring About the Impact of Crime on Victims: Results From an Intervention for Justice-Involved Youth. *Youth Violence and Juvenile Justice*. Advance online publication. DOI: 10.1177/15412040241305327

Hickey, A., & Wallis, R. (2023). *Why the Australian media aren't helping to solve the 'youth crime crisis' they're reporting*. Retrieved 19 November from https://theconversation.com/why-the-Australian media-arent-helping-to-solve-the-youth-crime-crisis-theyrereporting-208947

Higginson, A., Eggins, E., & Mazerolle, L. (2017). *Investigating Serious Violent Crime: What works, what doesn't and for what crime types?* www.aic.gov.au/about-us/governance/criminology-research-advisory-council

Hoehn, E., & De Young, A. (2024). *QMHC Trauma Strategy - Infant and Early Childhood*. Retrieved 7 March from https://www.qmhc.qld.gov.au/

Hoeve, M., Semon-Dubas, J., Eichelsheim, V. I., van der Laan, P. H., Smeenk, W., & Gerris, J. R. M. (2009). The relationship between Parenting and Delinquency: A Meta-analysis. *Journal of Abnormal Child Psychology, 37*(1), 749–775.

Hoge, R. D., & Andrews, D. A. (2021). *YLS/CMI 2.0 User Manual*. www.EPIC-21-11-05-DC-DYRS-FOIA-20211130-YLS-CMI-User-Manual

Homel, R., & Thomsen, L. (Eds.). (2017). *Developmental Crime Prevention* (2nd ed.). Routledge.

Hopper, E. K., Bassuk, E. L., & Olivet, J. (2009). Shelter from the Storm: Trauma-Informed Care in Homelessness Services Settings. *The Open Health Services and Policy Journal*, *3*(1), 131–151.

Hoskins, Z. (2022). Public Reason and the Justification of Punishment. *Criminal Justice Ethics*, •••, 1–21. DOI: 10.1080/0731129x.2022.2102838

Huebner, B. M. (2013). *Appendix B: The Missouri Model: A Critical State of Knowledge*. Department of Criminology and Criminal Justice, University of Missouri Retrieved 16 October from https://www.nap.edu/read/14685/chapter/16

Jankowski, M. K., Schifferdecker, K. E., Butcher, R. L., Foster-Johnson, L., & Barnett, E. R. (2019). Effectiveness of a Trauma-Informed Care Initiative in a State Child Welfare System: A Randomized Study. *Child Maltreatment*, *24*(1), 86–97. DOI: 10.1177/1077559518796336

Johnson, S. M. (2003). Introduction to Attachment. In Johnson, S. M., & Whiffen, V. E. (Eds.), *Attachment processes in couple fna family therapy*. Guildford Press.

Joshi, A., & Truong, M. (2024). *The role of adverse childhood experiences (ACEs) in adolescent use of violence*. Australian Institute of Family Studies. www.aifs.gov.au/resources/policy-and-practice-papers/role-adverse-childhood-experiences-aces-adolescent-use

Justice Reform Initiative. (2023). *Alternatives to incarceration in Queensland* www.justicereforminitiative.org.au

Kahn, R. E., Jackson, K., Keiser, K., Ambroziak, G., & Levenson, J. S. (2020). Adverse Childhood Experiences Among Sexual Offenders: Associations With Sexual Recidivism Risk and Psychopathology. *Sexual Abuse*, *33*(7), 839–866. DOI: 10.1177/1079063220970031

Kelley, T. M., Pransky, J., & Sedgeman, J. A. (2014). Realizing Resilience in Trauma Exposed Juvenile Offenders: A Promising New Intervention for Juvenile Justice and Prevention Professionals. *Journal of Child & Adolescent Trauma*, *7*(3), 143–151. DOI: 10.1007/s40653-014-0018-8

Kerr-Davis, A., Hillman, S., Anderson, K., & Cross, R. (2023). Introducing Routine Assessment of Adverse Childhood Experiences For Looked-After Children: The Use and Properties of the Trauma and Adverse Life Events (TALE) Screening Tool. *Journal of Child & Adolescent Trauma*, *16*(4), 981–994. DOI: 10.1007/s40653-023-00559-5

King, A. R. (2020). The ACE Questionnaire and Lifetime Physical Aggression. *Journal of Aggression, Maltreatment & Trauma*, •••, 1–18. DOI: 10.1080/10926771.2020.1796875

Kinniburgh, K. J., Blaustein, M., Spinazzola, J., & van der Kolk, B. A. (2005). Attachment, Self-Regulation, and Competency: A comprehensive intervention framework for children with complex trauma. *Psychiatric Annals*, *35*(5), 424–430. DOI: 10.3928/00485713-20050501-08

Knight, B. (2024). *Victorian government cops criticism over youth crime as crucial debate over justice bill approaches*. https://www.abc.net.au/news/2024-08-13/victoria-youth-crime-age-of-criminal-responsibility-inspotlight/104215232

Krushas, A. E., Kulig, T. C., & Goslar, M. (2025). Advancing the Study of Adverse Childhood Experiences: An Examination of Measurement and Latent Classes. *Justice Quarterly*, •••, 1–37. DOI: 10.1080/07418825.2025.2451311

Kurlychek, M. C., & Johnson, B. D. (2019). Cumulative Disadvantage in the American Criminal Justice System. *Annual Review of Criminology*, *2*(1), 291–319. DOI: 10.1146/annurev-criminol-011518-024815

Lacey, R. E., Howe, L. D., Kelly-Irving, M., Bartley, M., & Kelly, Y. (2020). The Clustering of Adverse Childhood Experiences in the Avon Longitudinal Study of Parents and Children: Are Gender and Poverty Important? *Journal of Interpersonal Violence*, •••, 1–24. DOI: 10.1177/0886260520935096

Leitch, L. (2017). Action steps using ACEs and trauma-informed care: A resilience model. *Health & Justice*, *5*, 1–5. DOI: 10.1186/s40352-017-0050-5

Leiting, M., Beck, K., Bürgin, D., Fegert, J. M., Jenkel, N., Boonmann, C., Schmeck, K., Grob, A., & Schmid, M. (2024). Adverse Childhood Experiences, Quality of Life and the Australian mediating Roles of Self-Efficacy and Self-Directedness in Youth Residential Care Leavers. *Applied Research in Quality of Life*, *19*(6), 3479–3499. DOI: 10.1007/s11482-024-10392-z

Li, N., Shelton, M., & Grigorenko, E. L. (2025). Adverse childhood experiences, anger, and violence among justice-involved youth: A network analysis. *Child Abuse & Neglect*, *161*, 107301. DOI: 10.1016/j.chiabu.2025.107301

Lujan, M. J. W. M., & Fanniff, A. M. (2018). Justice for All: Trauma and the Need for Safety and Fairness Within Juvenile Justice Facilities. *Criminal Justice and Behavior*, *46*(1), 63–81. DOI: 10.1177/0093854818796060

Lynch, N., van den Brink, Y., & Forde, L. (2022). Introduction. In *Responses to Serious Offending by Children* (pp. 1–8). Routledge., DOI: 10.4324/9781032107707-1

Malvaso, C., Day, A., Cale, J., Hackett, L., Delfabbro, P., & Ross, S. (2022a). Adverse Childhood Experiences and Trauma among Young People in the Youth Justice System. *Trends and Issues in Crime and Criminal Justice*, *651*(202206), 1–19.

Malvaso, C., Day, A., Cale, J., Hackett, L., Delfabbro, P., & Ross, S. (2022b). Adverse childhood experiences and trauma among young people in the youth justice system. *Trends and Issues in Crime and Criminal Justice*, *651*(June), 1–19.

Malvaso, C., Harris, D., McGee, T. R., & Craig, J. (2023). The Implications of Adverse Childhood Experiences (ACEs) Research in the Treatment and Prevention of Offending Behaviour. In *Frontiers in Developmental and Life-Course Criminology* (pp. 102–114). Routledge., DOI: 10.4324/9781003294740-10

Malvaso, C. G., Cale, J., Whitten, T., Day, A., Singh, S., Hackett, L., Delfabbro, P. H., & Ross, S. (2021). Associations Between Adverse Childhood Experiences and Trauma Among Young People Who Offend: A Systematic Literature Review. *Trauma, Violence & Abuse*, *23*(5), 1677–1694. DOI: 10.1177/15248380211013132

Malvaso, C. G., Day, A., & Boyd, C. M. (2024). The Outcomes of Trauma-Informed Practice in Youth Justice: An Umbrella Review. *Journal of Child & Adolescent Trauma*, *17*(3), 939–955. DOI: 10.1007/s40653-024-00634-5

Malvaso, C. G., Delfabbro, P. H., & Day, A. (2019). Adverse childhood experiences in a South Australian sample of young people in detention. *Australian and New Zealand Journal of Criminology*, *52*(3), 411–431. DOI: 10.1177/0004865818810069

Marrow, M. T., Knudsen, K. J., Olafson, E., & Bucher, S. E. (2014). The Value of Implementing TARGET within a Trauma-Informed Juvenile Justice Setting. *Journal of Child & Adolescent Trauma*, *5*(3), 257–270. DOI: 10.1080/19361521.2012.697105

Matza, D. (1990). *Delinquency & Drift*. Transactions Publishers.

McAra, L., & McVie, S. (2023). Raising the minimum age of criminal responsibility: Lessons from the Scottish experience. *Current Issues in Criminal Justice*, *36*(4), 386–407. DOI: 10.1080/10345329.2023.2272362

McGuire, A., Singh, M., & Jackson, Y. (2024). Let it go, let it go: Stop measuring child maltreatment as a binary yes/no. *Child Abuse & Neglect*, *155*, 106994. DOI: 10.1016/j.chiabu.2024.106994

McGuire, D. R. (2019). *A Blueprint for Change: Adapting the lessons of the Spanish Youth Justice System to the Northern Territory - Report of Diagrama visit*. https://www.diagramafoundation.org.uk/

McLachlan, K. J. (2024a). *Trauma-informed Criminal Justice Towards a More Compassionate Criminal Justice System*. Springer Nature., DOI: 10.1007/978-3-031-59290-4

McLachlan, K. J. (2024b). *Trauma-Informed Criminal Justice: Towards a More Compassionate Criminal Justice System*. Palgrave MacMillan.

McLennan, J. D., Gonzalez, A., MacMillan, H. L., & Afifi, T. O. (2024). Routine screening for adverse childhood experiences (ACEs) still doesn't make sense. *Child Abuse & Neglect*, (106708), 1–7. Advance online publication. DOI: 10.1016/j.chiabu.2024.106708

Merlo, A. V. (2024). Progress and Persistent Challenges in the Juvenile Justice System. *Justice Evaluation Journal, Advance online publication*, 1-19. https://doi.org/DOI: 10.1080/24751979.2024.2444923

Modrowski, C. A., Sheerin, K., Grant, M., Collibee, C., & Kemp, K. A. (2023). Applying the Exploration, Preparation, Implementation, and Sustainment Framework to Trauma-Focused Screening in the Juvenile Legal System: Considerations and Recommendations for Future Research. *Psychological Injury and Law*, *17*(3), 245–258. DOI: 10.1007/s12207-023-09482-4

Moffitt, T. E. (1993). Adolescence-Limited and Life-Course Persistent Antisocial Behavior: A Developmental Taxonomy. *Psychological Review*, *100*(4), 674–701.

Morgan, N. (2017). *Behaviour management practices at Banksia Hill Detention Centre*. www.oics.wa.gov.au

Moss, D., & Klapdor, C. (2022). *Working with children to prevent self-blame after disclosures of child sexual abuse*. www.emergingminds.com.au

Muncie, J. (2015). *Youth & Crime* (4th ed.). Sage Publications Ltd.

National Center for Juvenile Justice. (2010). *Finding your ACE score*. https://www.ncjfcj.org/publications/finding-your-ace-score/

National Child Traumatic Stress Network. (2016). *Structured Psychotherapy for Adolescents Responding to Chronic Stress (SPARCS)*. National Child Traumatic Stress Network. Retrieved 11 March 2016 from www.NCTSN.org

Noel, M. E., Gatewood, B. J., Turner, S. M., & Muhammad, B. (2024). "We Have Unique Experiences": Familial Socialization of Children of Incarcerated Parents. *Criminal Justice and Behavior*, *51*(7), 1012–1031. DOI: 10.1177/00938548241240063

Novak, A. (2022). The Association Between Adverse Childhood Experiences, Neuropsychological Deficits, and Experiences of Exclusionary Discipline in Early Childhood. *Journal of Developmental and Life-Course Criminology*, ●●●, 1–31. DOI: 10.1007/s40865-022-00192-0

Ogilvie, J., Thomsen, L., Barton, J., Harris, D. A., Rynne, J., & O'Leary, P. (2022). Adverse childhood experiences among youth who offend: Examining exposure to domestic and family violence for male youth who perpetrate sexual harm and violence. www.anrows.org.au/publication/adverse-childhood-experiences-among-youth-who-offend-examining-exposure-to-domestic-and-family-violence-for-male-youth-who-perpetrate-sexual-harm-and-violence/

Oostermeijer, S., & Dwyer, M. (2019). *Design Guide for Small-scale Local Facilities.* https://localtime264843868.wordpress.com/wp-content/uploads/2019/11/localtime_designguide_v1-2.pdf

Peltonen, K., Tammilehto, J., Flykt, M., Vanska, M., Kuppens, P., Bosmans, G., & Lindblom, J. (2024). Adverse childhood experiences and emotion dynamics in daily life: A two sample study. *Cognition and Emotion*, ●●●, 1–21. Advance online publication. DOI: 10.1080/02699931.2024.2434153

Perez, N. M., Jennings, W. G., & Baglivio, M. T. (2018). A Path to Serious, Violent, Chronic Delinquency: The Harmful Aftermath of Adverse Childhood Experiences. *Crime and Delinquency*, *64*(1), 3–25. DOI: 10.1177/0011128716684806

Perry, B. D. (2008). Child Maltreatment: A Neurodevelopmental Perspective on the Role of Trauma and Neglect in Psychopathology. In Hinshaw, T. B. S. P. (Ed.), *Child and Adolescent Psychopathology* (pp. 93–129). John Wiley & Sons.

Perry, B. D., Griffin, E., Davis, G., Perry, J. A., & Perry, R. D. (Eds.). (2018). *The Impact of Neglect, Trauma and Maltreatment on Neurodevelopment: Implications for Juvenile Justice Practice, Programs and Policy*. John Wiley & Sons, Ltd., https://doi.org/https://doi.org/10.1002/9781118650868.ch31

Peters, M. A., & Mika, C. T. (2017). Aborigine, Indian, indigenous or first nations? *Educational Philosophy and Theory*, *49*(13), 1229–1234. DOI: 10.1080/00131857.2017.1279879

Pettus, C. A. (2023). Trauma and Prospects for Reentry. *Annual Review of Criminology*, *6*(1), 423–446. DOI: 10.1146/annurev-criminol-041122-111300

Phoenix, J. (2016). Against Youth Justice and Youth Governance, for Youth Penalty. *British Journal of Criminology*, *56*(1), 123–140. DOI: 10.1093/bjc/azv031

Pickens, I. (2016). Laying the Groundwork: Conceptualizing a Trauma-Informed System of Care in Juvenile Detention. *Journal of Infant, Child, and Adolescent Psychotherapy; JICAP, 15*(3), 220–230. DOI: 10.1080/15289168.2016.1214452

Porges, S. W. (2020). *Polyvagal Theory and Protective Responses.* Retrieved 21 April from https://www.presence.academy/porges-poly-vagal/

Portwood, S. G., Lawler, M. J., & Roberts, M. C. (2023). *Handbook of Adverse Childhood Experiences: A Framework for Collaborative Health Promotion.* Springer.

Powers, P., & Act, R. (2000). https://www.legislation.qld.gov.au/view/html/inforce/current/act-2000-005

Productivity Commission. (2024). *Report on Government Services 2024.* www.pc.gov.au/ongoing/report-on-government-services/2024/community-services

Psychology Training and Supervision. (2023). *Trauma-Focused Cognitive-Behavioral Therapy.* www.tfcbtaustralia.com.au/resources

Public Sector Ethics Act, 1994. https://www.legislation.qld.gov.au/view/html/inforce/current/act-1994-067

QFCC. (2024). *Crossover Cohort: Young people under youth justice supervision and their interaction with the child protection system* www.qfcc.qld.gov.au

Queensland Government. (2023). *Code of Conduct For the Queensland Public Service.* www.forgov.qld.gov.au/pay-benefits-and-policy/public-service-values-and-conduct/public-service-code-of-conduct

Queensland Government Statistician's Office. (2021). *Youth offending: Research brief.* https://www.qgso.qld.gov.au › crime-justice-research

Quinn, K., Pacella, M. L., Dickson-Gomez, J., & Nydegger, L. A. (2017). Childhood Adversity and the Continued Exposure to Trauma and Violence Among Adolescent Gang Members. *American Journal of Community Psychology, 59*(1-2), 36–49. DOI: 10.1002/ajcp.12123

Riddle, S., Hickey, A., Pocock, C., McKee, A., Skye, D., & Wallis, R. (2024). Moving beyond deficit Australian media figurations of young people: Troubling the contemporary 'youth crime crisis'. *Continuum, 37*(6), 756–769. DOI: 10.1080/10304312.2024.2313565

Robinson, M. (2016). *To examine trauma-informed models of youth detention and bring back findings.* www.churchilltrust.com.au/fellow/murray-robinson-vic-2015/

Rose, B., Kuiper, M. E., Reinders Folmer, C., & van Rooij, B. (2024). Can criminology sway the public? How empirical findings about deterrence affect public punishment preferences. *Crime Science, 13*(1), 43. DOI: 10.1186/s40163-024-00240-8

Roy, C., Castonguay, A., Fortin, M., Drolet, C., Franche-Choquette, G., Dumais, A., Lafortune, D., Bernard, P., & Geoffrion, S. (2019). The Use of Restraint and Seclusion in Residential Treatment Care for Youth: A Systematic Review of Related Factors and Interventions. *Trauma, Violence & Abuse, 22*(2), 318–338. DOI: 10.1177/1524838019843196

Schiraldi, V., Hayes, D., & McGuire, D. R. (2021). *Youth Justice in The Netherlands & Spain.* https://justicelab.columbia.edu/content/netherlands-experience-emerging-adult-justice

Schmidt, A. T., Duron, J., Bergquist, B. K., Bammel, A. C., Maloney, K. A., Williams-Butler, A., & Hanten, G. R. (2023). Prosocial attributes relate to lower recidivism in justice-involved youth: Preliminary evidence using a novel measure of prosocial functioning. *Journal of Public Mental Health, 22*(4), 202–215. DOI: 10.1108/jpmh-02-2023-0012

Sirhan, N., Mufarreh, A., Lee, Y., Mishreky, C., Hunt, B., Anderson, T., & Bailey, B. A. (2024). Adverse Childhood Experiences in the Post-COVID Era. *Journal of Aggression, Maltreatment & Trauma*, •••, 1–13. DOI: 10.1080/10926771.2024.2404002

Sparks, B. (2021). Attitudes toward the Punishment of Juvenile and Adult Sexual Offenders in Canada: The Roles of Sentencing Goals and Criminal Justice Motivations. *Journal of Child Sexual Abuse, 30*(2), 125–145. DOI: 10.1080/10538712.2020.1862947

Sroufe, L. A., Carlson, E. A., Levy, A. K., & Egeland, B. (1999). Implications of attachment theory for developmental psychopathology. *Development and Psychopathology, 11*, 1–13.

Stathis, S. L., Letters, P., Doolan, I., Fleming, R., Heath, K., Arnett, A., & Cory, S. (2008). Use of the Massachusetts Youth Screening Instrument to assess mental health problems in young people within an Australian youth detention centre. *Journal of Paediatrics and Child Health, 44*(7-8), 438–443. DOI: 10.1111/j.1440-1754.2008.01324.x

Stewart, A. L., Livingston, M., & Dennison, S. (2008). Transitions and turning points: Examining the links between child maltreatment and juvenile offending. *Child Abuse & Neglect, 32*(1), 51–66. DOI: 10.1016/j.chiabu.2007.04.011

Swedo, E. A., Holditch Niolon, P., Anderson, K. N., Li, J., Brener, N., Mpofu, J., Aslam, M. V., & Underwood, J. M. (2024). Prevalence of Adverse Childhood Experiences Among Adolescents. *Pediatrics*. Advance online publication. DOI: 10.1542/peds.2024-066633

Thomas, J. L., Keenan-Miller, D., Sumner, J. A., & Hammen, C. (2021). Early Life Adversity and Clinical Intimate Partner Violence in Adulthood: The Australian mediating Role of Interpersonal Conflict in Adolescence. *Journal of Interpersonal Violence, 8862605211057267*. Advance online publication. DOI: 10.1177/08862605211057267

Thomsen, L., & Homel, R. (2024). Cumulative Sociodemographic Risk as a Predictor of Adolescent Antisocial Behaviour. *Child Indicators Research*, *17*(5), 2123–2148. DOI: 10.1007/s12187-024-10157-y

Tonry, M., & Farrington, D. (1995). Strategic Approaches to Crime Prevention. *Crime and Justice*, *19*(1).

Upton, F. (2023). Addressing Challenges and Opportunities in Juvenile Justice: Meeting the Needs of Incarcerated Adolescent Populations. *Psychological Science in the Public Interest*, *24*(3), 127–132. DOI: 10.1177/15291006231218669

Urquhart, C., & Jasiura, F. (2013). *Trauma Informed Practice Guide*. www.cewh .ca/wp-content/uploads/2012/05/2013_TIP-Guide.pdf

Usher, K., Jackson, D., Walker, R., Durkin, J., Smallwood, R., Robinson, M., Sampson, U. N., Adams, I., Porter, C., & Marriott, R. (2021). Indigenous Resilience in Australia: A Scoping Review Using a Reflective Decolonizing Collective Dialogue. *Frontiers in Public Health*, *9*, 1–17. DOI: 10.3389/fpubh.2021.630601

Van der Kolk, B. A. (Ed.). (2007). *Developmental impact of Childhood Trauma*. Cambridge University Press.

Van Der Kolk, B. A., McFarlane, A. C., & Weisaeth, L. (1996). Background Issues and History. In Van Der Kolk, B. A., & McFarlane, A. C. (Eds.), *Traumatic Stress: The Effects of Overwhelming Experience on Mind, Body, and Society*. Guilford Publications.

Van Wyk, J. A. (2023). ACEs and Angst: Adverse Childhood Experiences, General Strain Theory, and Adolescent Male Suicidal and Violent Behaviors. *SAGE Open*, *13*(2), 1–19. DOI: 10.1177/21582440231176710

Vardon, C. (2021). *Changing the Sentence: Overseeing Queensland's youth justice reforms*. https://www.qfcc.qld.gov.au/

Vidal, S., Connell, C. M., Prince, D. M., & Tebes, J. K. (2019). Multisystem-Involved Youth: A Developmental Framework and Implications for Research, Policy, and Practice. *Adolescent Research Review*, *4*(1), 15–29. DOI: 10.1007/s40894-018-0088-1

Vincent, G. M., Drawbridge, D. C., Lawson, S. G., Todorovic, K., & Perrault, R. T. (2024). Sustainability of Evidence-Based Practices: Risk-Need-Responsivity in Probation 7 Years Later. *Criminal Justice and Behavior*, *51*(5), 643–666. DOI: 10.1177/00938548241229193

White, M., & Gooda, M. (2017). *Royal Commission and Board of Inquiry into the Protection and Detention of Children in the Northern Territory: Final Report*. Darwin, Australia Retrieved from https://www.royalcommission.gov.au/royal-commission-detention-and-protection-children-northern-territory

Whitten, T., McGee, T. R., Homel, R., Farrington, D. P., & Ttofi, M. M. (2018). Comparing the criminal careers and childhood risk factors of persistent, chronic, and persistent–chronic offenders. *Australian and New Zealand Journal of Criminology*, *52*(2), 151–173. DOI: 10.1177/0004865818781203

Williams, B. T. (2023). *Effectiveness of staff training on Trauma-Informed Care*. The University of Southern Mississippi., https://aquila.usm.edu/cgi/viewcontent.cgi?article=1272&context=dnp_capstone

Wolff, K. T., Baglivio, M. T., & Intravia, J. (2022). Adverse childhood experiences (ACEs), psychotropic medication prescription, and continued offending among youth with serious offending histories in juvenile justice residential placement. *Journal of Criminal Justice*, *83*(November-December), 1–13. DOI: 10.1016/j.jcrimjus.2022.101922

Wolff, K. T., Cuevas, C., Intravia, J., Baglivio, M. T., & Epps, N. (2018). The Effects of Neighborhood Context on Exposure to Adverse Childhood Experiences (ACE) Among Adolescents Involved in the Juvenile Justice System: Latent Classes and Contextual Effects. *Journal of Youth and Adolescence*, *47*(11), 2279–2300. DOI: 10.1007/s10964-018-0887-5

Wood, S., Janssen, H., Hughes, K., Passmore, J., & Bellis, M. A. (2023). *A practical handbook on Adverse Childhood Experiences (ACEs) Delivering prevention, building resilience and developing trauma-informed systems*. Retrieved 26 December from https://phwwhocc.co.uk

Yannon, M. G., Decrop, R., Le, M., Beery, S., & Tompsett, C. J. (2024). Cumulative Adverse Childhood Experiences (ACEs) and Recidivism: A Meta-Analysis. *Criminal Justice and Behavior*, *51*(11), 1696–1714. DOI: 10.1177/00938548241267230

Yoder, J. R., Hodge, A. I., Ruch, D., & Dillard, R. (2018). Effects of Childhood Polyvictimization on Victimization in Juvenile Correctional Facilities: The Australian mediating Role of Trauma Symptomatology. *Youth Violence and Juvenile Justice*, *17*(2), 129–153. DOI: 10.1177/1541204018757038

Zettler, H. R., & Craig, J. M. (2022). Residentially-Placed Youth and the Adverse Childhood Experiences-Recidivism Relationship: Considering Racial/Ethnic and Sex Differences. *American Journal of Criminal Justice*, *48*(2), 530–544. DOI: 10.1007/s12103-021-09667-0

Zettler, H. R., & Craig, J. M. (2024). The Prevalence of Trauma Among Participants in a Juvenile Mental Health Court. *Criminal Justice and Behavior*, *51*(3), 401–419. DOI: 10.1177/00938548231222619

Zettler, H. R., Wolff, K. T., Baglivio, M., Craig, J. M., & Epps, N. (2017). The Racial and Gender Differences in the Impact of Adverse Childhood Experiences on Juvenile Residential Placement. *Youth Violence and Juvenile Justice*, *16*(3), 319–337. DOI: 10.1177/1541204017698213

Chapter 4
The Role of Adverse Childhood Experiences in Offender Rehabilitation:
Insights From Singapore's Correctional System

Liangyu April Lin
https://orcid.org/0009-0002-1618-4310
Singapore Prison Service, Singapore

Ace Ong
https://orcid.org/0009-0005-5434-3767
Singapore Prison Service, Singapore

Fann Yunfan Jiang
https://orcid.org/0009-0002-1618-4310
Singapore Prison Service, Singapore

Camelia Liow
https://orcid.org/0009-0008-8579-2831
Singapore Prison Service, Singapore

ABSTRACT

This chapter examines Adverse Childhood Experiences (ACEs) within Singapore's correctional system, focussing specifically on youth and women offenders, who are two distinct populations with a higher number of ACEs as compared to the general population. These populations demonstrate trauma profiles and rehabilitation needs that align with findings in international literature, warranting targeted intervention approaches. Understanding the needs of the two specialised populations, Singapore

DOI: 10.4018/979-8-3373-9524-1.ch004

Prison Service adopts a tailored approach to address the responsivity factor in rehabilitation. Through analysis of international research and local evidence, including the implementation of the T-care framework by SPS, we explore how trauma-informed practices can enhance rehabilitation outcomes for these vulnerable populations.

INTRODUCTION

Understanding ACEs in Correctional Populations

ACEs, including abuse, neglect, and household dysfunction, have increasingly been recognised as significant predictors of criminal justice involvement. A groundbreaking ACEs study by Felitti et al., (1998) laid the foundation for subsequent research highlighting the cumulative impact of early trauma on adult functioning, including a heightened risk of incarceration. A robust body of international literature has linked ACEs with developmental disruptions, mental health disorders, substance use and antisocial behaviour. In correctional populations, the prevalence rates and impact of ACEs are magnified. Studies have shown that individuals in prison often report significantly higher rates of ACEs than the general population, with certain subgroups such as women and youth offenders bearing a disproportionate number (Wolff & Shi, 2012; Baglivio et al., 2015).

The Singapore Prison Service is a department under the Ministry of Home Affairs that operates Singapore's correctional system with a mission to protect society through the safe custody and rehabilitation of offenders. SPS manages multiple correctional institutions and focusses on a comprehensive approach that combines secure custody with rehabilitation programmes aimed at reducing reoffending rates. The service emphasises evidence-based practices in correctional management, offering educational and vocational as well as rehabilitation and family programmes to address offenders' needs. SPS adopts a throughcare approach in offender rehabilitation and works closely with community partners and volunteers to support the successful reintegration of offenders into the community after their release.

PREVALENCE AND IMPACT OF ACES IN YOUTH AND WOMEN OFFENDERS

Prevalence of ACEs in Youth Offenders

Youth offenders show elevated levels of childhood adversity compared to their peers in the general population. A meta-analysis conducted in 2021 found that up to

90% of juvenile offenders reported at least one ACE, with more than 60% reporting four or more ACEs (Fox, et al., 2021). Another systematic review reported that over 85% of justice-involved youths had experienced at least one ACE (Malvaso et al., 2024). Each additional ACE increases juvenile recidivism risk by 35%, which highlights the significant impact of cumulative childhood trauma on the likelihood of persistent and severe offending behaviours among youths (Fox et al., 2015).

In the same vein, 93% of youths in Singapore's juvenile justice system reported experiencing at least one type of ACE, with youth-specific factors such as family criminality, substance abuse and parental loss strongly linked to earlier and more persistent reoffending (Jiang et al., 2025). These youths often exhibit behavioural dysregulation, impulsivity and defiance, which lead to early criminal justice involvement and complicated journeys in rehabilitation.

Impact of ACEs on Youth Development

Extant literature has identified ACEs as significant risk factors for reoffending among youth offenders (Baglivio et al., 2014). A meta-analysis by Yohros (2023) showed that experiencing a greater number of ACEs increases the likelihood of reoffending in youths by 4.4%. According to the developmental and life-course criminology (DLC) theories that seek to understand the individual causes of criminal (re)offending and how these individual factors are differentially associated with (re)offending at various stages of life (Farrington, 2003), there is a cumulative effect of disadvantage brought about by ACEs. This in turn elevates the potential of youths' first contact point with the criminal justice system as well as their sequential involvement due to recidivism (Kurlychek & Johnson, 2019). The strong relationship between ACEs and offending could be attributed to the impact ACEs have on brain development, specifically in areas related to executive functioning, emotional regulation and stress response (Anda et al., 2006; Teicher & Samson, 2016). These could in turn heightens the youth's likelihood of engaging in delinquent behaviours such as using violence or substances as a coping mechanism. Hence, interventions addressing the impact of ACEs on stress and coping are imperative to mitigate delinquent behaviours.

Local Studies on ACEs in At-risk Children and Youth Offenders

Given the high prevalence of ACEs in youth offenders documented in international literature, local studies have been conducted to understand their impact on at-risk children and youth offenders. Studies of Singapore's child protection cases have shown that maltreatment at an earlier age predicts greater externalising behaviours in children (Chen, 2016), while a higher number of ACEs was found to contribute to increased levels of aggressive behaviours (Lim, 2017). The pathway from trauma to offending is complicated. Research has shown that more than one third of children in foster care and voluntary children's homes has experienced multiple incidences of maltreatment, demonstrated poorer life functioning and presented with more behavioural and emotional needs (Liu et al., 2016).

Local research conducted on juvenile offenders found that youths with a history of ACEs were 1.38 times more likely to reoffend compared to youths without ACEs over a 7.4-year follow-up period (Li et al., 2015). Chng et al., (2016) showed that youth offenders with ACEs had poorer recidivism outcomes as compared to other youths. Similarly, Yao et al., (2022) found that the ACE of losing a biological parent serves as a risk factor, while Baglivio et al., (2014) found that having a parent with a criminal history serves as a risk factor for youth offending. These findings indicate that the presence of ACEs increases the risk of reoffending and serves as a barrier to desistance for youth offenders.

SPS conducted a study to explore how factors such as ACEs, social support and agency influence the desistance journey of youth offenders in Singapore. Youth reoffenders and youth desistors completed a survey assessing their ACEs, agency to desist and perceived social support from six sources: peers, family, workplace, school, community and Rehabilitation Officer (RO)/Correctional Rehabilitation Specialist (CRS). Youth reoffenders reported a greater exposure to ACEs relative to youth desistors. This aligns with a growing body of research indicating that cumulative childhood adversity increases the risk of reoffending among both young and adult offenders (Moore & Tatman, 2016; Weber & Lynch, 2021; Yohros, 2023).

Additionally, among youth reoffenders, higher levels of ACEs were found to be linked to significantly lower agency to desist as compared to youth desistors. This suggests that accumulated trauma may reduce the likelihood of desistance for youth offenders by diminishing their hope for the future.

With regards to social support, youth reoffenders reported perceiving less social support from significant others and RO/CRS than youth desistors. However, support from the community was positively associated with the agency to desist from crime among this group of youth offenders. This suggests that community support may be particularly important for youths who have experienced setbacks in their desistance journey, as it can influence their belief in their ability to stop offending. This study found significance for the role of ACEs in the desistance journey of youth offenders in Singapore.

Local and international evidence highlighted the high prevalence of ACEs among youth offenders and their impact on their social and emotional development, predisposing them to aggression and violence and elevating their risk of offending. Rehabilitation of youth offenders must be trauma-informed and youth-centric to address the impact of ACEs.

Prevalence of ACEs in Women Offenders

Women offenders often present with unique and complex pathways into the criminal justice system, shaped by extensive histories of trauma and victimisation (Covington, 2001; Schonbrun et al., 2016). ACEs have emerged as powerful predictors of criminal behaviours and offending in women. Recent international and local research documents the prevalence of ACEs among women offenders and elucidates their impact on offending trajectories.

The prevalence of emotional, physical and sexual abuse is reported to be at between 77% and 90% of women in prison respectively (Australian Institute of Family Studies, 2012; Messina & Grella, 2006). Friestad et al., (2012) found high rates of emotional abuse (39%), physical abuse (36%) and sexual abuse (19%) among women prisoners in Norway, with 34% reporting more than five ACEs. Levenson et al., (2015) reported that 50% of U.S. women sex offenders had experienced childhood sexual abuse, and 41% reported four or more ACEs, far exceeding rates in the general female population. Australian research by Fischer et al., (2024) similarly highlighted that 94% of incarcerated women experienced at least one ACE, with a median of six. Aboriginal women were disproportionately exposed to familial incarceration, compounding intergenerational trauma. Miller and Najavits (2012) noted estimates of up to 90% of women in prison experiencing interpersonal or sexual violence, consistent with findings by Grella et al., (2013) showing incarcerated women had significantly higher risk of trauma exposure as compared with controls in the general population, with odds ranging from of 1.7 to 3.7.

These traumatic experiences contribute to both initial offending and continued involvement in the justice system and strongly correlate with substance dependence, emotional dysregulation and institutional behaviour problems, which present significant barriers to rehabilitation. In Singapore, local research revealed that about 50% of incarcerated women reported abuse histories, with many remaining in abusive adult relationships (Chong et al., 2004;). Leung et al., (2015) noted that nearly half of women drug offenders cited previous abuse as a motivator for their drug-abusing behaviours.

Impact of ACEs on Women Offending

ACEs significantly influence pathways into offending, especially for women. Numerous research articles have shown that a history of abuse is related to the probability of a woman abusing alcohol and other drugs to regulate their emotions (Covington, 2008; Poole & Greaves, 2012). Intervention for women's substance abuse was found to be ineffective unless it acknowledged the complexity and issues of a woman's life and her vulnerability, which include being more susceptible to violence and other types of abuse (Covington, 2008). Friestad et al., (2012) found that the number of ACEs predicted suicide attempts and drug abuse in adulthood, both factors linked to criminal justice involvement. Levenson et al., (2015) also showed that higher ACEs scores correlated with younger victims among women sex offenders, indicating how childhood trauma may distort interpersonal relationships and offending patterns.

Hardyman and Van Voorhis (2004) and Salisbury and Van Voorhis (2009) emphasised that trauma and victimisation are stronger predictors of recidivism for women than for men. Childhood victimisation increases the risk of delinquency (Chesney-Lind & Shelden, 2004), while adult victimisation sustains ongoing offending behaviours (Bloom et al., 2003; Covington, 1998). Grella et al., (2013) underscored how trauma exposure significantly elevated the odds of post-traumatic stress disorder (PTSD), with substance use emerging as a maladaptive coping strategy and a strong predictor of continued criminal involvement.

Local Study on Trauma in Incarcerated Mothers

SPS conducted a study on incarcerated mothers to understand their history of ACEs, mental health difficulties and challenges related to being an incarcerated parent. The study found 81.1% of incarcerated mothers in Singapore had experienced at least one ACE. This prevalence rate exceeded that reported in the local general population of 63.9% (Subramaniam et al., 2020) and aligned with rates found in the incarcerated population in the United States of 80.0% (Levenson et al., 2015). Of the incarcerated mothers in the study, 37.8% had experienced at least four ACEs, which was also higher than the local general population of 13.1% (Subramaniam et al., 2020) but lower than the incarcerated population in Japan of 48.4% (Sasaki et al., 2023). In addition to the high rates of ACEs, this study also found that close to one-third of the sample reported post-traumatic stress symptoms, which is higher than rates reported in other countries such as Spain and the United States.

In addition, the study found that an incarcerated mother's exposure to ACEs predicted her experience of higher levels of trauma and anxiety symptoms, but it did not predict depression or stress symptoms. This could be attributed to a stronger relationship between trauma and anxiety versus trauma and depression, as observed in extant literature. The study found that the incarcerated mother's ACEs level was found to be significantly predictive of their children's scores on PEARLS (Paediatric Adverse Childhood Experiences). This finding suggests that the risk of children being exposed to similar adverse experiences increases when their mothers are also exposed to ACEs.

ACEs are alarmingly prevalent among women offenders, contributing to the development of mental health issues, substance abuse and offending behaviours.

Effective rehabilitation must prioritise trauma-informed, gender-responsive and culturally sensitive interventions that address the profound and enduring effects of childhood adversity. Such approaches are essential to breaking cycles of trauma and criminalisation.

ACEs AS RESPONSIVITY FACTORS IN REHABILITATION

The Risk-Need-Responsivity (RNR) model (Andrews & Bonta, 2010) underscores the importance of addressing personal characteristics that influence treatment responsiveness. According to the "responsivity" principle, ACEs and trauma would likely affect offenders' capacity to engage in and benefit from interventions. Unresolved trauma can manifest as hypervigilance, mistrust, aggression and avoidance behaviours, which are often misinterpreted as resistance or noncompliance within the correctional setting (Levenson, 2015). Research by Marzano et al., (2011) suggested that ACEs are risk factors for poor mental health in adulthood. Offenders who experienced multiple ACEs are more likely to engage in self-harm behaviour and experience mental illness under confinement (Ford et al., 2020). Taking into account such correlation, intervention programmes will need to be responsive to the offender's ACEs, trauma history and mental health conditions and will need to engage each offender differently.

Failure to address trauma related to ACEs in a timely and adequate manner may result in treatment dropout, institutional misconduct and increased recidivism. Trauma-responsive interventions that incorporate psychoeducation, emotional regulation and relational safety can significantly enhance programme engagement and outcomes (Wilson et al., 2015).

TRAUMA-INFORMED CARE (TIC) IN A CORRECTIONAL SETTING

TIC has been widely adopted in youth and adult correctional facilities. Adopting TIC means training correctional staff, redesigning environments and policies to reflect trauma awareness and embedding trauma-informed programming alongside traditional security-focussed goals (Miller, & Najavits, 2012). Some juvenile detention facilities have implemented trauma-informed milieu intervention, including staff training and youth-focussed TIC skills training co-led by trained staff, which showed significant reductions in facility violence when at least 15% of youths went through the intervention (Baetz, et al., 2019). Another study examining a trauma-informed unit (TRU) vs. a standard unit (TAU) found that staff in the TAU experienced injuries at nine times the rate of those in the TRU, and TRU staff felt better supported and safer (Hashweh et al., 2024). These studies highlight the benefit of having trauma-trained staff and youth programming to improve both safety and climate in youth detention facilities. While the effects of Post Traumatic Stress Disorder (PTSD) symptom reduction were small to moderate and had inconsistent effects on recidivism and delinquency, gains were clearer in emotion regulation and safety (Malvaso et al., 2024).

Turning to adult corrections, emerging empirical studies suggest that TIC approaches in correctional environments enhance rehabilitation among women offenders by targeting the high co-occurrence of PTSD and substance use that typifies this population. For instance, group-based *Seeking Safety* interventions have demonstrated significant reductions in PTSD symptoms at three-month follow-ups among incarcerated women, as well as reductions in substance use and an improved ability to cope (Zlotnick et al., 2003; Zlotnick & Najavits, 2009). A randomised controlled pilot study further indicated that, although both *Seeking Safety* and the usual care and treatment alone yielded long-term improvements in PTSD and psychopathology, greater session attendance correlated with enhanced outcomes among women in the *Seeking Safety* programme (Zlotnick & Najavits, 2009).

Furthermore, a study employing a gender-responsive intervention involving the *Helping Women Recover* and *Beyond Trauma* curricula reported that participants had significantly lower rates of reincarceration within 12 months post-release (31% vs. 45%) and longer stays in aftercare programmes compared to controls (Messina et al., 2010). Findings show the beneficial effects of treatment components oriented toward women's needs and support the integration of Gender-responsive Treatment (GRT) in prison programmes for women. Collectively, these findings indicate that structured, trauma-informed and gender-responsive treatments can improve clinical outcomes and reduce short-term reoffending among women offenders, although further large-scale and long-term evaluations are warranted.

In summary, TIC in correctional facilities has shown promising results in addressing the impact of trauma on stress reactions, self-regulation and mental health as well as reducing institutional violence in youth and women offenders, when implemented through combined staff training and offender-focussed interventions.

ADOPTION OF T-CARE IN SPS

As correctional systems worldwide increasingly recognise the importance of TIC, SPS has adopted T-care as a structured de-escalation and engagement model for youth and women populations. T-care is a trauma-informed care framework designed to empower the dedicated personnel (who work with traumatised children, youth, adults and families) by providing a user's guide to the brain's stress system and a set of practical, efficient tools for preventing and managing stress reactions (Advanced Trauma Solutions Professionals, n.d.). It recognises the widespread impact of trauma and understands how it can affect a person's behaviour, physical and mental health, and interactions with systems (Advanced Trauma Solutions Professionals, n.d.). T-care teaches four practical skills to help individuals manage stress reactions: 1) notice alarm reactions, 2) recognise alarm triggers, 3) define goals and 4) focus on the mind: slow down, orient, self-check. It provides practical language and skills to enhance self-regulation, behavioural self-control and the ability to cope in stressful events.

T-care emerged as an adaptation of the TARGET (Trauma Affect Regulation – Guide for Education and Therapy) model (Ford & Russo, 2006). While maintaining the theoretical foundations of trauma-informed care, T-care was specifically modified to enable implementation by non-clinical correctional staff, setting it apart from TARGET, which requires clinically trained personnel (Advanced Trauma Solutions Professionals, n.d.). Although T-care is grounded in trauma-related theories, it serves as a trauma-informed approach rather than a trauma treatment intervention. The implementation of T-care in SPS was based on several key attributes that aligned with the service's rehabilitation objectives. These include its trauma-informed foundation, strength-based approach, cultural sensitivity and relational focus. Through T-care, staff learned to help individuals develop better behavioural self-control and enhance their coping strategies during stressful encounters. In addition, staff members also benefitted from applying T-care skills in their own coping and self-management strategies.

The decision to pilot T-care with youth and women populations in SPS was strategically driven by evidence of the populations' heightened vulnerability to trauma related to ACEs. Local research indicates that these groups not only show higher prevalence of ACEs but also demonstrate distinct trauma manifestations that significantly impact their rehabilitation journey. Youth offenders, being at a critical developmental stage, present a unique opportunity for early intervention, while women offenders including incarcerated mothers often exhibit complex trauma histories intertwined with relationships and caregiving roles. These populations also typically show greater receptivity to relationship-based interventions, making them ideal candidates for testing the effectiveness of T-care's trauma-informed approach in the correctional setting.

YOUTH OFFENDERS

Developmentally Informed Care for Youth Offenders

Youths in the justice system differ significantly from adult offenders in terms of cognitive, emotional and neurological development (Calleja, 2022). This difference makes it essential for officers to be trauma-informed when working with youths and to adopt approaches that are responsive to their developmental stage. Standard interventions designed for adults are often ill-suited for this population and may cause further harm or disengagement if applied without proper adaptation (Calleja, 2022; Jackson et al., 2023).

Research has increasingly demonstrated that traditional treatment models for adolescent offenders have relied heavily on cognitive-behavioural approaches originally developed for adults (Schmucker & Lösel, 2015; ter Beek et al., 2018). However, these models often fail to account for the distinct developmental needs of adolescents. The Forward-Focused Model (FFM), evaluated in Michigan, aimed to address this gap by incorporating developmentally tailored cognitive-behavioural therapy (CBT) interventions. This model emphasises prosocial development and targets trauma, substance use and mental health conditions that frequently co-occur among justice-involved youth (Calleja, 2022). In a study comparing the FFM to treatment-as-usual in secure residential programmes, adolescents receiving the specialised model had substantially lower rates of recidivism, with a sexual recidivism rate of just 2.9% over a three-year follow-up period. This was nearly half the rate of those receiving standard treatment (Calleja, 2022).

These findings illustrate the value of treatment models that are not only evidence-based but also developmentally responsive. These findings align with advances in neuroscience research, where studies have shown that the youth brain undergoes prolonged development, with the prefrontal cortex, which governs decision-making and impulse control, not reaching maturity until the mid- to late twenties (Giedd et al., 1999; Sowell et al., 1999, 2001). Consequently, youths are more susceptible to risk-taking behaviour, especially in the presence of peers, and tend to respond differently to perceived rewards and consequences than adults (Chein et al., 2011; Gardner & Steinberg, 2005; Pfeifer et al., 2011; Steinberg, 2005). This developmental context underscores the need for interventions that consider cognitive and emotional immaturity rather than treating youths offending in the same way as adult criminal behaviour.

Trauma-informed Care for Youth Offenders

Youth offenders also experience significantly higher levels of trauma compared with their peers in the general population (Ford et al., 2007; Jackson et al., 2023). In the United States, studies have shown that over 90% of youth in residential treatment facilities (RTFs) report experiencing at least one traumatic event. Moreover, rates of PTSD in these youths are four to eight times higher than in community-based samples (Cohen et al., 2016; Everhart Newman et al., 2018). This elevated trauma exposure creates challenges for rehabilitation and underscores the critical need for trauma-informed interventions specifically designed for this vulnerable population.

Cohen et al., (2016) conducted a study across 18 RTF programmes in Connecticut, New Hampshire and Vermont, testing the implementation of trauma-focused cognitive behavioural therapy (TF-CBT) with adjudicated youth. TF-CBT is an evidence-based treatment that includes core components such as psychoeducation, affective modulation, trauma narration and safety planning. This structured approach aimed to address both the cognitive and emotional aspects of trauma recovery. The study found that youths who received TF-CBT showed significant and clinically meaningful improvements in both PTSD and depressive symptoms. These improvements were most notable when therapists received both online and in-person training, along with regular consultation to maintain fidelity to the model. The findings highlight the importance of comprehensive training and ongoing support for practitioners implementing trauma-informed interventions.

In a separate study by Everhart Newman et al., (2018), conducted in a secure residential facility in the southeastern United States, TF-CBT was implemented with youths who had engaged in illegal sexual behaviour. This group is known to experience disproportionately high rates of trauma, particularly sexual and physical abuse. The study found that TF-CBT led to a reduction in PTSD symptoms among the youths and was feasible to implement in secure treatment settings where treatment is often mandated by the court. These findings suggest that trauma-informed treatment can be successfully delivered even in highly controlled environments if staff are trained and the therapeutic approach is well supported. Furthermore, these results demonstrate that even youths with complex trauma histories and challenging behaviours can benefit from evidence-based trauma interventions when implemented with appropriate clinical oversight and institutional support.

T-care Pilot for Youth Offenders at a Reformative Training Centre (RTC)

Recognising these vulnerabilities and the neurodevelopmental impact of ACEs, SPS has piloted programmes that prioritise emotional safety, engagement and therapeutic alliance. From March to September 2022, a T-care pilot was conducted at the RTC, a dedicated youth rehabilitation facility for youth offenders between the ages of 16 to 21. A total of eight youth offenders, four correctional officers and two Correctional Rehabilitation Specialist (CRS) professionals participated in the T-care pilot implementation. The CRS professionals were trained in psychology, counselling, or social work, and were primarily responsible for delivering rehabilitative interventions to the youths. They assisted with training correctional officers in the delivery of T-care skills and supported the officers in engagement with youth offenders. Through the T-care pilot, participating youths were introduced to practical tools aimed at enhancing their emotional self-regulation, while officers used a trauma-informed lens to guide their interactions and engagement with the offenders. This dual approach ensured that both staff and the youths benefitted from trauma-informed principles, creating a more therapeutic environment within the correctional setting.

The pilot evaluation was conducted to (1) understand the impact of T-care on youth offenders and correctional officers' stress and mental health, and (2) identify the facilitators and barriers towards implementation of T-care in the RTC. The self-reported questionnaires were administered at pre- and post-time points. Youth offenders' level of depression, anxiety and stress; hopelessness; and distress were measured on the Depression Anxiety Stress Scale 21 (DASS-21), Beck Hopelessness Scale (BHS) and Impact of Event Scale (IES) respectively. The officers' level of job stress, overall level of stress and mental well-being were measured on the Job Stress Scale (JSS), Perceived Stress Scale (PSS) and Mental Health Continuum-Short Form (MHC-SF) respectively. To complement the quantitative data, focus group discussions were conducted with youth offenders and officers at the end of the pilot to understand their experiences of using T-care as well as to gather implementation challenges from their perspectives. In addition, biweekly reflection was conducted with youth offenders to discuss the impact of applying T-care skills on them.

Given the small sample size of participating youths, no statistical analysis was conducted on the quantitative measures. However, the Reliable Change, Clinically Significant Change (Jacobson & Truax, 1991) was used to compare the pre-post differences in level of depression, anxiety, stress, hopelessness and distress. It was found that three out of eight youths reported reliable improvement in their level of distress as measured by the Impact of Event Scale (IES), three showed reliable reduction in the level of depression, anxiety and stress, and two had improvement in the hope scale. Complementing the quantitative findings, qualitative data showed that, with good understanding of stress and trauma, youth participants were able to acquire new coping strategies that helped them manage interpersonal conflicts and institutional rules in the RTC. Most youths attempted to apply T-care skills, including managing stress, grounding techniques and reframing maladaptive thoughts, and were able to better control their emotions.

Nevertheless, there was a subset of youths who encountered difficulties in consistently applying these strategies, particularly in high-stress or emotionally triggering situations. This challenge highlights the complexity of behavioural change in adolescents with significant trauma histories. In addition, with regards to the implementation process, the support from CRS professionals in training dedicated officers helped to translate T-care concepts into everyday practice. However, a lack of protected time due to competing demands of officers and absence of common T-care language in the RTC were challenges that could have hindered the effectiveness of the T-care pilot.

Narratives by Officers Regarding T-care Implementation in Youths

The implementation of T-care brought valuable insights from both ground officers and CRS trainers. Their experiences highlight the programme's impact on both staff and youth offenders in Reformative Training (RT) while also revealing practical challenges in its implementation. These firsthand accounts provide crucial perspectives on how trauma-informed approaches can be integrated into correctional practice.

An officer who worked directly with RTs during the T-care implementation, observed how the concept of trigger and awareness resonated strongly with many of them:

"Some RTs shared that it helped them reframe their reactions. They would tell themselves, 'This is no big deal, I don't need to react violently to this situation.'"

The programme also transformed the officers' perspectives about the youths' behaviours and deepened their level of understanding.

"It deepened my understanding of RT behaviour. Their actions weren't necessarily targeted at us personally but rather influenced by their past experiences. While I already understood that experiences shape behaviour, T-care provided a framework that enhanced my understanding."

A T-care CRS trainer Lucy (pseudonym) emphasised that the programme's most significant impact was on the officers themselves.

"Incarceration itself is a traumatic experience. When officers understand how traumatic experiences can trigger certain responses, it enhances their empathy and changes their approach to RT engagement. This builds stronger officer-RT relationships."

Lucy also noted how T-care's accessible language, for instance the term "alarm reaction", provided a common vocabulary that RTs could readily understand and relate to. This shared terminology facilitated more effective communication between staff and the youths, creating a foundation for meaningful therapeutic interactions.

However, the implementation came with its own challenges. One officer, Roxy (pseudonym), described how they needed to adapt their approach for RTs with different learning capabilities.

> *"Some of them faced challenges in adopting T-care practices. Some of the RTs took longer to learn. So, we need to remind them ... Although some infographics were used, the content was quite dry."*

Roxy found that small group sessions of up to five participants proved most effective, particularly when RTs were grouped by similar comprehension levels to facilitate engagement. While the programme used infographics as teaching aids, Roxy suggested that more diverse and engaging content, such as videos, could have enhanced learning. The resource-intensive nature of providing individualised attention often required officers to extend their work time beyond their regular working hours to ensure proper support. These implementation challenges highlight the need for adequate staffing resources and flexible delivery methods when implementing trauma-informed programmes in correctional settings.

These narratives underscore how T-care not only provided practical tools for RTs to manage their stress and behaviours at the institution but also fostered a more nuanced understanding among staff around the impact of trauma on a youth's emotional and behavioural reactions. Staff members learned ways to support RTs in managing their reactions towards stressful situations, ultimately contributing to a more therapeutic correctional environment.

Implications of the T-care Pilot on Youths

These findings point to the necessity for ongoing, iterative support structures that reinforce skill application over time. Moreover, the findings suggest that trauma-informed interventions for youth offenders must be developmentally attuned and flexible in delivery. In line with this developmental approach, the RTC has implemented holistic programmes that address both the educational and psychosocial needs of youth offenders. This model recognises that effective rehabilitation requires addressing not only trauma symptoms but also the broader developmental, educational and social needs of adolescents. Each youth offender is assigned a dedicated CRS and regular individual sessions to ensure their needs are met and to provide consistent support throughout their rehabilitation journey. The individualised sessions allow for personalised trauma-informed interventions that can be adapted based on each youth's specific trauma history, developmental stage and progress. Educational opportunities, such as GCE O-levels, N-levels and A-levels, are provided to help youth offenders resume their academic journey, which may have been disrupted prior to incarceration. Understanding the crucial role of family support in youth rehabilitation, the RTC conducts family engagement sessions where correctional officers and CRS professionals meet with parents or caregivers to discuss the youth's progress and explore ways to better support their development.

Understanding youths' needs for peer acceptance and identity formation, the RTC provides structured out-of-cell time for sports and prosocial programmes, where youth offenders develop healthy camaraderie through group activities and competitions. These peer interactions provide opportunities for participants to practise the emotional regulation and interpersonal skills learned in a supportive, supervised environment. Age-appropriate education on relationships and sexual health is provided, and the institution also demonstrates attention to physical development by providing milk supplements to meet nutritional needs during this critical growth period. This holistic approach extends beyond the period of incarceration, with ROs working closely with families to ensure effective supervision and support when youths are released on supervision. The strong emphasis on family reintegration reflects the commitment in the RTC's approach, in which successful rehabilitation requires sustained family involvement and support throughout each youth's correctional journey. This approach demonstrates how the lessons learned from the T-care pilot have been integrated into a broader rehabilitative philosophy that addresses the complex needs of youth offenders with trauma histories.

WOMEN OFFENDERS

Local Evidence of Trauma among Women Offenders

While youth offenders demonstrate distinct trauma manifestations linked to developmental stages, women offenders represent another critical population where ACEs significantly shape offending pathways. Local studies in Singapore align with international findings where Chong et al., (2004) reported that 49.5% of 208 women offenders disclosed a history of abuse, with many remaining in abusive relationships. Another SPS study (SPS, 2013) found that 54% of women inmates reported some form of trauma. Leung et al., (2015) observed that nearly half (48%) of women in the female prison interviewed for a study on drug use motivations had histories of abuse, further supporting the connection between early trauma, substance misuse and offending.

Implications for Rehabilitation and Intervention

These findings highlight the importance of trauma-informed correctional care. Miller and Najavits (2012) stressed that effective rehabilitation must acknowledge histories of interpersonal violence and complex trauma. Correctional environments that ignore these realities may exacerbate symptoms and increase recidivism. Incorporating trauma-specific interventions, as advocated by Grella et al., (2013), can help women develop healthier coping mechanisms and address the root causes of their offending. Additionally, Fischer et al., (2024) noted the need for culturally responsive approaches, particularly for populations like Aboriginal women, who face unique intergenerational trauma linked to systemic inequities.

Gender-responsive Rehabilitation for Women Offenders with an Emphasis on Trauma-informed Care

Over the past decade, SPS has adopted the comprehensive 5Ps approaches (Purpose, People, Programmes, Processes and Place) in building a transformational environment for rehabilitation, while adhering to the principles of gender responsivity. Taking a Gender Responsive (GR) approach acknowledges that correctional practices designed for male offenders are not as effective when applied to women offenders. Thus, the general principles of being gender responsive include understanding gendered pathways of offending; paying attention to the unique needs and challenges of women; valuing their perspectives and experiences; and being relational, culturally sensitive and trauma informed. This approach contributed to a steady decrease in recidivism rates in women. The two-year recidivism rate for women offenders has continued to decrease since the 2016 release cohort. It has dropped from 21% for the cohort released in 2016 to 15.3% for the cohort released in 2021 (Yusof, 2024).

The intervention programmes given to women offenders, which include Psychological-based Correctional Programmes (PCPs), Family and Reintegration Programmes and Personal Development Programmes, were created with the governing principles of GR. The gender-specific PCP programme is known as the 4C (Catch it, Check it, Change it, Cast it), which specifically addresses trauma, emotional regulation and relational needs unique to women offenders.

The service has also invested significantly in the people aspect, through staff development in Gender-Responsive Integrated Training, enabling staff, officers and rehabilitation partners to manage conflicts and emotional situations with greater sensitivity and understanding. Understanding the crucial role of family connections, the prison service has established robust partnerships with community agencies and self-help groups to provide mothering/caregiving and family support programmes to help women rebuild healthy relationships with their children and families.

As part of the processes and partnerships, throughcare services were provided to women offenders as they transited to the aftercare phase. There is close collaboration between the Singapore Prison Service and community partners to support women offenders as they resume their roles as mothers, wives and daughters in the community (Nurazafirah, 2025). Community partners deliver family and parenting programmes to women offenders prior to their release and continue providing case management support in the community to facilitate successful reintegration. These services focus on strengthening family relationships and addressing potential conflicts that may arise when women return to live with their families.

T-Care Pilot for Women Offenders in SPS

Trauma-informed care is integrated as part of the Gender-Responsive care in the SPS women's institution. Acknowledging the need for a tailored approach towards women offenders with past traumatic experiences, a similar T-care pilot was implemented from January to August 2023 at the A4 institution, which is a women's prison. Drawing on insights from the limited sample size of the previous RTC pilot, the women's prison pilot recruited a greater number of women offenders. The programme was conducted with a total of 18 women offenders and four women officers. Similar to the RTC pilot, this pilot evaluation was conducted to understand (1) the impact of T-care on the women offenders and the officers' stress and mental health, and (2) identify the facilitators and barriers towards implementation of T-care in the women's prison.

Self-reported questionnaires were administered at pre- and post-timepoints to measure the offenders' level of depression, anxiety and stress; hopelessness; and distress on the Depression Anxiety Stress Scale 21 (DASS-21), Beck Hopelessness Scale (BHS) and Impact of Event Scale (IES) respectively. The officers' level of job stress, overall level of stress and mental well-being were measured on the Job Stress Scale (JSS), Perceived Stress Scale (PSS) and Mental Health Continuum-Short Form (MHC-SF) respectively. In addition, focus group discussions were conducted with the women offenders and the officers to gather qualitative data on their experiences of using T-care and to understand implementation challenges from their perspectives.

Due to the small sample size, non-parametric tests and reflexive thematic analysis were utilised to analyse the quantitative and qualitative data respectively. Quantitatively, there were significant reductions in the offenders' sense of depression, stress and hopelessness following the T-care pilot. Qualitatively, the offenders expressed increased hope, awareness of their stress triggers and the ability to manage stressors using T-care strategies.

Narratives by Offenders and Officers regarding T-care Implementation

The offenders and officers involved in the pilot were asked to further substantiate the qualitative evaluation through narratives and feedback. In general, participants reported increased hope and reduced negative thoughts.

> *"Now I think positive only. No matter what, nothing is impossible in our life. When I go back, I start back my new life."*

> *"I believe that after this, (I) can face stress outside; opposed to outside run away from problems"*

In addition, there was increased awareness of personal stress triggers, and an improved capacity for emotional regulation through the application of T-care strategies.

> *"T-care officer helped me to understand that I was more sensitive and easily triggered ... Realised what she said is true so will take a step back and think about own reaction."*

> *"It makes me realise that what I'm feeling, or thought is just the reaction to my problem. There is where I know my main goal is calming me down to stay away from making the problem worse."*

Similarly, an evaluation was conducted with the prison officers who were taught T-care skills in their engagement with the women offenders. While the quantitative measures of well-being did not reflect statistically significant changes in stress levels or overall mental health (as measured by the Mental Health Continuum Short Form), qualitative reports highlighted important shifts in the officers' self-perception. Specifically, officers noted greater self-awareness of their own emotional responses and stress reactions, which impacted how they responded to offenders.

> *"After going through T-care, I learned how to identify my stress and how I usually react to it. Some of the reaction is not good and by identifying it early, I can prevent it from happening. This is extremely useful in life not only when working with offenders."*

Some officers also expressed enhanced confidence in implementing trauma-informed approaches and improved understanding and relational dynamics between staff and offenders.

> *"I am able to understand better why certain inmates get agitated easily. For example, waiting for us to get back to them/trust issues. They might have past experiences of being betrayed/lied to."*

Officers observed that offenders were more capable of modulating their emotions and managing interpersonal conflicts within the institutional setting. One officer noted the leaps in improvement.

> *"For some of them go from "zero to hero". One of my girls never self-inflict, (after) started (T-care) in February, until now no reports."*

The evaluation results showed that T-care as a trauma informed approach was effective as it benefitted both offenders and officers and enhanced inmate management. Additionally, it was noted that support systems like training and coaching are essential for effective and sustainable implementation of such skills.

Implications of the T-care Pilot on the Women Prison Population

The creation of a psychologically safe environment, coupled with support provided by correctional officers at the A4 institution created mutual respect and improved professional relationship between staff and offenders. Early evaluation suggests that T-care has improved inmate-staff rapport and reduced behavioural incidents, aligning with international findings on trauma-informed correctional practices (Konecky & Lynch, 2019).

For successful implementation, strong management supported effective delivery of the sessions, and the officers provided a safe space, which contributed to the effective implementation of T-care. However, time constraints in applying T-care as an inmate engagement tool and having to manage difficult inmates added to the officers' stress.

The findings indicated that T-care helped women offenders identify and manage stress and mental health more effectively, which led to better offender management. Implementation of T-care could be further enhanced by refining support structures to suit the operational environment and participants' needs, such as providing protected time for officers to conduct T-care sessions with offenders and allowing extended and more in-depth sessions to enable quality discussion and in-session practices.

Implications of T-care in the Singapore Prison Service

The implementation of the T-care pilot in selected youth and women offenders at the Singapore Prison Service revealed several key insights into trauma-informed corrections. Both groups of participants demonstrated meaningful improvements in emotional regulation and stress management, with reduced behavioural incidents and enhanced engagement in rehabilitation. Common success factors included the creation of psychologically safe environments, consistent staff support and the development of practical coping strategies. However, challenges persisted across both groups, particularly in terms of operational constraints and the need for protected time for officers to implement trauma-informed practices effectively. Staff training emerged as crucial for both groups, with officers reporting improved understanding of the impact of trauma on behaviour and enhanced confidence in managing challenging situations. These learnings suggest that while population-specific adaptations are necessary, the fundamental principles of trauma-informed care remain effective across different offender groups. The experiences from both pilots provide valuable guidance for expanding trauma-informed practices across the broader correctional system.

FUTURE DIRECTIONS FOR TRAUMA-INFORMED CORRECTIONS IN SINGAPORE

The path forward for trauma-informed corrections in Singapore requires a multi-faceted approach that builds upon current successes while addressing existing gaps. A primary focus should be expanding comprehensive ACE prevalence assessments across the adult offender population, moving beyond the current understanding of youth and women offenders. This broader assessment would provide valuable insights into how trauma manifests across different offender groups and inform the development of targeted interventions.

Future Research for Evidence-informed Practices

Research priorities should extend to examining the complex relationships between ACEs and comorbid conditions, particularly mental health disorders, substance use patterns and violent behaviour manifestations. Understanding these interconnections would enable more nuanced and effective rehabilitation approaches.

Staff Training and Practice

Institutional transformation remains a critical goal, requiring systematic integration of trauma-informed principles across all aspects of correctional operations. This includes expanding staff training in trauma literacy, developing trauma-responsive security procedures and creating environments that support psychological safety while maintaining necessary security measures. The successful implementation of T-care pilots at the youth and women institutions provides a foundation for this expansion, but sustained effort is needed to embed these practices throughout the system.

Integrating Process with Operations

Aftercare case management strategies must also evolve to incorporate trauma-informed principles more fully. This involves strengthening partnerships with community organisations, developing trauma-responsive supervision practices and ensuring continuity of care for offenders transitioning back into the community.

Special attention should be paid to supporting families affected by incarceration, recognising the intergenerational impact of trauma and the importance of family systems in rehabilitation.

CONCLUSION

The examination of ACEs in Singapore's correctional system has revealed both the profound impact of early trauma on offending behaviour and the transformative potential of trauma-informed interventions. Through focussed studies of youth and women offenders, we have gained crucial insights into how trauma shapes different pathways to offending and requires tailored rehabilitation approaches. The successful implementation of T-care pilots demonstrates that trauma-informed practices can be effectively integrated into correctional settings, leading to improved outcomes in the emotion regulation, behavioural management and rehabilitation engagement of youth and women offenders. In addition, staff members have developed a more nuanced understanding of trauma and its impact on offenders' emotions and behaviours and have acquired skills to help youths and women manage their stress.

Implementation experiences across both populations have revealed critical success factors, including the creation of psychologically safe environments, comprehensive staff training and the fostering of strong staff-offender relationships. While challenges such as operational constraints and resource limitations persist, these experiences provide valuable lessons for scaling trauma-informed practices across the correctional system.

Looking ahead, the continued development of evidence-based, trauma-informed approaches within Singapore's correctional system represents an important step in enhancing rehabilitation outcomes. Success will require sustained institutional commitment, continued research investment and enhanced collaboration between correctional services and community partners. The ongoing transformation of correctional practice, grounded in understanding and addressing the impact of ACEs, offers a more humane and effective approach to rehabilitation.

This evolution in correctional practice acknowledges that behind every offender lies a history that, when understood and addressed, can open pathways to meaningful change. By continuing to build on current successes while addressing emerging challenges, Singapore's correctional system can further strengthen its trauma-informed approach, ultimately promoting successful rehabilitation and facilitating desistance while breaking intergenerational cycles of trauma and offending.

REFERENCES

Advanced Trauma Solutions Professionals. (n.d.). *TARGET curricula*. Retrieved from http://www.advancedtrauma.com/

Anda, R. F., Felitti, V. J., Bremner, J. D., Walker, J. D., Whitfield, C., Perry, B. D., Dube, S. R., & Giles, W. H. (2006). The enduring effects of abuse and related adverse experiences in childhood: A convergence of evidence from neurobiology and epidemiology. *European Archives of Psychiatry and Clinical Neuroscience, 256*(3), 174–186. DOI: 10.1007/s00406-005-0624-4

Andrews, D. A., & Bonta, J. (2010). *The psychology of criminal conduct* (5th ed.). LexisNexis Matthew Bender.

Australian Institute of Family Studies. (2012). *Addressing women's victimisation histories in custodial settings*. (no. 13). Canberra: Australian Government. https://aifs.gov.au/publications/addressing-womens-victimisation-histories-custodial-settings/profile-women-prison

Baetz, C. L., Surko, M., Moaveni, M., McNair, F., Bart, A., Workman, S., Tedeschi, F., Havens, J., Guo, F., Quinlan, C., & Horwitz, S. M. (2019). Impact of a trauma-informed intervention for youth and staff on rates of violence in juvenile detention settings. *Journal of Interpersonal Violence*, *36*(17–18). Advance online publication. DOI: 10.1177/0886260519857163

Baglivio, M. T., Epps, N., Swartz, K., Huq, M. S., Sheer, A., & Hardt, N. S. (2014). The prevalence of adverse childhood experiences (ACE) in the lives of juvenile offenders. *Journal of Juvenile Justice*, *3*(2), 1–23.

Baglivio, M. T., Wolff, K. T., Piquero, A.R., & Epps, N. (2015) The relationship between Adverse Childhood Experiences (ACE) and juvenile offending trajectories in a juvenile offender sample. *Journal of Criminal Justice, 43*(3), 229-241. https://doi.org/. 2015.04.012.DOI: 10.1016/j.jcrimjus

Bloom, B., Owen, B., & Covington, S. (2003). *Gender-responsive strategies: Research practice and guiding principles for women offenders*. Department of Justice, National Institute of Corrections.

Calleja, N. G. (2022). Developmentally informed treatment for adolescent sex offenders: An effectiveness evaluation of the Forward-Focused Model. *Journal of Offender Rehabilitation*, *61*(2), 106–120.

Chein, J. M., Albert, D., O'Brien, L., Uckert, K., & Steinberg, L. (2011). Peers increase adolescent risk taking by enhancing activity in the brain's reward circuitry. *Developmental Science, 14*(2), F1–F10. DOI: 10.1111/j.1467-7687.2010.01035.x

Chen, J. (2016). Maltreatment Onset and Subtypes Predict Internalising and Externalising Symptomatology in Maltreated Children. (Unpublished master's thesis), James Cook University.

Chesney-Lind, M., & Shelden, R. G. (2004). *Girls, delinquency, and juvenile justice* (3rd ed.). Thompson Wadsworth.

Chng, G. S., Chu, C. M., Zeng, G., Li, D., & Ting, M. H. (2016). A Latent Class Analysis of Family Characteristics Linked to Youth Offending Outcomes. *Journal of Research in Crime and Delinquency, 53*(6), 765–787. DOI: 10.1177/0022427816644947

Chong, F. P., Samion, S., Teo, L. P., Goh, E. K., Basir, S. K., & Won, T. L. (2004). *A study on the programming needs of women offenders in Changi Women's Prison.* Singapore Prison Service.

Cohen, J. A., Mannarino, A. P., Jankowski, K., Rosenberg, S., Kodya, S., & Wolford, G. L. (2016). A Randomized Implementation Study of Trauma-Focused Cognitive Behavioural Therapy for Adjudicated Teens in Residential Treatment Facilities. *Child Maltreatment, 21*(2), 156–167. DOI: 10.1177/1077559515624775

Covington, S. (1998). The relational theory of women's psychological development: Implications for the criminal justice system. In Zaplin, R. T. (Ed.), *Female offenders: Critical perspectives and effective interventions* (pp. 113–128). Aspen Publishing.

Covington, S. S. (1998). Women in prison: Approaches in the treatment of our most invisible population. *Women & Therapy, 21*(1), 141–155.

Covington, S. S. (2001). *A Woman's journey home: Challenges for female offenders and their children [Commissioned paper].* From Prisons to Home: The Effect of Incarceration and Reentry on Children, Families, and Communities Conference. https://aspe.hhs.gov/reports/womans-journey-home-challenges-female-offenders-their-children

Covington, S. S. (2008). Women and addiction: A trauma-informed approach. *Journal of Psychoactive Drugs,* (Suppl 5), 377–385. DOI: 10.1080/02791072.2008.10400665

Everhart Newman, J. L., Falligant, J. M., Thompson, K. R., Gomez, M. D., & Burkhart, B. R. (2018). Trauma-focused cognitive behavioural therapy with adolescents with illegal sexual behaviour in a secure residential treatment facility. *Children and Youth Services Review, 91*, 431–438. DOI: 10.1016/j.childyouth.2018.06.028

Farrington, D. P. (2003). Developmental and Life Course Criminology: Key Theoretical and Empirical Issues – *The 2002 Sutherland Award Address. Criminology, 41*, 221–225. https://doi.rog/10.1111/j.1745-9125.2003.tb00987.x

Felitti, V. J., Anda, R. F., Nordenberg, D., Williamson, D. F., Spitz, A. M., Edwards, V., Koss, M. P., & Marks, J. S. (1998). Relationship of childhood abuse and household dysfunction to many of the leading causes of death in adults: The Adverse Childhood Experiences (ACE) Study. *American Journal of Preventive Medicine, 14*(4), 245–258. DOI: 10.1016/S0749-3797(98)00017-8

Fischer, L., Wilson, M., Schofield, P. W., Jones, J., Kariminia, A., Barrett, E., Dean, K., Sullivan, E., Covington, S., & Butler, T. (2024). Exposure to childhood adversity and intimate partner violence in a sample of incarcerated women in Australia. *International Journal of Offender Therapy and Comparative Criminology*, •••, 1–18. DOI: 10.1177/0306624X241270577

Ford, J. D., Chapman, J. F., Hawke, J., & Albert, D. (2007). *Trauma among youth in the juvenile justice system: Critical issues and new directions*. National Center for Mental Health and Juvenile Justice Research.

Ford, J. D., & Russo, E. (2006). Trauma-focused, present-centered, emotional self-regulation approach to integrated treatment for posttraumatic stress and addiction: Trauma adaptive recovery group education and therapy (TARGET). *American Journal of Psychotherapy, 60*(4), 335–355.

Ford, K., Bellis, M. A., Hughes, K., Barton, E. R., & Newbury, A. (2020). Adverse childhood experiences: A retrospective study to understand their associations with lifetime mental health diagnosis, self-harm or suicide attempt, and current low mental wellbeing in a male Welsh prison population. *Health & Justice, 8*(1), 13. DOI: 10.1186/s40352-020-00115-5

Fox, B. H., Perez, N., Cass, E., Baglivio, M. T., & Epps, N. (2015). Trauma changes everything: Examining the relationship between adverse childhood experiences and serious, violent and chronic juvenile offenders. *Child Abuse & Neglect, 46*, 163–173. DOI: 10.1016/j.chiabu.2015.01.011

Friestad, C., Rustad, A. B., & Kjelsberg, E. (2012). Adverse childhood experiences among women prisoners: Relationships to suicide attempts and drug abuse. *The International Journal of Social Psychiatry, 60*(1), 40–46. DOI: 10.1177/0020764012461235

Gardner, M., & Steinberg, L. (2005). Peer influence on risk taking, risk preference, and risky decision making in adolescence and adulthood: An experimental study. *Developmental Psychology, 41*(4), 625–635. DOI: 10.1037/0012-1649.41.4.625

Giedd, J. N., Blumenthal, J., Jeffries, N. O., Castellanos, F. X., Liu, H., Zijdenbos, A., Paus, T., Evans, A. C., & Rapoport, J. L. (1999). Brain development during childhood and adolescence: A longitudinal MRI study. *Nature Neuroscience*, *2*(10), 861–863. DOI: 10.1038/13158

Grella, C. E., Lovinger, K., & Warda, U. S. (2013). Relationships among trauma exposure, familial characteristics, and PTSD: A case-control study of women in prison and in the general population. *Women & Criminal Justice*, *23*(1), 63–79. DOI: 10.1080/08974454.2013.743376

Hardyman, P. L., & Van Voorhis, P. (2004). *Developing gender-specific classification systems for women offenders*. U.S. Department of Justice, National Institute of Corrections.

Hashweh, N., Johnson, F., Chrusciel, T., & Barnes, A. (2024). Effect of trauma-informed supervision in youth detention center: A retrospective study. *Journal of Family Trauma, Child Custody & Child Development*, *21*(1), 96–109. DOI: 10.1080/26904586.2023.2218856

Jackson, R. D., Kethineni, S., & Cao, Y. (2023). Hopes for healing: An exploratory study of trauma-informed care training and the juvenile justice system. *Children and Youth Services Review*, *148*, 1–9. DOI: 10.1016/j.childyouth.2023.106877re

Jacobson, N. S., & Truax, P. (1991). Clinical significance: A statistical approach to defining meaningful changes in psychotherapy research. *Journal of Consulting and Clinical Psychology*, *59*(1), 12–19. DOI: 10.1037//0022-006x.59.1.12

Jiang, F. Y., Wijayaratne, D. C., Choo, J., Lin, A. L., & Tay, A. (2025). From adversity to desistance: An exploratory study of adverse childhood experiences, agency, and social support among justice-involved youths. *Advancing Corrections*, *19*, 81–94.

Konecky, E. M., & Lynch, S. M. (2019). Cumulative trauma exposure, emotion regulation, and posttraumatic stress disorder among incarcerated women. *Journal of Traumatic Stress*, *32*(5), 806–811. DOI: 10.1002/jts.22443

Kurlychek, M. C., & Johnson, B. D. (2019). Cumulative disadvantage in the American criminal justice system. *Annual Review of Criminology*, *2*, 291–319. DOI: 10.1146/annurev-criminol-011518-024815

Leung, C. C., Goh, J. H., & Chionh, Y. J. S. (2015). *Drug motives study: Comparing the profiles and drug motives of drug offenders and penal offenders with concurrent drug consumption record* [PowerPoint slides]. Singapore Prison Service.

Leung, S., Goh, E., & Chionh, Y. (2015). *Motivations for drug use among female inmates.* Singapore Prison Service. *Research Bulletin (International Commission for the Northwest Atlantic Fisheries).*

Levenson, J. S., Willis, G. M., & Prescott, D. S. (2015). Adverse childhood experiences in the lives of female sex offenders. *Sexual Abuse*, *27*(3), 258–283. DOI: 10.1177/1079063214544332

Li, D., Chu, C. M., Goh, J. T. L., Ng, I. Y., & Zeng, G. (2015). Impact of childhood maltreatment on recidivism in youth offenders: A matched-control study. *Criminal Justice and Behavior*, *42*(10), 990–1007.

Lim, R. W. (2017). *Adverse Childhood Experiences and Aggression in Juvenile Offenders in Singapore: Exploring the Moderating Influence of Prosocial Peers and Social Support*. Singapore Prison Service.

Liu, D., Chu, C. M., Neo, L. H., Ang, R. P., Tan, M. Y., & Chu, J. (2016). Multiple trauma exposure and psychosocial functioning in Singaporean children in out -of-home care. *Psychological Trauma: Theory, Research, Practice, and Policy*, *8*(4), 431–438. DOI: 10.1037/tra0000098

Malvaso, C. G., Day, A., & Boyd, C. M. (2024). The outcomes of trauma-informed practice in youth justice: An umbrella review. *Journal of Child & Adolescent Trauma*, *17*(3), 939–955. DOI: 10.1007/s40653-024-00634-5

Marzano, L., Hawton, K., Rivline, A., & Fazel, S. (2011). Psychosocial influences on prisoner suicide: A case-control study of near-lethal self-harm in women prisoners. *Social Science & Medicine*, *72*, 874–883. DOI: 10.1016/j.socscimed.2010.12.028

Messina, N., Burdon, W., Hagopian, G., & Prendergast, M. (2010). A randomized experimental study of gender-responsive substance abuse treatment for women in prison. *Journal of Substance Abuse Treatment*, *38*(2), 97–107. https://pubmed.ncbi.nlm.nih.gov/20015605/

Messina, N., & Grella, C. E. (2006). Childhood trauma and women's health outcomes in a California prison population. *American Journal of Public Health*, *96*(10), 1842–1848. DOI: 10.2105/AJPH.2005.082016

Miller, N. A., & Najavits, L. M. (2012). Creating trauma-informed correctional care: A balance of goals and environment. *European Journal of Psychotraumatology*, *3*, 17246. Advance online publication. DOI: 10.3402/ejpt.v3i0.17246

Moore, M. D., & Tatman, A. W. (2016). Adverse Childhood Experiences and Offender Risk to Re-offend in the United States: A quantitative examination. *International Journal of Criminal Justice Sciences*, *11*(2), 148–158.

Pfeifer, J. H., Masten, C. L., Moore, W. E., Oswald, T. M., Mazziotta, J. C., Iacoboni, M., & Dapretto, M. (2011). Entering adolescence: Resistance to peer influence, risky behaviour, and neural changes in emotion reactivity. *Neuron, 69*(5), 1029–1036. DOI: 10.1016/j.neuron.2011.02.019

Poole, N., & Greaves, L. (2012). *Becoming Trauma Informed.* Centre for Addiction and Mental Health.

Salisbury, E. J., & Van Voorhis, P. (2009). Gendered pathways: An empirical investigation of women probationers' paths to incarceration. *Criminal Justice and Behavior, 36*, 541–566.

Sasaki, A., Mochizuki, A., & Yoshihara, D. (2023). Gender Differences in Abusive Parenting among Incarcerated Parents in Japan. *The Prison Journal, 103*(1), 45–67. DOI: 10.1177/00328855221139865

Schmucker, M., & Lösel, F. (2015). The effects of sexual offender treatment on recidivism: An international meta-analysis of sound quality evaluations. *Journal of Experimental Criminology, 11*(4), 597–630. DOI: 10.1007/s11292-015-9241-z

Schonbrun, Y. C., Johnson, J. E., Anderson, B. J., Caviness, C., & Stein, M. D. (2016). Hazardously Drinking Jailed Women: Post-Release Perceived Needs and Risk of Reincarceration. *International Journal of Offender Therapy and Comparative Criminology, 61*(16), 1819–1832. https://doi.org/ (Original work published 2017). DOI: 10.1177/0306624X16634702

Sowell, E. R., Thompson, P. M., Holmes, C. J., Jernigan, T. L., & Toga, A. W. (1999). In vivo evidence for post-adolescent brain maturation in frontal and striatal regions. *Nature Neuroscience, 2*(10), 859–861. DOI: 10.1038/13154

Sowell, E. R., Thompson, P. M., Tessner, K. D., & Toga, A. W. (2001). Mapping continued brain growth and gray matter density reduction in dorsal frontal cortex: Inverse relationships during postadolescent brain maturation. *The Journal of Neuroscience : The Official Journal of the Society for Neuroscience, 21*(22), 8819–8829. DOI: 10.1523/JNEUROSCI.21-22-08819.2001

Steinberg, L. (2005). Cognitive and affective development in adolescence. *Trends in Cognitive Sciences, 9*(2), 69–74.

Subramaniam, M., Abdin, E., Seow, E., Vaingankar, J. A., Shafie, S., Shahwan, S., Lim, M., Fung, D., James, L., Verma, S., & Chong, S. A. (2020). Prevalence, sociodemographic correlates and associations of adverse childhood experiences with mental illnesses: Results from the Singapore Mental Health Study. *Child Abuse & Neglect, 103*, 104447. Advance online publication. DOI: 10.1016/j.chiabu.2020.104447

Teicher, M. H., & Samson, J. A. (2016). Annual research review: Enduring neurobiological effects of childhood abuse and neglect. *Journal of Child Psychology and Psychiatry, and Allied Disciplines*, *57*(3), 241–266. DOI: 10.1111/jcpp.12507

Ter Beek, E., Spruit, A., Kuiper, C. H. Z., van der Rijken, R. E. A., Hendriks, J., & Stams, G. J. J. M. (2018). Treatment effect on recidivism for juveniles who have sexually offended: A multilevel meta-analysis. *Journal of Abnormal Child Psychology*, *46*(3), 543–556. DOI: 10.1007/s10802-017-0308-3

Weber, S., & Lynch, S. (2021). Understanding the relations among adverse childhood experiences (ACE), substance use, and reoffending among detained youth. *Child Abuse & Neglect*, *120*. Advance online publication. DOI: 10.1016/j.chiabu.2021.105211

Wilson, L. C., Fauci, J. E., & Goodman, L. A. (2015). Bringing trauma-informed practice to domestic violence programs: A Qualitative Analysis of Current Approaches. *The American Journal of Orthopsychiatry*, *86*(6), 586–599. DOI: 10.1037/ort0000098

Wolff, N., & Shi, J. (2012). Childhood and adult trauma experiences of incarcerated persons and their relationship to adult behavioural health problems and treatment. *International Journal of Environmental Research and Public Health*, *9*, 1908–1926.

Women in Prison Project. (2006). *Fact sheet: Why focus on women in prison*. Correctional Association of New York. http://www.correctionalassociation.org

Yao, X., Zhang, H., & Zhao, R. (2022). Does Trauma Exacerbate Criminal Behavior? An Exploratory Study of Child Maltreatment and Chronic Offending in a Sample of Chinese Juvenile Offenders. *International Journal of Environmental Research and Public Health*, *19*(18), 11197. DOI: 10.3390/ijerph191811197

Yohros, A. (2023, July). Examining the relationship between Adverse Childhood Experiences and Juvenile Recidivism: A systematic review and meta-analysis. *Trauma, Violence & Abuse*, *24*(3), 1640–1655. DOI: 10.1177/15248380211073846

Yusof, Z. M. (2024, August 7). Rehabilitation programmes for women offenders help drive down two-year recidivism rate. *The Straits Times*. https://www.straitstimes.com/singapore/rehabilitation-programmes-for-women-offenders-see-two-year-recidivism-rate-drop-for-5-straight-years

Zlotnick, C., & Najavits, L. M. (2009). Randomized controlled pilot study of cognitive-behavioral therapy in a sample of incarcerated women with substance use disorder and PTSD. *Behavior Therapy*, *40*(3), 325–336. https://pubmed.ncbi.nlm.nih.gov/19892078/

Zlotnick, C., Najavits, L. M., Rohsenow, D. J., & Johnson, D. M. (2003). A cognitive-behavioral treatment for incarcerated women with substance abuse disorder and posttraumatic stress disorder: Findings from a pilot study. *Journal of Substance Abuse Treatment*, *25*(2), 99–105.

Chapter 5
Cumulative Adversity and Pathways to Coercive Recruitment:
Gang Affiliation, Trafficking, and Forced Servitude

Andrew Lowe
https://orcid.org/0009-0006-6069-2987
University of Southern Queensland, Australia

ABSTRACT

The disadvantage and adversity that predisposes a child to abuse and neglect may in fact be just as damaging to lifespan development and wellbeing as the abuse itself. Essentially, risk factors, victimization experiences and victimization types are significantly more predictive and more valuable, in research and in practice, when considered cumulatively. With regard to pathways to coercive recruitment, particularly into criminal activity (Gangs, violent extremism, smuggling and drug-muling), the research regarding 'cross over kids' highlights the importance of cumulative harm in explaining the outcomes observed among crossover children (Bromfield & Miller, 2012). These experiences, in turn, can result in young people turning to gangs and crime as a means of gaining love, respect and power.

INTRODUCTION

As risk accumulates for a young person experiencing maltreatment, so too does the harm endured through childhood adversity. Bromfield, Higgins and Gillingham (2007), coined the term cumulative harm to describe the profound and exponential

DOI: 10.4018/979-8-3373-9524-1.ch005

effects of an accumulation of adverse experience in a child's life. Bromfield, Higgins and Gillingham (2007) proposed that for many children "victimization is more of a condition than an event" (p.9).

> *Persistence is a pathway in which child maltreatment, domestic violence, family conflict, and disruption propel children into an intensively and generalized victimized condition that in turn generates anger and aggression, which, by fueling and sustaining defiant, challenging, rule-violating behaviour, tends to lock then into an even more persistent victimized condition. (Finkelhor et al., 2007b, p.493).*

Baidawi and Sheehan (2019) draw attention to this accumulation specifically as it relates to what is termed 'cross over kids', those juveniles who are engaged with both the child protection system and the youth justice system. Baidawi and Sheehan (2019) engaged in a detailed case audit of 300 cross over children in the Victorian youth justice system and found that the mean number of adverse childhood experiences (ACEs) was 5.4, and 68 percent of children had experienced five or more ACEs. These results were consistent with that of the North American study of 930 crossover children which identified a mean of 4.8 ACEs (Baglivio et al., 2016). These findings collectively point to the importance of cumulative harm, encompassing chronic adverse experiences and experiences of multiple harm types, in explaining the outcomes observed among crossover children (Bromfield & Miller, 2012). The disadvantage and adversity that *predisposes* a child to abuse and neglect may in fact be just as damaging to lifespan development and wellbeing as the abuse itself. Essentially, risk factors, victimization experiences and victimization types are significantly more predictive and more valuable, in research and in practice, when considered cumulatively. With regard to pathways to coercive recruitment, particularly into criminal activity (Gangs, violent extremism, smuggling and drug-muling), the research regarding 'cross over kids' highlights the importance of cumulative harm in explaining the outcomes observed among crossover children (Bromfield & Miller, 2012). These experiences, in turn, can result in young people turning to gangs and crime as a means of gaining love, respect and power.

COERCIVE RECRUITMENT

Coercive recruitment (also referred to as coerced recruitment) is the act of compelling an individual to join a group, organization, or enter into labour or service through the use of force, threats, intimidation, or deception, thereby violating their free will. Coercive recruitment is defined as a broad category of tactics involving all forms of pressure—be it social, psychological, or physical—used to induce individuals to join a violent or unlawful group and take actions they otherwise would not (Eck, 2014). Eck (2014) conceptualize this as a continuum of violence that ranges from voluntary enlistment at one end to highly violent forced recruitment at the other. This process is a form of modern slavery and exploitation where individuals do not offer their participation voluntarily. Eck (2014) argues that trauma and coercion are inextricably linked in the context of recruitment to violent or criminal groups. Trauma acts both as a precursor that makes individuals susceptible to coercive pressure and as a deliberate tool used by groups to ensure compliance and prevent defection (Eck, 2014). Given what we now know and accept about the characteristics of coercion, the strategies involved in recruiting an individual in a controlling and coercive manner may be subtle. Thus, coercive recruitment exists on a continuum, ranging from explicit physical violence to more subtle psychological and social pressures. Coercive recruitment is like a predatory trap. Social entrapment is the slow-closing door that gradually removes a person's exit options until they are stuck inside. Forced recruitment is the iron cage that physically snaps shut, using violence and chains to keep the person there against their will. In both cases, the person remains in the 'room' not because they want to be, but because the cost of trying to leave has been made terrifyingly high. Common tactics include:

Threats and Intimidation: This involves explicit or implicit threats of harm to the individual, their family, or their property if they do not comply.

- **Deception:** Recruiters might make false promises about the nature, location, or pay of a job. Once the person accepts, the actual conditions are different, and they are then trapped through debt bondage, confiscation of documents, or other coercive means.
- **Abuse of Power/Vulnerability:** Perpetrators exploit a person's vulnerability, such as an insecure immigration status, poverty, or lack of social support, to force them into an agreement they would not otherwise accept.
- **Isolation:** The individual is isolated from friends, family, and their support networks, making them more dependent and less likely to seek help.
- **Psychological Manipulation:** Tactics like gaslighting, humiliation, and love bombing are used to break down an individual's cognitive processes, self-esteem, and ability to think critically, making them easier to control.

Coercive recruitment is found in various contexts:

- **Armed Conflict:** Rebel groups sometimes use violent or forced recruitment tactics (conscription) to bolster their numbers, particularly when under pressure or facing high attrition rates.
- **Workplace/Labour:** In legitimate or semi-legitimate employment, coercion can involve employers using their position of authority to force employees to

perform tasks outside their role through threats of termination, demotion, or other negative consequences.

- **High-Control Groups:** Cults or high-control groups (including gangs) use manipulative practices, starting with excessive warmth (love bombing) that transitions into control and isolation, to demand obedience and loyalty from new members.

In all contexts, the key element is the removal of a person's freedom of choice and the use of power to force action against their will.

PERSONAL, COLLECTIVE AND HISTORICAL TRAUMA

Personal trauma refers to traumatic experiences that an individual has directly experienced. A primary subset of personal trauma discussed in the report is Adverse Childhood Experiences (ACEs), which are specific events occurring before age 18—such as abuse, neglect, or household dysfunction—that can lead to toxic stress and maladaptive psychological outcomes (Felitti et al., 1998; Baglivio et al., 2021; Lewis & Marsden, 2021). Collective trauma is defined as a collective complex trauma inflicted on a group of people who share a specific group identity or affiliation, such as their ethnicity, nationality, or religious affiliation (Evans-Campbell, 2008; Lewis & Marsden, 2021). Historical trauma is a specific form of intergenerational trauma. It is defined as the lasting effects of a "mass trauma experience"—such as war, political violence, or the subjugation of a population by a dominant group—that are transmitted across generations (Heberle et al., 2020).

VIOLENT EXTREMISM AND GANG AFFILIATION

From a criminogenic perspective, gangs are groups which espouse some kind of unified purpose, and involve criminal activity, often taking the form of drug distribution, money lending, intimidation and coercion, violence and general disruption (Petherick & Sinnammon, 2013). Similarly, violence extremism (VE) includes "any group or individual defined as extreme on a given scale (such as religious or political), adopting the threat or use of illegal force and violence to attain a political, economic, religious or social goal through fear, coercion and/or intimidation" (LaFree et al., 2018, p.233). In contemporary Western, democratic discourse, violent extremism is often divided into four categories: right-wing, left-wing, Islamic and termed 'single-issue extremism', such as animal rights and environmentalism (Gill et al., 2014). According to Carlsson et al., (2020), research indicates a relationship exists between VE and age, whereby VE behaviour seems to increase through the later stages of adolescence and into emerging adulthood, followed by a decrease throughout adulthood. In a study of Swedish foreign fighters travelling to Syria and Iraq, Gustafsson and Ranstorp (2017) identified an "overwhelming majority of youths and young adults" (p.81). This finding has been confirmed by others, encompassing a range of VE forms (Rostami et al., 2018; Silke, 2008; Kimmel, 2018). There is no single route to extremism. For some, the path is driven by ideological attitudes and a desire for power; for others, it is a "vulnerability route" where childhood trauma and peer exploitation lead to group membership and eventually extremist action (Clemmow et al., 2025). The link between cumulative adversity and maltreatment in childhood and violent extremism (VE) is profound, Honnavalli et al. (2019) explicitly define the involvement of children in extremist groups as a complex and multifaceted form of child abuse. Early traumatic experiences do not determine who will engage in violent extremism; rather, they culminate in a significantly greater risk of initial involvement. Involvement in extremism is a complex process influenced by a combination of events, experiences, personal factors, and social-political contexts (O'Driscoll, 2017). While an accumulation of negative experiences over time generally makes a person more susceptible to the "pull" of violent groups, recent research (O'Driscoll, 2017; Marchment et al., 2025) emphasizes that the specific configurations of trauma offer more explanatory power than simple ACE counts. Marchment et al. (2025) identified four distinct clusters of Adverse Childhood Experiences (ACEs) that provide a more nuanced and accurate understanding of risk. These include Child Abuse Victimization (direct psychological and physical abuse); Unstable Home (chaotic environment with drug use or mental health issues); High ACEs (severe, cumulative trauma); with Low ACEs generally predict significantly lower susceptibility to violent extremism compared to other trauma-informed profiles.

Rather than being separate issues, violent extremism facilitates various types of maltreatment that align with the World Health Organisation's (WHO) classifications of abuse, further perpetuating the accumulation of adversity and trauma for children recruited into VE. The recruitment and presence of children in violent extremist groups is viewed, in itself, as a form of exploitation and physical abuse. Even when children articulate a desire to join, their capacity to make such a choice is considered specious, meaning they should primarily be viewed as victims of their circumstances. Groups like ISIS and the LTTE have historically exploited children's impressionable nature to ensure a constant, low-cost supply of recruits.

Reflective of Agnew's strain theory (2015) which purports that certain criminogenic strains can motivate delinquent behaviours in order to 'cope' with these tensions, attachment difficulties can drive youth to commit crimes to meet the need for acceptance, belonging and connection. Childhood adversity and diminished parental attachment can disrupt the development of self-concept and identity and may foster delinquent associations and beliefs which are favorable to crime, as young people search for a meaningful group (Bryce & Schaffer, 2024). According to Alleyene and Wood (2010), a juvenile with low self-esteem and a need for belonging, may seek out gang membership to obtain the emotional support lacking in the other aspects of their life. This is particularly relevant in uncertain and dangerous environments, where membership to a gang or violent group may provide some order, protection and human connection (Littman, 2017).

Joining criminal networks, gangs or VE groups can be motivated by a need to address a gap in a young person's development, such as their relational development, meaning making, and social problems solving (Bryce & Schaffer, 2024). Peers who are already aligned with a violent gang or extremist group serve as role models and signals of social norms, not available to a young person in their familial environment (Littman, 2017). Evidence of the influence of peers in introducing young people to VE groups and gangs can be found in those who join Al-Qaida or Islamic State (IS) where three quarters of members are considered to be recruited by peers (Atran, 2015). A study of ex-neo-Nazis in Scandinavia revealed prior experiences of victimization and marginalization drove them to 'search' or seek' a group to which they could belong (Kimmel, 2018). The role VE groups and gangs play in assisting young people to extricate themselves from their difficult and turbulent home lives, providing a 'safe place' to land after leaving, and providing physical and psychological support is central to understanding the way in which attachment drives the need for belonging, and motivates criminal behaviour.

As espoused throughout this chapter, adversity and its influence on behaviour is cumulative. Early experiences with trauma and victimization accumulate and can transition a young people from stability to instability, positioning gangs and VE groups as attractive means of coping, in part, by fostering positive feeling of belonging and acceptance, to counter-balance the negative affect (Bryce & Schaffer, 2024; O'Driscoll, 2017; Simi, Windisch & Sporer, 2016; Simi, Bubolz & Sporer, 2016). According to Simi, Bubolz & Sporer, (2016), narratives of youth involved in VE "highlight the importance of childhood trauma as a series of destabilizing experiences that generate cumulative disadvantage" (p. 126). Amassing an accumulation of social risk factors, including exposure to violence, separation from family, poverty, and maltreatment, in childhood, increases a juvenile's likelihood of involvement in gangs and membership to VE groups (Simi et al., 2016; Littman, 2017). Gangs provide an opportunity for young men to explore and assert power, and, within this, harsher violent masculinities are valorized, and promoting gendered violence and increasing the risk of femicide (Baird, 2012)

While many children join through the psychological "pull" factors mentioned above, many are still forcibly recruited or abducted. Even when a child appears to "choose" to join, the sources note that this decision is almost always made under some degree of duress or due to a lack of safer alternatives. For example, the Lord's Resistance Army (LRA) would abduct children and then purposely disorient them—taking them far from home and marching them in circles—to make escape seem impossible (Beber and Blattman, 2013).

Recruitment Strategies which Leverage Cumulative Vulnerability.

Non-state armed groups (NSAGs) and VEs use a variety of tactics to recruit children, ranging from direct physical coercion to sophisticated psychological manipulation that exploits the developmental needs of adolescents (Littman, 2017). Extremist groups psychologically abuse children through indoctrination and brainwashing, often using the internet to disseminate propaganda. This process is designed to create perfect fighters who are isolated from mainstream values and willing to die for the group's cause (Honnavalli et al., 2019). Prolonged exposure to violence—such as witnessing or participating in executions—desensitizes children to suffering, which is detrimental to their moral and psychological development.

Violent extremism interferes with a child's attachment stability by uprooting them from their homes and families, leading to long-term psychological distress and difficulty forming healthy relationships. Involvement in conflict zones results in the loss of fundamental rights, including the right to education, healthcare, and a safe living environment. In many conflict zones, girls are abducted to become "wives" for combatants or are raped as a form of punishment or as a tool to subdue them. Boys have also been reported as victims of sexual abuse while in detention. Children from disadvantaged backgrounds—such as orphans, refugees, or those from lower socio-economic strata—are more easily "poached" and manipulated by extremist groups. In some cases, parents may even encourage involvement because they believe it offers their children a higher social status or protection they cannot otherwise provide (Honnavalli et al., 2019).

According to Littman (2017), the primary tactics for recruiting children include:

- **Exploiting the Fundamental "Need to Belong"**: Recruiters capitalize on the human drive for social connection, which is particularly intense during adolescence as young people struggle with identity. NSAGs offer a "ready-made community" and a clear identity to children who may feel uncertain about their place in the world. In dangerous or unstable contexts, commanders present their groups as providing a sense of order and human connection that is otherwise missing. Some leaders have used specific spiritual practices to create new social bonds among group members and instil an artificial sense of belonging.

- **The "Quest for Significance" and Strategic Communication:** Recruiters use strategic communications to convince children that joining the group will make their lives matter. Groups exploit feelings of humiliation, deprivation, and frustration. By framing their activities as high-level, significant missions, recruiters offer children a way to feel respected and meaningful, especially after they have been exposed to trauma.
- **Leveraging Peer and Kinship Networks:** The sources highlight that peer influence is one of the most powerful recruitment tactics because children are highly sensitive to social norms. Children are significantly more likely to join if they have friends or relatives already in the group this is often referred to as 'social signalling'. In some contexts, such as IS or Al-Qaida in Europe, an estimated three-quarters of members were brought in through peers. Recruiters may offer immediate rewards that appeal to adolescent impulsivity, a state often heightened when peers are present.
- **Encouraging Rebellion and Autonomy:** For children who feel they lack control in their personal lives, recruitment is framed as an act of independence. Recruiters appeal to the adolescent desire to react against traditional authority figures (like parents or teachers). Capitalizing on Domestic Discord: Groups like IS capitalize on domestic discord and specifically use recruitment to encourage children to rebel against their parents, depicting the act of joining as a demonstration of personal agency.
- **Identity Imposition and Indoctrination:** Because children's identities are less entrenched than those of adults, recruiters find it easier to impose a new "warrior" or "group" identity on them. By integrating children into the group's narrative, recruiters make violent behaviour seem typical and desirable and normalised. In some cases, forcing children to commit violence is used as part of the indoctrination process to increase their identification and allegiance to the group.
- **Online Recruitment Tactics:** Extremist and terrorist organisations are taking advantage of technology and social media platforms due to the utility of having access to millions of individuals, especially children who are unaware and unmonitored in this environment. Children are increasingly being targeted and victimised by terrorism and evidence shows that children are becoming more engaged with extremist related content (United Nations Interregional Crime and Justice Research Institute, 2025). Research conducted by the Anti-Defamation League (2024) found that 15% of adults and 9% of children had been exposed to right-wing extremist ideology specifically while online gaming. Such developments within the technological and gaming space allows for extremist organisation to spread propaganda more easily, tailor narratives to a certain group of people and create cohesion among on-

line communities (Belova-Dalton, 2023). The radicalisation of youth in the online gaming environment is quickly evolving and the radicalisation process can be occurring without youth realising it.

TRAFFICKING AND FORCED SERVITUDE

Cockburn and Olver (2019) argued that child abuse and neglect are significant factors that increase a child's susceptibility to being trafficked. This vulnerability is not a single isolated factor but rather part of a complex interplay of situational and historical considerations that traffickers exploit. The following points explain how prior abuse facilitates trafficking (Cockbain & Olver, 2019):

- **Pre-existing Histories of Maltreatment**: Research (Cockbain & Olver, 2019) into internal sex trafficking and "county lines" drug exploitation in the UK shows that many victims have documented histories of prior abuse or neglect. These histories are often linked to other risk factors, such as social services involvement and youth offending, which traffickers use to identify and target vulnerable targets.
- **The Grooming Process**: Traffickers often use sophisticated grooming techniques to manipulate children who may be seeking the stability or attention they lacked due to prior abuse. In "county lines" activity, children—predominantly boys—are groomed to transport and sell drugs, a process that is highly effective on those with prior histories of neglect.
- **Escapism and Going Missing:** Children who have experienced abuse or neglect are more likely to go missing from home or residential care. This behavior significantly heightens their exposure to traffickers, as they are often isolated from protective adult figures and are operating "in the margins of society".
- **Institutional Vulnerability:** In cases of domestic servitude, insufficient oversight of private fostering arrangements can leave children particularly vulnerable. When children are placed in unofficial care settings without proper monitoring, traffickers can easily hide abuse and exploitation behind closed doors in private households.
- **Reduced Credibility and Disclosure Barriers:** A history of abuse can make children less likely to self-identify as victims or seek help from authorities. Furthermore, professionals sometimes worry that children with complex backgrounds—including prior abuse and social services involvement—may not be viewed as credible witnesses, which can impede the criminal justice response and leave the child trapped in an exploitative cycle.

Types of Trafficking

Trafficking is a broad and varied issue that can be categorized by the geographical movement involved or the specific purpose of the exploitation. According to the Cockbain & Olver (2019), trafficking is best viewed as a process consisting of an act, a means, and a purpose, though for children, the "means" (such as deception or force) is not legally required to qualify the act as trafficking.

The following are the primary types of trafficking identified by Cockbain and Olver (2019):

Dimensions of Movement

- **International (Transnational) Trafficking**: This involves moving victims across national borders. Countries in this process are often categorized as source, transit, or destination points, though many nations now fulfill all three roles simultaneously.
- **Internal (Domestic) Trafficking**: This occurs within the borders of a single country. In the UK, this is increasingly recognized in cases of child sexual exploitation and "county lines" drug operations.

Types of Exploitation by Purpose

Cockbain and Olver (2019) proffer a wide array of contexts in which individuals, particularly children, are exploited:

Sexual Exploitation: This includes the exploitation of the prostitution of others and other forms of commercial or non-commercial sexual abuse. It is a dominant form of recorded trafficking, particularly for girls and women.

Forced Labour and Services: This is a broad category covering work in various licit and illicit sectors. Specific examples include:

- **Agriculture and Fishing:** Traditional sectors for forced labour.
- **Drug Cultivation:** Such as children trafficked to work as "gardeners" in illegal **cannabis factories**.
- **Construction and Factory Work:** Exploitation in industrial or manual labour settings.

Criminal Exploitation: This involves forcing victims to commit crimes for the benefit of others.

- **'County Lines':** A specific UK phenomenon where young people are manipulated to transport and sell drugs from urban hubs to provincial areas (e.g. muling and smuggling).
- **Forced Begging and Theft:** Using victims to generate income through street-level crimes or shoplifting.
- **Benefit Fraud:** Exploiting a victim's identity or status to illegally claim government funds.

Domestic Servitude: This type of trafficking is uniquely hidden because it occurs behind closed doors in private households. Victims are often socially and physically isolated, forced to work long hours under poor conditions.

Specialized and Emerging Forms: The sources also identify less common but severe forms of trafficking, including:

- **Child Soldiering:** Primarily associated with war-torn regions.
- **Organ Harvesting:** Trafficking for the removal of organs.
- **Forced Marriage and Illegal Adoption:** Using trafficking to facilitate unauthorized familial or marital structures.
- **Camel Jockeying:** A form of exploitation historically associated with specific regions like the Middle East.

UNDERSTANDING VULNERABILITY TO INFORM PREVENTION AND INTERVENTION

Understanding vulnerability is critical to preventing recruitment and radicalization because it allows practitioners to move beyond treating children and young people as "willing participants" and the reactive rescue model and instead address the underlying socio-psychological and environmental drivers and systems of cumulative disadvantage that traffickers and extremist groups exploit. By framing recruitment and radicalization as a form of child maltreatment, practitioners and researchers alike, can develop earlier, more effective, humane, and targeted interventions and close the implementation gaps that leave children exposed. Lewis and Marsden (2021) argue for trauma-informed frameworks to advance the understanding of radicalization by examining the direct and indirect impacts of personal, collective, and intergenerational trauma. These Authors highlight that while Adverse Childhood Experiences (ACEs) and exposure to collective violence are significant push factors for violent extremism, they typically act as "conditioning experiences" that lead to maladaptive coping mechanisms or a search for identity rather than being definitive predictors on their own. Lewis and Marsden (2021) advocate for a shift from a deficit-based "vulnerability" model toward a strengths-based, socio-ecological approach that addresses stressors across micro, meso, and macro levels of an individual's life. Furthermore, their report (2021) suggests that aligning Violent Extremism intervention and prevention efforts with the principles of trauma-informed care—such as safety, trustworthiness, and empowerment—can enhance procedural justice and improve public cooperation with counter-terrorism systems. Oberg et al. (2023) stress the importance of systemic, uniform training in trauma-informed practices for all Countering Violent Extremism (CVE) practitioners. While practitioners widely agree that understanding the impacts of trauma is a critical skill for effectively engaging with clients and helping them think critically about their beliefs, their study (Oberg et al., 2023) found significant disparities in training and resources across different states and jurisdiction. They emphasise the importance of holistic client formulation whereby practitioners move beyond a focus on criminal behaviour to incorporate an individual's trauma history allows for a more "whole client" view. This shift from wanting to punish to wanting to understand is seen as essential for successful rehabilitation and community reintegration. This also addresses the risk of over-securitization where punitive actions, such as house raids, can be counterproductive by contributing to the trauma of children and families and reinforcing a sense of "othering," which may increase radicalization risks (Oberg et al., 2023).

Research (Cockbain & Olver, 2019; Honnavalli et al., 2019; Lewis & Marsden, 2021; Oberg et al., 2023) suggests that understanding vulnerability prevents recruitment and radicalization through the following methods:

1. Identifying the "Push" and "Pull" Factors

To undermine recruitment, practitioners must first understand the specific reasons why children become involved. Push factors include poverty, conflict, prior histories of abuse, and neglect. Pull Factors include the search for better opportunities, stability, or employment. By addressing these root causes—such as providing better economic prospects for children who might otherwise migrate "willingly" into debt bondage—prevention efforts can stop the trafficking process before the "act" of recruitment begin.

These include:

- **Socio-Economic Needs:** Many children, particularly orphans or refugees, are "poached" because they come from lower socio-economic strata where joining a group is seen as a way to gain social status or basic necessities.

- **The Search for Identity:** Extremist groups exploit the adolescent need for a "personalized entity" and self-esteem. By recognizing that a child's "choice" to join is often "specious" (misleading) due to their circumstances, authorities can focus on providing healthy alternatives for belonging.

2. Implementing "Bio-Psychosocial" Interventions

Understanding vulnerability shifts the focus from simple security measures to a holistic care model.

- **Beyond Physical Needs:** Prevention must address spiritual, intellectual, and emotional growth rather than just immediate physical health.
- **Critical Thinking:** Intervention programs should prioritize developing critical thinking and resilient coping strategies to help vulnerable individuals resist ideological indoctrination.

3. Utilizing Mentorship and Community Models

Recognizing that radicalization often happens through social isolation or peer influence allows for community-based prevention.

- **The Aarhus Model:** This approach (Agerschou, 2014) uses mentorship and local community **collaboration** (including mosques and cultural societies) to create a safe platform for at-risk individuals to recover from trauma and build resilience. The Aarhus model is a specialized intervention framework developed in Denmark designed to support individuals who are either radicalized or at high risk of becoming so. Rather than relying solely on security-based measures, this model focuses on the rehabilitation and social reintegration of vulnerable individuals through a community-centric approach
- **Dialogue:** Engaging in dialogue with major players in the community helps identify vulnerable individuals before they are fully radicalized.

4. Reducing Stigma to Prevent "Re-radicalization"

Understanding a child's vulnerability helps the community view them as victims rather than criminals.

- **Breaking the Climate of Fear:** If a community is distrustful or fearful of children returning from conflict zones, that alienation acts as an obstacle to reintegration and may drive the child back to the extremist group.

- **Public Awareness:** Raising awareness that these children were groomed and exploited—often through internet propaganda or physical coercion—is essential for successful social reintegration.

5. Personalized and Rigorous Assessment

Because the types of abuse and vulnerability differ for every individual, understanding the specific "history of the crack" is vital for treatment.

• **Tailored Treatment:** Prevention and rehabilitation require personalized treatment determined by rigorous assessment of the child's degree of agency and their specific exposure to trauma.

• **Multidisciplinary Teams:** Effective prevention involves experts from various fields (psychology, legal, and community leadership) to manage the safe reintegration of vulnerable youth.

6. Strengthening Institutional Oversight

Certain institutional arrangements act as facilitators for trafficking. Understanding these specific vulnerabilities allows for systemic fixes (Cockbain & Olver, 2019):

- **Private Fostering**: Insufficient oversight of private fostering arrangements can leave children vulnerable to domestic servitude. Better monitoring of these arrangements can prevent children from being hidden "behind closed doors".
- **Residential Care:** Many children go missing from residential care after being rescued, only to be re-trafficked. Understanding that these children require specialized safeguarding rather than just "rescue" is vital to breaking the cycle of exploitation.

7. Re-framing Criminality as Exploitation

A major hurdle in prevention is the criminalization of victims. Understanding vulnerability helps authorities recognize that criminal behaviour is often a symptom of trafficking:

- **Victim-Offender Overlap**: In "county lines" activity, children are often groomed to sell drugs and may even recruit others as they ascend the gang hierarchy.
- **Statutory Defence**: By understanding that these children are acting under compulsion or as a "direct result" of being trafficked, the legal system can use

tools like Section 45 of the Modern Slavery Act 2015 to protect them rather than prosecute them, which encourages victims to come forward without fear

8. Tailoring Interventions to Specific Trafficking Types

Prevention is not a "one-size-fits-all" endeavour. Understanding the specific vulnerabilities associated with different types of trafficking allows for more nuanced responses:

- **Internal Sex Trafficking:** Vulnerabilities often include histories of youth offending and social services involvement.
- **Cannabis Cultivation:** This is often linked to specific ethnic backgrounds (e.g., Vietnamese) and the exploitation of illegal migration routes.
- **County Lines:** This predominantly targets 15-17 year old boys who are groomed through sophisticated social manipulation.

CONCLUSION

The research (Bryce & Schaffer, 2024; Cockbain & Olver, 2019; Honnavalli et al., 2019; Littman, 2017;Oberg et al., 2023; United Nations Interregional Crime and Justice Research Institute, 2025) pertaining to various forms of coercive recruitment collectively call attention to the intersection of childhood adversity, exploitation, and violent behaviour, framing the involvement of minors in trafficking, extremism, and forced criminal activity as a consequence of cumulative vulnerability rather than inherent criminality. Child trafficking is defined as a multi-stage process of exploitation—ranging from sexual exploitation, domestic servitude and "county lines" drug operations—where prior histories of maltreatment and institutional gaps leave children susceptible to manipulation. Similarly, the recruitment of children into violent extremism is categorized as a severe form of child abuse under World Health Organisation standards, with groups exploiting developmental needs for belonging and significance through indoctrination and physical coercion. This pattern of vulnerability extends to gang violence, where affiliation and lethal violence is frequently motivated by developmental strains, insecure attachment styles, and environmental stressors such as poverty or bullying. Ultimately, the literature (Bryce & Schaffer, 2024; Cockbain & Olver, 2019; Honnavalli et al., 2019; Littman, 2017; United Nations Interregional Crime and Justice Research Institute, 2025) emphasize that addressing these complex issues requires a shift from strictly punitive measures to a more holistic, bio-psychosocial interventions that recognizes the “victim-offender overlap” and prioritizes trauma informed practice and trauma recovery, critical thinking, and social reintegration.

REFERENCES

Agerschou, T. (2014). Preventing radicalization and discrimination in Aarhus. *Journal for Deradicalization*, (1), 5–22.

Agnew, R. (2015). General strain theory and delinquency. The handbook of juvenile delinquency and juvenile justice, 2, 239-256.

Anti-Defamation league. (2024). Addressing extremism in online games through platform policies. https://www.adl.org/resources/report/addressing-extremism-online-games-through-plaform-policies

Atran, S. (2015). Role of youth: Countering violent extremism, promoting peace, addressing the UN Security Council. *Psychology Today*.

Baglivio, M. T., & Epps, N. (2016). The interrelatedness of adverse childhood experiences among high-risk juvenile offenders. *Youth Violence and Juvenile Justice*, *14*(3), 179–198.

Baglivio, M. T., Wolff, K. T., & Epps, N. (2021). Violent juveniles' adverse childhood experiences: Differentiating victim groups. *Journal of Criminal Justice*, *72*, 101769.

Baidawi, S., & Sheehan, R. (2019). *Cross-over kids': Effective responses to children and young people in the youth justice and statutory child protection systems. Report to the Criminology Research Advisory Council.* Australian Institute of Criminology.

Baird, A. (2012). The violent gang and the construction of masculinity amongst socially excluded young men. *Safer Communities*, *11*(4), 179–190.

Beber, B., & Blattman, C. (2013). The logic of child soldiering and coercion. *International Organization*, *67*(1), 65–104.

Belova-Dalton, O. (2023). The impact of new media and the internet on terrorism. Estonian Academy of Security Sciences. https://doi.org/DOI: 10.15158/0skz-3a87

Bromfield, L., & Miller, R. (2012). *Cumulative harm: Best interests case practice model.* Victorian Government Department of Human Services.

Bromfield, L. M., Gillingham, P., & Higgins, D. J. (2007). Cumulative harm and chronic child maltreatment. Developing practice: the child youth and family work journal, 19, 34-42.

Bryce, I., & Schaffer, K. (2024). Motivations for Juvenile Offending Behaviour and Femicide. In *Forensic Victimology and Femi (ni) cide: A Transdisciplinary Approach on Forensic Evidence and its Contexts* (Vol. II, pp. 165–188). Springer Nature Switzerland.

Carlsson, C., Rostami, A., Mondani, H., Sturup, J., Sarnecki, J., & Edling, C. (2020). A Life-Course Analysis of Engagement in Violent Extremist Groups. *British Journal of Criminology*, *60*(1), 74–92.

Clemmow, C., Fowler, N., Seaward, A., & Gill, P. (2025). Risk of What and Why? Disaggregating Pathways to Extremist Behaviours in Individuals Susceptible to Violent Extremism. *Behavioral Sciences & the Law*, *43*(2), 228–247. PMID: 39645658

Cockbain, E., & Olver, K. (2019). Child trafficking: characteristics, complexities, and challenges. In *Child abuse and neglect* (pp. 95–116). Academic Press.

Eck, K. (2014). Coercion in rebel recruitment. *Security Studies, 23*(2), 364-398.
Evans-Campbell, T. (2008). Historical trauma in American Indian/Native Alaska communities: A multilevel framework for exploring impacts on individuals, families, and communities. *Journal of Interpersonal Violence*, *23*(3), 316–338.

Felitti, V. J., Anda, R. F., Nordenberg, D., Williamson, D. F., Spitz, A. M., Edwards, V., & Marks, J. S. (1998). Relationship of childhood abuse and household dysfunction to many of the leading causes of death in adults: The Adverse Childhood Experiences (ACE) Study. *American Journal of Preventive Medicine*, *14*(4), 245–258. PMID: 9635069

Finkelhor, D., Ormrod, R. K., & Turner, H. A. (2007b). Re-victimization patterns in a national longitudinal sample of children and youth. *Child Abuse & Neglect*, *31*(5), 479–50. PMID: 17537508

Gill, P., Horgan, J., & Deckert, P. (2014). Bombing Alone: Tracing the Motivations and Antecedent Behaviors of Lone-Actor Terrorists. *Journal of Forensic Sciences*, *59*, 425–435. PMID: 24313297

Gustafsson, L., & Ranstorp, M. (2017). Swedish foreign fighters in Syria and Iraq: An analysis of open-source intelligence and statistical data.

Heberle, A. E., Obus, E. A., & Gray, S. A. (2020). An intersectional perspective on the intergenerational transmission of trauma and state-perpetrated violence. *The Journal of Social Issues*, *76*(4), 814–834.

Honnavalli, V., Neo, L. S., Gan, R., Tee, S. H., Khader, M., & Chin, J. (2019). Understanding violent extremism and child abuse: A psychological analysis. In *Child Abuse and Neglect* (pp. 79–94). Academic Press.

Kimmel, M. S. (2018). *Healing from Hate: How Young Men Get Into—and Out Of—violent Extremism*. University of California Press.

LaFree, G. (2018). *Losing legitimacy: Street crime and the decline of social institutions in America*. Routledge.

Lewis, J., & Marsden, S. (2021). Trauma, adversity, and violent extremism. *Centre for Research and Evidence on Security Threats, 9*.

Littman, R. (2017). Children and Extreme Violence: Insights from Social Science on Child Trajectories Into and Out Of Non-State Armed Groups.

Marchment, Z., Clemmow, C., & Gill, P. (2025). Adverse Childhood Experiences and Susceptibility to Violent Extremism. *Terrorism and Political Violence*, •••, 1–15.

O'Driscoll, D. (2017). Links between childhood experience of violence and violent extremism. *Helpdesk report. Available online:* https://assets. publishing. service. gov. *uk/media/5c1903f740f0b60c2c1c798a/248_Childhood_Experience_of_Violence_and _Violent_Extremism. pdf (accessed on 15 December 2024).*

Oberg, G., Adams, B., & Stahl, G. (2023). The role of trauma and mental health in violent extremism: The perceptions of countering violent extremism (CVE) practitioners and why we can't get it wrong. *Journal of Aggression, Maltreatment & Trauma*, *32*(12), 1744–1762.

Petherick, W., & Sinnamon, G. (2013). *Motivations: Offender and victim perspectives*. Elsevier.

Rostami, A., Sturup, J., Mondani, H., Thevselius, P., Sarnecki, J. and Edling, C. (2018), 'The Swedish Mujahideen: An Exploratory Study of 41 Swedish Foreign Fighters Deceased in Iraq and Syria', Studies in Conflict and Terrorism, 1–14. Published Online, doi: .DOI: 10.1080/1057610X.2018.1463615

Silke, A. (2008). Holy Warriors: Exploring the Psychological Processes of Jihadi Radicalization. *European Journal of Criminology*, *5*, 99–123.

Simi, P., Sporer, K., & Bubolz, B. F. (2016). Narratives of Childhood Adversity and Adolescent Misconduct as Precursors to Violent Extremism: A Life-Course Criminological Approach. *Journal of Research in Crime and Delinquency*, *53*(4), 536–563. DOI: 10.1177/0022427815627312

Simi, P., Windisch, S., & Sporer, K. (2016). *Recruitment and Radicalization among US Far Right Terrorists*. START.

United Nations Interregional Crime and Justice Research Institute. (2025). Children and Counter-Terrorism. https://unicri.org/sites/default/files/2019-10/Children_counter_terrorism.pdf

Chapter 6
Adverse Childhood Experiences and the Development of Serial Killers

Hannah Lewis
https://orcid.org/0009-0009-1454-2082
Charles Sturt University, Australia

ABSTRACT

This chapter will discuss the incidence of adverse childhood experiences amongst adult serial killers and how the cycle of violence impacts on future violent criminal behaviour. By considering the Trauma-Control Model (Hickey, 1997), issues relating to the ability to cope with the accumulation of adverse childhood trauma and the response undertaken through serial homicide, can help to identify potential triggers in individuals at higher risk of engaging in this behaviour and develop effective interventions to prevent the incidence of serial homicide.

INTRODUCTION

The early life experiences of serial killers are frequently marked by profound adversity. Numerous studies have found that adverse childhood experiences (ACEs), including abuse, neglect, and exposure to dysfunctional family environments, are disproportionately common among serial homicide offenders (LaBrode, 2007; Mitchell & Aamodt, 2005). While not all individuals exposed to trauma go on to engage in violent behaviour, the cumulative impact of such experiences can shape cognitive, emotional, and behavioural responses in ways that elevate the risk of ex-

DOI: 10.4018/979-8-3373-9524-1.ch006

treme violence. This chapter examines the incidence of ACEs among serial killers and explores how unresolved trauma may contribute to homicidal behaviour. Using Hickey's Trauma-Control Model (Hickey, 1997, 2016) as a theoretical framework, it considers how serial homicide can emerge as a maladaptive coping mechanism in individuals unable to manage internalised trauma. The chapter then integrates this perspective with the broader "cycle of violence" literature to investigate the developmental pathways from victimisation to violent offending. Gender differences, model limitations, and implications for prevention and intervention are also discussed.

The developmental histories of serial murderers – those who kill two or more victims in separate events (Morton & Hilts, 2008) – and other violent offenders often includes adverse childhood experiences, including various forms of child abuse and multitype maltreatment (Brantley & Kosky, 2005; Harrison et al., 2015; Mitchell & Aamodt, 2005). Adverse childhood experiences (ACEs) are broadly defined as experiences in childhood or adolescence (under 18 years) involving "potentially traumatic events, or household or environmental factors that threaten their safety, stability, or social bonds" (Jones & Hoffmann, 2024, p. 349). While definitions of these experiences can vary across studies, it is essential to clarify the specific meanings used in this chapter to ensure consistency and clarity. Accordingly, the following definitions of abuse are drawn from the *Australian Child Maltreatment Study* (Haslam et al., 2023, pp. 6-7) and will be used throughout this section to describe key forms of childhood maltreatment:

- *Physical Abuse*: involves the use of physical force against a child that causes injury, harm, pain, or a breach of dignity, or has a high likelihood of resulting in these, where it is clearly not reasonable corporal punishment, or done reasonably while engaging in any other legitimate context such as a sport or pastime.
- *Sexual Abuse*: includes any sexual act inflicted on a child by any adult or other person, including contact and non-contact acts, for the purpose of sexual gratification, where true consent[1] by the child is not present.
- *Psychological and Emotional Abuse*: involves non-physical interactions with the child which convey to a child that they are worthless, flawed, unloved, unwanted, endangered, or only of value in meeting another's needs.
- *Neglect*: involves the failure to provide the child with the basic necessities of life, as suited to the child's developmental stage, and as recognised by the child's culture context.
- *Exposure to Domestic Violence*: occurs when a child sees or hears acts of violence towards other family members in the child's home.
- *Multitype Maltreatment* - experiencing more than one different type of maltreatment, which can include any combination of the types of abuse.

Understanding the multifaceted impact of ACEs requires not only recognition of their psychological and biological consequences but also an examination of their prevalence and manifestation within specific populations. Therefore, this chapter now turns to an analysis of the rates and patterns of ACEs among serial killers, drawing on empirical research to illuminate the types and frequencies of childhood maltreatment that characterise this group. By exploring these patterns, we can gain deeper insight into the developmental contexts that may contribute to the emergence of serial homicidal behaviour.

RATES AND PATTERNS OF ADVERSE CHILDHOOD EXPERIENCES AMONG SERIAL KILLERS

Understanding the prevalence and patterns of adverse childhood experiences (ACEs) among serial killers is essential for identifying the ways in which early trauma contributes to later violent behaviour. While ACEs are not unique to offenders, existing research suggests that serial killers demonstrate disproportionately high rates of abuse, neglect, and family dysfunction compared to the general population (Mitchell & Aamodt, 2005). Examining these patterns allows for the identification of recurring themes, such as parental rejection, abandonment, and inconsistent caregiving, which appear to shape the developmental trajectories of many offenders. By situating serial killers within the broader literature on ACEs, this section explores how the frequency and forms of abuse they experience may underpin their later violent behaviour.

The lack of adjustment to the trauma and ability to overcome the emotional and psychological damage of the abuse is more likely to result in someone becoming a serial killer (Brantley & Kosky, 2005; Hickey, 2016). This trauma is a result of some abuse characteristics such as rejection, abandonment, and neglect (Hickey, 2010, p. 221). Many serial killers kill as a result of this rejection and abandonment in childhood (Hickey, 2010, p. 5). Dutton and Hart's (1992) research into the impact of childhood abuse and neglect on serial killers concluded that abused children (physically, sexually, and emotionally) were three times more likely than non-abused adults to act violently as adults. Knight (2006, p. 1191) states that some of the main characteristics of sexually motivated serial killers include the notion that as children, serial killers engage in aggressive play, come from dysfunctional families where there is neglect and abuse (Keppel & Birnes, 2003; Schlesinger, 2000), fathers are absent or controlling and authoritative, with the mothers being rejecting, punitive, hated, or controlling (Hickey, 1997; Miller, 2000, 2014). Noting previous studies, Leary et al. (2017, p. 630) discuss parental abuse and summarise the following:

Ressler and Shachtman (2002) reported that over 40% of serial murderers reported childhood psychological abuse; Mitchell and Aamodt (2005) found that 70% of serial killers were abused as children, either psychologically (50%), physically (36%), or sexually (26%); Borja and Ostrosky (2013) extrapolated a strong alignment between parental victimization/abuse and severe psychopathy (e.g., serial killing). Such findings suggest potentially lethal outcomes associated with highly dysfunctional, abusive parental relationships. Stein (2009) found that 80% of 65 violent offenders were subject to extreme levels of abuse as children and attributed the offenders' outcomes to the underlying deviance of early attachments, making their interpersonal landscapes highly toxic.

Evidently, a large number of studies have attempted to measure the rates of child abuse, particularly amongst serial killers, and all studies indicate that the rate of child abuse is significantly higher than the general population, as demonstrated in Table 1 below.

Table 1. Type and prevalence of childhood abuse among general populations (USA, Australia, Great Britain) and serial killers

Type of Abuse	General USA Population (%)[1]	General Australian Population (%)[2]	General Great Britain Population (%)[3]	Serial Killer Population (%)[4]
Physical	6	9.1	7.6	48.9
Sexual	3	7.5	11.5	26.4
Psychological/Emotional	2	N/A	11.8	48.7
Neglect	18	8.9	1.2	18[5]
No Abuse Reported	70	N/A	N/A	26.8

Note. [1] General USA population data from Mitchell & Aamodt (2005); [2] General Australian population data from Australian Bureau of Statistics (2021-22); [3] General Great Britain population data from Office for National Statistics (2020); [4] Serial killer population data from Aamodt et al. (2023); [5] Neglect percentage in the Serial Killer column adapted from Mitchell & Aamodt (2005), because Aamodt et al. (2023) did not report this category.

Interestingly, the rate of neglect in the U.S. general population and the serial killer population were reported at the same level. One possible explanation for this finding lies in definitional issues, as the rates of neglect in the Australian and Great Britain general populations were more consistent with patterns observed across other forms of maltreatment. However, this similarity cannot be fully accounted for by differences in data sources, as both sets of figures were drawn from the same study (Mitchell & Aamodt, 2005). Notably, Mitchell and Aamodt (2005) themselves acknowledge that neglect "seems greatly underrepresented" in the serial killer population (p. 44).

While neglect appears underreported in the U.S. serial killer data, other forms of childhood experiences, such as witnessing or being exposed to domestic violence, are captured in the Australian and Great Britain datasets. These differences in reporting highlight both cross-national variations in data collection and the challenges of drawing direct comparisons between populations. Examining exposure to domestic violence provides additional insight into the environmental and familial factors that may contribute to the development of violent behaviour in serial killers.

The role of exposure to, and witnessing of, domestic violence and abuse in the home is increasingly acknowledged and recognised as an ACE (Felitti et al., 1998; Jones & Hoffman, 2024; McKinley, 2020). In Australia, the ABS (2021-22) reported that 13.3 per cent of the general population has observed domestic violence, while in Great Britain 9.8 per cent of the general population reported witnessing such violence (ONS, 2020). Exposure to domestic violence was the most common form of maltreatment reported by the *Australian Child Maltreatment Study* (Haslam et al., 2023) and the research by Nation et al. (2023). Outcomes of this exposure include an increased likelihood of becoming domestic violence perpetrators themselves, or, in the case of females, victims themselves (Strickland, 2008). The theory of intergenerational transmission of violence provides a useful framework for understanding how these early experiences may shape later violent behaviour. Grounded in Bandura's (1961, 1977) social learning theory, the theory posits that children learn behaviours by observing and internalising the actions of key adults in their lives. Research by Straus (1979) and Walker (1979) further suggests that exposure to family violence during childhood not only increases the likelihood of adolescents imitating violent behaviours, but can also establish enduring patterns of aggression that persist into adulthood. Consistent with this framework, empirical evidence from Poland has shown that individuals exposed to family violence face a significantly heightened risk of engaging in homicide offending as adults (Boduszek et al., 2012), and Reid et al. (2019) also found that 34 per cent of male sexual serial killers were exposed to domestic violence. Within this framework, the high rates of ACEs observed among serial killers may be understood as part of a developmental trajectory in which early exposure to violence, coupled with modelling by caregivers, facilitates the internalisation of violent fantasies and the eventual enactment of extreme violence in the form of serial homicide. This perspective helps explain by serial killers often exhibit complex patterns of aggression and control, reflecting the learned behaviours and maladaptive coping mechanisms established in their formative years.

Multitype maltreatment, as defined above, refers to the coexistence of one or more of the types of child maltreatment, and is distinct from "multiple victimisation" as this term may refer to multiple experiences of the same type of maltreatment, either from the same or different perpetrators (Higgins & McCabe, 2001; Paquette et al., 2025). Individuals with more extensive ACEs tend to exhibit more severe behavioural problems, and tend to have more serious, violent, and extensive criminal careers (DeLisi & Beauregard, 2018). In their study, Reid et al. (2019) reported that

79 per cent of participants had experienced multitype maltreatment, while Duke et al. (2010) found that each additional type of ACE reported by youth increased the risk of violent perpetration by 35% to 114%.

Additionally, the accumulation of multitype maltreatment was associated with greater impairment and adjustment problems, than those that experienced only one form of neglect or abuse (Higgins & McCabe, 2001; Weatherby et al., 2009). Considered a "dose-response" relationship, as the number of ACEs increase, the likelihood of experiencing negative outcomes also increases (Forster et al., 2020; Jones & Hoffman, 2024). Jones and Hoffman (2024) also report that ACEs are highly interrelated and those that report at least one ACE are likely to experience other types of ACEs. From this, those exposed to multitype maltreatment are at an increased risk of engaging in maladaptive behaviours. This was demonstrated by DeLisi and Beauregard (2018) who found that the accumulation of ACEs in offenders increased the risk of a homicide being perpetrated and that exposure alone was unlikely to lead to homicide, in particular, sexual homicide offending.

Beyond the direct experience of multitype maltreatment, exposure to ACEs can influence a range of developmental and psychosocial outcomes, including aspects of brain function, emotional regulation, attachment and mental health, which in turn are associated with aggression, reduced empathy, and the emergence of antisocial traits. ACEs are reported to have a negative effect on brain development and cognitive processing, leading to aggressive thought patterns and a lack of emotional regulation (Marono et al., 2020). Deprivation in childhood is a significant risk factor for changes in brain functioning in later life and can impact on the way that the brain develops (Heide & Solomon, 2006; Reid et al., 2019; Schimmenti et al., 2021). This has been explained in relation to serial killers as being "pathologically maladjusted" (Deepak & Ramdoss, 2021, p. 1449).

Alongside the effects on brain development, some other key issues emerge relating to attachment, bonding and socialisation. As previously mentioned, parental rejection or growing up in with parents who lack warmth and responsiveness and do not provide a safe and secure environment leads to an inability or impairment to engaging in healthy relationships (Reid et al., 2019). The most frequently observed expression of childhood trauma is rejection (Arrigo & Purcell, 2001). Rejected children are linked to being more aggressive, hostile and have an absence of positive self-esteem (Rohner et al., 2005). They lack the regulation of emotion, exhibit aggressive behaviour and lack the ability to form empathetic, compassionate and healthy attachments (Borja & Ostrosky, 2013; Heide & Solomon, 2006). Rejection most commonly comes from parents or caregivers (Purcell & Arrigo, 2006), but can also come from peers and can lead to poor social relationships, and diminished social support (McDermott, 2004), which in turn, results in delinquent and deviant behaviour. Hickey (1997) reported that 48 per cent of male serial killers had been rejected by a parent or other significant person in their lives. Similarly, Reid et al. (2019) found that 71 per cent of male sexual serial killers were loners in school and were actively rejected by peers and 90 per cent described feelings of social isolation throughout their childhood (p. 1638).

Children who experienced parental rejection were more likely to have personality and psychological disorders (Rohner et al., 2005) including psychopathy and anti-social personality disorder (APD) (Dowdell et al., 2022; Schimmenti et al., 2021). Psychopathy appears to play a significant role in homicide offenders, particularly sexual homicide offenders (Chopin et al., 2023; Meloy, 2000). Chopin et al. (2023) reported that the presence of ACEs increase the risk of a number of personality disorders and psychopathy, and lead indirectly to the perpetration of homicide, particularly if problem behaviours emerge during adolescence.

The association between ACEs and aggression is well established, with evidence indicating that these patterns can first manifest during children's social play. Such play functions as an important mechanism for processing fears and other emotional challenges, while supportive peer relationships contribute to the development of resilience and facilitate healthy socialisation. However, for serial homicide offenders, this positive play is not usually present. They often lack the ability to engage in appropriate play and form social bonds and as a result, experience high levels of social isolation, solitary play, and loneliness (Reid et al., 2019). As they aged, their substance use and abuse heightened as did their engagement with violent fantasy and play. For some serial killers and other violent offenders, this displacement of aggression can culminate in animal cruelty (Jones & Hoffman, 2024; Knight, 2006; Arrigo & Purcell, 2001; Trentham et al., 2018). From this, serial killers shift their aggression from animals to humans, potentially after becoming desensitised from violence (Trentham et al., 2018). Another feature evident in serial homicide offenders includes overkill – where more violence and torture are inflicted on the victim more than was necessary to result in death (Chopin & Beauregard, 2021; Marono et al., 2020; Ressler et al., 1988). An identified link has been reported between exposure to traumatic events and the degree of psychopathy (Borja & Ostrosky, 2013). In their study, Borja and Ostrosky (2013) found that inmates with high levels of psychopathy who were convicted of violence offences, including homicide, reported significant victimisation and greater exposure to stressful experiences, including both physical and sexual abuse. Notably, the cumulative number of traumatic events, together with experiences of emotional abuse, was correlated with higher psychopathy scores. Even in juvenile homicide offenders, both serial and sexual, reported high psychopathic personality traits (Myers, 2004). Myers (2004) also reported 94 per cent of juvenile offenders experienced a dysfunctional family system, 94 per cent experienced a history of child abuse, 88 per cent reported family violence, and 81 percent reported paternal abandonment/neglect. Of the 16 juvenile sexual homicide offenders, all had an impaired capacity to feel guilt.

Exposure to ACEs has been associated with higher rates of mental illness and substance abuse. Psychological abuse, in particular, has been significantly linked to "child adjustment problems including internalizing and externalizing problems such as depression, self-destructive behaviour, eating disorders, attention deficit disorders, drug and alcohol problems" (Reid et al., 2019, p. 1633). Ongoing and repeated exposure to ACEs have been shown to increase the risk of post-traumatic stress disorder (PTSD), depression, and other mental illnesses (Heide & Solomon, 2006; McDermott, 2004).

These psychological consequences highlight how early trauma can shape the cognitive and emotional processes, fostering maladaptive coping strategies, distorted attachment patterns, and the development of violent fantasies. Such patterns provide a conceptual bridge to Hickey's (1997) Trauma-Control Model, which situates early life trauma as a central factor in the emergence of serial homicide behaviour.

TRAUMA-CONTROL MODEL

Hickey (1997) proposed a Trauma-Control Model (TCM) that early life trauma, or adverse childhood experiences, play a central role in the eventual development of serial homicide offenders. According to this model, trauma acts as a catalyst that, when combined with certain psychological predispositions and social and environmental factors, may lead a person down a path of increasingly violent fantasies and, eventually, serial murder. Perpetrators find themselves in a self-generating and self-perpetuating cycle of violent fantasy and sadistic offending (Purcell & Arrigo, 2006).

In relation to the TCM, a *destabilising event* or *traumatisation* must occur, which often manifests through an "unstable home life, death of parents, divorce, corporal punishments, sexual abuse, and other negative events that occur during the formative years of the offender's life" (Hickey, 2016, p. 148). These traumatic events cause deep psychological wounds and contribute to a sense of powerlessness, shame, and rage. Most often, these traumas take the form of abuse, neglect, or rejection, from which dysfunctional coping mechanisms may emerge. One such mechanism is the development of violent fantasies, which allow the individual to mentally explore aggressive impulses and exert a sense of control that is absent in real life. Over time, these fantasies can become elaborate, obsessive, and sexually charged, particularly when the underlying trauma involves humiliation or sexual abuse. Engaging with these fantasies can provide a temporary sense of relief and gratification, reinforcing maladaptive cognitive and emotional patterns, and setting the stage for the eventual enactment of violent behaviour. These patterns may later be amplified by facilitators, often alcohol, drugs, pornography and books on the occult (Hickey, 2016), which further disinhibit behaviour and intensify the fantasies.

The trauma experienced by serial killers is often unresolved and inadequately addressed (Arrigo & Purcell, 2001). In response, individuals may continue to turn inward, developing violent fantasies as a coping mechanism. Over time, these fantasies become increasingly ritualised and compulsive, with offenders mentally rehearsing violent acts before attempting to replicate them. The resultant murders are often ritualistic, repetitive, and serve to relieve psychological tension, although the outcome rarely meets the expectations of the fantasy, as the offender cannot fully control the victim's response (Prentky et al., 1989). Following each act, a 'cooling-off period'[2] typically ensues, after which fantasy and tension build again, often resulting in shorter intervals between killings as the psychological need intensifies. These fantasies rarely exist in isolation; they are often reinforced and intensified by external facilitators, such as alcohol, drugs, and pornography, which serve to disinhibit behaviour and further fuel the offender's violent and sexually motivated fantasies.

Facilitators

As mentioned, facilitators play a significant role in the transformation of childhood trauma into serial killing. These facilitators function to "further shape the personality, promote predatory inclinations, and enable the individual to act out his fantasies" (DeFronzo & Prochnow, 2004, p.104). The main facilitators for this are alcohol, drugs, pornography and exposure to violent subcultures (DeFronzo et al., 2007; Homant & Kennedy, 2009; Levin & Fox, 2017), which may amplify violent fantasies and normalise the use of violence as a strategy for achieving dominance and power (DeFronzo et al., 2007). In particular, alcohol and drugs decrease inhibitions and compromise moral awareness and acceptable behavioural boundaries (Purcell & Arrigo, 2006; Weatherby et al., 2009), while pornography further fuels growing fantasies of violence (Arndt et al., 2004; Hickey, 2016) and may serve to reinforce and sustain the elaborate fantasy lives of serial killers (Weatherby et al., 2009). For example, sadistic violence and the objectification of women in pornography, video games and broader society can influence a young person's mind, especially when combined with prior trauma (Miller, 2014). As fantasies evolves, so too does engagement with facilitators. Increasing use can result in a loss of potency desensitization, potentially leading to addiction (Arndt et al., 2004). Importantly, research has demonstrated a positive correlation with these facilitators and both sexual offending and serial homicide, highlighting the role they play in transforming fantasy into violent action (Arrigo & Purcell, 2001; Weatherby et al., 2009).

Fantasy

Fantasy is a crucial component of Hickey's model, representing a key psychological mechanism through which individuals process unresolved trauma and adverse childhood experiences. Within this model, violent fantasies serve as an internal and controlled mental space in which aggressive impulses and feelings of powerlessness can be explored, rehearsed, and gradually integrated into the individual's emerging identity. Over time, these fantasies often become increasingly elaborate and compelling, frequently combining elements of both violence and sexuality, which may amplify the intensity and appeal of the imagined scenarios. Fantasy thus functions not only as a means of emotional release, but also as a source of gratification, reinforcing maladaptive cognitive and affective patterns that can shape behaviour and motivation.

Linking to childhood traumas, one study found that male serial killers described having violent fantasies about their mothers, with whom they had an abusive relationship (Reid et al., 2019). In these fantasies, there was initially more focus on escape and freedom rather than the infliction of pain; however, they reflected the powerlessness and lack of control these men experienced and represented a reversal of their real-life helplessness. Over time, these escapist fantasies may intensify, incorporating elements of domination, humiliation, and sexual aggression. The avenues of escape gradually substitute for social relationships the individual has failed to create or sustain (Purcell & Arrigo, 2006), and in doing so, the fantasies evolve into increasingly sadistic and violent scenarios in which control, suffering, and sexualised violence were central. In this way, what begins as a psychological refuge can transform into a compulsive rehearsal for aggression, normalising violent behaviour and lowering the threshold for translating fantasy into real-world acts of harm.

As violent and sexually charged fantasies become more elaborate and compulsive, they begin to shape the offender's perceptions, motivations, and behavioural scripts. Over time, these mental rehearsals not only provide gratification and a sense of control but also reduce the psychological barriers to enacting real-world violence. The progression from imagination to action is gradual, with offenders often experimenting with minor acts or testing boundaries before moving toward more severe behaviours. Ultimately, the development and reinforcement of these fantasies lay the groundwork for homicidal behaviour, as the individual seeks to translate imagined scenarios into reality (Hickey, 2016).

What develops from these fantasies is the homicidal behaviour. As fantasies become increasingly violent, and often sexual, they exhibit the underlying context of control. From this, fantasy itself fails to achieve the sense of satisfaction it once did, and the actual enactment of the fantasy becomes irresistible. Since the fantasy is never fully achievable, due to factors such as unsatisfaction and lack of control of the victim's response, the perpetrator may kill the victim. Because killing fails to fully relieve negative emotions, the process becomes cyclical: an ongoing attempt to fill feelings of emptiness through the domination and destruction of others. As desensitisation and acclimation return, the act no longer provides the desired relief, leading to increased severity and frequency (Purcell & Arrigo, 2006). Ultimately, this cycle often concludes with a period of decline and deterioration, sometimes resulting in a final frenzied episode (Arndt et al., 2004).

Criticisms and Limitations of Hickey

While Hickey's TCM provides a compelling framework for understanding the interplay between early trauma, facilitators, and fantasy in the development of serial homicide, it is not without limitations. For example, Pollock (1995) argued that escalation is not a universal trajectory, pointing to instances where homicidal behaviour manifested instead as spree killing, thereby challenging the assumption that all offenders progress through increasingly violent stages. However, more recent scholarship has suggested that spree and serial killings may exist along a continuum, rather than as wholly distinct phenomena, meaning Pollock's critique does not necessarily undermine the model so much as highlight variation in offender pathways. Similarly, Homant and Kennedy (2009) contend that Hickey's framework lacks conceptual clarity, particularly in distinguishing between predispositions and traumas, and in identifying where traumatisations end and stresses or facilitators begin. These ambiguities suggest that, while the model offers valuable insights, it may oversimplify the complex and overlapping factors that contribute to serial homicide.

While Hickey's Trauma Control Model offers a psychological roadmap for understanding how early trauma, fantasy and behavioural facilitators can culminate in serial homicide, it does not exist in isolation. Rather, it can be seen as a specific, individualised manifestation of a broader theoretical framework – the cycle of violence. This cycle, grounded in developmental criminology and psychology, posits that individuals who experience victimisation in childhood are more likely to become perpetrators of violence themselves. By situating Hickey's model within this wider context, it becomes possible to explore how ACEs not only shape internal psychological processes, but also contribute to broader patterns of violent behaviour across the life course.

CYCLE OF VIOLENCE

The cycle of violence theory, which essentially argues that violence begets violence, has been supported by numerous studies demonstrating that childhood abuse is associated with an increased risk of violent and aggressive behaviour in adulthood (Dutton & Hart, 1992; Widom, 1989). This empirical pattern aligns with theoretical perspectives such as the intergenerational transmission of violence, which suggest that early exposure to abuse can normalise violent behaviours. Widom's (1989) landmark study was one of the first large-scale empirical investigations to demonstrate that individuals who experience abuse and neglect in childhood are significantly more likely to engage in violent behaviour later in life. Using court-substantiated cases of childhood maltreatment matched with control groups, she found that children who had experienced abuse or neglect were nearly twice as likely to be arrested for violent crimes as adults. This foundational work gave rise to the term "cycle of violence," capturing the idea that victimisation can perpetuate itself across time, with those once harmed becoming perpetrators of harm.

Widom and Maxfield's (2001) follow-up study, conducted through the U.S. National Institute of Justice, re-examined the same cohort two decades later, revealing that the connection between early maltreatment and later criminal behaviour persisted well into adulthood. Crucially, this longitudinal research revealed gendered pathways: while males exposed to childhood trauma were more likely to become violent offenders, females often displayed internalising behaviours such as depression or substance abuse. These findings support a developmental and cumulative model of violence, where trauma shapes long-term behavioural, emotional, and relational trajectories. These insights align closely with the ACE framework, which further broadens the scope by including not just physical and sexual abuse, but also emotional neglect, domestic violence exposure, parental incarceration, and household dysfunction. This convergence of findings from both the ACEs literature and Widom's longitudinal work strongly supports the premise that early trauma is not only a risk factor but a foundational component in the developmental pathway toward violence.

Dutton and Hart's (1992, p.135) study also showed that certain types of abuse were associated with specific offending. For example, childhood sexual abuse increased the odds of committing sexual offences in adulthood. Similarly, more recent research has found that serial killers who suffered physical abuse were more likely to demonstrate overkill, and those that engaged in mutilation, torture or binding of the victim were more likely to have experienced sexual abuse during childhood (Marono et al., 2020). Importantly, a number of studies have also indicated that exposure to parental violence is related to violent behaviour (Heide, 1999; Reid et al., 2019; Smith & Thornberry, 1995). Children who witness family violence are likely to demonstrate diminished social competence and behavioural problems which has a significant effect on them (Jaffe et al., 1986). Webster-Stratton (1985) similarly found that a coercive cycles of family violence, combined with low family income, were highly correlated with negative and controlling interactions. Furthermore, parents who reported being victims of physical abuse in childhood were more likely to engage in similar abusive behaviours towards the next generation, perpetuating the cycle of violence (Krischer et al., 2021).

Beyond empirical correlations, research has examined the psychological mechanisms underlying the cycle of violence. Children may learn to interpret threats as pervasive and personal, responding to stress or interpersonal conflict with aggression. Repeated reinforcement of these patterns can normalise violent behaviour, reduce empathic concern, and inhibit the development of moral reasoning, creating a developmental trajectory in which violence becomes a habitual, learned response.

In the context of serial homicide, the cycle of violence may interact with pre-existing psychological predispositions, such as impulsivity or psychopathy, and environmental factors to produce extreme behavioural outcomes (Hickey, 2016; Purcell & Arrigo, 2006). High rates of childhood abuse among serial killers suggest that repeated trauma contributes not only to violent tendencies but also to the development of sadistic fantasies, overkill, and ritualised violence (Marono et al., 2020; Reid et al., 2019). These findings indicate that the cycle of violence is not limited to generalised aggression but can escalate into specialised, premeditated patterns of lethal behaviour.

While the cycle of violence provides a robust framework for understanding the development of violent behaviour, research consistently indicates that its manifestation is influenced by gender. Males who experience childhood abuse are generally more likely to externalise aggression, engaging in violent offending, whereas females often display internalising behaviours such as depression, self-harm, or substance abuse (Widom & Maxfield, 2001). These gendered pathways suggest that the interplay between early trauma, socialisation, and biological factors shapes not only the likelihood of later violence but also the form it may take. Examining these differences is essential for understanding why males are disproportionately represented among serial killers and provides a foundation for the next section exploring gender-specific patterns of childhood adversity and offending trajectories.

GENDER DIFFERENCES IN ACES AND SERIAL KILLING

Some studies have noted the greater the exposure to more severe forms of abuse, neglect, victimisation and deprivation are at an increased risk for numerous issues – behavioural, mentally and emotionally, and medically (DeLisi & Beauregard, 2018). This includes substance abuse, depression, suicidal ideations, externalising behaviours and violence. Some differences in these expressions are found in relation to gender. For example, Keeney and Heide (1994) found childhood abuse to be a common background factor among both male and female serial murderers, but their analysis revealed significant gender differences in how serial violence is enacted, for example, through methods, victim selection, and psychological traits), underscoring that similar trauma histories can diverge into very different behavioural outcomes depending on gender.

Although research consistently shows that women are more likely than men to experience certain forms of childhood abuse, in particular sexual abuse and intrafamilial victimisation, this disparity is not reflected in the gender distribution of serial homicide offenders, who are overwhelmingly male (Hickey, 2016). One explanation for this apparent contradiction lies in how trauma is processed and expressed differently across genders, namely the internal and external indicators.

Internal/External Manifestations

Carmen, Rieker, and Mills (1984), in their study of psychiatric inpatients, found that female victims of abuse were significantly more likely to internalise their trauma, exhibiting symptoms such as depression, anxiety, low self-esteem, and difficulties forming trusting relationships. These internalised patterns of coping stood in contrast to the externalised responses observed in male patients, who more often demonstrated aggression, antisocial behaviours, and increased contact with the criminal justice system. Notably, abused male patients were more likely to display violent behaviour toward others (60 per cent of abused males versus only 17 per cent of abused females) highlighting a gendered difference in behavioural outcomes following trauma.

This divergence suggests that while ACEs are common across both genders, the pathways from trauma to violence may differ significantly. Males may be more likely to respond with outward aggression, shaped in part by social norms that discourage vulnerability and emotional expression (Pollack, 2000). Over time, these externalised coping strategies may escalate toward violent or even homicidal behaviour in a small subset of individuals. In extreme cases, particularly when combined with other risk factors, this pattern can evolve into chronic violence, including homicidal behaviour. This was seen in Reid et al's. (2019) study whereby serial killers often felt unable to fit the image of masculinity as expected, encouraged or enforced by their fathers. Conversely, females are more likely to direct trauma responses inward, which can manifest in self-destructive behaviours, psychiatric illness, or chronic relational instability rather than outward violence (Widom & Maxfield, 2001).

This gendered difference in the psychological expression of trauma may partly explain why rates of early abuse do not correlate proportionally with rates of serial killing. Instead, they point to the importance of how trauma is processed, expressed, and shaped by gendered socialisation, which can lead to markedly different long-term outcomes for male and female victims.

Somewhat compounding this is the fact that serial homicide often reflects masculine-coded forms of violence such as domination and control, further aligning with socially sanctioned narratives of male power (Jenkins, 1994; Leyton, 1986). This has been seen in a number of different contexts, including Brazilian youths and Chinese triad youth gangs (Gerard & Khachatryan, 2024). In contrast, girls are encouraged to internalise distress, leading to different psychiatric and behavioural outcomes even when exposed to similar traumatic conditions. As such, the observed gender disparity in serial homicide cannot be understood solely through individual trauma histories. Instead, it must be situated within broader sociocultural frameworks that shape how trauma is internalised and externalised.

With respect to Hickey's (2016) TCM, he observed differences between male and female serial killers, although the core psychological mechanisms remain broadly applicable to both. The nature of the trauma, expression of fantasies, facilitators and cyclic behaviour was identified as key differences between male and female serial killers.

- **Nature of the Trauma:** Hickey (2016) noted that males are more likely to experience overt physical abuse, sexual abuse, and bullying which often lead to violent, sexually sadistic fantasies. Females experienced trauma that was more relational or emotional, such as neglect, domestic violence, or co-dependent relationships, rather than overt physical abuse. In some cases, female offenders were victimised alongside male partners (for example, in team killings) or grew up in environments marked by exploitation or instability (Hickey, 2016).
- **Expression of Fantasies:** Males tended toward sexually aggressive, sadistic, and dominance-based fantasies, often escalating to hands-on, personal forms of murder (for example, strangulation or stabbing). On the other hand, females had less overtly violent fantasies, when present. This is reflected in the methodology of female serial killers, where they are more likely to kill for profit, use covert or passive methods to kill (e.g. smothering, poisoning), and target vulnerable people or family members.
- **Facilitators:** Men more commonly use pornography, drugs, or alcohol to reinforce or act out their fantasies. Women less commonly show evidence of these external facilitators, and instead, trauma and situational factors may play a stronger role (for example, financial stress and abusive relationships).
- **Cyclical Behaviour:** Male serial killers more often fit the classic pattern of cyclical killings with "cooling-off periods" and escalating violence.

Alternatively, female serial killers may kill over longer spans (often years), without clearly defined cycles, and their killings may appear more opportunistic or goal-driven than compulsive.

An overview of these differences is noted in Table 2 below.

Table 2. Comparison of male and female serial killers in the trauma-control model

Aspect	Male Serial Killers	Female Serial Killers
Typical Early Trauma	Physical/sexual abuse, bullying, rejection	Emotional abuse, neglect, domestic violence
Coping Mechanism	Fantasies of power, control, and sadistic violence	Detachment, manipulation, or passive-aggression
Fantasy Content	Sexual domination, torture, sadism	Control over others, profit, revenge, caretaking distortions
Facilitators	Pornography, alcohol, drugs	Less commonly present; sometimes toxic relationships
Victim Type	Strangers, particularly women and sex workers	Family members, dependents, patients
Killing Method	Hands-on (strangling, stabbing, shooting)	Indirect (poisoning, suffocation, overdose)
Motivation	Sexual gratification, power, dominance	Profit, attention, control, "mercy" or revenge
Cycle Pattern	Clear fantasy-build-release pattern; shorter intervals	Longer intervals, less ritualistic, less overt fantasy
Public vs Private	Often kills in public or isolated outdoor spaces	Kills in domestic or caregiving settings
Detection	Often through forensic or behavioural patterns	Often detected late due to trust and role invisibility

Note. Adapted from *Serial Murderers and Their Victims* (7th ed.) by E. W. Hickey, 2016.

Hickey's (2016) analysis, complemented by the table of gender differences, underscores that males and females not only experience adverse childhood experiences differently but also manifest the effects of trauma in distinct ways. Males are more likely to externalise, exhibiting aggression, violent offending, and other outwardly harmful behaviours, whereas females tend to internalise, presenting with depression, anxiety, self-harm, or substance misuse. These patterns illustrate how gender can shape the expression of early trauma, and suggest that the developmental pathways leading to serial homicide are influenced by both biological and sociocultural factors. However, while these findings are informative, they also highlight key limitations in the existing literature. The studies on gender differences often rely on relatively small sample sizes, retrospective reporting, or documented histories of abuse, which may underrepresent the true prevalence of certain adverse experiences. Additionally, the focus on extreme outcomes, such as sexual or homicidal offending, can obscure the nuanced ways in which trauma manifests across genders and may not account for protective factors or resilience in some individuals.

It is also important to note that the vast majority of individuals who experience severe ACEs, including women who disproportionately face sexual and relational trauma, do not become violent offenders. Protective factors such as supportive relationships, access to therapeutic interventions, and socialisation that encourages prosocial coping strategies can mitigate the trajectory from victimisation to violence. Acknowledging resilience alongside risk reinforces that ACEs are significant predictors, but not inevitabilities, in the development of serial homicide.

LIMITATIONS AND CONSIDERATIONS

The most glaring limitation that needs to be acknowledged is twofold – that not all abused children become serial killers, and not all serial killers have documented histories of trauma. This would indicate that other factors come into play when looking at the drivers behind serial homicide. Some studies have attempted to address this complexity by examining the interplay of biological, psychological, and sociocultural factors (Hickey, 2016). These approaches highlight that while adverse childhood experiences are significant, they represent only one component of a multifactorial pathway to serial homicide.

Another limitation of the role that child abuse plays in relation to serial murder is the lack of explanation behind why males are more frequently the perpetrators of serial homicide, yet females experience certain types of child abuse (sexual, neglect, emotional) at higher rates. This can be partially explained by the internal versus external manifestations of ACEs (for example, higher rates of self-harm as opposed to outward harm towards another person), however does not explain this to the level that would indicate childhood trauma is the sole cause of serial homicide. Further research into the coping skills and mechanisms adopted by females would benefit our understanding of how similar adverse experiences can lead to divergent behavioural outcomes. Such research may also illuminate protective factors that mitigate the trajectory from victimisation to serial homicide perpetration, thereby contributing to a more nuanced understanding of gender differences in the pathways from childhood trauma to serial killing.

One other important limitation to consider is the framing of ACEs as direct causes of serial killing, which risks oversimplifying complex human behaviour and may unintentionally imply that individuals with such experiences are destined to become offenders – the theory of determinism. The deterministic perspective can also contribute to stigmatising survivors of childhood abuse by associating victimhood with future violence, which is inaccurate. Whilst it is important to examine ACEs in relation to understanding potential risk factors for serial homicide occurring, it is necessary to avoid making deterministic assumptions about childhood adversity victims.

Most of the studies done on serial killers with histories of ACEs have primarily focused on sexual homicide (Burgess et al., 1986; DeLisi & Beauregard, 2018; Mitchell & Aamodt, 2005; Reid et al., 2019; Ressler et al., 1986; Ressler et al., 1988). This emphasis on sexually motivated offenders has consequently limited the generalisability of findings to serial murderers whose crimes are not sexually driven, such as those motivated by power, control or financial gain. The predominance of sexual homicide research may reinforce a narrow typology of serial killers, obscuring the broader spectrum of motivations, behavioural patterns and psychological profiles that exist. Expanding research to include non-sexually motivated serial murderers is therefore essential to fully understand the multifactorial pathways between childhood adversity and the development of serial homicide behaviour.

Of interest, the USA government does not routinely collect statistics about the general population experiencing child maltreatment, and as such, the statistics used to report the prevalence (Table 1) came from an academic source and is quite outdated (2005). The collection of child abuse statistics like that collected by the Australian Bureau of Statistics (ABS) and the Office of National Statistics (ONS) would be beneficial for better comparisons across nations. Additionally, it is often reported that incidents of child abuse frequently go unreported and are underestimated (Dong et al., 2003; Felitti et al., 1998; Mitchell & Aamodt, 2005; Strickland, 2008). This can be related to the consideration that the treatment people received as children were not abusive (Harrison et al., 2015), were commonplace, and characteristic for their generation (Mitchell & Aamodt, 2005, p. 44). These are reflective of the challenges in defining and measuring ACEs, particularly in relation to historical cases. Furthermore, some individuals do not wish to disclose abuse for protection of their parents, siblings, or others (Mitchell & Aamodt, 2005). In addition to this, there are limitations relating to self-reported data and retrospective profiling, something adopted by most of the studies on ACEs. In addition, there is a potential publication bias in existing research: offenders with well-document or extreme histories of trauma are more likely to be studied and published on, while cases without clear abuse backgrounds may be underrepresented. This imbalance risks overstating the strength of the trauma-serial homicide link and underscores the need for broader sampling across offender populations.

While this chapter focused on the rates and patterns of adverse childhood experiences among serial killers, it is important to recognise that severe childhood abuse also exerts profound biological effects. Research has shown that such abuse can disrupt normal brain development, leading to significantly smaller total brain and cerebral volumes, impaired functioning of limbic system pathways, and alterations in neurotransmitter systems (Heide & Solomon, 2006) and other poor physical health outcomes (Afifi et al., 2022). Although these neurobiological impacts are beyond the scope of the present discussion, they underscore the complex interplay between early trauma and later behavioural outcomes, warranting further exploration in future research.

Although there have been several limitations in existing research and theoretical models, it is nonetheless important to recognise that such insights can inform preventative strategies. By identifying the pathways through which ACEs, maladaptive coping mechanisms, and psychosocial factors contribute to violent offending, it becomes possible to develop targeted interventions aimed at reducing the risk of future violence, including serial homicide. Some of these include assessment and early identification and intervention (Dowdell et al., 2022), dedicated resources to assist with healthy adaptation and recovery, including trauma-informed responses (Afifi et al., 2022; Royal Commission into Institutional Responses to Child Sexual Abuse, 2017).

CONCLUSION

This chapter has examined the incidence and impact of adverse childhood experiences (ACEs) among serial killers, drawing on theoretical frameworks, empirical findings, and comparative analyses to better understand the developmental pathways that can lead from early victimisation to extreme violence. Evidence consistently demonstrates that serial killers experience disproportionately high rates of childhood maltreatment, including physical, sexual, and emotional abuse, neglect and exposure to domestic violence. These experiences not only increase the likelihood of maladaptive coping strategies but also appear to underpin the development of violent fantasies, social isolation, psychopathy, and the ritualised forms of violence that characterise serial homicide.

The Trauma-Control Model offers a compelling psychological account of how trauma interacts with fantasy and facilitators to produce cycles of violence. Within this framework, unresolved trauma fuels compulsive and sexually charged fantasies that eventually find expression in serial murder. Yet, when situated alongside the broader "cycle of violence" theory, it becomes clear that ACEs are not only individualised triggers but part of an intergenerational and cumulative process through which violence begets violence. Together, these perspectives suggest that serial homicide represents an extreme endpoint of developmental trajectories shaped by rejection, abuse, and exposure to violence during childhood.

Gender emerged as an important variable in shaping these pathways. While both male and female serial killers frequently report histories of childhood trauma, the expression of these experiences differs markedly. Men are more likely to externalise their trauma, manifesting it in violent and sadistic behaviours, while women often internalise theirs, leading to depression, self-harm, or less overtly violent forms of killing, such as poisoning. These findings highlight the importance of considering not only the prevalence of ACEs but also how gendered socialisation influences the processing of trauma and subsequent behavioural outcomes. They also point to the need for criminological analyses that situate serial homicide within broader cultural narratives of masculinity, domination, and control.

At the same time, several limitations complicate the interpretation of these findings. Not all individuals exposed to ACEs become violent offenders, and not all serial killers have documented histories of trauma. This underscores the multifactorial nature of serial homicide, in which biological predispositions, psychological vulnerabilities, social contexts, and cultural narratives all interact with early adversity to shape behavioural outcomes. Moreover, the predominance of research on sexually motivated offenders risks obscuring the diversity of motives and trajectories within serial homicide. Expanding empirical studies to include non-sexual, financially motivated, or partner-assisted offenders is essential to produce a more nuanced picture.

Despite these challenges, the study of ACEs in relation to serial homicide offers important implications for prevention and intervention. Recognising that trauma is neither a necessary nor sufficient cause of serial murder, but rather a significant risk factor, allows for early identification of vulnerable individuals without falling into deterministic explanations. Trauma-informed approaches to education, child protection, and mental health services can mitigate the long-term effects of adversity, reducing the likelihood that unresolved trauma will manifest in maladaptive coping or violent behaviour. Equally, policies aimed at addressing domestic violence, improving family stability, and strengthening protective factors such as social support and resilience can disrupt the intergenerational transmission of violence.

Ultimately, serial homicide represents the extreme tail of a much broader continuum of violence linked to adverse childhood experiences. While rare, these crimes illuminate the destructive potential of unresolved trauma and underscore the urgency of addressing child maltreatment as a matter of public health, social justice, and crime prevention. By integrating psychological models with criminological frameworks, researchers and practitioners can move beyond simplistic causal accounts and toward a more comprehensive understanding of how trauma, gender, culture, and social conditions converge to shape pathways into violence. In doing so, the criminological study of ACEs and serial homicide not only advances academic knowledge but also informs practical strategies to prevent violence, intervene earlier, and foster resilience among those most at risk.

REFERENCES

Aamodt, M. G., Leary, T., & Girimurugan, S. (2023). *Radford/FGCU Annual Report on Serial Killer Statistics: 2023*. Radford University.

Afifi, T. O., Stewart-Tufescu, A., Taillieu, T., Salmon, S., Fortier, J., & Roos, L. E. (2022). Adverse childhood experiences. In Asmundson, G. J. G., & Noel, M. (Eds.), *Comprehensive clinical psychology* (2nd ed., Vol. 11, pp. 1–16). Elsevier., DOI: 10.1016/B978-0-12-818697-8.00038-8

Arndt, W. B., Hietpas, T., & Kim, J. (2004). Critical characteristics of male serial murderers. *American Journal of Criminal Justice, 29*(1), 117–131. DOI: 10.1007/BF02885707

Arrigo, B. A., & Purcell, C. E. (2001). Explaining paraphilias and lust murder: Toward an integrated model. *International Journal of Offender Therapy and Comparative Criminology, 45*(1), 6–31.

Australian Bureau of Statistics. (2021-22). *Childhood abuse*. ABS. https://www.abs.gov.au/statistics/people/crime-and-justice/childhood-abuse/2021-22

Bandura, A. (1961). *Psychological foundations of thought and action: A social learning analysis*. Prentice-Hall.

Bandura, A. (1977). *Social learning theory*. Prentice-Hall.

Boduszek, D., Hyland, P., & Bourke, A. (2012). An investigation of the role of personality, familial, and peer-related characteristics in homicidal offending using retrospective data. *Journal of Criminal Psychology, 2*(2), 96–106. DOI: 10.1108/20093821211264468

Borja, K., & Ostrosky, F. (2013). Early traumatic events in psychopaths. *Journal of Forensic Sciences, 58*(4), 927–931. DOI: 10.1111/1556-4029.12104

Brantley, A. C., & Kosky, R. H. (2005). Serial murder in the Netherlands: A look at motivation, behavior, and characteristics. *FBI Law Enforcement Bulletin, 74*(1), 26–32. DOI: 10.1037/e559082006-004

Burgess, A. W., Hartman, C. R., Ressler, R. K., Douglas, J. E., & McCormack, A. (1986). Sexual homicide: A motivational model. *Journal of Interpersonal Violence, 1*(3), 251–272.

Carmen, E. H., Rieker, P. P., & Mills, T. (1984). Victims of violence and psychiatric illness. *The American Journal of Psychiatry, 141*(3), 378–383. DOI: 10.1176/ajp.141.3.378

Chopin, J., & Beauregard, E. (2021). Patterns of overkill in sexual homicides. *Journal of Criminal Psychology*, *11*(1), 44–58. DOI: 10.1108/JCP-10-2020-0045

Chopin, J., DeLisi, M., & Beauregard, E. (2023). Developmental sequela for sexual homicide: Testing an integrated multi-theoretical model. *Journal of Interpersonal Violence*, *38*(7-8), 5721–5747. DOI: 10.1177/08862605221127199

Deepak, S. A., & Ramdoss, S. (2021). The life-course theory of serial killing: A motivation model. *International Journal of Offender Therapy and Comparative Criminology*, *65*(13-14), 1446–1472. DOI: 10.1177/0306624X20981030

DeFronzo, J., Ditta, A., Hannon, L., & Prochnow, J. (2007). Male serial homicide: The influence of cultural and structural variables. *Homicide Studies*, *11*(1), 3–14. DOI: 10.1177/1088767906297434

DeFronzo, J., & Prochnow, J. (2004). Violent cultural factors and serial homicide by males. *Psychological Reports*, *94*, 104–108. DOI: 10.2466/pr0.94.1.104-108

DeLisi, M., & Beauregard, E. (2018). Adverse childhood experiences and criminal extremity: New evidence for sexual homicide. *Journal of Forensic Sciences*, *63*(2), 484–489. DOI: 10.1111/1556-4029.13584

Dong, M., Anda, R. F., Dube, S. R., Giles, W. H., & Felitti, V. J. (2003). The relationship of exposure to childhood sexual abuse to other forms of abuse, neglect, and household dysfunction during childhood. *Child Abuse & Neglect*, *27*(6), 625–639. DOI: 10.1016/S0145-2134(03)00105-4

Dowdell, E. B., Freitas, E., Owens, A., & Greenle, M. M. (2022). School shooters: Patterns of adverse childhood experiences, bullying, and social media. *Journal of Pediatric Health Care*, *36*(4), 339–346. DOI: 10.1016/j.pedhc.2021.12.004

Duke, N. N., Pettingell, S. L., McMorris, B. J., & Borowsky, I. W. (2010). Adolescent violence perpetration: Associations with multiple types of adverse childhood experiences. *Pediatrics*, *125*(4), e778–e786. DOI: 10.1542/peds.2009-0597

Dutton, D. G., & Hart, S. D. (1992). Evidence for long-term, specific effects of childhood abuse and neglect on criminal behaviour in men. *International Journal of Offender Therapy and Comparative Criminology*, *36*(2), 129–137. DOI: 10.1177/0306624X9203600205

Egger, S. A. (2002). *The killers among us: An examination of serial murder and its investigation*. Prentice Hall.

Felitti, V. J., Anda, R. F., Nordenberg, D., Williamson, D. F., Spitz, A. M., Edwards, V., Koss, M. P., & Marks, J. S. (1998). Relationship of childhood abuse and household dysfunction to many of the leading causes of death in adults: The adverse childhood experiences (ACE) study. *American Journal of Preventive Medicine*, *14*(4), 245–258. DOI: 10.1016/S0749-3797(98)00017-8

Forster, M., Gower, A. L., McMorris, B. J., & Borowsky, I. W. (2020). Adverse childhood experiences and school-based victimization and perpetration. *Journal of Interpersonal Violence*, *35*(3-4), 662–681. DOI: 10.1177/0886260517689885

Gerard, F. J., & Khachatryan, N. (2024). Youth homicide offenders: A review of recent literature. In Burgason, K. A., & DeLisi, M. (Eds.), *Routledge Handbook of Homicide Studies* (pp. 188–213). Routledge., DOI: 10.4324/9781003399476-12

Harrison, M. A., Murphy, E. A., Ho, L. Y., Bowers, T. G., & Flaherty, C. V. (2015). Female serial killers in the United States: Means, motives, and makings. *Journal of Forensic Psychiatry & Psychology*, *26*(3), 383–406. DOI: 10.1080/14789949.2015.1007516

Haslam, D., Mathews, B., Pacella, R., Scott, J. G., Finkelhor, D., Higgins, D. J., Meinck, F., Erskine, H. E., Thomas, H. J., Lawrence, D., & Malacova, E. (2023). *The prevalence and impact of child maltreatment in Australia: Findings from the Australian Child Maltreatment Study: Brief Report*. Australian Maltreatment Study. http://doi.org/DOI: 10.5204/rep.eprints.239397

Heide, K. M. (1999). Youth homicide. In Smith, M. D., & Zahn, M. A. (Eds.), *Studying and preventing homicide: Issues and challenges* (pp. 175–196). Sage Publications.

Heide, K. M., & Solomon, E. P. (2006). Biology, childhood trauma, and murder: Rethinking justice. *International Journal of Law and Psychiatry*, *29*, 220–233. DOI: 10.1016/j.ijlp.2005.10.001

Hickey, E. (1997). *Serial murderers and their victims* (2nd ed.). Wadsworth.

Hickey, E. (2010). *Serial murderers and their victims* (5th ed.). Cengage.

Hickey, E. (2016). *Serial murderers and their victims* (7th ed.). Cengage.

Higgins, D. J., & McCabe, M. P. (2001). Multiple forms of child abuse and neglect: Adult retrospective reports. *Aggression and Violent Behavior*, *6*, 547–578. DOI: 10.1016/S1359-1789(00)00030-6

Homant, R. J., & Kennedy, D. B. (2009). Understanding serial sexual murder: A biopsychosocial approach. In Petherick, W. (Ed.), *Profiling and Serial crime: Theoretical and practical issues* (pp. 341–372). Elsevier.

Jaffe, P., Wolfe, D., Wilson, S., & Zak, L. (1986). Similarities in behavioural and social maladjustment among child victims and witnesses to family violence. *The American Journal of Orthopsychiatry*, *56*(1), 142–146. DOI: 10.1111/j.1939-0025.1986.tb01551.x

Jenkins, P. (1994). *Using murder: The social construction of serial homicide*. Aldine de Gruyter.

Jones, M. S., & Hoffman, J. P. (2024). Adverse childhood experiences and homicide. In Burgason, K. A., & DeLisi, M. (Eds.), *Routledge handbook of homicide* (pp. 349–368). Routledge., DOI: 10.4324/9781003399476-19

Keeney, B. T., & Heide, K. M. (1994). Gender differences in serial murderers: A preliminary analysis. *Journal of Interpersonal Violence*, *9*(3), 383–398. DOI: 10.1177/088626094009003007

Keppel, R. D., & Birnes, W. J. (2003). *The psychology of serial killer investigations: The grisly business unit*. Academic Press.

Knight, Z. G. (2006). Some thoughts on the psychological roots of the behaviour of serial killers as narcissists: An object-relations perspective. *Social Behaviour and Personality: An International Journal*, *34*(10), 1189–1206. DOI: 10.2224/sbp.2006.34.10.1189

Krischer, M. K., Sevecke, K., & Lehmkuhl, G. (2021). Family upbringing: Family factors as predictors for the development of antisocial behaviour and psychopathy dimensions. In A. R. Felthous & H. Sab (Eds.), *The Wiley International Handbook on Psychopathic Disorders and the Law: Volume 1 Diagnosis and Treatment* (2nd ed., pp. 389-402). John Wiley and Sons Ltd.

LaBrode, R. T. (2007). Etiology of the psychopathic serial killer: An analysis of antisocial personality disorder, psychopathy, and serial killer personality and crime scene characteristics. *Brief Treatment and Crisis Intervention*, *7*(2), 151–160. DOI: 10.1093/brief-treatment/mhm004

Leary, T., Southard, L., Hill, J., & Ashman, J. (2017). The Macdonald triad revisited: An empirical assessment of relationships between triadic elements and parental abuse in serial killers. *North American Journal of Psychology*, *19*(3), 627–640.

Levin, J., & Fox, J. A. (2017). Multiple homicide: Understanding serial and mass murder. In F. Brookman., E. R. Maguire & M. Maguire. (Eds.), *The handbook of homicide*, (pp. 249-267). John Wiley & Sons, Incorporated.

Leyton, E. (1986). *Compulsive killers: The story of modern multiple murder*. New York University Press.

Marono, A. J., Reid, S., Yaksic, E., & Keatley, D. A. (2020). A behavior sequence analysis of serial killers' lives: From childhood abuse to methods of murder. *Psychiatry, Psychology, and Law : an Interdisciplinary Journal of the Australian and New Zealand Association of Psychiatry, Psychology and Law*, *27*(1), 126–137. DOI: 10.1080/13218719.2019.1695517

McDermott, B. M. (2004). Child and youth emotional trauma: An explanatory model of adverse outcomes. *Psychiatry, Psychology, and Law : an Interdisciplinary Journal of the Australian and New Zealand Association of Psychiatry, Psychology and Law*, *11*(2), 269–279. DOI: 10.1375/pplt.2004.11.2.269

McKinley, A. (2020). Vulnerability to fatal violence: Child sexual abuse victims as homicide participants in Australia. In Bryce, I., & Petherick, W. (Eds.), *Child Sexual Abuse: Forensic Issues in Evidence* (pp. 351–372). Impact, and Management., DOI: 10.1016/B978-0-12-819434-8.00017-9

Meloy, J. R. (2000). The nature and dynamics of sexual homicide: An integrative review. *Aggression and Violent Behavior*, *5*(1), 1–22. DOI: 10.1016/S1359-1789(99)00006-3

Miller, L. (2000). The predator's brain: Neuropsychodynamics of serial killing. In Schlesinger, L. B. (Ed.), *Serial Offenders: Current though, recent findings* (pp. 135–166). CRC Press.

Miller, L. (2014). Serial killers: II. Development, dynamics, and forensics. *Aggression and Violent Behavior*, *19*(1), 1–11. DOI: 10.1016/j.avb.2013.11.002

Mitchell, H., & Aamodt, M. G. (2005). The incidence of child abuse in serial killers. *Journal of Police and Criminal Psychology*, *20*(1), 40–47. DOI: 10.1007/BF02806705

Morton, R. J., & Hilts, M. A. (Eds.). (2008). *Serial murder: Multi-disciplinary perspectives for investigators*. Federal Bureau of Investigation; Behavioral Analysis Unit-2; National Center for the Analysis of Violent Crimes.

Myers, W. C. (2004). Serial murder by children and adolescents. *Behavioral Sciences & the Law*, *22*(3), 357–374. DOI: 10.1002/bsl.590

Nation, A., Pacella, R., Monks, C., Mathews, B., & Meinck, F. (2023). Prevalence of violence against children in the United Kingdom: A systematic review and meta-analysis. *Child Abuse & Neglect*, *146*, 106518. DOI: 10.1016/j.chiabu.2023.106518

Office for National Statistics. (2020). *Child abuse in England and Wales: March 2020*. ONS. https://www.ons.gov.uk/peoplepopulationandcommunity/crimeandjustice/bulletins/childabuseinenglandandwales/march2020

Paquette, S., Chopin, J., & Fortin, F. (2025). *Online sexual crimes, offenders, and victims: Theory, research, and practice*. Routledge., DOI: 10.4324/9781003512653-8

Pollack, W. S. (2000). *Real boys: Rescuing our sons from the myths of boyhood*. Owl Books.

Prentky, R. A., Burgess, A. W., Hartman, C. R., Lee, A., Rokous, F., Douglas, J. E., & Ressler, R. (1989). The presumptive role of fantasy in serial sexual homicide. *The American Journal of Psychiatry, 146*(7), 887–891. DOI: 10.1176/AJP.146.7.887

Purcell, C., & Arrigo, B. A. (2006). *The psychology of lust murder: Paraphilia, sexual killing, and serial homicide*. Elsevier.

Reid, S., Katan, A., Ellithy, A., Della Stua, R., & Denisov, E. V. (2019). The perfect storm: Mapping the life course trajectories of serial killers. *International Journal of Offender Therapy and Comparative Criminology, 63*(9), 1621–1662. 10.1177%2F0306624X19838683

Ressler, R. K., Burgess, A. W., & Douglas, J. (1988). *Sexual homicide: Patterns and motives*. Free Press.

Ressler, R. K., Burgess, A. W., Douglas, J. E., Hartman, C. R., & D'Agostino, R. B. (1986). Sexual killers and their victims: Identifying patterns through crime scene analysis. *Journal of Interpersonal Violence, 1*(3), 288–308. DOI: 10.1177/088626086001003003

Ressler, R. K., & Shachtman, T. (2002). *Whoever fights monsters*. St. Martins.

Rohner, R. P., Khaleque, A., & Cournoyer, D. E. (2005). Parental acceptance-rejection: Theory, methods, cross-cultural evidence, and implications. *Ethos (Berkeley, Calif.), 33*(3), 299–334. DOI: 10.1525/eth.2005.33.3.299

Royal Commission into Institutional Responses to Child Sexual Abuse. (2017). *Final Report: Impacts* (Vol. 3). Commonwealth of Australia. https://www.childabuseroyalcommission.gov.au/final-report

Schimmenti, A., Carabellese, F. F., & Caretti, V. (2021). Child maltreatment and psychopathy. In A. R. Felthous & H. Sab (Eds.), *The Wiley International Handbook on Psychopathic Disorders and the Law: Volume 1 Diagnosis and Treatment* (2nd ed., pp. 403-419). John Wiley and Sons Ltd.

Schlesinger, L. B. (2000). Serial homicide: Sadism, fantasy and a compulsion to kill. In Schlesinger, L. B. (Ed.), *Serial Offenders: Current though, recent findings* (pp. 3–22). CRC Press.

Smith, C., & Thornberry, T. P. (1995). The relationship between childhood maltreatment and adolescent involvement in delinquency. *Criminology*, *33*(4), 451–481.

Stein, A. (2009). From their cradle to your grave: How child abuse and dissociation drive violent crime. *The Journal of Psychohistory*, *36*(4), 320–327.

Straus, M. A. (1979). Measuring intrafamily conflict and violence: The conflict tactics (CT) scales. *Journal of Marriage and Family*, *41*(1), 75–88. DOI: 10.2307/351733

Strickland, S. M. (2008). Female sex offenders: Exploring issues of personality, trauma, and cognitive distortions. *Journal of Interpersonal Violence*, *23*(4), 474–489. DOI: 10.1177/0886260507312944

Trentham, C. E., Hensley, C., & Policastro, C. (2018). Recurrent childhood animal cruelty and its link to recurrent adult interpersonal violence. *International Journal of Offender Therapy and Comparative Criminology*, *62*(8), 2345–2356. DOI: 10.1177/0306624X17720175

Walker, L. E. (1979). *The battered woman*. Harper & Row.

Weatherby, G. A., Buller, D. M., & McGinnis, K. (2009). The Buller-McGinnis model of serial homicidal behavior: An integrated approach. *Journal of Criminology and Criminal Justice Research & Education*, *3*(1), 1–21.

Webster-Stratton, C. (1985). Comparison of abusive and non-abusive families with conduct-disordered children. *The American Journal of Orthopsychiatry*, *55*(1), 59–69. DOI: 10.1111/j.1939-0025.1985.tb03421.x

Widom, C. S. (1989). The cycle of violence. *Science*, *244*(4901), 160–166.

Widom, C. S., & Maxfield, M. G. (2001). *An update on the "cycle of violence"*. National Institute of Justice. https://nij.ojp.gov/library/publications/update-cycle-violence

Yaksic, E. (2022). *Killer data: Modern perspectives on serial murder*. Routledge.

Yaksic, E., Simkin, M., & Roychowdhury, V. (2021). A statistical study of the time intervals between serial homicides. *Journal of Criminal Justice*, *73*, 101751.

ENDNOTES

1. True consent will not be present where the child either lacks capacity to give consent, or has capacity but does not give full, free, and voluntary consent.

2 The presence of a 'cooling-off period' is a contentious issue in serial homicide. Traditionally it is said to encompass a serial killer returning to their 'normal' lives, however some researchers argue that many serial killers never truly "cool off" (Egger, 2002; Yaksic, 2022; Yaksic et al., 2021)

Chapter 7
Theoretical Insights Into Cumulative Childhood Adversity and Homicide Victimization:
A Conditional Vulnerability Approach

Amber C. McKinley
https://orcid.org/0000-0001-5637-7198
Charles Sturt University, Australia

ABSTRACT

Individuals who experience homicide often have backgrounds marked by extensive childhood adversity—such as abuse, neglect, and household dysfunction—which undermines psychological resilience and support. The CDC-Kaiser ACE Scale provides a tool for quantifying such early trauma, yet research more frequently explores its links to offending than to victimisation. This chapter addresses the gap by reviewing evidence that higher ACE scores elevate the risk of homicide victimisation, examining how overlapping adversities foster psychological vulnerabilities and risky behaviours. Highlighting gradient effects and the conditional vulnerability model, the chapter offers insights into pathways from childhood trauma to fatal outcomes, identifying high-risk populations and discussing crucial implications for prevention, intervention, and policy.

DOI: 10.4018/979-8-3373-9524-1.ch007

INTRODUCTION

Among homicide victims, research consistently identifies several adverse childhood factors as highly prevalent. Notably, physical and emotional abuse, chronic neglect, and repeated exposure to household dysfunction. Such dysfunction often includes parental substance abuse, mental illness, domestic violence, and parental separation or incarceration, all of which contribute to the long-term vulnerability of the individual. Physical abuse and witnessing violence, especially within the home, are amongst the most frequently reported experiences in the backgrounds of homicide victims (Jobe-Shields, Elzy, Swiecicki & Seals, 2017). Sexual abuse and emotional neglect also surface frequently, compounding trauma and diminishing support networks throughout a person's development. Together, these adversities cluster to create cumulative trauma, which not only erodes psychological resilience and healthy attachment, but also heightens susceptibility to violence and risky environments later in life (Burke et al., 2023; Jahic et al., 2021; Laajasalo, Pajunen, Martikainen & Kivivuori, 2025; Malvaso, Day, Delfabbro, Cale, Hackett, Delfabbro & Ross, 2022; Muller, 2019).

For the purposes of this chapter, and within the context of this book, Adverse Childhood Experiences (ACEs) can include:

- Death of a parent or caregiver.
- Emotional (psychological) abuse.
- Emotional neglect.
- Experiencing discrimination or racism.
- Exposure to community violence.
- Having a household member incarcerated.
- Household mental illness.
- Household substance (alcohol or drug) abuse.
- Living in poverty, homelessness, or unstable housing.
- Parental separation or divorce.
- Physical abuse.
- Physical neglect.
- Sexual abuse.
- Witnessing domestic violence.

The CDC-Kaiser Adverse Childhood Experiences (ACE) Scale is a foundational tool in understanding the profound and lasting impact of early life adversity on later health, behaviour, and social outcomes. Developed through a landmark study conducted by Kaiser Permanente in collaboration with the Centers for Disease Control and Prevention from 1995 to 1997, the ACE Scale quantifies exposure to ten categories of childhood trauma that occur before the age of 18. These categories are grouped into three main types: abuse (emotional, physical, sexual), neglect (emotional, physical), and household challenges (domestic violence, parental substance abuse, mental illness, incarceration, and parental separation or divorce) (Centers for Disease Control and Prevention, 2024; Pennsylvania Coalition Against Domestic Violence. (n.d.); Stevens, (n.d.)). Each type of adversity counts as one point, resulting in an individual's ACE score, which can range from zero to ten. The higher the score, the greater the cumulative exposure to adversity.

The cumulative impact of ACEs has been extensively linked to the violent behaviours of adults in later life (Almeida, Silva & Gouveia-Pereira, 2024; Krieg, Murphy & Elliott, 2022; Reiniger & Zemp, 2021). Critically, this phenomenon is not restricted to offenders, consideration must be given to possibility that multiple and cumulative ACEs could also increase the likelihood of an individual becoming the victim of violent crimes, specifically homicide. Current peer-reviewed research primarily establishes that ACEs significantly increase the risk of *perpetrating* violent crime, including homicide (Bauer, Martins, Hammerton, Hoffmann, Cardoso, Colvara, Hartmann, Calegaro, Perrone, Aurélio, Menezes & Murray, 2024), rather than specifically becoming a *victim* of homicide. The evidence base is robust regarding the pathway from ACEs to violent offending, but direct links to homicide victimisation are not well documented in the literature. Therefore, this book chapter will explore the compelling evidence linking cumulative ACEs with an increased risk of homicide victimisation. It will provide an overview of the ACE framework, illustrate how exposure to multiple childhood adversities—such as abuse, neglect, or household dysfunction—may significantly elevate the likelihood of later homicide victimisation.

Drawing on contemporary peer-reviewed studies, the chapter will examine the mechanisms by which repeated or combined early-life trauma can foster psychological vulnerabilities, behavioural maladaptation, and environments that heighten susceptibility to extreme violence. Special attention will be given to gradient effects, where risks for homicide victimisation intensify with each additional ACE, and how these patterns persist even when monitoring for other risk factors. Further, the chapter will utilise *conditional vulnerability theory* to explain the ebb and flow of vulnerabilities. Ultimately, the chapter aims to clarify the pathways connecting childhood trauma to fatal victimisation, highlight population groups at elevated risk, and discuss the broader implications for prevention, intervention, and policy development.

Understanding ACEs in the context of violent outcomes—particularly homicide victimisation—is crucial because ACEs represent foundational risk factors that shape vulnerability to violence across the individuals lifespan. Early exposure to trauma, abuse, neglect, or household dysfunction disrupts healthy emotional, social, and cognitive development, often resulting in maladaptive coping mechanisms, impaired judgement, and difficulty forming safe relationships (Scottish Government, 2018). These pathways elevate the likelihood of entanglement in high-risk situations and contribute to the social and environmental conditions that perpetuate cycles of victimisation. Recognising the profound influence of ACEs enables practitioners, policymakers, and communities to implement targeted screening, trauma-informed care, and holistic prevention strategies—ultimately reducing the burden of violence and breaking the intergenerational transmission of risk associated with homicide victimisation (Anda et al., 2009; Jahic et al., 2021, Jones & Hoffmann, 2024).

ACEs increase the risk of becoming a homicide victim primarily by raising the likelihood of repeated violence victimisation, fostering risky behaviours and environments, and impairing emotional and behavioural regulation. The more ACEs a person experiences, the greater the risk; both directly, through increased exposure to violence, and indirectly, through behavioural and developmental pathways that heighten vulnerability. Growing up in environments where violence is normalised can lead to increased risk of both offending and victimisation, as individuals may be more likely to live in or return to unsafe communities as adults (Freeze, 2019). ACEs can cause neurological, psychological, and biological changes that affect impulse control, emotional regulation, and stress responses (Joshi & Truong, 2025). These changes can increase the likelihood of engaging in risky behaviours or forming relationships and associations that elevate exposure to violence (Joshi & Truong, 2025).

Individuals who score high ACEs may have difficulties avoiding dangerous situations or may be more likely to be involved in high-risk social networks, both of which can increase the risk of violent victimisation. ACEs are more prevalent among individuals from disadvantaged backgrounds, who are also statistically at higher risk for being victims of violent crime (Luby, Baram, Rogers & Barch, 2021). Further, clustering ACEs and socioeconomic disadvantage can lead to cycles of violence within communities, increasing the overall risk of homicide victimisation exposure for all residents, including those with a history of ACEs.

THEORETICAL FRAMEWORK

Victimological theories seek to understand the causes, patterns, and consequences of victimisation, examining how and why certain individuals or groups become victims of crime. These theories explore factors such as social, psychological, and situational dynamics, highlighting the roles of victim behaviour, offender motivation, and broader societal structures in shaping experiences of victimisation. By highlighting these complexities, victimological theories provide a critical foundation for effective crime prevention, victim support, and the advancement of justice policy.

The following six theories are the most significant for victimology:

1. Biopsychosocial theory (Engel, 1977)
2. Deviant Place (Stark, 1987).
3. Lifestyle theory (Hindelang et al., 1978) updated to Schreck's self-control theory in 1999.
4. Propinquity effect (Festinger et al., 1950).
5. Routine Activity theory (Cohen & Felson, 1979).
6. Victim Precipitation theory (Wolfgang, 1957), superseded by Herman (1992) trauma theory.

All these victimological theories share a focus on how individual characteristics, behaviours, and daily circumstances interact with environmental and situational factors to influence one's risk of crime victimisation. Whether emphasising personal psychology and biology (biopsychosocial theory), the role of proximity and exposure to potential offenders (propinquity effect), how victims might actively or passively contribute to their own victimisation (trauma theory), or how personal routines, lifestyles, and the environments frequented shape vulnerability (self-control, routine activity, and deviant place theories), each framework illustrates that victimisation is not solely a random event. Instead, these theories argue that victimisation often arises from a convergence of personal, social, and environmental elements—in which the potential victim's actions, associations, and surroundings increase their risk. Collectively, they underscore the importance of a holistic perspective that accounts for both the choices individuals make and the broader contexts in which they live, while cautioning against attributing blame to victims (Hannis, 2015; Siegel, 2017; Walsh, 2019).

Building on this, the concept of "Conditional Vulnerability" (CV) emerged to address the limitations of single-theory explanations by highlighting the complex interplay between individual agency and the situational or contextual factors that shape victimisation. CV was developed by McKinley (2024) in response to the inability of any one criminological theory to fully describe how a person becomes a victim across certain situations and contexts. Moreover, the individual theories did not fully explain the nuances of the different crime typologies. Therefore, the theoretical basis for CV is building upon the biopsychosocial theory (Engels, 1977) informed by and drawing upon five prominent and well-established criminological theories. The following sections will provide a brief explanation of each of the theories upon which conditional vulnerability theory is based.

1. **Biopsychosocial theory (Engel, 1977)** posits that health/illness are understood via the interplay of biological, psychological, and social factors[1].
2. **Deviant place theory (Stark, 1987)** argues that certain urban neighbourhoods persistently exhibit high crime rates not because of the types of people who live there, but due to specific ecological and structural characteristics of the place itself. Stark (1987) identifies five key traits: high population density, poverty, mixed land use (residential and commercial), transience (rapid turnover of residents), and dilapidation. These conditions foster social disorganisation, reduce effective social control, and increase opportunities and motivations for deviance[2].
3. **Self-control theory (Schreck, 1999)** expanding on the original *Lifestyle exposure theory* (Hindelang, Gottfredson, and Garofalo, 1978), positing that low self-control is a key cause of exposure to risky situations and lifestyle choices that heighten victimization risk. The theory posits that these risky behaviors are rooted in a general tendency to pursue immediate gratification with little regard for long-term consequences, mirroring the logic of self-control theory's explanation of criminal behavior. While Gottfredson and Hirschi's *General Theory of Crime* (1990) focused mainly on offending, Schreck systematically argued that these same traits predispose individuals to become crime victims because their impulsivity and riskiness lead them into dangerous environments and associations.
4. **The Propinquity Theory (Festinger, Schachter and Back, 1950)** posits that physical and psychological proximity—or frequent, close contact—significantly increases the likelihood of relationships forming, as familiarity and such encounters breed intimacy and trust.
5. **Routine Activities Theory (RAT) (Cohen and Felson, 1979)** explains crime as a situational event requiring three key elements to converge in time and space: a motivated offender, a suitable target, and the absence of a capable guardian[3].
6. **Trauma Theory (Herman, 1992)** - due to the age and related controversies associated with Wolfgang's *victim precipitation theory* that holds that in certain crimes, especially violent ones like homicide, the victim plays an active role by initiating or provoking the criminal act[4]; the conditional vulnerability theory has altered to include the more victim-centric trauma theory. Herman's (1992) trauma theory explicates the pathways between adverse experiences and lethal violence exposure. Individuals with complex trauma histories demonstrate heightened vulnerability to homicide victimization through impaired risk assessment, maladaptive relationship patterns, and compromised safety-seeking behaviours.

CONDITIONAL VULNERABILITY

Conditional vulnerability as a theory illustrates that victimisation risk is not caused by a single factor but is multifaceted and complex. CV aims to describe an individual's risk of victimisation based on the notion that the more interaction between specific factors, the more vulnerable a person becomes. This theory describes the range of internal and external factors that can contribute to a person's risk of harm and suggests these factors are dynamic. CV explains cumulative ACEs and homicide victimisation by illustrating how biological vulnerabilities (e.g., stress reactivity), psychological impacts (e.g., maladaptive coping, trauma symptoms), and social factors (e.g., family dysfunction, community violence) interact to heighten risk.

The relationship between ACEs and violence is thought to be mediated by neurological, psychological, and biological changes resulting from prolonged exposure to stressors during critical developmental periods (Herzog & Schmahl, 2018). ACEs can lead to behavioural changes (such as increased risk-taking or difficulty forming healthy relationships) and social circumstances (such as ongoing deliberate exposure to unsafe environments), both of which contribute to a higher risk of adult sexual victimisation (Hughes et al, 2017). Chronic stress and trauma from ACEs can alter brain development, emotional regulation, and stress responses, making individuals more vulnerable to further victimisations (Hughes et al, 2017; Su & Stone, 2020).

Multiple ACEs disrupt development across these domains, increasing impulsivity, emotional dysregulation, and exposure to unsafe environments, thus elevating vulnerability to lethal violence. Additionally, cumulative ACEs—often concentrated in such environments—heighten homicide victimisation risk: for example: children repeatedly exposed to unsafe, stressful, and violent surroundings experience multiple adversities that cumulatively increase their vulnerability to becoming victims of violence, including homicide, due to constant proximity to danger and weakened protective social structures, as originally described by Stark (1987).

Further, children exposed to repeated adversity often adopt high-risk lifestyles, such as associating with violent peers, living in unsafe environments, or lacking guardianship, which elevate their likelihood of encountering dangerous situations and, consequently, homicide victimisation (Schreck, 1999). Thus, cumulative ACEs shape vulnerable lifestyles that increase both exposure to and risk of lethal violence. Proximity and frequent exposure to adversity increase the odds of forming risky or dangerous relationships, perpetuating intergenerational cycles of violence and vulnerability, especially in environments where protective factors are absent or weakened.

Moreover, propinquity provides a social-psychological lens for understanding how cumulative ACEs can translate into increased homicide victimisation risk. Propinquity can explain why children exposed to multiple adversities might be at higher risk. Individuals raised in environments with high propinquity to violence, neglect, or other adverse circumstances are continuously exposed to interpersonal relationships marked by abuse, trauma, or crime (Holt, Buckley & Whelan, 2008). Dense proximity to harmful individuals or situations—often shaped by family structure, neighbourhood environments, or peer associations—can normalise or reinforce violent behaviours, heightening risk for both perpetration and victimisation of crimes including homicide (Foell, Pitzer, Nebbitt, Lombe, Yu, Villodas & Newransky, 2021).

Additionally, elements specific to the Routine Activities Theory, explains cumulative ACEs and homicide victimisation by highlighting how ACEs can increase exposure to risky environments, weaken protective guardianship, and make individuals more likely targets for violence. Children with repeated ACEs may develop daily routines or social patterns—such as unsupervised activity and associating with high-risk peers—that heighten their vulnerability to potential offenders, fulfilling the theory's triad (motivated offender, suitable target, lack of capable guardianship) and thus elevating homicide victimisation risk.

Finally, Herman's (1992) trauma theory provides a contemporary psychological framework that complements and moves on from Wolfgang's (1957) victim precipitation theory by explaining the underlying mechanisms that create vulnerability to homicide victimization. While Wolfgang identified behavioral patterns in victim-precipitated homicides—such as initiating physical altercations—Herman's (1992) work elucidates how traumatic experiences fundamentally alter neurobiological and psychological functioning, potentially increasing impulsive, aggressive, or risk-taking behaviors that Wolfgang observed. Trauma theory reframes victim precipitation through a lens of psychological sequelae rather than personal culpability, suggesting that prior victimization experiences may create hypervigilance, emotional dysregulation, and maladaptive coping strategies that inadvertently increase exposure to dangerous situations. This theoretical integration transforms Wolfgang's descriptive observations into a more nuanced understanding of how cumulative trauma creates pathways to lethal victimization without attributing blame to victims.

THE EPIDEMIOLOGY OF HOMICIDE VICTIMISATION

Homicide victimisation displays substantial variation across age, gender, ethnicity, and social class, shaped by global, regional, and local dynamics—and deeply influenced by intersectional factors that define high-risk groups. Globally, the overall homicide rate varies significantly by region. The Americas[5] have the highest rate, at about 17.2 victims per 100,000 population, notably higher than Africa (13.0) and Europe (3.0) (United Nations Office on Drugs and Crime, 2023). Patterns indicate that homicide overwhelmingly affects younger populations and males: about 77.7%

of US homicide victims from 2000 to 2019 were male, and 69.8% were aged 15 to 44 (GBD US Health Disparities Collaborators, 2025).

Related to the US homicide rates, the highest homicide rates are concentrated among males of colour aged 15–24 (74.6 per 100,000) and 25–44 (70.0 per 100,000), and among American Indian and Alaska Native males in the same age brackets. Among females, American Indian or Alaska Native women aged 25–44 and women of colour aged 15–44 also face disproportionately high rates (GBD US Health Disparities Collaborators, 2025).

Social class and neighbourhood deprivation play significant roles, as homicide rates are persistently higher in communities marked by poverty, disadvantage, and social exclusion (Fabio, Tu, Loeber & Cohen, 2011; Gjelsvik, Zierler, Blume & Nie, 2004; Mohammadi & Ceccato, 2022). Firearms remain the leading method of homicide in most high-rate regions, such as the Americas, exacerbating risks in marginalised localities (Hart, 2015). From an intersectional perspective, risk is not uniform but layered, shaped by the convergence of race, gender, class, and social marginalisation. Men of colour are at the greatest risk for both chronic and acute victimisation, but women of colour including Indigenous women often face persistent, and sometimes rising, chronic victimisation across their lives (Semenza, Testa & Jackson, 2022). Structural inequalities, including historical racism, restricted access to support systems, and stereotypes that criminalise or marginalise minorities, further concentrate victimisation risk in these groups (Egede, 2023).

Research consistently demonstrates significant gender-based disparities in both the exposure to and consequences of ACEs, with differential pathways to violent outcomes including femicide and homicide. Females report substantially higher rates of childhood adversity, with 39% of females experiencing multiple ACEs compared to 21% of males and demonstrate more complex patterns of childhood trauma characterised by increased likelihood of sexual abuse, physical neglect, and dysfunctional family environments (Lu et al., 2023). This heightened exposure to ACEs creates distinct vulnerability patterns, with females experiencing significantly stronger associations between childhood trauma and subsequent violent behaviour than their male counterparts.

The relationship between cumulative ACEs and female homicide victimisation represents a critical yet underexplored area within victimology research. Emerging evidence demonstrates that women exhibit more complex patterns of childhood adversity than men, with these experiences creating distinct pathways to later victimisation (Burke et al., 2023). Zhu, Exner-Cortens, Dobson, Wells, Noel & Madigan (2024) presented in their meta-analytic research confirms that ACEs are positively associated with intimate partner violence (IPV) victimization among women ($r = .20$), with dose-response relationships indicating that each additional ACE increases vulnerability.

Women experiencing eight or more ACEs are 3.5 times more likely to experience adult IPV victimisation, while cumulative ACE scores significantly predict both physical and sexual IPV victimization (aOR = 1.43) (Cprek et al., 2021). Burke et al. (2022) identified that women are more negatively impacted by ACEs than men, with pathways to violent victimisation mediated through prior victimization experiences, mental illness, and substance use disorders. Similarly, Kubiak et al. (2017) found that childhood adversity's effects on violence among women were mediated by victimization, mental illness, substance use, and anger expression, rather than through direct pathways.

Research with incarcerated populations reveals that 94% of women who used violence experienced at least one childhood adversity, suggesting cumulative trauma creates vulnerability to both victimisation and violent contexts (Fischer et al., 2024). These findings underscore the necessity for trauma-informed interventions that address the complex interplay between childhood adversity and women's heightened risk for lethal victimisation.

ACES AND GIRLS' VULNERABILITY TO HOMICIDE AND FEMICIDE: A GLOBAL PERSPECTIVE

ACEs create complex pathways that significantly increase a girls' vulnerability to homicide and femicide victimization. Research demonstrates that females experience more severe long-term consequences from childhood trauma than males, with these effects extending to violent crime victimization (Thompson et al., 2004). The relationship between ACEs and violence follows a dose-response pattern, where cumulative childhood adversities exponentially increased risk for future victimization and violence involvement (Anda et al., 2006).

Studies reveal that girls with multiple ACEs face heightened vulnerability to violence perpetration and victimization (Zuo et al., 2021). In China, sex-stratified analyses indicate that girls were more vulnerable to the negative effects of ACEs, with higher risks of perpetration among those exposed to distinctive subtypes or multiple adversities (Zuo et al., 2021). This vulnerability extends to intimate partner violence, where women with childhood histories of severe maltreatment combined with household dysfunction demonstrate elevated odds of adult victimization (Negriff, 2019).

Global South perspectives highlight unique cultural and structural factors. In sub-Saharan Africa, 72% of females experience at least one ACE, with physical violence affecting 36.5% of girls (Amene et al., 2024). Research from Cambodia demonstrates how gendered social scripts legitimize violence against women and children, creating environments where ACEs normalize male aggression and female subordination (Miedema et al., 2023). Similarly, studies from Pakistan reveal that 58% of women experienced childhood adversity, with home violence being the most prevalent form (Chung et al., 2023).

The femicide epidemic in Latin America exemplifies these dynamics, where countries like El Salvador and Guatemala maintain the highest global femicide rates (Trejo et al., 2024). These patterns underscore the critical need for gender-sensitive interventions addressing both individual trauma histories and broader structural inequalities that perpetuate violence against women and girls (Ullman et al., 2025).

In the Pacific region, women and girls with multiple adverse childhood experiences (ACEs) face significantly heightened vulnerability to both violence perpetration and victimization. Research examining Pacific populations reveals alarmingly high rates of childhood trauma exposure, with up to 84% of women in Bougainville, Papua New Guinea reporting childhood trauma experiences (Fulu et al., 2017). A latent class analysis of young Cambodian women identified that 17% experienced combined physical, sexual, and emotional abuse during childhood, and these women demonstrated substantially elevated risks for both perpetrating and experiencing intimate partner violence (IPV) in adulthood compared to those with low ACE exposure. This bidirectional relationship between cumulative childhood adversity and adult violence is further evidenced across Pacific Island nations, where women experiencing IPV are significantly more likely to have histories of childhood sexual abuse, witnessed maternal abuse, or experienced multiple forms of childhood maltreatment. The structural pathways between childhood trauma and violence against women reveal an intergenerational cycle whereby multiple ACEs create compounding effects that fuel both victimization and subsequent perpetration of violence. In contexts where baseline rates of intimate partner violence already reach 60-68% across Kiribati, Fiji, Solomon Islands, and Vanuatu, the cumulative burden of multiple childhood adversities amplifies women's and girls' vulnerability within already high-risk environments, underscoring the critical need for integrated violence prevention approaches that address childhood trauma exposure (Miedema, Le, Chiang, Ngann & Shortt, 2023; Secretariat of the Pacific Community, n.d.).

Research from the Oceania region reveals that girls experiencing multiple adverse childhood experiences (ACEs) demonstrate heightened vulnerability to both violence victimization and perpetration. In a Shanghai-based study examining early adolescents, sex-stratified analyses indicated girls were significantly more vulnerable to violence perpetration when exposed to distinctive ACE subtypes or multiple adversities. Girls with high ACE exposure demonstrated an adjusted odds ratio of 11.95 for perpetration compared to those with low exposure, while no significant correlation was found among boys (Fischer et al., 2024). Furthermore, girls experiencing multiple ACEs faced dramatically elevated risks of becoming victim-perpetrators, with those exposed to high levels of adversity showing 35 times greater odds compared to girls with minimal ACE exposure. Australian research on incarcerated women corroborates this pattern, demonstrating that 94% reported experiencing at least one childhood adversity, with a median of six ACEs, and an association between increased ACE scores and subsequent intimate partner violence victimization and perpetration. The cumulative effects were particularly pronounced among girls, who exhibited greater vulnerability to negative ACE effects through developing attachment difficulties, poor emotional regulation, and diminished trust, making them susceptible to violence involvement. These findings underscore the critical need for gender-responsive interventions addressing childhood trauma in Pacific populations (Zuo, Zhang, Yan, Lian, Yu, Tu, & Lou, 2021).

REVIEW OF KEY STUDIES LINKING CUMULATIVE ACES TO INCREASED HOMICIDE VICTIMISATION RISK

As previously stated, a growing body of research has demonstrated a robust association between cumulative ACEs and an increased risk of homicide victimisation (Bauer, et al., 2024; Hughes, et al., 2017; Silva et al., 2024). Key studies have consistently found that individuals exposed to a higher number of ACEs—such as physical, emotional, or sexual abuse, neglect, and family dysfunction—are at significantly elevated risk for both perpetration and victimisation of severe violence, including homicide (Anda et al., 2006; DeLisi & Beauregard, 2018; Mathews et al., 2023). Data from large cohorts, including adjudicated delinquents and high-risk youth, underscore a notable graded or dose-response relationship: with each additional ACE, the likelihood of involvement in serious violence—including homicide—rises substantially (DeLisi & Beauregard, 2018; Jahic et al., 2021; Muller, 2019; Pessoa & Almeida, 2024). For example, a large-scale analysis reported that each extra traumatic experience increased the odds of serious, violent, and chronic delinquency by 35%, with some forms of adversity—such as exposure to household violence, incarcerated family members, or severe physical abuse—showing the strongest correlations to violent offending and victimisation (DeLisi & Beauregard, 2018; Jahic et al., 2021).

Exposure to ACEs can diminish an individual's ability to recognise risk, limit coping mechanisms, and increase susceptibility to dangerous interpersonal situations, thereby escalating their risk of becoming homicide victims. There is also evidence that family members in households with high ACEs scores face increased risks of premature death, including homicide, further supporting the intergenerational impact of adversity (Anda et al., 2009). It is important to note, however, that while the cumulative burden of ACEs strongly predicts increased risk, not all individuals with high ACEs experience later violence, and the pathway from childhood adversity to lethal outcomes is often indirect, mediated by subsequent trauma, poverty, and community context (Jones & Hoffmann, 2024; Malvaso et.al, 2022).

DOSE-RESPONSE RELATIONSHIPS: HOW RISK ESCALATES WITH MORE ACES

Cumulative risk models explain increased vulnerability with multiple ACEs by demonstrating a dose-response relationship: as the number of adverse experiences rises, so does the risk for negative outcomes, regardless of the specific type of adversity. These models treat each additional ACE as incrementally increasing vulnerability, capturing the compounded impact of multiple traumas or stressors. This accumulation overwhelms coping mechanisms, heightens emotional and behavioural difficulties, and leads to a greater likelihood of later health, social, and behavioural problems, including violence and victimisation, compared to experiencing a single adversity. Thus, cumulative risk models highlight that the total burden of adversity is a key driver of greater lifelong risk (Hales et al., 2023; LaNoue et al., 2020; Wiens et al., 2020).

The original CDC-Kaiser study and subsequent research has shown that ACEs are common—almost two-thirds of participants reported at least one ACE, and over one in five reported three or more—but they also tend to cluster, with many individuals experiencing multiple forms of adversity (Massachusetts Association for Mental Health. (n.d.); Pennsylvania Coalition Against Domestic Violence. (n.d.)). This clustering is crucial, as the cumulative effect, rather than any single event, is most predictive of long-term harm.

This pattern of clustering not only amplifies the overall risk of adverse outcomes but also creates complex pathways in which multiple adversities interact, often compounding their effects over time. As a result, the cumulative burden of ACEs intersects with a range of mediating factors that can shape the likelihood and nature of long-term consequences—including the emergence of substance use, criminal involvement, and mental health issues.

Mediating factors such as substance use, criminal involvement, and mental health play a critical role in the pathway from cumulative ACEs to homicide victimisation. Individuals exposed to multiple ACEs are more likely to develop substance use problems, which not only increase the risk for risky behaviours and association with criminogenic environments but also heighten the probability of involvement in violence, either as perpetrators or victims (Douglas et al., 2010; Mongan et al., 2025).

Mental health disorders—especially depression, Post Traumatic Stress Disorder (PTSD) and other psychiatric conditions—are common consequences of cumulative ACEs and can further mediate the relationship by exacerbating vulnerability to victimisation and impairing decision-making or coping strategies (Burke et al., 2023; Day et al., 2013; He et al., 2022; Muller, 2019). Additionally, early criminal involvement and the development of aggressive or antisocial behaviours serve as mediators; exposure to childhood trauma and dysfunction raises the risk for later criminality, which in turn increases the likelihood of both offending and violent victimisation, including homicide (Burke et al., 2023; Doelman et al., 2023; Muller, 2019). These mediating mechanisms highlight the complex, multifaceted ways in which the effects of childhood adversity can elevate the risk of deadly victimisation throughout the life course.

MECHANISMS LINKING ACES TO HOMICIDE VICTIMISATION

ACEs are linked to homicide victimisation through multiple interrelated mechanisms, beginning with biological effects. Traumatic and chronic stress in childhood, such as abuse or neglect, disrupts healthy brain development and the stress response system. This can alter brain structure—impacting areas involved in emotion regulation, impulse control, and threat perception—and cause persistent changes in hormonal stress responses, particularly the hypothalamic-pituitary-adrenal (HPA) axis and cortisol levels (Barboza Solís et al., 2015). As a result, individuals with high ACE exposure may develop diminished emotional regulation, increased impulsivity, and an exaggerated physiological response to stress, all of which raise the risk of aggressive behaviour and difficulties in conflict de-escalation, subsequently heightening victimisation in violent settings (Burke et al., 2023; Herzog & Schmahl, 2018).

Further, intergenerational transmission of trauma plays a crucial role: children raised in environments marked by violence, neglect, or trauma are more likely to experience and perpetrate violence themselves, creating a cycle that perpetuates across generations (Hashemi, Fanslow, Gulliver & McIntosh, 2022; Reese, Chang, Zauszniewski & Brown, 2022). This process involves both learned behaviours (whereby violence is modelled and normalised) and the cascading impact of untreated trauma, which can manifest as poor emotional regulation, substance abuse, and involvement with the justice system.

Additionally, cumulative exposure to ACEs further amplifies these risks, as multiple, intersecting adversities (e.g., witnessing domestic violence, parental substance misuse, and direct abuse) have an additive effect, intensifying behavioural and psychological vulnerabilities that increase homicide victimisation and perpetuate violence from one generation to the next (Burke et al, 2023; Joshi & Truong, 2025; Keynejad & Howard, 2025).

PROTECTIVE FACTORS AND RESILIENCE

Despite high exposure to ACEs, several factors can mitigate the risk of later homicide victimisation. Research highlights the critical protective influence of positive childhood experiences, such as supportive adult relationships, strong peer or school connections, safe neighbourhoods, and family resilience. These positive factors not only promote emotional wellbeing but can break cycles of trauma by fostering resilience. The presence of such supportive relationships has been consistently linked to reduced engagement in risky behaviours—including violence and substance misuse—among individuals with high ACE exposure, thus lowering their risk of becoming homicide victims (Almeida et.al, 2024; Bellis et al., 2017; Emerging Minds, n.d.; Suh, Gallaway & Celaya, 2024).

Supportive adults play a pivotal role in buffering the negative impact of ACEs. Trusted relationships with caregivers, mentors, or other caring adults can foster a sense of security and trust, promote healthy coping strategies, and model non-violent conflict resolution. Studies have found that even one caring adult can significantly decrease the adoption of harmful behaviours and improve mental health outcomes. School connectedness and strong peer support further amplify these benefits, strengthening emotional regulation and social skills that help prevent involvement in violent situations (Bellis et.al., 2017; Suh et.al., 2024).

Community resources, such as accessible after-school programs, mental health services, and safe recreational spaces, also act as protective buffers. These resources give young people opportunities to build skills, develop positive relationships, and access support networks beyond their immediate family. Trauma-informed approaches within these community services are especially beneficial: providers trained to recognise and respond to histories of trauma can help young people process their experiences, avoid re-traumatisation, and redirect behaviours that arise from adverse backgrounds. Access to transportation and the availability of relevant services have been found to significantly mitigate the disadvantage associated with high ACE loads (Blair, Marryat & Frank, 2019; Joshi & Truong, 2025; Lopez-Tamayo et al., 2022)

Successful intervention programs include trauma-informed care initiatives, mentoring schemes, and community-based prevention models. Notable examples are after-school activities that focus on social-emotional learning, volunteer opportunities that foster engagement, and family resilience-building programs. Parenting interventions that reduce child maltreatment and support positive attachment have demonstrated success in lowering antisocial and violent behaviours. These approaches, backed by evidence, show that even for those with cumulative ACE exposure, strengthening protective factors at individual, relational, and community levels can meaningfully reduce the risk of homicide victimisation and promote safer, healthier trajectories

(Campbell, Fernando, Gassner, Hill, Seidler & Summers, 2024; Emerging Minds, n.d.; Scottish Government, 2018; yourtown, 2023).

POLICY AND PRACTICE IMPLICATIONS

Cumulative ACEs play a significant role in increased homicide victimisation risk, stressing the vital need for prevention-focused policies. Early screening for ACEs allows for prompt intervention before trauma manifests as mental or behavioural health issues or increases vulnerability to violence (Silva et al., 2024). Universal screening in clinical and community settings aids in identifying at-risk children and connecting them to timely support, improving clinical decision-making and helping prevent negative long-term health and safety outcomes. These screenings are not only diagnostic but act as critical entry points for positive interventions, especially when paired with the promotion of positive childhood experiences to foster resilience (ACEs Aware, 2021; Kistin & Brotanek, 2022).

Trauma-informed care is an essential practice implication derived from understanding the impact of cumulative ACEs. Practitioners in health, education, and justice sectors must recognise trauma's pervasive effects, responding with sensitivity to avoid re-traumatisation and address the unique needs of affected individuals. Training staff in trauma-informed care principles—such as establishing safety, building trust, and collaborating with patients—ensures services are empathetic and culturally responsive. This approach is particularly important for children and adolescents exhibiting violence or behavioural dysregulation as trauma coping mechanisms, where building lasting trust and rapport is crucial for any intervention's success (Huang et al., 2019; National University, n.d.).

Support systems and cross-sector coordination are key for effective prevention and intervention. Early interventions, such as creating safe environments, providing cross-sector support (e.g., case management and multidisciplinary teams), and implementing wraparound models, have demonstrated improvements for at-risk children. Justice, health, and social service systems should collaborate to develop universal and targeted interventions informed by ACE screening (Walker & Matarese, 2011). This might involve mental health and substance use screening at all juvenile justice intercepts, along with coordinated care planning involving families, schools, and community organisations. Special focus must be given to disproportionately impacted populations, ensuring culturally tailored, relationship-based services that span the family, school, and wider community contexts.

Addis (2021) argues that at the community and societal level, comprehensive approaches are required. Community-based interventions that build collective resilience—such as mentoring, after-school programs, and family resource hubs—

strengthen protective factors and mitigate immediate harm from ACEs. Societal strategies should aim to address root causes by strengthening family economic supports, promoting positive social norms, supporting parent and youth skill-building, and intervening early through high-quality childcare and home visitation programs. Policy reforms aimed at justice, health, and social systems must seek to reduce inequities and foster safe, stable, nurturing relationships and environments, as these are fundamental to breaking the cycle connecting ACEs to violence, including homicide victimisation (Addis, 2021).

FUTURE DIRECTIONS AND RESEARCH GAPS

Future research on the relationship between cumulative ACEs and homicide victimisation must prioritise longitudinal and cross-cultural studies. Additionally, most ACEs research has focused on Western samples. Expanding to low- and middle-income countries will shed light on how cultural, social, and economic contexts shape both the prevalence of ACEs and their later outcomes, as evidence suggests patterns of exposure and impact differ significantly by country, gender, and socioeconomic status. Integrating diverse international samples and socio-cultural variables will enable the development of more globally relevant models of risk and resiliency.

Future investigation should also clarify how poly-victimisation and exposure (versus direct victimisation) contribute differently to risk pathways and develop culturally sensitive and nuanced tools to enable targeted intervention. Overall, the field needs methodological innovation and broader sampling frames to answer crucial questions about how, when, and for whom ACEs amplify the risk of homicide.

CONCLUSION

While studies consistently show that ACEs increase the risk of violent *behaviour* and criminal justice involvement, they also note that individuals with high ACEs are more likely to be exposed to violence in adulthood (Edalati & Nicholls, 2017; Graf et al., 2021; Ogilvie et al., 2022; Saxena & Messina, 2021). This increased exposure logically extends to a higher risk of serious victimisation, including homicide, though direct statistical evidence is lacking in current research. Extant research suggests that as ACE scores increase, so does the risk of negative health and social outcomes, including premature mortality, which may include homicide among other causes (Brown et al., 2009; Campbell et al., 2016; Fox et al., 2015; Yu et al., 2022).

In conclusion, growing evidence underscores the profound connection between cumulative Adverse Childhood Experiences (ACEs) and the heightened risk of homicide victimisation. Research demonstrates that each additional ACE not only compounds an individual's risk of exposure to violence but also interacts with other social determinants—such as poverty, discrimination, and systemic inequality—to further intensify vulnerability. This graded, dose-response relationship makes clear that the impacts of early adversity are both profound and far-reaching, shaping neurodevelopment, psychological wellbeing, and behavioural patterns in ways that echo across the lifespan. The clustering of ACEs, alongside other risk factors like community violence and chronic stress, amplifies the pathways through which cycles of trauma and lethal violence are perpetuated across generations.

Addressing these complex realities demands a truly multidisciplinary approach. Effective prevention must bridge disciplines, integrating insights from public health, law enforcement, education, social work, mental health, and community organisations. Interventions should move beyond the individual to confront the systemic and structural forces that cluster and magnify risk—advocating for policies that address inequality, invest in trauma-informed care, and bolster protective factors in families and communities. Collaborative, culturally-informed strategies are essential, with a priority placed on supporting marginalised populations who most acutely bear the burden of cumulative adversity.

REFERENCES

Addis, S. (2021). What Works to Prevent Adverse Childhood Experiences (ACEs) at the Community Level? An Evidence Review and Mapping Exercise – Executive Summary. *Public Health Wales* https://phwwhocc.co.uk/wp-content/uploads/2022/02/What-Works-to-Prevent-ACEs-at-the-Community-Level.-An-Evidence-Review-Mapping-Exercise-Executive-Summary.pdf

Almeida, T. C., Cardoso, J., Matos, A. F., Murça, A., & Cunha, O. (2024). Adverse childhood experiences and aggression in adulthood: The moderating role of positive childhood experiences. *Child Abuse & Neglect*, *154*, 106929.

Almeida, T. C., Silva, C. C., & Gouveia-Pereira, M. (2024). Adverse childhood experiences and aggression in adulthood. *Children and Youth Services Review*, *157*, 107530. DOI: 10.1016/j.childyouth.2024.107530sciencedirect

Amene, E. W., Tao, G., Okello, F., Finlay, J. E., Babalola, S., & Vandevanter, N. (2024). Prevalence of Adverse Childhood Experiences in sub-Saharan Africa: A multicountry analysis of the Violence Against Children and Youth Surveys. *Child Abuse & Neglect*, *155*, 106778. DOI: 10.1016/j.chiabu.2023.106778

Anda, RF, Dong M, Brown DW, Felitti VJ, Giles WH, Perry GS, Valerie EJ, Dube SR. (2009). The relationship of adverse childhood experiences to a history of premature death of family members. BMC Public Health. Apr 16; 9:106. doi: . PMID: 19371414; PMCID: PMC2674602.DOI: 10.1186/1471-2458-9-106

Anda, R. F., Felitti, V. J., Bremner, J. D., Walker, J. D., Whitfield, C. H., Perry, B. D., & Giles, W. H. (2006). The enduring effects of abuse and related adverse experiences in childhood: A convergence of evidence from neurobiology and epidemiology. *European Archives of Psychiatry and Clinical Neuroscience*, *256*(3), 174–186.

Barboza Solís, C., Kelly-Irving, M., Fantin, R., Darnaudéry, M., Torrisani, J., Lang, T., & Delpierre, C. (2015). Adverse childhood experiences and physiological wear-and-tear in midlife: Findings from the 1958 British birth cohort. *Proceedings of the National Academy of Sciences of the United States of America*, *112*(7), E738–E746.

Bauer, A., Martins, R. C., Hammerton, G., Hoffmann, M. S., Cardoso, A. S., Colvara, C., Hartmann, C. F., Calegaro, G., Perrone, L. R., Aurélio, N., Menezes, A. M. B., & Murray, J. (2024, April). Adverse childhood experiences and crime outcomes in early adulthood: A multi-method approach in a Brazilian birth cohort. *Psychiatry Research*, *334*, 115809. https://pmc.ncbi.nlm.nih.gov/articles/PMC10985840/. DOI: 10.1016/j.psychres.2024.115809

Bellis, M. A., Hardcastle, K., Ford, K., Hughes, K., Ashton, K., Quigg, Z., & Butler, N. (2017, March 23). Does continuous trusted adult support in childhood impart life-course resilience against adverse childhood experiences - a retrospective study on adult health-harming behaviours and mental well-being. [Erratum in: BMC Psychiatry. 2017 Apr 13;17] [1] [:140. doi: 10.1186/s12888-017-1305-3. PMID: 28335746; PMCID: PMC5364707]. *BMC Psychiatry*, *17*(1), 110. DOI: 10.1186/s12888-017-1260-z

Blair, A., Marryat, L., & Frank, J. (2019). How community resources mitigate the association between household poverty and the incidence of adverse childhood experiences. *International Journal of Public Health*, *64*(7), 1059–1068. DOI: 10.1007/s00038-019-01258-5

Brown, D. W., Anda, R. F., Tiemeier, H., Felitti, V. J., Edwards, V., Croft, J. B., & Giles, W. H. (2009). Adverse childhood experiences and the risk of premature mortality. *American Journal of Preventive Medicine*, *37*(5), 389–396. DOI: 10.1016/j.amepre.2009.06.021library.csp+1

Burke, C., Conn, B. M., Sutter, M., Willmott, J. A., & Chandler, J. (2022). Adverse childhood experiences and pathways to violent reoffending. *Criminal Justice and Behavior*, *49*(8), 1157–1177.

Burke, C., Ellis, J. D., Peltier, M. R., Roberts, W., Verplaetse, T. L., Phillips, S., Moore, K. E., Marotta, P. L., & McKee, S. A. (2023). Adverse childhood experiences and pathways to violent behaviour for women and men. *Journal of Interpersonal Violence*, *38*(3-4), 4034–4060. DOI: 10.1177/08862605221113012

Campbell, E., Fernando, T., Gassner, L., Hill, J., Seidler, Z., & Summers, A. O. (2024). *Unlocking the prevention potential: Accelerating action to end domestic, family and sexual violence. Report of the Rapid Review of Prevention Approaches.* Department of the Prime Minister and Cabinet. https://www.pmc.gov.au/sites/default/files/resource/download/unlocking-prevention-potential.pdf

Campbell, J. A., Walker, R. J., & Egede, L. E. (2016). Associations between adverse childhood experiences, high-risk behaviors, and morbidity in adulthood. *American Journal of Preventive Medicine*, *50*(3), 344–352. 022guides.library.uq+1DOI: 10.1016/j.amepre.2015.07.

Centers for Disease Control and Prevention. (2024). *About the CDC-Kaiser ACE Study*. U.S. Department of Health & Human Services. https://www.cdc.gov/violenceprevention/aces/about.html

Chung, E. O., LeMasters, K., Nisar, Y. B., Kim, H., & Ji, Y. (2023). Maternal adverse childhood experiences on child growth and development in rural Pakistan. *PLOS Global Public Health*, *3*(10), e0001669. DOI: 10.1371/journal.pgph.0001669

Cohen, L. E., & Felson, M. (1979). Social change and crime rate trends: A routine activity approach. *American Sociological Review*, *44*(4), 588–608. DOI: 10.2307/2094589

Cprek, S. E., Fisher, B. S., McDonald, M. J., McDaniel, H. M., Williamson, L., & Williams, C. M. (2021). Adverse childhood experiences and interpersonal violence among college students: Does a relationship exist? *Journal of American College Health*, *69*(8), 913–920. DOI: 10.1080/07448481.2020.1715413

Day, D. M., Hart, T. A., Wanklyn, S. G., McCay, E., Macpherson, A., & Burnier, N. (2013). Potential mediators between child abuse and both violence and victimization in juvenile offenders. *Psychological Services*, *10*(1), 1–11. DOI: 10.1037/a0028057

DeLisi, M., & Beauregard, E. (2018). Adverse childhood experiences and criminal extremity: New evidence for sexual homicide. *Journal of Forensic Sciences*, *63*(2), 484–489. DOI: 10.1111/1556-4029.13584

Doelman, E. H., Luijk, M. P., Haen Marshall, I., Jongerling, J., Enzmann, D., & Steketee, M. J. (2023). The association between child maltreatment and juvenile delinquency in the context of Situational Action Theory: Crime propensity and criminogenic exposure as mediators in a sample of European youth? *European Journal of Criminology*, *20*(2), 528–547.

Douglas, K. R., Chan, G., Gelernter, J., Arias, A. J., Anton, R. F., Weiss, R. D., & Kranzler, H. R. (2010). Adverse childhood events as risk factors for substance dependence: Partial mediation by mood and anxiety disorders. *Addictive Behaviors*, *35*(1), 7–13.

Edalati, H., & Nicholls, T. L. (2017). The effects of adverse childhood experiences on risk of criminal justice involvement and victimization among homeless adults with mental illness. *Child Abuse & Neglect*, *72*, 20–29. DOI: 10.1016/j.chiabu.2017.07.020 5

Egede, L. E. (2023). Addressing structural inequalities, structural racism, and health disparities: A perspective for moving toward health equity. *Ethnicity & Disease*, *33*(3), 302–308. DOI: 10.18865/ed.33.3.302

Engel, GL., (1977). The need for a new medical model: a challenge for biomedicine. Science. Apr 8;196(4286):129-36. doi: 10.1126/science.847460. PMID: 847460.

Fabio, A., Tu, X., Loeber, R., & Cohen, J. (2011). Neighborhood socioeconomic disadvantage and the shape of the age–crime curve. *American Journal of Public Health, 101*(s1), S325–S332. DOI: 10.2105/AJPH.2011.300238

Festinger, L., Schachter, S., & Back, K. (1950). Social pressures in informal groups: A study of human factors in housing (pp. x, 240). Harper.

Fischer, L., Wilson, M., Schofield, P. W., Jones, J., Kariminia, A., Barrett, E., Dean, K., Sullivan, E., Covington, S., & Butler, T. (2024). Exposure to childhood adversity and intimate partner violence in a sample of incarcerated women in Australia. *Journal of Interpersonal Violence*. Advance online publication. DOI: 10.1177/0306624X241270577

Foell, A., Pitzer, K. A., Nebbitt, V., Lombe, M., Yu, M., Villodas, M. L., & Newransky, C. (2021). Exposure to community violence and depressive symptoms: Examining community, family, and peer effects among public housing youth. *Health & Place, 69*, 102579. DOI: 10.1016/j.healthplace.2021.102579

Fox, B. H., Perez, N., Cass, E., Baglivio, M. T., & Epps, N. (2015). Trauma changes everything: Examining the relationship between adverse childhood experiences and serious, violent, and chronic juvenile offenders. *Child Abuse & Neglect, 46*, 163–173. DOI: 10.1016/j.chiabu.2015.01.011library.csp+1

Freeze, C. (9 April 2019). Adverse Childhood Experiences and Crime FBI Law Enforcement Bulletin. https://leb.fbi.gov/articles/featured-articles/adverse-childhood-experiences-and-crime

Fulu, E., Miedema, S., Roselli, T., McCook, S., Chan, K. L., Haardörfer, R., Jewkes, R., Warner, X., Lang, J., Naved, R. T., Huque, H., Farah, S., Shuvra, M. M. R., Erken, A., Wang, X., Gang, F., Li, H., Mudrovcic, Z., & Hua, W. UN Multi-Country Study on Men and Violence study team. (2017). Pathways between childhood trauma, intimate partner violence, and harsh parenting: Findings from the UN Multi-country Study on Men and Violence in Asia and the Pacific. *The Lancet. Global Health, 5*(5), e512–e522. DOI: 10.1016/S2214-109X(17)30103-1

GBD US Health Disparities Collaborators, Strassle, P. D., Kendrick, P., Baumann, M. M., Kelly, Y. O., Li, Z., Schmidt, C., Sylte, D. O., Compton, K., Bertolacci, G. J., La Motte-Kerr, W., Daoud, F., Naghavi, M., Rodriquez, E. J., Mensah, G. A., Murray, C. J. L., Mokdad, A. H., Dwyer-Lindgren, L., & Pérez-Stable, E. J. (2025). Homicide rates across county, race, ethnicity, age, and sex in the US: A Global Burden of Disease Study. *JAMA Network Open, 8*(2), e2462069. DOI: 10.1001/jamanetworkopen.2024.62069

Gjelsvik, A., Zierler, S., Blume, J., & Nie, N. (2004). Homicide risk across race and class: A small-area analysis in Massachusetts and Rhode Island. *Journal of Urban Health, 81*(3), 372–382. DOI: 10.1093/jurban/jth130

Gottfredson, M. R., & Hirschi, T. (1990). *A general theory of crime*. Stanford University Press.

Graf, G. H. J., Simoes, C., & Koerting, J. (2021). Adverse Childhood Experiences and Justice System Contact: A Systematic Review. *Pediatrics, 147*(1), e2020021030. DOI: 10.1542/peds.2020-021030 3

Hales, G., Debowska, A., Rowe, R., Boduszek, D., & Levita, L. (2023). Comparison of person-centered and cumulative risk approaches in explaining the relationship between adverse childhood experiences and behavioral and emotional problems. *Journal of Interpersonal Violence, 38*(13-14), 8065–8087. DOI: 10.1177/08862605231153877

Hannis, C. K. (2015). *Understanding the victim-offender overlap: An exploratory study* (Master's thesis, Missouri State University). MSU Graduate Theses, 2840. https://bearworks.missouristate.edu/theses/2840

Hart, R. (2015). *An analysis of global homicide patterns* (Undergraduate honors thesis, University of California, Berkeley). https://econ.berkeley.edu/sites/default/files/HART-Honors%20Thesis.pdf

Hashemi, L., Fanslow, J., Gulliver, P., & McIntosh, T. (2022). Intergenerational impact of violence exposure: Emotional-behavioural and school difficulties in children aged 5–17. *Frontiers in Psychiatry, 12*, 771834. DOI: 10.3389/fpsyt.2021.771834

He, J., Yan, X., Wang, R., Zhao, J., Liu, J., Zhou, C., & Zeng, Y. (2022). Does childhood adversity lead to drug addiction in adulthood? A study of serial mediators based on resilience and depression. *Frontiers in Psychiatry, 13*, 871459.

Herman, J. L. (1992). *Trauma and recovery: The aftermath of violence—from domestic abuse to political terror*. Basic Books.

Herzog, J. I., & Schmahl, C. (2018). Adverse childhood experiences and the consequences on neurobiological, psychosocial, and somatic conditions across the lifespan. *Frontiers in Psychiatry, 9*, 420. DOI: 10.3389/fpsyt.2018.00420

Hindelang, M. J., Gottfredson, M. R., & Garofalo, J. (1978). *Victims of personal crime: An empirical foundation for a theory of personal victimization*. Ballinger Publishing Co.

Holt, S., Buckley, H., & Whelan, S. (2008). The impact of exposure to domestic violence on children and young people: A review of the literature. *Child Abuse & Neglect, 32*(8), 797–810. DOI: 10.1016/j.chiabu.2008.02.004

Huang, H., Sim, Y., & Draper, R. (2019). Adverse Childhood Experiences and Trauma-Informed Care in Rehabilitation Counseling. *Rehabilitation Research, Policy, and Education, 33*(2), 103–118. DOI: 10.1891/2168-6653.33.2.103

Hughes, K., Bellis, M. A., Hardcastle, K. A., Sethi, D., Butchart, A., Mikton, C., Jones, L., & Dunne, M. P. (2017). The effect of multiple adverse childhood experiences on health: A systematic review and meta-analysis. *The Lancet. Public Health, 2*(8), e356–e366. DOI: 10.1016/S2468-2667(17)30118-4

Jahic, I., Trulson, C. R., Caudill, J. W., Bonner, T., Slemaker, A., & DeLisi, M. (2021). Adverse childhood experiences and forensic typologies: Getting specific about trauma among institutionalized youth. *International Journal of Environmental Research and Public Health, 18*(21), 11307. DOI: 10.3390/ijerph182111307

Jobe-Shields, L., Williams, J., & Hardt, M. (2017). Predictors of emotional security in survivors of interpersonal violence. *Journal of Child and Family Studies, 26*(10), 2834–2842.

Jones, M. S., & Hoffmann, J. P. (2024). Adverse childhood experiences and homicide. In Burgason, K. A., & DeLisi, M. J. (Eds.), *Routledge Handbook of Homicide Studies* (pp. 349–368). Routledge., DOI: 10.4324/9781003399476-19

Joshi, A., & Truong, M. (2025). The role of adverse childhood experiences (ACEs) in adolescent use of violence. Child Family Community Australia (CFCA) Australian Institute of Family Studies (AIFS).https://aifs.gov.au/resources/policy-and-practice-papers/role-adverse-childhood-experiences-aces-adolescent-use

Keynejad, R. C., & Howard, L. M. (2025). Intergenerational "transmission" of intimate partner violence and abuse: Interpretations and implications. *The Lancet Regional Health. Europe, 53*, 101299. DOI: 10.1016/j.lanepe.2025.101299

Kistin, C., & Brotanek, J. (2022). Screening for Adverse Childhood Experiences in Children. *JAMA Pediatrics, 176*(2), e220121. DOI: 10.1001/jamapediatrics.2022.0121

Krieg, S. M., Murphy, L., & Elliott, J. C. (2022). Adverse childhood experiences and pathways to violent behavior in adults: A latent class analysis. *Frontiers in Psychology, 13*, 9852029. DOI: 10.3389/fpsyg.2022.9852029pmc.ncbi.nlm.nih

Kubiak, S. P., Kasiborski, N., & Schmittel, E. (2017). Assessing long-term outcomes of an intervention designed to reduce child maltreatment among parents involved in the child welfare system. *Journal of Public Child Welfare, 11*(2), 131–149.

Laajasalo, T., Pajunen, T., Martikainen, P., & Kivivuori, J. (2025). Adverse childhood experiences (ACEs) and juvenile violent delinquency in multiple successive birth cohorts. *Nordic Journal of Criminology, 26*(2), 1–14. DOI: 10.18261/njc.26.2.3

LaNoue, M. D., George, B. J., Helitzer, D. L., & Keith, S. W. (2020). Contrasting cumulative risk and multiple individual risk models of the relationship between Adverse Childhood Experiences (ACEs) and adult health outcomes. *BMC Medical Research Methodology, 20*(1), 239. DOI: 10.1186/s12874-020-01120-w

Lopez-Tamayo, R., Suarez, L., Simpson, D., & Volpe, K. (2022). The impact of adverse childhood experiences and community violence exposure on a sample of anxious, treatment-seeking children. *Journal of Child & Adolescent Trauma, 15*(4), 1081–1093. DOI: 10.1007/s40653-022-00447-4

Lu, Mueser, Rosenberg, & Jankowski. (2023). Variety of ACEs and risk of anxiety-depression: Females demonstrated higher rates and more complex trauma profiles. *Frontiers in Psychiatry, 14*, 1233981.

Luby, J. L., Baram, T. Z., Rogers, C. E., & Barch, D. M. (2021). Adverse Childhood Experiences in a low-income Black cohort: Prevalence, sex differences, and links to violent crime exposure. *Child and Adolescent Psychiatry and Mental Health, 15*, 35. Advance online publication. DOI: 10.1186/s13034-021-00390-y

Malvaso, C., Day, A., Delfabbro, P., Cale, J., Hackett, L., & Ross, S. (2022). *Adverse childhood experiences and trauma among young people in the youth justice system* (Report to the Criminology Research Advisory Council, Grant: CRG 12/18–19). Australian Institute of Criminology. https://www.aic.gov.au/sites/default/files/2022-06/crg_1218_19_adverse_childhood_experiences_v8.pdf

Massachusetts Association for Mental Health. (n.d.). *CDC-Kaiser ACEs Study*. https://www.mamh.org/advocacy/prevention/impact-of-traumatic-experiences/cdc-kaiser-aces-study

Mathews, B., Pacella, R., Dunne, M., & Higgins, D. (2023). The Australian Child Maltreatment Study: Prevalence, outcomes and implications. *The Medical Journal of Australia, 218*(9), 420–424. DOI: 10.5694/mja2.51971acms+1

McKinley, A. (2024). Homicide Solvability. In Perez, O. (Ed.), *Ciencias Forenses y Femicidio/Feminicidio: Evidencia y Contextos "Forensic Sciences & Femicide/Feminicide: Evidence & Contexts"*.

Miedema, S. S., Le, V. D., Chiang, L., Ngann, T., & Shortt, J. W. (2023). Adverse childhood experiences and intimate partner violence among youth in Cambodia: A latent class analysis. *Journal of Interpersonal Violence*, *38*(3-4), NP1446–NP1472. DOI: 10.1177/08862605221090573

Minds, E. (n.d.). Adverse childhood experiences (ACEs): Summary of evidence and impacts. Emerging Minds. https://emergingminds.com.au/resources/adverse-childhood-experiences-aces-summary-of-evidence-and-impacts/

Mohammadi, A., & Ceccato, V. (2022). Homicide rates are spatially associated with built environment, socioeconomic and demographic conditions in Toronto neighbourhoods. *Scientific Reports*, *12*, 13398. DOI: 10.1038/s41598-022-17718-5

Mongan, D., Millar, S. R., Brennan, M. M., Doyle, A., Galvin, B., & McCarthy, N. (2025). Associations and mediating factors between adverse childhood experiences and substance use behaviours in early adulthood: A population-based longitudinal study. *Addictive Behaviors*, *161*, 108194. DOI: 10.1016/j.addbeh.2024.107869

Muller, W. (2019). The relation between adverse childhood experiences and types of offending: A literature review (Bachelor thesis, Tilburg University). Retrieved from http://arno.uvt.nl/show.cgi?fid=150029

National University. (n.d.). *A Guide to Trauma Informed Care Principles*. https://www.nu.edu/blog/trauma-informed-care-principles/

Negriff, S. (2019). ACEs are not equal: Examining the relative impact of adversity type and multiple adversities on adolescent health and violence outcomes. *Child Abuse & Neglect*, *98*, 104208. DOI: 10.1016/j.chiabu.2019.104208

Ogilvie, J. M., Stewart, A. L., Chan, M., & Shinkfield, A. J. (2022). The relationship between adverse childhood experiences and adolescent violence: An Australian study. *Children and Youth Services Review*, *134*, 106352. DOI: 10.1016/j.childyouth.2021.106352 2

Pennsylvania Coalition Against Domestic Violence. (n.d.). *About the ACE study* [PDF]. https://www.pcadv.org/wp-content/uploads/ACE-Handount.pdf

Pessoa, T. M. G., & Almeida, T. C. (2024). The Link Between Adverse Childhood Experiences and Mental Health in Offenders: A Systematic Review. *Crime and Delinquency*, *0*(0). Advance online publication. DOI: 10.1177/00111287241242478

Reese, E. M., Chang, D., Zauszniewski, J. A., & Brown, H. L. (2022). Intergenerational transmission of trauma: The mediating role of family health. *BMC Public Health*, *22*, 976. Advance online publication. DOI: 10.1186/s12889-022-13431-9

Reiniger, B., & Zemp, M. (2021). When problems only get bigger: The impact of adverse childhood experiences related to maltreatment and violence in adulthood. *Frontiers in Psychology, 12*, 693420. DOI: 10.3389/fpsyg.2021.693420frontiersin

Saxena, P., & Messina, N. (2021). Adverse Childhood Experiences and Pathways to Violent Behavior: Examining Gender Differences Among Justice-Involved Adults. *Journal of Interpersonal Violence, 36*(7–8), 4042–4066. DOI: 10.1177/0886260518777551

Schreck, C. J. (1999). Criminal victimization and low self-control: An extension and test of a general theory of crime. *Justice Quarterly, 16*(3), 633–654. DOI: 10.1080/07418829900094291

Scottish Government. (2018). *Understanding childhood adversity, resilience and crime*. Justice Analytical Services. https://www.gov.scot/binaries/content/documents/govscot/publications/research-and-analysis/2018/05/understanding-childhood-adversity-resilience-crime/documents/00535550-pdf/00535550-pdf/govscot:document1

Secretariat of the Pacific Community. (n.d.). *Thematic brief: Ending violence against women in the Pacific*. https://pacificdata.org/data/dataset/acf42df5-54c0-43e2-98c4-e2afefb1bce0/resource/4cf275c7-ea06-419f-845e-7b49cff21e96/download/spc-pwl_thematicbrief_evawg.pdf

Semenza, D. C., Testa, A., & Jackson, D. B. (2022). Intersectional differences in serious violent victimization trajectories across the life course. *Preventive Medicine Reports, 26*, 101732. Advance online publication. DOI: 10.1016/j.pmedr.2022.101732

Siegel, L. J. (2017). *Criminology: Theories, patterns, and typologies* (13th ed.). Cengage Learning.

Silva, C., Moreira, P., Sá Moreira, D., Rafael, F., Rodrigues, A., Leite, Â., & Lopes, S. (2024). Impact of adverse childhood experiences in young adults and adults: A systematic literature review. *Pediatric Reports, 16*(2), 461–481. DOI: 10.3390/pediatric16020040

Stark, R. (1987). Deviant Places: A Theory of the Ecology of Crime. *Criminology, 25*(4), 893–910. DOI: 10.1111/j.1745-9125.1987.tb00824.x

Stevens, J. E. (n.d.). Got your ACE score? ACEs Too High. Retrieved July 6, 2025, from Suh, B. C., Gallaway, M. S., & Celaya, M. F. (2024). Supportive relationships mitigate the effect of cumulative exposure to adverse childhood experiences on depression, anxiety, stress, and suicide considerations: The Arizona Youth Risk Behavior Survey. *Children, 11*(2), 161. https://doi.org/ /DOI: 10.3390/children-11020161https://acestoohigh.com/got-your-ace-score

Su, W. M., & Stone, L. (2020). Adult survivors of childhood trauma: Complex trauma, complex needs. *Australian Journal of General Practice*, *49*(7), 423–430.

Suh, B. C., Gallaway, M. S., & Celaya, M. F. (2024). Supportive relationships mitigate the effect of cumulative exposure to adverse childhood experiences on depression, anxiety, stress, and suicide considerations: The Arizona Youth Risk Behavior Survey. *Children (Basel, Switzerland)*, *11*(2), 161. DOI: 10.3390/children11020161

Thompson, M. P., Kingree, J. B., & Desai, S. (2004). Gender differences in long-term health consequences of childhood physical abuse. *American Journal of Public Health*, *94*(4), 660–665. DOI: 10.2105/ajph.94.4.660

Trejo, B. G., Mendoza, F., & Lamas, H. (2024). Characterising the killing of girls and women in urban settings in Latin America, 2000–2019: An analysis of variability and time trends using mortality data from vital registration systems. *BMJ Public Health*, *2*(1), e000985. DOI: 10.1136/bmjph-2023-000985

Ullman, C., Amin, A., Bourassa, A., Chandarana, S., Dutra, F., & Ellsberg, M. (2025). Interventions to prevent violence against women and girls globally: A global systematic review of reviews to update the RESPECT women framework. *BMJ Public Health*, *3*(1).

United Nations Office on Drugs and Crime. (2023). *Global Study on Homicide 2023*. United Nations. https://www.unodc.org/unodc/en/data-and-analysis/global-study-on-homicide.html

Walker, J. S., & Matarese, M. (2011). Family Voice with Informed Choice: Coordinating Wraparound with Research-Based Treatment for Children and Youth with Complex Needs. *Journal of Child and Family Studies*, *22*(1), 6–18. DOI: 10.1007/s10826-011-9456-2

Walsh, A. (2019). Section Three: Victimology. In Introduction to Criminology (4th ed., pp. 76–90). SAGE Publications.https://us.sagepub.com/sites/default/files/upm-binaries/90401_Section_Three_Victimology_Exploring_the_Experience_of_Victimization.pdf

Wiens, K., Gillis, J., Nicolau, I., & Wade, T. J. (2020). Capturing risk associated with childhood adversity: Independent, cumulative, and multiplicative effects of physical abuse, sexual abuse, and family violence on mental disorders and suicidality. The Permanente Journal, 24, 19.079. https://doi.org/DOI: 10.7812/TPP/19.079

Wolfgang, M. E. (1957). Victim Precipitated Criminal Homicide. The Journal of Criminal Law, Criminology, and Police Science, 48(1), 1–11. https://doi.org/ ACEs Aware. (2021). *Your ACE Screening & Clinical Response Approach*. California Department of Health Care Services. https://www.acesaware.org/wp-content/uploads/2021/09/Stage-2-Workbook.pdfDOI: 10.2307/1140160

yourtown. (2023, January). *Adverse childhood experiences: What works papers*. https://www.yourtown.com.au/sites/default/files/document/Adverse%20Childhood%20Experiences%20-%20What%20Works%20Papers,%20January%202023.pdf

Yu, Z., Noll, J. G., & Putnam, F. W. (2022). Adverse childhood experiences and homicide victimization: A population-based study. *Child Abuse & Neglect, 127*, 105607. . 105607guides.library.uq+1DOI: 10.1016/j.chiabu.2022

Zhu, J., Exner-Cortens, D., Dobson, K., Wells, L., Noel, M., & Madigan, S. (2024). Adverse childhood experiences and intimate partner violence: A meta-analysis. *Development and Psychopathology*, *36*(2), 929–943.

Zuo, X., Lou, C., Gao, E., Lyu, S., Guida, J., Hallman, K., & Li, S. (2021). Childhood adversity subtypes and violence victimization and perpetration among early adolescents in Shanghai, China. *PLoS One*, *16*(9), e0256800.

ENDNOTES

1 Biological aspects include genetics, physiology, and physical health; psychological factors involve thoughts, emotions, and behaviours; social influences encompass relationships, cultural background, and socioeconomic status.

2 Crime persists even as populations change, suggesting that the environment, not the individuals, is the primary driver of deviant behaviour in such areas.

3 The theory emphasises that criminal opportunities arise from the everyday routines and activities of individuals, such as predictable schedules or unprotected environments.

4 This theory emphasises the complex interaction between victim and offender, rather than viewing victims as purely passive, and has been foundational in

victimology, though it remains controversial due to concerns about victim blaming.

5 The Americas include the following countries: United States; Brazil; Mexico; Colombia; Argentina; Canada; Peru; Venezuela; Chile; Ecuador; Guatemala; Bolivia; Haiti; Cuba; Dominican Republic; Honduras; Paraguay; El Salvador; Nicaragua; Costa Rica; Panama; Uruguay and Jamaica.

Chapter 8
Cumulative Harm for Children Involved in Family Law Proceedings

Susan De Campo
https://orcid.org/0009-0006-6734-6008
LifeCare Consultancy, Australia

ABSTRACT

Cumulative harm refers to the impact of several adverse experiences, on an individual's well-being. Within the family law system in Australia, although the impact of high conflict separation has attracted research, cumulative harm in circumstances where a child has not seen a parent for a period of time and is then reunified with them, has not been extensively explored. Other aspects of potential harm for children who become embroiled in the adversarial family law system has not been considered in a collective context. There are distinct touchpoints of potential harm that ought to be subjected to cumulative harm evaluation if the long term consequences are to be mitigated.

INTRODUCTION

Cumulative harm refers to the impact of several adverse experiences, on an individual's well-being (Bryce, et al., 2023). It is distinguished from single-incident trauma where there is a single traumatic event that is specific and time-limited (Briere et al., 2025). The concept of cumulative harm emerged decades ago (Khan, 1963), and has attracted considerable attention since this time. Researchers and social scientists have explored cumulative harm within the child protection sector where the incidents were connected to long-standing parental risk factors (Tustin & Tustin,

DOI: 10.4018/979-8-3373-9524-1.ch008

2024b). Certainly in this sector either dysfunctional or inadequate parenting can underpin identifiable parental risk factors including generational trauma and abuse, multiple notifications to child protection authorities, substance misuse, privileging other adult relationships over parenting their child and a lack of knowledge around optimal or functional parenting (Younas & Gutman, 2023). Whilst it is accepted that children can be or are resilient (Goldstein & Brooks, 2005), there is on-going debate around when and why this resilience wanes (Tustin & Tustin, 2024b). Researchers are increasingly calling for cumulative harm to be overtly acknowledged and considered in all facets of the social sciences involving children (Bryce, 2018).

Within the family law system in Australia, although the impact of high conflict separation, for example, has attracted research (Akin Ojelabi & Gutman, 2020; Lange et al., 2022; Shumaker & Kelsey, 2020), cumulative harm as a construct has not been extensively researched. Apart from high-conflict separation (there are other harms that a child *may* have been exposed to that could be included in a discussion about outcomes of cumulative harm. These include, but are not limited to, pre-separation conflict and/or family violence, substance and alcohol misuse, significant lifestyle changes, mental health issues, unjustified parental absence, involvement in family court processes such as a child impact report interview, family report interviews, systemic harms, participation in court-ordered family therapy, possible attendance at a contact centre and, in circumstances where a child has not seen a parent for a period of time and is then reunified with them, participate in a court-ordered reunification process, noting, of course, that there is no formally recognised or evidenced-based process for such a process (Kempf & Outlaw, 2023). On occasion there may be a reversal of care where a child is ordered to reside with the parent who they have been estranged from. There is no data available regarding how often such a process is therapeutically supported. In Australia, it appears that judicial officers rely on a word-of-mouth/reputation system for assigning families to practitioners to undertake processes such as reunification therapy.

Following a brief explanation of the family law system in Australia, this chapter will explore each of these potential harm touch points and consider the current mechanisms employed to address the impact of harm for children in the family law system. Although courts exercising family law jurisdiction are required to consider safety or protection from harm, this is arguably undertaken in a more siloed manner than a cumulative or systemic manner (Meier & Sankaran, 2021). In the case of domestic and family violence, for example, physical abuse can be visible and quantifiable, can lead to protective interventions more quickly, can result in criminal charges and tangible consequences for the perpetrator whereas emotional abuse is more nebulous, more difficult to quantify and possibly more difficult to demonstrate. This, of course, is particularly problematic when research confirms that the impact of emotional abuse can be lifelong (Colton, Cao, & Davies, 2025). Such realities underpin the challenges of considering cumulative harm.

THE AUSTRALIAN FAMILY LAW SYSTEM

In Australia, family law is governed by federal laws that are applied by the Federal Circuit and Family Court of Australia (FCFCOA) (Division 1) and the FCFCOA (Division 2). Broadly, family law covers legal separation, the dissolution of marriage, the division of property and the arrangements for parenting after separation. Legal obligations and the rights of family members are also considered (Parkinson, 2023). The family law system is adversarial; this means that the parties, typically the parents or the separated individuals, outline issues in contention and the court acts as a neutral adjudicator. Active pursuit of the truth, the premise of an inquisitorial system, is not the focus. This system, by its very nature creates a competitive dynamic and is increasingly thought to be problematic for marginalised or vulnerable litigants, such as survivors of domestic and family violence or those without legal representation. The system lends itself to a focus on 'winning', and by default, the other party 'losing' (Dodds, et al., 2023).

The Australian system is informed by the tenets of the *Family Law Act 1975* and its subsequent amendments. The principals enshrined therein are, amongst others, that following separation both parents have responsibilities to their children (unless orders state otherwise), and that a child's safety is prioritised ("*Family Law Act 1975,* (Cth),"). Although about 70 percent of couples who separate devise parenting arrangements without involvement in the family court system (Kaspiew, 2016), those who become involved in the system are likely dealing with issues that have the potential to place the child at risk of some form of harm.

The dominant guiding principle for family law in Australia concerns what arrangements are deemed to be in 'the best interest of the child'. This concept attracted considerable research in the 90's. In more recent times it includes consideration of the impact on children whose parents have differing religious views (Beyene, 2024), the gender of carers (Bergström et al., 2020), and the diminishing of parental responsibility or freedom to autonomously parent their child (Đerlek, 2024). Nonetheless, the principle continues to ensure that a child's physical, emotional and psychological well-being are prioritised; they are protected from harm, abuse, neglect and (direct or indirect) exposure to violence; their physical, psychological and educational needs are supported, and that their views and wishes are considered in accordance with their age, stage and development (Daly, 2018).

Debate regarding the utility of 'the system' has been on-going for almost twenty years and invariably seeks to improve systems and interventions that privilege more child-focused outcomes (McIntosh et al., 2008). Detractors and critics of an adversarial approach point to realities such as a situation where a father who uses violence/abuse/coercive control and can afford highly skilled, adept and convincing legal counsel to present his case to the court, litigating against a self-represented mother who alleges she and the children are survivors of said violence or abuse. Such realities have led to procedural and policy changes such that parties are now, unless contraindicated for safety reasons, required to participate in processes such as mediation and dispute resolution.

Data on these aforementioned processes reveals that approximately 3% of separated families utilise court (Kaspiew, 2016; Kaspiew & Carson, 2019). According to the most recent statistics, the number of divorces granted in 2024 was over 47,000 and there are approximately 1500 anonymised judgments published each year. Not all these judgments involve children, however a high portion do involve children. Moreover, the judgments only reflect matters that have proceeded to trial, and were not resolved prior to the conclusion of trial; children may well have been involved in family court proceedings that settle by consent (AustLii, 1998 - 2025). Such children will have undoubtedly been impacted by some, if not all, the following challenges.

SIGNIFICANT LIFESTYLE CHANGES

When parents separate, they are not only required to consider a parenting arrangement that is in the best interests of the child, there is also commonly a division of property, and obviously, changes in living arrangements. Some of these changes can be experienced as extremely challenging, if not traumatic, for children (Mannarino & Cohen, 2011; Newell & Moss, 2011). They may have to relocate, they may have to change schools, they may/probably have to sleep at the other parent's place of residence anywhere between one and seven nights per fortnight, they will have to adjust to the different ways that every day events are experienced – parent-teacher interviews, award days, school photo days, Easter, Christmas, birthdays, family gatherings, funerals. They might have to adjust to different meal preparation/cooking/lunchbox skills, different house-keeping standards, different hair-styling skills, different expectations around discipline, screen-time, chores and homework, not having their favourite pet for x number of days/fortnight, not even speaking with the 'other' parent for days at a time.

The aforementioned adjustments that children of separated parents may be required to process are also dependent on other issues they have been exposed to, their resilience and the impact of cumulative harm. It is also the case that 'change' is sometimes inextricably linked to 'loss' (Cronin Favazza & Munson, 2010; Mannarino & Cohen, 2011). This means, of course, that the child will experience a grieving process associated with the changes; the trajectory of this process is highly variable and will add to the other issues facing the child (Fiorini & Mullen, 2006).

Importantly, significant changes for neurodiverse children, can be even more difficult to manage and if not factored into post-separation parenting arrangements, there is a high likelihood the child will suffer (Afifi et al., 2022; Jennings, 2005). Given the diversity of training, experience and expertise of social science experts who provide recommendations and opinions to the court (Rathus, 2021), it may be that that recommendations are not adequately informed by current expertise and knowledge about neurodiversity. It is noted, of course that there has been an enormous increase in research in this area in the past five to ten years (Chung et al., 2024; Evans et al., 2024). There is a dearth of research pertaining to post-separation parenting arrangements for a neurodiverse child. Accordingly, potential harms for this specific cohort are largely unknown. Although there is some grey literature pertaining to, say, autistic children, published research is not abreast of current trends. One example of this concerns the so-called labelling issue. The neurodiversity movement (VanDaalen et al., 2025), promotes the use of identity first language: an autistic person, as opposed to a person with autism. Papers from less than a decade ago, do not align with such preferences and refer to 'disorders' in their analyses and commentary (Birnbaum & Lach, 2016). Although not the focus of this chapter, it is possible that inadvertent harms are being caused to neurodiverse individuals by virtue of such issues as language use, mislabelling and stigmatisation.

Exposure to Pre-Separation Conflict

It is possible, if not likely, that prior to parents separating, there has been conflict in the family home. Of course, some conflict exists in most relationships so it is important to distinguish between types of conflict. Interparental conflict (IPC) can be categorised as destructive – where prolonged anger, rage, hostility, discord and unresolved tension is pervasive (Harold & Sellers, 2018) or constructive IPC, characterised by conflict resolution, the use of respectful problem-solving skills and communication. It is unsurprising that the former type of ICP leads to poorer outcomes, whereas the latter invariably leads to better psychological outcomes for young people (Cummings & Davies, 2011). The impact of destructive IPC on children has been researched for decades, most particularly in the post-no fault divorce era. The 1970's saw the introduction of "the no-fault revolution" (Oren, 2018); that is, the imperative to provide a verifiable reason for divorce, saw a significant rise in research around both family conflict and the impact of divorce on children. By the mid-eighties, the negative impact of parental conflict on children was widely acknowledged (Noonan, 1985). Subsequent research has confirmed that exposure to significant levels of verbal and physical conflict or abuse in either intact families or separated families leads to poorer outcomes for children across a range of measures such as compromised immune health, sleep disorders, chronic health challenges, relational difficulties and emotional control (Vandana, 2023).

Although undertaken some decades ago, one longitudinal study concluded that parental conflict and marital discord lead to an increase in anxiety and depression in children aged between six and fourteen years (Jekielek, 1998). This study marked an increased awareness that outcomes for children were worse if children were exposed to conflict on a longer term basis where parents remained married than if the parents separated and the children were not exposed to conflict; divorce may result in improved emotional well-being of children previously exposed to conflict (Westrupp et al.,, 2018).

More recently, a review of studies published between 2012 and 2023, explored the consequences of exposure to IPC across three key areas: young people's mental health, reactivity and coping, and parenting and family ramifications (Colton et al., 2025). Fifty papers assessed the connection between IPC and children's mental health. Unsurprisingly, the consensus is that children will have increased likelihood of 'internal' (depression, anxiety, low self-worth), 'external' (verbal and physical aggression) (Hosokawa & Katsura, 2019) and/or 'social' problems (difficulty forming relationships, social anxiety) (Jekielek, 1998; Lux et al., 2021). There is also consensus that destructive IPC contributes to a perpetuation of destructive IPC patterns within their family system such that the next generation of parents engage in harsh parenting, are less supportive and mindful parents and have less positive parent-child connection (Cheung & Chung, 2023).

The third domain that this 2025 paper explored was how a child's reactivity style and patterns and coping behaviours are affected by IPC. It is hypothesised that destructive IPC amplifies emotional reactivity and is a predictor for poorer mental health outcomes (Colton et al., 2025; Davies et al., 2020). Some of these outcomes depend on the extent of the exposure to IPC, the child's genetic make-up and their innate temperament (Hentges et al., 2015).

Exposure to High Conflict Separation/Divorce

High-conflict separation is characterised by on-going legal disputes, high relational conflict and heightened emotions (Anderson, 2022; Eddy, 2012; Schmidt & Grigg, 2023; Smyth & Moloney, 2019). When the construct of high conflict divorce was initially formalised in the nineties (Johnston, 1994), it was thought that about 10% of couples remained in high conflict. In more recent times, estimates are that 20 – 40% of couples engage in high conflict and that this number is increasing (Schmidt & Grigg, 2024). Another feature of HCS is the presence of high levels of retaliation alongside of low levels of reparation such that the resultant simmering terror leads to further conflict, projection and an inability to resolve issues (Saini & Birnbaum, 2007). The issue of property settlement or division of assets and financial support for children post-separation also features in such matters. The more satisfied a parent feels about the financial support they receive, the better the co-parenting relationship (Bonach, 2005). Finally, it is acknowledged that HCS has many confounding variables such as mental health issues, family violence, poorly executed legal processes and substance and alcohol misuse (Smyth & Moloney, 2019).[1]

In conjunction with the awareness of the negative impacts of destructive IPC, the damaging impact of HCS on children has attracted attention for many years. The seminal text: '*In the Name of the Child: A Developmental Approach to Understanding and Helping Children of Conflicted and Violent Divorce*" (Johnston et al., 2009), utilises three decades of research and clinical expertise to address the impact of and support for children of HCS. In Australia, respected researchers also seek to highlight the negative impacts of HCS, noting that if a dispute remains highly conflictual for longer than five years, the issues are no longer the issues; rather, there is likely to be the presence of interparental hatred (Smyth & Moloney, 2019). The specific consequences of a 'hating' parent in the post-separation space have not been explored. Nonetheless, it could be reasonably assumed that this is likely to impact on a child's identity development. Moreover, such dynamics likely fall into an overall impact of the psychological well-being of the child (D'Onofrio & Emery, 2019).

The consequences for children of HCS are so significant that some believe that child protection agencies probably ought to be more proactively engaged with these families (Joyce, 2016). It has been widely established that HCS affects social engagement, parent-child relationships, emotional wellbeing, academic performance and long-term adjustment and coping (J. Johnston et al., 2009; J. R. Johnston, 1994). More specifically, children may experience increased levels of anxiety, depression and distress (Pellón, Martínez-Pampliega, & Cormenzana, 2024); they may have lower feelings of self-worth due to feeling responsible for the IPC (Daklallah, 2022; Esmaeili & Yaacob, 2012). Children may have divided loyalties, feel caught in the middle of their parents or feel pressure to favour one parent over the other (Baker & Brassard, 2013; Grape et al., 2024). Exposure to dysfunctional dynamics may lead to weakened or disrupted sibling bonds (Poortman & Voorpostel, 2009) and the emotional burden and toll can lead to compromised ability to focus at school (Laletas & Khasin, 2021).

It is inevitable that children are cognisant of the negative opinions the parents have toward each other (Vandana, 2023). Some of the behaviours that a child might witness, be indirectly exposed to or directly face include: denigration of the other parent, insisting the child act as a messenger or spy, misinform a child with the goal of causing conflict between the child and the other parent, parentify the child, seek emotional support from the child, demean the other parent's parenting ability, and denigrate the other parent's family (Tustin & Tustin, 2024a).

The widely accepted consequences of HCS were a key consideration in the formation of Family Relationship Centre in Australia. These 65 centres followed the 2006 amendments to the *Family Law Act* 1975 where there is a strong emphasis on promoting and facilitating a more cooperative, less litigious approach to post-separation parenting (Moloney, 2013; Smyth & Moloney, 2019).

Substance and Alcohol Misuse

Although there are some long-standing common reasons for couples to separate or divorce – lack of appreciation, sexual rejection, infidelity and family violence or abuse, research also acknowledges the negative impact of substance and/or alcohol misuse in families and on children (Smith et al., 2016). Parental substance and alcohol misuse, is most certainly identified as a key issue in HCS (Kaspiew, 2016). These impacts for children are far-reaching and include psychological issues such as depression and anxiety, increased risk of developing drug and alcohol problems as a child matures, behavioural issues, poorer academic performance (Harwin et al., 2010). Of course, the immediate impacts are impaired parenting ability, compromised focus and attention, and neglect (Velleman & Templeton, 2016). In in-tact families, the effects of substance misuse may be ameliorated if the other parent is functional and adopts the primary parenting role, however, in separated families, protective measures for children may be less present.

If it is determined that substance or alcohol misuse is an issue in the family court litigation arena, it is possible that the child may only spend time with that parent at a children's supervised contact centre (Commerford & Hunter, 2015). Although it is assumed that the parent will not be substance affected during the visit, this industry is not regulated; the processes and procedures vary greatly across services and there is no established best practice that the service must adhere to (Schindeler, 2019; Stern & Oehme, 2002).

Parent's Mental Health

Although divorce/separation can be a highly stressful experience for children and parents, this is compounded if a parent is suffering from poor mental health (Barnes, 2020). It is noted that up to one in five young people live in families with a parent who has a mental illness (Reupert et al., 2013); this likely translates into one in five young people of separated families are faced with this issue. Despite efforts to de-stigmatise mental illness, shame, embarrassment and misinformation continue to pervade this issue; children of divorced parents where mental illness is a factor are particularly vulnerable to these feelings and can blame themselves for somehow contributing to their parent's challenges (Reupert et al., 2015). Moreover, children of parents with a mental illness are at greater risk of developing psychological problems themselves later in life

Given that a parent who has unstable mental health or mental illness may not be able to provide optimal parenting, there is also a risk that the child will be subjected to neglect – a form of harm (Lauritzen et al., 2014). Further, recent research suggests that parents who alienate their children from the other parent have certain personality traits, if not personality disorders that contribute to this form of emotional abuse of children (Roma et al., 2022). So, not only is the child influenced to feel negatively toward the other parent – the far-reaching consequences of which are noted below – this manipulation is being done by a parent with problematic personality traits (Fares et al., 2023).

Exposure to Forensic Processes

Although there is an increasing emphasis on having children's views and wishes considered in post-separation parenting arrangements (Quigley & Cyr, 2018), this may come with negative consequences, despite the aim of empowering a child or respecting their rights. Typically, if the child's views and wishes are sought, this occurs via child-inclusive mediation, a child-impact report, a family report and/or via an independent children's lawyer (Fernando, 2013). Affording a child the opportunity to provide their wishes may assist in decision-making skills, provide a sense of control or personal agency and may communicate that what they think and how they feel, matters (Smart & Neale, 2000).

Researchers have identified several challenges or potentially problematic aspects of obtaining a child's wishes about post-separation parenting arrangements. Many children feel as though they are being asked to choose between their parents, they worry about how a parent might feel about their views and wishes, they do not want a parent to feel rejected and they can feel pressured to ensure a fair arrangement – *for the parent* (Cashmore, 2011). A problematic aspect of condoning a child's views and wishes occurs in cases where a parent has unjustifiably negatively influenced a child against a parent (Rowlands et al., 2022; Warshak, 2003). Interviewing a child who, for nefarious reasons, has to reiterate to a forensic investigator (such as a family report writer), an imposed view can reinforce dissonance the child is already experiencing about their parents' conflict (Warshak, 2018).

Problematically, despite knowledge of appropriate child interviewing techniques within the child protection and criminal arena, this information has not been formally introduced into the family law context in Australia. We do not know, for sure, *what effect* a particular interviewing technique has on children, *how* they are being interviewed and how the vested parties can ensure that best practice is being employed (Turoy-smith & Powell, 2017). There is some research to suggest that children believe they are asked questions designed to "trick" them (Trinder, 1997), and that they are required to give their opinion to too many people (Fernando, 2013). Ultimately, it appears that the balance between hearing the voice of the child and protecting them from parental conflict is unlikely to have been achieved (Dimopoulos et al., 2025).

Systemic Harms

In Australia, family law mostly operates under an adversarial system whereby the parties/parents provide the court with their evidence, and an outcome decision is made – either by consent or ordered by a judicial officer. The judicial officer does not undertake independent investigations and in accordance with the rules of evidence and procedure, makes decisions based on the information or evidence that is presented to them (Chisholm, 2007). Some researchers argue that a system where legally trained professionals who make psychosocial decisions for children, may potentially result in a violation of the child's rights (Dodds et al., 2023). For those parents who do proceed to court and the very few who then proceed to trial (less than 3% of 30%) of separated couples, the dynamic is such that the parties are essentially pitted against each other – one person wins, the other loses, decisions about parenting may be made by people who have no direct or long-standing knowledge of the child(ren), the extent to which the child's views and wishes are considered is likely variable and the proceedings can continue for years (Kaspiew & Carson, 2019). A potential by-product of this process is that the child is 'in the middle'.

The potential harm caused to children as a result of the nature of the system is such that academics in the field believe that family matters involving children ought to be less adversarial (Harrison, 2007). It is acknowledged that an adversarial system promotes conflict rather than reduces it; this is particularly problematic in family law because disputes between spouses is different to disputes between parties who are not known to each other (Sowter, 2018). Moreover, once the legal dispute is settled, after many months, if not years (R. Kaspiew et al., 2015), the former adversaries are supposed to co-parent their child in such a manner that the child is not negatively impacted. Research pertaining to outcomes for children involved in the system for many years is limited. It seems reasonable to conclude the consequences are in accordance with those found in HCS.

Unjustified Parental Absence

Unjustified parental absence concerns the divisive topic of parental alienation (PA). Briefly, research explains that PA is a process whereby one parent influences a child to reject the other parent (Georgeta et al., 2021; Bentley & Matthewson, 2020; Bernet & Greenhill, 2022; Haines et al., 2019; Harman et al., 2022; Kelly & Johnston, 2001). Several authors refer to markers of PA in a child. These are, the child resists or refuses to have a relationship/contact with one parent, the child previously enjoyed a positive relationship with that parent, there is no evidence of or corroborated details regarding abuse, highly dysfunctional or neglectful parenting, the campaign of denigration or negative influence occurs across several platforms (affidavits, social media, social settings, information to teachers), the child displays several behavioural examples of being alienated (for example, trivial reasons for the rejection, absence of guilt about the rejection, narratives that are identical to the alienating parent's, claiming their position is independent of any influence) (Bernet & Greenhill, 2022; Greenberg & Schnider, 2020).

Research pertaining to the consequences of alienating behaviours for children has increased markedly in the past decade or so. Even the most ardent detractors of the construct now concede that children can be manipulated or influenced to reject a previously loved parent (Meland, Furuholmen, & Jahanlu, 2024). The consequences for children have been likened to other forms of severe child abuse and include affective disorders, poor self-worth, substance misuse, dysfunctional parentification and/or adultification, 'loss of childhood'(Fidler & Bala, 2020) (Hine, 2024), pseudo-maturity disenfranchised grief and ambiguous loss (Harman et al., 2022).

It is likely difficult to quantify the lifelong consequences of PA, however, research in this area confirms that they are comparable to other forms of childhood abuse or trauma (Verhaar et al., 2022). Some research suggests that, in a similar vein to generational trauma, alienating behaviours are repeated in subsequent generations (Matthewson, 2023). A relatively recent systematic literature review found that adults who experienced PA as children experience depression and anxiety, poorer self-esteem, increased risk of psychopathology, higher substance misuse, higher divorce and separation rates and parental relationship challenges (Miralles et al., 2023). PA has been described by some as a "poorly understood form of violence" (Harman et al., 2019). Notably, when a mother is alienated, such alienation is more readily accepted as a form of violence against the mother and abuse of the child (Morris, 2009).

The impact of PA on a child's self-esteem occurs due to four inter-related areas. Firstly, when a child (incorrectly) receives a message that the targeted parent does not love the child, they readily conclude that they are not lovable. Then, when given messages that the targeted parent is flawed, dysfunctional, bad, they conclude that part of them must also be flawed. Thirdly, the child receives the message that receiving love from the alienating parent is contingent upon their embracing of the negative messages about the targeted parent; that is, the alienating parent hates the other parent more than they love their child. Finally, the child is manipulated to believe that the alienating parent knows their feelings, thoughts and needs better than the child themselves does. Such tactics may be covert or overt and the impacts can be subconscious or palpable (Baker & Ben-Ami, 2011).

Despite some controversy about definitions, insufficient research, and weaponising PA by abusive fathers (Mercer & Drew, 2021), there is increasing qualitative and quantitative research regarding its legitimacy and the outcomes for alienated children (Hine, 2024). Australian and international research is increasing, and subsequent findings are being grappled with in the family law system (Rathus et al., 2019).

REVERSAL OF CARE, REUNIFICATION THERAPY AND MORATORIUM OF TIME

In circumstances where there has been unjustified parental absence as outlined above, the court may order the child to live with the alienated parent and the perpetrating parent to not see the child for a period of time, usually some months. Certainly, this response is quite drastic and considered to be a last resort (Birnbaum & Bala, 2024). This study notes that there is limited research on the impact of reversal of care or, as it is referred to in other countries, reversal of custody. Nonetheless, the six children that were interviewed, shared information pertaining to the difficult experience of being alienated from one of their parents. All six young people had not had significant contact with the previously favoured parent for an average of five years since the reversal. It was noted that this was the case despite the current custodial parent encouraging them to do so; the no contact decision was linked to the child's wishes, or the previously favoured parent's wishes.

Given that a reversal of care only occurs in extreme cases, where resist-refuse dynamics are seen or where it has been determined that a child has been influenced to reject a previously loved parent (alienation), the court may also order the child and parent to participate in reunification therapy.

A challenge in providing an agreed, evidenced-based definition of 'reunification therapy' likely reflects the discretionary ways in which the practice is undertaken. Faust (2017), defines *Reunification Family Therapy*, as "a therapeutic process designed to repair relationships between parents and children in an attempt to restore not only physical contact but meaningful social, emotional, and interpersonal exchanges between parents and children" (p. 3). Clawar (2020) states it is "the process, techniques, methods, and theories that are employed to repair, reconnect, rebuild, heal, normalize, and/or stabilize a relationship between a parent and child that has become damaged, distant, absent, and/or alienated" (p. 5). In the Australian context, a standardised definition and the resultant processes arising from any definition have not been extensively researched or published.

The specifically labelled RT was not a feature of therapeutic family law work in Australia until the late 1990s. International publications that speak to the definition of RT, where and when it is undertaken and frameworks have originated from Canada, the United States of America, the United Kingdom, Brazil, Mexico, and New Zealand, to name a few (Joshi, 2021). One of the earliest references to reunifications in Australia is found in a 1998 publication that explored the activities of children's supervised contact centres. This publication noted that contact centres is one of the places that fathers could reunite with their child(ren) (Szirom, 1998).

If there is no agreed definition of what reunification therapy is, and if there are no best-practice guidelines pertaining to how it ought to be delivered, it is possible that it is being undertaken by people who are not appropriately skilled, qualified or experienced. Moreover, it is possible that there are instances where it is harmful. In 2023, a de-identified psychologist was recorded undertaking RT. Some of this recording was aired on the national broadcaster. The processes used by the therapist were described as unorthodox and possibly unethical (Davoren, 2023). Again, the possible harm caused to this child is unknown, although the journalist who reported this case, notes that all parties felt upset and concerned about the processes the therapist insisted were followed.

Problematically, although RT is regularly ordered, despite the lack of an agreed practice framework (Polak, 2020), the number of reversals of care that are therapeutically supported versus those that occur without therapeutic support, is unknown. It could be argued that if a child has been exposed to dynamics that are so fraught that a judicial officer has determined that the child is at greater risk of harm by remaining with the primary parent, than being summarily placed in the care of someone with whom they have had minimal time with, that child is highly psychologically vulnerable. It is critical that the (reversal of care) process *must* be therapeutically supported. Not providing therapeutic support is another potential source of harm. Disappointingly, such scenarios have not been researched.

Alongside a reversal of custody or care, the court may order a moratorium of time whereby the child does not see the previously favoured parent. The justification of course being that if a child has been negatively influenced against the other parent, then they need to be protected from that parent whilst they are re-establishing their previously positive relationship with the now-primary parent. A moratorium also provides a reprieve from negative messages about the other parent, it reduces the manifestation of loyalty conflicts and it provides a boundaried time-frame for therapeutic interventions to occur (Gottlieb, 2017; Gottlieb, 2012). Again, despite what might sound 'logical', there is a lacuna of evidence that upholds the necessity for a moratorium. This reality may underpin models of RT that do not require a 'parentectomy' (Polak et al., 2020). This latter model of RT involves a reversal of care, mandated therapeutic support for both the child and the parent and a pro-active approach to involving the favoured parent, noting that if a parentectomy occurs, resumption of a close relationship with the favoured parent after a moratorium is not guaranteed.

There are other models of RT that have been researched and utilised throughout the world. One such model of RT has been proposed by practicing clinical psychologist Kathleen Reay. Her Family Reflections Reunification Program (FRRP) was piloted in 2012 with 22 children. Three, six, nine and twelve month follow-ups demonstrated a 95% success rate; that is, the alienated children and previously rejected parent had sustained an on-going relationship (Reay, 2015). This author also notes that there are at least ten compelling reasons as to why traditional therapy will not only be unsuccessful, delivering traditional therapy can make the situation "catastrophically worse" (p.200). It is worth noting that international research about RT has often been undertaken by the program or process designer; the issue of confirmation bias should therefore, be considered (McSweeney, 2021).

IMPLICATIONS FOR PRACTICE AND POLICY

As noted earlier, issues facing children embroiled in the family law system have been identified, considered, and researched on an issue-by-issue basis; consideration of cumulative harm has not been afforded comparable attention Certainly, in the child protection system, cumulative harm is recognised as a significant issue requiring improved acknowledgement and consideration from both the legislative and judicial contexts (Sheehan, 2019). Importantly, unless key stakeholders, such as expert witnesses, family law professionals and the judiciary not only understand the enormous consequences of cumulative harm and are taught how to measure it, the devastating consequences for the subject children will continue unabated.

Although not extensively tested, replicated, or utilised, there are ways that cumulative harm can be measured (Bryce et al., 2024). It is hoped that the suggestions offered in this research be considered as a mandatory tool for children within the family law system. This would result in early intervention known to decrease harm (Sheehan, 2019), and improved or at least, less problematic outcomes for children involved in the family law system.

CONCLUSION

The potential impact of cumulative harm in the family law system cannot be overstated. This chapter has highlighted several touchpoints that children are potentially exposed to and noted the importance of acknowledging cumulative harm in family law matters. These touch points relate to inter or intra-personal factors such as pre-separation parental conflict, high conflict separation, unjustified parental absence/parental alienation and compromised parenting. There are also external factors, processes or parties that potentially case harm, including the consequences of an adversarial family law system that pits parents against each other, forensic processes, reunification and/or court-ordered therapy and reversal of care and moratorium of time orders without therapeutic support. There is scope for the construct of cumulative harm to be further investigated, acknowledged and addressed within this system and the stakeholders involved. Initially this would involve mechanisms to collect data relating to the issues raised in this chapter.

The following concluding de-identified case study provides an example of the possible consequences of cumulative harm that can occur to children embroiled in family law disputes. We see a child who has witnessed parental conflict, experienced significant lifestyle changes, separation of her parents, subsequent high conflict separation, forensic processes and perhaps, an inadequate assessment regarding the impact all these realities have had on her. Certainly, the impact of cumulative harm has not been adequately considered.

> *Alice's parents separated when she was seven years old, in 1997. She recalls that they fought a great deal prior to the actual separation – about so many things – such that when they told her they were separating, there was a part of her that actually felt relieved. She'd miss her father but was reassured she'd see him regularly. Alice, her mother and two older brothers, remained in the same house she'd always lived in despite her mother telling her that her father was trying to sell the house and didn't care where they lived. Alice worried about this and was confused about why her father would threaten such a thing. Although she enjoyed seeing him, the things her mother was telling her about him, made her angry. If you asked the mothers of Alice's friends, they would say she was quiet but sometimes had angry outbursts.*
>
> *When Alice was eight, she mentioned, almost in passing, that she didn't really like her grandmother's new husband and she especially didn't like that he tickled her even when she asked him to stop. After that, literally everything seemed to change. Her mother seemed angry with her, her father was 'weird', her brothers were doing their own thing, and she was told she'd have to talk to someone about where she wanted to live.*
>
> *Alice recalls that this is the time for her when the relief changed to confusion, worry and a knotted stomach. For the first time ever, she did not get any A's on her report and her teachers started reprimanding her about not paying attention in class.*
>
> *Alice recalls speaking with (who she now knows) to be a social worker. He was not very friendly; she remembers being told that whatever she said to him, he*

would be telling a judge and her parents would get to read his report. She recalls feeling really worried that she was going to say the wrong thing. She did not want either of her parents to be angry with her; she wanted both of them to love her and she wanted to stop feeling like she had to make sure they were happy. Alice was never entirely sure what the point of the conversation was. She knows however, that she never saw her step-grandfather again until she was a teenager. Alice thinks she talked about how much she loved her mum and her dad, but she sometimes forgot to take things from one house to the other. She also preferred the pillows at her mum's. Her dad was better at cooking, her mum was better at making school lunches. She hated that now her parents weren't 'a team 'and there was no part of her life that was how it was before they separated.

Alice is now 35 years old, has a 10 year old son and seven year old daughter. She has recently separated from her husband of 15 years and is seeking therapy to ensure her children are not subjected to "whatever I went through". Alice describes an adolescence where her self-esteem was poor, she did not achieve well at school, she was diagnosed with anxiety, she knew her parents "hated each other", her mother was constantly worried about money, and she disliked her father's new partner. She married her first boyfriend despite not loving him deeply but feeling as though he was as good as she'd get. Alice knows that her parents' divorce affected her, however she has not explored the reasons for this or the ways in which she has been impacted. Therapy will explore the impact of cumulative harm on Alice.

REFERENCES

Afifi, T. D., Mazur, A., Otmar, C., Wagner, A. C., Papernow, P. L., Methikalam, B., & Peightal, B. M. (2022). Coparenting: A focus on divorced families, stepfamilies, intergenerational families, and families with a child on the autism spectrum.

Akin Ojelabi, L., & Gutman, J. (2020). Family dispute resolution and access to justice in Australia. *International Journal of Law in Context, 16*(2), 197–215. DOI: 10.1017/S1744552320000142

Alina Georgeta, S., Mona, V., Luca, T., Adelina Mihaela, ., Otilia Ioana, T., Beatrice, M., & Roxana Andreea, T. (2021). Parental Alienation-Development and Validation of a Behavioral Anchor Scale. *Sustainability (Basel, Switzerland), 13*(316), 316. DOI: 10.3390/su13010316

Anderson, K. B. (2022). *Determining The Antecedents That Lead To High Conflict Domestic Disputes In Couples With Children.* Oakland University, AustLii. (1998 - 2025). AustLii (Research infrastructure facility). Retrieved from https://www .austlii.edu.au. from Faculties of Law, UTS & UNSW https://www.austlii.edu.au

Baker, A. J., & Brassard, M. R. (2013). Adolescents caught in parental loyalty conflicts. *Journal of Divorce & Remarriage, 54*(5), 393–413.

Baker, A. J. L., & Ben-Ami, N. (2011). To Turn a Child Against a Parent Is To Turn a Child Against Himself: The Direct and Indirect Effects of Exposure to Parental Alienation Strategies on Self-Esteem and Well-Being. *Journal of Divorce & Remarriage, 52*(7), 472–489. DOI: 10.1080/10502556.2011.609424

Barnes, G. G. (2020). Parental mental illness and extra difficulties for children when parents divorce. In *Building Children's Resilience in the Face of Parental Mental Illness* (pp. 90–109). Routledge.

Bentley, C., & Matthewson, M. (2020). The Not-Forgotten Child: Alienated Adult Children's Experience of Parental Alienation. *The American Journal of Family Therapy, 48*(5), 509–529. DOI: 10.1080/01926187.2020.1775531

Bergström, H., Westberg-Broström, A., & Eidevald, C. (2020). Swedish media discourses about child sexual abuse in preschools: The best interest of the child and continued trust in male teachers. *Early Child Development and Care, 190*(12), 1878–1886. DOI: 10.1080/03004430.2018.1544128

Bernet, W., & Greenhill, L. L. (2022). The Five-Factor Model for the Diagnosis of Parental Alienation. *Journal of the American Academy of Child and Adolescent Psychiatry, 61*(5), 591–594. DOI: 10.1016/j.jaac.2021.11.026

Beyene, M. (2024). Secular Interpretation of the Best Interest of the Child: CCI's Decision on Child Custody in the Context of Divorced Parents (Case Comment). *Mizan law review, 18*(2), 447-456. doi:DOI: 10.4314/mlr.v18i2.8

Birnbaum, R., & Bala, N. (2024). A Retrospective Study of Outcomes of Custody Reversal in Parental Alienation Cases. *University of New Brunswick Law Journal, 75*, 62.

Birnbaum, R., & Lach, L. M. (2016). Children With Neurodevelopmental Disorders in Parental Separation. *Parenting plan evaluations: Applied research for the family court*, 205.

Bonach, K. (2005). Factors contributing to quality coparenting: Implications for family policy. *Journal of Divorce & Remarriage, 43*(3-4), 79–103.

Briere, J., Scott, C., & Sage, p. (2025). *Principles of trauma therapy: a guide to symptoms, evaluation, and treatment* (Third edition. ed.). Thousand Oaks, California: SAGE.

Bryce, I. (2018). Cumulative risk and harm: The condition of accumulation in child maltreatment. *Communities, Children and Families Australia, 12*(1), 7–22.

Bryce, I., Beccaria, G., McIlveen, P., & Du Preez, J. (2023). When quantity takes on a quality of its own: A retrospective exploration of the lived experience of cumulative harm. *Child Abuse Review, 32*(4), e2800.

Bryce, I., Collier, S., Harris, L., Higgins, D., & Toohey, J. (2024). Measuring accumulation: Constructing a tool for evaluating cumulative harm in children engaged with an intensive family support service. *Child abuse review (Chichester, England: 1992), 33*(5), n/a. doi:DOI: 10.1002/car.2897

Cashmore, J. (2011). Children's participation in family law decision-making: Theoretical approaches to understanding children's views. *Children and Youth Services Review, 33*(4), 515–520.

Cheung, R. Y. M., & Chung, K. K. H. (2023). Interparental conflict and mindful parenting practices: Transactional effects between mothers and fathers. *Journal of Marriage and Family, 85*(1), 280–292. DOI: 10.1111/jomf.12868

Chisholm, R. (2007). 'Less adversarial' proceedings in children's cases. *Family Matters (Melbourne, Vic.)*, (77), 28–32.

Chung, K. M., Chung, E., & Lee, H. (2024). Behavioral Interventions for Autism Spectrum Disorder: A Brief Review and Guidelines With a Specific Focus on Applied Behavior Analysis. *Soa--ch'ŏngsonyŏn chŏngsin ŭihak = Journal of child & adolescent psychiatry, 35*(1), 29-38. doi:DOI: 10.5765/jkacap.230019

Clawar, S. S. (2020). *Parent-Child Reunification: A Guide to Legal and Forensic Strategies*. ABA Book Publishing.

Colton, K. C., Cao, V. T., & Davies, P. T. (2025). The Impact of Parental Conflict and Emotional Abuse on Children and Families. *Partner Abuse, 16*(1), 173–202. DOI: 10.1891/PA-2024-0042

Commerford, J., & Hunter, C. (2015). Children's Contact Services. *Key issues (Report no 35 2015). Australia, Melbourne: Australian Institute of Family Studies.*

Cronin Favazza, P., & Munson, L. J. (2010). Loss and grief in young children. *Young Exceptional Children, 13*(2), 86–99.

Cummings, E. M., & Davies, P. T. (2011). *Marital conflict and children: An emotional security perspective*. Guilford Press.

D'Onofrio, B., & Emery, R. (2019). Parental divorce or separation and children's mental health. *World Psychiatry; Official Journal of the World Psychiatric Association (WPA), 18*(1), 100–101. DOI: 10.1002/wps.20590

Daklallah, M. (2022). *Attachment style, self-esteem, and locus of control in adult children of divorce.*

Daly, A. (2018). *Children, autonomy and the courts: beyond the right to be heard.* Brill Nijhoff.

Davies, P. T., Thompson, M. J., Hentges, R. F., Coe, J. L., & Sturge-Apple, M. L. (2020). Children's Attentional Biases to Emotions as Sources of Variability in Their Vulnerability to Interparental Conflict. *Developmental Psychology, 56*(7), 1343–1359. DOI: 10.1037/dev0000994

Davoren, H. (2023, 5 October). False Witness. *Background Briefing*. Retrieved from https://www.abc.net.au/news/2023-06-19/family-court-report-writer-recording-expert-witness-ahpra/102185414

Đerlek, M. (2024). DEPRIVATION OF PARENTAL RIGHTS AND "THE BEST INTEREST OF THE CHILD". *Pravo, teorija i praksa, 41*(1), 151-163. doi:DOI: 10.5937/ptp2401151D

Dimopoulos, G., Hew, E., Vosz, M., & Walsh, H. (2025). 'Talk to Us, Not About Us': Children's Understandings and Experiences of Participation in Australian Family Law. *Child & Family Social Work*. Advance online publication. DOI: 10.1111/cfs.13275

Dodds, L., Creamer, C., Powell, Z., & Davis, C. (2023). "Stay in Your Own Lane" the Inherent Flaws Undermining Children's Rights Within Australia's Family Law System: A Perspective from the Field. *Journal of Human Rights and Social Work, 8*(4), 370–375.

Eddy, B. (2012). *High conflict people in legal disputes*. Unhooked Books.

Esmaeili, N. S., & Yaacob, S. N. (2012). Correlates of self-esteem among adolescents of divorced families. *Archives des Sciences, 65*(8), 52–59.

Evans, J. A., Krumrei-Mancuso, E. J., & Rouse, S. V. (2024). What you are hiding could be hurting you: Autistic masking in relation to mental health, interpersonal trauma, authenticity, and self-esteem. *Autism in Adulthood: Challenges and Management, 6*(2), 229–240.

Family Law Act 1975, (Cth).

Fares, R., Najem, R., Hallit, S., Pelissolo, A., Haddad, G., & Naja, W. J. (2023). Parental alienation in Lebanon: A case report. *Journal of Medical Case Reports, 17*(1), 164–167. DOI: 10.1186/s13256-023-03911-3

Faust, J. (2017). *Reunification family therapy: A treatment manual.* Hogrefe Publishing.

Fernando, M. (2013). Children's direct participation and the views of Australian judges. *Family Matters (Melbourne, Vic.)*, (92), 41–47.

Fidler, B. J., & Bala, N. (2020). Concepts, controversies and conundrums of "alienation:" Lessons learned in a decade and reflections on challenges ahead. *Family Court Review, 58*(2), 576–603.

Fiorini, J. J., & Mullen, J. A. (2006). Understanding grief and loss in children. *Vistas Online*, 31-33.

Goldstein, S., & Brooks, R. B. (2005). Resilience in children. *New York: Springer. Gooding, HC, Milliren, CE, Austin, SB, Sheridan, MA, & McLaughlin, KA (2016). Child abuse, resting blood pressure, and blood pressure reactivity to psychological stress. Journal of Pediatric Psychology, 41*, 5–12.

Gottlieb, L. (2017). Turning points for families: A therapeutic vacation. *Retrieved from End Parental Alienation:* http://endparentalalienation. weebly. com

Gottlieb, L. J. (2012). *The parental alienation syndrome: A family therapy and collaborative systems approach to amelioration*. Charles C Thomas Publisher.

Grape, L., Skoglund, J., Haugen, G. M. D., & Thørnblad, R. (2024). Adolescents' Negotiations of Loyalty and Fairness in Relation to Parents' Separation Process. *Child & Family Social Work*.

Greenberg, L. R., & Schnider, R. A. (2020). We're still taking x-rays but the patient is dying: What keeps us from intervening more quickly in resist-refuse cases? *Family Court Review*, *58*(2), 488–506. DOI: 10.1111/fcre.12484

Haines, J., Matthewson, M., & Turnbull, M. (2019). *Understanding and managing parental alienation: A guide to assessment and intervention*. Routledge.

Harman, J. J., Bernet, W., & Harman, J. (2019). Parental Alienation: The Blossoming of a Field of Study. *Current directions in psychological science: a journal of the American Psychological Society, 28*(2), 212-217. doi:DOI: 10.1177/0963721419827271

Harman, J. J., Warshak, R. A., Lorandos, D., & Florian, M. J. (2022). Developmental psychology and the scientific status of parental alienation. *Developmental Psychology*, *58*(10), 1887–1911. DOI: 10.1037/dev0001404

Harman, Matthewson, M. L., & Baker, A. J. (2022). Losses experienced by children alienated from a parent. *Current Opinion in Psychology*, *43*, 7–12.

Harold, G. T., & Sellers, R. (2018). Annual research review: Interparental conflict and youth psychopathology: An evidence review and practice focused update. *Journal of Child Psychology and Psychiatry, and Allied Disciplines*, *59*(4), 374–402.

Harrison, M. (2007). Finding a better way: A bold departure from the traditional common law approach to the conduct of legal proceedings.

Harwin, J. P., Madge, N. P., & Heath, S. (2010). Children affected by parental alcohol problems (ChAPAPs).

Hentges, R. F., Davies, P. T., & Cicchetti, D. (2015). Temperament and Interparental Conflict: The Role of Negative Emotionality in Predicting Child Behavioral Problems. *Child Development*, *86*(5), 1333–1350. DOI: 10.1111/cdev.12389

Hine, B. A. (2024). Parental Alienation-What Do We Know, and What Do We (Urgently) Need to Know? A Narrative Review. *Partner Abuse*, *15*(3), 362–396. DOI: 10.1891/PA-2023-0015

Hosokawa, R., & Katsura, T. (2019). Exposure to marital conflict: Gender differences in internalizing and externalizing problems among children. *PLoS One*, *14*(9), e0222021.

Jekielek, S. M. (1998). Parental conflict, marital disruption and children's emotional well-being. *Social Forces*, *76*(3), 905–936.

Jennings, S. (2005). AUTISM IN CHILDREN AND PARENTS. Unique Considerations for Family Court Professionals. *Family Court Review*, *43*(4), 582–595. DOI: 10.1111/j.1744-1617.2005.00057.x

Johnson, H. (2013). The gendered nature of violence: An international focus. In *Routledge international handbook of crime and gender studies* (pp. 91–119). Routledge.

Johnston, J., Roseby, V., & Kuehnle, K. (2009). *In the Name of the Child: A Developmental Approach to Understanding and Helping Children of Conflicted and Violent Divorce* (2nd ed.). Springer Publishing Company, Incorporated.

Johnston, J. R. (1994). High-conflict divorce. *The Future of Children*, ●●●, 165–182.

Joshi, A. (2021). Parental Alienation Is Real: Exposing the Myth of the Woozle. *Litigation*, *47*(3), 8–9.

Joyce, A. N. (2016). High-Conflict Divorce: A form of Child Neglect. *Family Court Review*, *54*(4), 642–656. DOI: 10.1111/fcre.12249

Kaspiew, R., Carson, R., Qu, L., Horsfall, B., Tayton, S., Moore, S., & Dunstan, J. (2015). *Court outcomes project*. Australian Institute of Family Studies.

Kaspiew. (2016). Separated parents and the family law system: what does the evidence say? Kaspiew, & Carson, R. (2019). *Parenting arrangments after separation: Evidence Summary*. Southbank: Commonwealth of Australia Retrieved from https://aifs.gov.au/sites/default/files/2022-06/1910_parenting_arrangements_after_separation.pdf

Kelly, J. B., & Johnston, J. R. (2001). THE ALIENATED CHILD:A Reformulation of Parental Alienation Syndrome. *Family Court Review*, *39*(3), 249–266. DOI: 10.1111/j.174-1617.2001.tb00609.x

Kempf, J. P., & Outlaw, B. D. (2023). Reunification therapy: A mechanism for managing the chaos. *Oklahoma Bar Journal, 94(9)*, 12 - 17. Retrieved from https://www.okbar.org/barjournal/november-2023/reunification-therapy-a-mechanism-for-managing-the-chaos/

Khan, M. M. R. (1963). The concept of cumulative trauma. *The Psychoanalytic Study of the Child*, *18*(1), 286–306.

Laletas, S., & Khasin, M. (2021). Children of high conflict divorce: Exploring the experiences of primary school teachers. *Children and Youth Services Review*, *127*, 106072.

Lange, A. M. C., Visser, M. M., Scholte, R. H. J., & Finkenauer, C. (2022). Parental Conflicts and Posttraumatic Stress of Children in High-Conflict Divorce Families. *Journal of Child & Adolescent Trauma, 15*(3), 615–625. DOI: 10.1007/s40653-021-00410-9

Lauritzen, C., Reedtz, C., Van Doesum, K. T. M., & Martinussen, M. (2014). Implementing new routines in adult mental health care to identify and support children of mentally ill parents. *BMC Health Services Research, 14*(1), 58–58. DOI: 10.1186/1472-6963-14-58

Lux, U., Christ, S. L., & Walper, S. (2021). Coparenting problems and parenting behavior as mediating links between interparental conflict and toddlers' adjustment difficulties in Germany. *Zeitschrift für Kinder- und Jugendpsychiatrie und Psychotherapie.*

Mannarino, A. P., & Cohen, J. A. (2011). Traumatic loss in children and adolescents. *Journal of Child & Adolescent Trauma, 4*(1), 22–33.

Matthewson, M. (2023). A qualitative exploration of reunification post alienation from the perspective of adult alienated children and targeted parents. *Frontiers in Psychology, 14 - 2023.* doi: https://doi.org/DOI: 10.3389/fpsyg.2023.1189840

McIntosh, J. E., Bryant, H. D., & Murray, K. (2008). Evidence of a different nature: The child-responsive and less adversarial initiatives of the Family Court of Australia. *Family Court Review, 46*(1), 125–136.

McSweeney, B. (2021). Fooling ourselves and others: Confirmation bias and the trustworthiness of qualitative research – Part 1 (the threats). *Journal of Organizational Change Management, 34*(5), 1063–1075. DOI: 10.1108/JOCM-04-2021-0117

Meier, J. S., & Sankaran, V. (2021). Breaking down the silos that harm children: A call to child welfare, domestic violence and family court professionals. *Va. J. Soc. Pol'y & L., 28*, 275.

Meland, E., Furuholmen, D., & Jahanlu, D. (2024). Parental alienation–a valid experience? *Scandinavian Journal of Public Health, 52*(5), 598–606.

Mercer, J., & Drew, M. (2021). *Challenging Parental Alienation.* Routledge.

Miralles, P., Godoy, C., & Hidalgo, M. D. (2023). Long-term emotional consequences of parental alienation exposure in children of divorced parents: A systematic review. *Current Psychology (New Brunswick, N.J.), 42*(14), 12055–12069. DOI: 10.1007/s12144-021-02537-2

Moloney, L. (2013). From Helping Court to Community-Based Services: The 30-Year Evolution of Australia's Family Relationship Centres. *Family Court Review, 51*(2), 214–223. DOI: 10.1111/fcre.12021

Morris, A. (2009). Gendered dynamics of abuse and violence in families: considering the abusive household gender regime. *Child abuse review (Chichester, England: 1992), 18*(6), 414-427. doi:DOI: 10.1002/car.1098

Newell, S., & Moss, A. (2011). *Supporting children and young people through change, loss and grief: An evaluation of the Seasons for Growth program*. Good Grief.

Noonan, L. P. (1985). *Effects of long-term parental conflict on personality functioning of children of divorce*. The Wright Institute.

Oren, L. (2018). No-Fault Divorce Reform in the 1950s: The Lost History of the "Greatest Project" of the National Association of Women Lawyers. *Law and History Review, 36*(4), 847–890. DOI: 10.1017/S0738248018000172

Parkinson, P. (2023). *Australian family law in context: commentary and materials* (8th edition. ed.). Sydney: Thomson Reuters Australia, Limited.

Pellón, I., Martínez-Pampliega, A., & Cormenzana, S. (2024). Post-divorce adjustment, coparenting and somatisation: Mediating role of anxiety and depression in high-conflict divorces. *Journal of Affective Disorders Reports, 16*, 100697.

Polak, S. (2020). Mental health professionals' practice of reintegration therapy for parent–child contact problems post-separation: A phenomenological study. *Journal of Divorce & Remarriage, 61*(3), 225–248.

Polak, S., Altobelli, T., & Popielarczyk, L. (2020). Responding to severe parent-child rejection cases without a parentectomy: A blended sequential intervention model and the role of the courts. *Family Court Review, 58*(2), 507–524. DOI: 10.1111/fcre.12496

Poortman, A.-R., & Voorpostel, M. (2009). Parental divorce and sibling relationships: A research note. *Journal of Family Issues, 30*(1), 74–91.

Quigley, C., & Cyr, F. (2018). The Voice of the Child in Parenting Coordination: Views of Children, Parents, and Parenting Coordinators. *Journal of Divorce & Remarriage, 59*(6), 501–527. DOI: 10.1080/10502556.2017.1403823

Rathus, Z. (2021). Social Scientists Operating in the Law: A Case Study of Family Assessment Experts in the Australian Family Law System. *International Journal of Law, Policy and the Family, 35*(1), ebab051.

Rathus, Z., Jeffries, S., Menih, H., & Field, R. (2019). "It's Like Standing on a Beach, Holding Your Children's Hands, and Having a Tsunami Just Coming Towards You": Intimate Partner Violence and "Expert" Assessments in Australian Family Law. *Victims & Offenders*, *14*(4), 408–440. DOI: 10.1080/15564886.2019.1580646

Reay, K. M. (2015). Family reflections: A promising therapeutic program designed to treat severely alienated children and their family system. *The American Journal of Family Therapy*, *43*(2), 197–207.

Reupert, A., Cuff, R., & Maybery, D. (2015). *Helping children understand their parent's mental illness*. Cambridge University Press.

Reupert, J., Maybery, D., & Kowalenko, N. M. (2013). Children whose parents have a mental illness: Prevalence, need and treatment. *The Medical Journal of Australia*, *199*(3), S7–S9. DOI: 10.5694/mja11.11200

Roma, P., Marchetti, D., Mazza, C., Ricci, E., Fontanesi, L., & Verrocchio, M. C. (2022). A Comparison of MMPI-2 Profiles Between Parental Alienation Cases and Custody Cases. *Journal of Child and Family Studies*, *31*(5), 1196–1206. DOI: 10.1007/s10826-021-02076-1

Rowlands, G. A., Warshak, R. A., & Harman, J. J. (2022). Abused and Rejected: The Link Between Intimate Partner Violence and Parental Alienation. *Partner Abuse*, *14*(1), 37–58.

Saini, M., & Birnbaum, R. (2007). Unraveling the label of" high conflict": What factors really count in divorce and separated families.

Schindeler, E. (2019). Family law court orders for supervised contact in custodial disputes - unanswered questions. *Children Australia*, *44*(4), 194–201. DOI: 10.1017/cha.2019.42

Schmidt, C. D., & Grigg, J. (2023). Counseling High Conflict: Navigating the Complexities of High Conflict Divorce. *The Family Journal (Alexandria, Va.)*, •••, 10664807231173689.

Schmidt, C. D., & Grigg, J. (2024). Counseling High Conflict: Navigating the Complexities of High Conflict Divorce. *The Family Journal (Alexandria, Va.)*, *32*(1), 71–80. DOI: 10.1177/10664807231173689

Sheehan, R. (2019). Cumulative Harm in Child Protection: The Hidden Concern. *Australian Social Work*, *72*(4), 434–446. DOI: 10.1080/0312407X.2019.1603316

Shumaker, D., & Kelsey, C. (2020). The existential impact of high-conflict divorce on children. *Person-Centered and Experiential Psychotherapies, 19*(1), 22–37. DOI: 10.1080/14779757.2020.1717985

Smart, P., & Neale, B. (2000). It's my life too'-Children's perspectives on post-divorce parenting. *FAMILY LAW-BRISTOL, 30*, 163–169.

Smith, V. C., Wilson, C. R., & Use, C. o. S., Prevention, Ryan, S. A., Gonzalez, P. K., . . . Walker, L. R. (2016). Families affected by parental substance use. *Pediatrics, 138*(2), e20161575.

Smyth, B. M., & Moloney, L. J. (2019). Post-separation parenting disputes and the many faces of high conflict: Theory and research. *Australian and New Zealand Journal of Family Therapy, 40*(1), 74–84.

Sowter, D. M. (2018). Advocacy in non-adversarial family law: A recommendation for revision to the model code. *Windsor Yearbook of Access to Justice, 35*, 401–432. DOI: 10.22329/wyaj.v35i0.5788

Stern, N., & Oehme, K. (2002). The troubling admission of supervised visitation records in custody proceedings. *Temple Law Review, 75*(2), 271–311.

Szirom, T., Jaffe, R., McIntosh, J., Holmes, L. (1998). Contact Services in Australia - Research and Evaluation Project.

Trinder, L. (1997). Competing constructions of childhood: Children's rights and children's wishes in divorce. *Journal of Social Welfare and Family Law, 19*(3), 291–305. DOI: 10.1080/09649069708415674

Turoy-smith, K. M., & Powell, M. B. (2017). Interviewing of Children for Family Law Matters: A Review. *Australian Psychologist, 52*(3), 165–173. DOI: 10.1111/ap.12193

Tustin, D., & Tustin, D. (2024a). *Common Co-Parenting Mistakes and Associated Orders*. Springer.

Tustin, D., & Tustin, D. (2024b). *Risk of Cumulative Harm for Children*. Springer.

VanDaalen, R. A., Vallefuoco, A. A., Fernandez, M. L., Liu, S. Y., & Lemaire, C. J. (2025). Public Perceptions of the Neurodiversity Movement: A Thematic Analysis. *Neurodiversity, 3*, 27546330251325973.

Vandana, N. (2023). Crisis of Parental Conflict: Impact on Children and Families. *Horyzonty Wychowania, 22*(64). Advance online publication. DOI: 10.35765/hw.2023.2264.08

Velleman, R., & Templeton, L. J. (2016). Impact of parents' substance misuse on children: An update. *BJPsych Advances*, *22*(2), 108–117.

Verhaar, S., Matthewson, M. L., & Bentley, C. (2022). The Impact of Parental Alienating Behaviours on the Mental Health of Adults Alienated in Childhood. *Children (Basel, Switzerland)*, *9*(4), 475. DOI: 10.3390/children9040475

Warshak. (2003). Payoffs and Pitfalls of Listening to Children. *Family relations, 52*(4), 373-384. doi:DOI: 10.1111/j.1741-3729.2003.00373.x

Warshak. (2018). Night shifts: Revisiting blanket restrictions on children's overnights with separated parents. *Journal of divorce & remarriage, 59*(4), 282-323.

Westrupp, E. M., Brown, S., Woolhouse, H., Gartland, D., & Nicholson, J. M. (2018). Repeated early-life exposure to inter-parental conflict increases risk of preadolescent mental health problems. *European Journal of Pediatrics, 177*(3), 419–427. DOI: 10.1007/s00431-017-3071-0

Younas, F., & Gutman, L. M. (2023). Parental risk and protective factors in child maltreatment: A systematic review of the evidence. *Trauma, Violence & Abuse, 24*(5), 3697–3714.

ENDNOTE

1 It is important to distinguish between family violence and high conflict as constructs. Labelling DFV as high conflict could lead to a perception of mutualising violence. This would be misleading given the highly gendered nature of DFV (Johnson, 2013).

Chapter 9
But It Is Only a Little Risk...
An Examination of Unacceptable Risk and Cumulative Risk in Australian Family Law

Isabelle Tiffany Chassain
https://orcid.org/0009-0002-6986-0888
Unique Minds Consultancy, Australia

ABSTRACT

When determining a child's best interests, safety remains a primary factor. The determination of safety is arguably the process of examining and weighing different factors to identify the child's best interests, with the understanding that safety should not be taken as having a fixed axis, content, or designated standard. The longstanding approach of M v M (1988) 166 CLR 69 reaffirmed in Isles v Nelissen [2022] FedCFamC1A 97 established that safety considerations will create circumstances of intolerable risk whereby it is "suffice to say that a conclusion of there being an unacceptable risk may be had from the cumulative consideration of factors." Arguably, Unacceptable risk is therefore the assessment and understanding of cumulative risk, where risk assessments are based on evidence-driven conclusions derived from known facts and circumstances. Drawing from Australian Family Law's conceptualisation of unacceptable risk, this article will further explore the interrelated nature of cumulative risk in the consideration of a child's best interests.

DOI: 10.4018/979-8-3373-9524-1.ch009

INTRODUCTION AND CONCEPTUAL FRAMEWORK

When determining parenting arrangements under Part VII of the *Family Law Act*, the Court must consider the child's best interests as paramount (Family Law Act, 1975, Section 60CA). However, the determination of best interests remains a subjective and normative process that requires careful, deliberate consideration of a multitude of factors (Australian Law Reform Commission, 1997) of which safety and risk are two. Since the amendments to the *Family Law Act i*n May 2024, specifically section 60CC, which sets out how a court determines the best interest of a child, it can be seen that the concept of ***promoting safety*** has become a pivotal factor, arguably more central. It has seen a move away from protecting the child from risk, harm, abuse and neglect to language that requires a more holistic, future-facing consideration of risk and its tolerance. Despite this, the High Court, in its 1988 decision of *M v M,* which introduced the accepted test of 'unacceptable risk' remains the basis for the relevant case law to consider when a harm to a child may be intolerable. This standard, established by *M v M* sets out the relevant test that the courts undertake when they are asked to determine and decide if a child may be exposed to unacceptable levels of risk of harm or risk, and what actions or processes (if any) could be undertaken to ameliorate it (*Demir v Ozden*, 2025; Fogarty, 2006). Within family law matters, the concept of unacceptable risk identifies that there is a level of safety that a child within their family unit should reasonably expect. It provides that the court has an obligation to ensure that it considers all potential harms, including their gravity, when considering their best interests.

In the context of family law, the concept of safety is not static, but rather is dynamic and context-dependent. Therefore, a nuanced understanding of the differences between risk and safety requires a clear delineation of the concepts – these terms are not interchangeable. Safety is a term with relatively new emphasis found within the *Family Law Act* and not defined by the legislation, despite its now central nature to section 60CC. As a term, it has been heavily examined by the judiciary as they attempt to determine its proper scope and intended application. Recent case law has shown that the consideration of safety requires significant discretion, with no fixed definition of what is meant by *"promote the safety*". However, despite there being no fixed definition or identified test, it has been understood that in order to promote the safety of a child the court must consider the relevant s 60CC factors in different degrees, and while the court may be informed by the characteristics of risk (*Heijman v D'Onofrio*, 2024) requiring assessments of risk (*AB v CD*, 2019) considerations of safety are not entirely based on risk alone. Instead, when determining best interests, it is the culmination of factors that must be considered as they are found in section 60CC (Family Law Act, 1975), which includes their effect and impact on the children. Helpfully, however, the courts, in their consideration of safety and its application to best interest, have identified that safety:

- "*is defined in the Oxford English Dictionary as the state of being protected from or guarded against hurt or injury; freedom from danger*" (*Paige v Muir*, 2025, para. [29]);
- is a term which is wide in nature, bound only by its object, which is to keep children, and those who care for them, from harm and ensuring that the arrangements meet their needs, therefore having no fixed content or standard (*Oyama v Oyama*, 2024);
- "*is a state in which hazards or conditions leading to the physical, psychological, or material harm are controlled in order to preserve the health and wellbeing of an individual.*" However, "*[i]t is not the complete elimination of risk of harm, but rather making such order as affords the child the most optimal protection from harm*" (*Denton v Denton (No 3)*, 2024, para. [30]); and
- is a "*means to advance the interest of and move to a stronger or more prominent position the safety (i.e., to be free from hurt, damage, harm or danger) of children and those who care for them*" (*Melounis v Melounis (No 4)*, 2024, para. [151]).

It can be seen from the above that each of these definitions, although not overtly specific, recognises that safety must be assessed based on the child's specific vulnerabilities and needs, rather than a rigid, one-size-fits-all standard. These interpretations of safety also align with Justice Nettle, in *AB v CD* (2019), who described safety as a "*protean*" concept, emphasising its fluidity and responsiveness to the unique circumstances of each case. What becomes apparent, when considering safety in the context of family law, is that when determining what orders allow for the promotion of safety for a child, it requires a court to consider which arrangements (Orders) give the child the strongest position and optimal protection from damage, harm or danger relating to their physical, emotional, psychological and general wellbeing and needs. This is important for understanding unacceptable risk, as it specifically relates to a safety threshold: the gravity of the harm and the possibility of it occurring, rather than the probability of its occurrence, are the significant factors in determining if there is unacceptable risk (*Isles v Nelissen*, 2022). It is the boundary identified by the Court whereby the existence of indicators of harm or the assessment of risk results in a conclusion to be drawn, based on the evidence, that the risk to the child is so great that it becomes intolerable for the child to be exposed or possibly be exposed to it, even if the risk has not yet materialised or the harm is only a possibility

(*Eastley v Eastley*, 2022; *Fitzwater v Fitzwater*, 2019; *Isles v Nelissen*, 2022; *M v M*, 1988; *Melounis v Melounis (No 4)*, 2024).

In family law matters, unacceptable risk has traditionally been considered in matters where 'big harm' or 'significant harm' (Fogarty, 2006) is identified, for example, when allegations of sexual abuse are raised (*Bead v Gaffin*, 2024; *Eastley v Eastley*, 2022; *Fitzwater v Fitzwater*, 2019; *Isles v Nelissen*, 2022; *M v M*, 1988) or there are concerns of significant psychological harm being done (*Bonney v Boone*, 2019; *Conte v Lachner*, 2024; *Demir v Ozden*, 2025; *Durante v Durante*, 2024); where there are allegations of significant and/or substantial family violence (*Dodd v Ferrell*, 2022) or other significant factors which will be of great detriment to the child, which warrant consideration as to whether they are intolerable (*Bant v Clayton*, 2015; *Rasheed v Galliano (No 2)*, 2024; *Reynolds v Reynolds*, 2025). However, this is not to say that unacceptable risk only occurs when a child is exposed to 'big harms/risks'; indeed, the cumulative nature of many risks or harms may, in some instances, result in a situation where the aggregation of risks makes the risks/harms collectively intolerable.

It is this potential application of unacceptable risk that this article seeks to explore further, as it is not clear from the case law whether it is contemplated by the family law courts in general consideration of safety or unacceptable risk tests, nor is it an area that has received any real academic consideration as it relates to family law. What this article seeks to start is the exploration of how the use of the unacceptable risk test could align with the social science theories and child protection understandings of cumulative risk, which clearly demonstrate that ongoing and repeated exposures to what may be considered 'little' risks or harms can have a lasting and profound impact on a child's emotional, psychological and developmental wellbeing and needs (Bryce, 2018a; Bryce et al., 2024; Gilmor, 2010; Miller, 2007, p. 1). In exploring cumulative risk in this manner, it suggests that it may be a further harm subset that should be considered in family law matters through the same test of unacceptable risk, should the factors present a situation where, cumulatively, they are so grave that one must determine whether they are intolerable to the child.

Traditional legal frameworks often aim to focus on tangible evidence of harm, identifiable through specific actions or observable outcomes; yet this fails to address how many forms of harm, including coercive control, emotional neglect, and situational instability, are less visible yet equally damaging. Recognising the impact of these subtle forms of harm requires a shift in legal perspective to include subjective experiences and the cumulative impact, which involves a consideration of social science research (Prout, 2005). However, the writer notes that, while not the subject of this specific article, this creates a legal conundrum itself, with the courts' use of extrinsic research being another area that must be grappled with to allow this to succeed. In the social sciences and interestingly in child welfare jurisdictions, cumulative harm, is an emerging term in that in this context refers to the accumulation of adverse childhood experiences (ACE) that may include abuse, neglect, adversity and dysfunction, with such occurring over a prolonged time or in a repetitive manner (Bryce, 2018a; Bryce et al., 2023; Bromfield et al., 2007; Edwards et al., 2003; Jonson-Reid et al., 2012). In these contexts, it also leads to consideration and exploration of other factors that impact it, including cultural, gender-related, and socio-economic factors that influence a child's safety in relation to the identified risk. For instance, cultural norms might shape perceptions of what constitutes acceptable behaviour, potentially concealing harmful practices; gender dynamics may influence the recognition and reporting of abuse, with societal biases sometimes minimising the experiences of certain groups; and socio-economic issues, such as poverty and limited access to resources, can heighten vulnerabilities and obstruct protective interventions. Understanding how these factors may affect the child is not always immediately evident to the court when assessing risk. However, they can significantly influence the child's and family's resilience and risk levels and may affect the orders a court may seek to issue to address and mitigate these risk factors.

Moreover, while not challenging the traditional focus of unacceptable risk in relation to these 'large risks'; considering unacceptable risk through the lens of cumulative harm/risk requires explicit attention to be had to the potential that when there are several 'little' risks identified, that the cumulative nature of those identified risks may become (in some instances) intolerable if they cannot be appropriately ameliorated. This shifts risk consideration to a continuum-based model that identifies risks as existing along a spectrum, enabling courts to identify patterns that may seem insignificant when considered individually but, when considered cumulatively, may pose a significant harm to a child (Chisholm, 2011; Bryce, 2018a, 2018b). Without incorporating cumulative risk analysis, the legal system may overlook the compounded effects of multiple low-level risk factors, where persistent exposure to seemingly minor adversities can accumulate, leading to significant harm over time.

Considering risk through the concept of a continuum also acknowledges the drafting of section 60CC of the *Family Law Act* (as well as the *United Nations Convention on the Rights of the Child*[1]) which provides for a non-hierarchical, non-exhaustive list of factors to be considered and weighed as is appropriate to the individual child (*Oyama v Oyama*, 2024). For example issues of safety as referred to in section 60CC(2)(a) can impact upon the capacity of a parent to provide for the psychological needs of a child (section 60CC(2)(d)) and in turn can impact upon the benefits of having a relationship with a parent (section 60CC(2)(e)) while views expressed by a child at section 60CC(2)(b) can be indicative of the emotional needs of the child under s 60CC(2)(c) (*Oyama v Oyama*, 2024; *Selwood v Selwood (No 2)*, 2024) and may provide insight as to the 'little' factors which are impacting the child. These factors then arguably impact considerations of unacceptable risk, for example, to promote the safety of the child, specifically with reference to their psychological needs, the relationship between a parent and a child may not be able to be supported (*Durante v Durante*, 2024). However, unless there are clear signs, like in *Durante v Durante* (2024), indicating that such a decision is necessary, the overall effect of the 'little harms' might not be considered in cases where the long-term impact is unknown or not yet apparent. This could lead to them being overlooked because they do not align with common legal definitions or perspectives, or the ongoing nature of the harm might be minimised and not fully recognised by the Court or Court experts. Courts can struggle to recognise and substantiate less visible harms, such as emotional abuse or coercive control, as these harms may lack physical evidence, making them more difficult to prove under traditional legal standards (Australian Law Reform Commission, 2019; Elizabeth et al., 2012; Rathus et al., 2019). Additionally, bias or a lack of awareness might lead to these harms being minimised or dismissed.

Yet interestingly, the unacceptable risk test offers a potential framework that could mitigate this. In understanding the application of the test of unacceptable risk, the court has identified that any risk assessment first involves predicting the likelihood of the potential event, the prospect, and the magnitude of the harm that may result from the event. It then involves weighing these two considerations to determine if the risk is acceptable in the circumstances (*Isles v Nelissen*, 2022; *Bant v Clayton*, 2015; *Hickson v Matthew*, 2022).[2] It is a predictive exercise influenced by factual findings from past events. It contemplates potential harm and views it as existing within a continuum - ranging from highly probable to remotely possible - and identifies a point on this continuum where the risk "*becomes so potent it cannot be tolerated*" (*Durante v Durante*, 2024, para. [193]; *Fitzwater v Fitzwater*, 2019, para. [148]-[149]). Judgements focus on the future, requiring significant value judgements, assumptions, as well as educated, uncertain predictions and intuitions (*Grella v Jamieson*, 2017; *Roberts v Short*, 2024).[3] Assessing risk in this manner aligns with the methods established by *M v M* (1988) and *Isles v Nelissen* (2022), which involve evaluating both the possibility of harm and its severity. However, together with these two considerations, it also necessitates explicitly considering the child's unique needs and development, as well as how the accumulation of 'little risks/harms' impacts the child holistically. This approach aims to ensure the most suitable environment for the child, taking into account their individual circumstances. For example, a child with a history of trauma, such as poverty or neglect, may be more vulnerable to specific risk factors and thus require a more cautious approach in care arrangements. This often involves a multidisciplinary understanding of the circumstances before the Court, along with consistent methodologies and processes.

I. THE EVOLUTION AND LEGAL FOUNDATIONS OF UNACCEPTABLE RISK

The legal standard for unacceptable risk remains deliberately flexible, enabling courts to adapt to the complexities of modern family dynamics. However, this flexibility also becomes its weakness, as without structured guidance, decision-making may become inconsistent or overly discretionary (D. J. Higgins & Kaspiew, 2011). Consequently, one judge's threshold for 'unacceptable' may differ markedly from another's (*CDJ v VAJ (No 1)*, 1998; *Kellerman v Kellerman*, 2024). This is especially important when applying the concept of cumulative risk to such situations, as perception of risk, or the accumulation of risks, based on their knowledge, experience, and understanding, varies (Fogarty, 2006). As *Deiter v Deiter* (2011) clarifies risk assessments have two elements, being the likelihood of the occurrence and the severity of the impact (*Deiter v Deiter*, 2011; *Durante v Durante*, 2024) and it becomes a balance act where some occurrence of the risk may be tolerable, but an unacceptably high risk of the same is not, or not in the circumstances of the individual child (*Deiter v Deiter*, 2011; *Demir v Ozden*, 2025; *Durante v Durante*, 2024, para. [80]-[81]; *Hasip v Ruwan*, 2024; *Isles v Nelissen*, 2022, para. [86]).

As detailed earlier, the concept of unacceptable risk was crystallised in the High Court decision of *M v M* in 1988, where the Court was tasked with determining the parenting arrangements for a family where allegations of sexual abuse were present; however, the evidentiary proof, considered sufficient in criminal matters, was lacking. In this case, the High Court was not satisfied on the evidence that the father was guilty of sexual abuse. Stating that "*... the court must determine on the evidence there is a risk of sexual abuse occurring if custody or access be granted and assess the magnitude of that risk... a court will not grant custody or access to a parent if that custody or access would expose the child to an unacceptable risk of sexual abuse*" (*M v M*, 1988, p. 582) yet they did not elaborate on how this would need to be established on the evidence (*Isles v Nelissen*, 2022, para. [5]). The High Court determined that, given the circumstances, no contact with the Father was in the child's best interests because the doubt which remained that the Father might have sexually abused the child was of *"sufficient strength to warrant the denial of access"*(*M v M*, 1988, p. 583). This ruling showed that the Court prioritised protecting the child from risk over the rights of the parents, particularly when the concerns were serious and well-founded, even if not definitively and conclusively proven (Chisholm, 2010; Parkinson, 2015).

The concept of unacceptable risk was later built upon by the Family Court, whereby the court determined that unacceptable risk was "*a balance between the risk of detriment to the child from sexual abuse and the possibility of benefit to the child from parental access*" (*In the Marriage of B*, 1993, p. 58) This was further considered in *Napier v Hepburn* (2006), where it was determined that the application of unacceptable risk required a consideration of both the magnitude of the harm which may occur to the child if abused in the way envisaged and the likelihood of such abuse occurring (*Napier v Hepburn*, 2006). Where the starting point was to recognise the chance of a future adverse event, even though it has not yet occurred and thus cannot be proven (*CDJ v VAJ (No 1)*, 1998; Riethmuller, 2023).

Since *M v M* (1988), there have been various interpretations of how unacceptable risk is determined. It has been recognised that a more nuanced approach is required, recognising that allegations and risk do not exist in isolation but must be viewed within the full context of the case before the Court. Recent decisions continue to support this view, understanding that safety is not a fixed idea but a "*protean or (variable) conception which is certainly informed by the nature and gravity of apprehended harm and the risk of its occurrence*"(*AB v CD*, 2019, para. [205]). For example, the 2022 decision of *Isles and Nelissen* saw an appeal dismissed by the Full Court in similar circumstances to *M v M* (1988), where the Father had been accused of the rape of a child, yet the criminal proceedings had been discontinued due to a *"lack of specificity"* (*Isles v Nelissen*, 2022, para. [63]). The Court determined that the *"possibility of abuse could be enough to vindicate a finding that an unacceptable risk of harm exists"* (*Isles v Nelissen*, 2022, para. [37]) and that it was not necessary to prove the harm on the balance of probabilities, as previously suggested (*Fitzwater v Fitzwater*, 2019; *Isles v Nelissen*, 2022, para. [6], [46], [50], [51], [81]).

The Court argued that expecting possibilities to be proven forensically is oxymoronic, stating that risks of harm are postulated from the known historical facts (which must be proven on the balance of probabilities) and current circumstances of the case (*Durante v Durante*, 2024; *Fitzwater v Fitzwater*, 2019; *Isles v Nelissen*, 2022) and must been heeded even if the concerned events are improbable eventualities (*Fitzwater v Fitzwater*, 2019; *Isles v Nelissen*, 2022). However, that an inability to prove past allegations of abuse does not result in that evidence becoming irrelevant to the assessment of future risks either (Parkinson, 2021; Riethmuller, 2023) For example in *Isles v Nelissen* (2022), in the original decision, while the trial judge could not make findings of specific sexual abuse, he did make findings that the father presented an unacceptable risk; with the Full Court agreeing on appeal with the primary judge that it was *"suffice to say that a conclusion of there being an unacceptable risk may be had from the cumulative consideration of factors"* (*Isles v Nelissen*, 2022, para. [71]). The Full Court confirmed that even if not proven on the balance of probabilities, evidence of past abuse is sufficient to assess potential future risk. To explain why unacceptable risk cannot be judged on the balance of probabilities, the Full Court used the follow hypothetical situation: *"imagine a child will be minded by one of three randomly allocated carers. Assume one of the carers would sexually abuse the child, but the other two would not, meaning the child stands a 33.33 per cent chance of being sexually abused if left in care. No sensible adult would take the risk of leaving the child in care because even though the prospect of sexual abuse is only possible but not probable, the risk is still too high to tolerate. In other words, it is unacceptable"* (*Isles v Nelissen*, 2022, para. [86]).

This was further reinforced in the 2022 decision of *Eastley v Eastley* (decided shortly after *Isles v Nelissen*), where the trial judge, although not satisfied that the requisite standard of proof had been met to make an affirmative finding of fact, was nonetheless not convinced on the balance of probabilities that the incidents did not occur. Consequently, the judge relied on the evidence presented when considering the future risk, despite it not being sufficient proof to establish a fact (*Eastley v Eastley*, 2022; Riethmuller, 2023). The 2024 decision of *Durante v Durante* (2024) also considered the process for determining unacceptable risk in the context of parental alienation, where it was found that the risk of the mother having a relationship with the children was unacceptable. In determining the parenting arrangements for two children, the Court found that the behaviour of the Father and the paternal grandparents had caused the children to be *"profoundly disturbed"* (*Durante v Durante*, 2024, para. [5]). The Court identified that despite the children experiencing harm in the Father's care, where they were considered to be *"well down the path of major psychiatric and personality problems"*, and where neither the Father nor the paternal grandparents understood the extraordinary damage which they had caused to the children's lives (*Durante v Durante*, 2024, para. [7]-[8]), the risk of them having a relationship with the mother outweighed the risk associated with them remaining in the Father's care.

As discussed above, the doctrine of unacceptable risk has developed from a judicial innovation in *M v M* (1988) into a flexible yet increasingly complex standard, as confirmed by *Isles v Nelissen* (2022) and more recent cases. Arguably, this is supported by the application of section 65D, which grants the Court the power to make any decisions it "thinks proper," ensuring that orders do not place children at unacceptable risk, as such decisions would not be considered proper (Riethmuller, 2023). Yet, despite this, some of its complexity arises because, although it is an accepted concept in family law, the *Family Law Act* does not legislate it, and case law is relied on to determine its application (Pierluigi, 2020; Riethmuller, 2023).[4] The unacceptable risk test remains a process in which the court is required to consider, first, what the risk is; second, the magnitude of harm that could result from it and whether it is intolerable; and finally, whether there is a reasonable way to mitigate the risk (*In the Marriage of B*, 1993; *Murphy v Murphy*, 2007; *Napier v Hepburn*, 2006; *W v W (Abuse Allegations: Unacceptable Risk)*, 2005; *Young v Young*, 2010; Pierluigi, 2020). Considering unacceptable risk in this manner, through these three steps, allows for a transition where it is not necessary to regard unacceptable risk as only occurring in 'big risks' as is traditionally considered in the case law; but instead to consider the combined effects of multiple smaller risks and whether reasonable measures can mitigate them, or if the overall accumulation of these risks exposes the child to potential harm that, if realised, would be intolerable. Therefore, it is necessary to understand cumulative risk and harm, and the impact they have on a child's best interests.

II. UNDERSTANDING CUMULATIVE RISK: LEGAL AND PSYCHOLOGICAL DIMENSIONS

Cumulative risk refers to the aggregation of multiple risk factors that, although individually may seem insignificant, collectively pose a substantial threat to a child's wellbeing and thus potentially result in cumulative harm. Cumulative harm is the "*effects of patterns of circumstances and events in a child life which diminish the child's sense of safety, stability and wellbeing. Cumulative harm is the existence of compounded experiences of multiple episodes of abuse or 'layers' of neglect*"(Bromfield et al., 2007; Bromfield & Higgins, 2005; Bryce, 2018b; Miller, 2007, p. 1). Although a relatively modern term, research suggests that cumulative harm may be as pervasive and catastrophic as other forms of maltreatment, potentially even more so (Bryce, 2018a); and while singular events of 'big' harm may present devastating impacts to a child, chronic experiences of 'little' harms are alarming more frequent than singular episodic 'big' events (Bromfield et al., 2007; Bromfield & Higgins, 2005; Edwards et al., 2003; Felitti et al., 1998; D. Higgins, 2004; D. J. Higgins & McCabe, 1998). Concerningly, research has identified that repetitive episodes of harm (which in isolation may not be considered detrimental) may have greater predictive power for adverse outcomes in children than singular larger risk factors when experienced over a prolonged period (Bath, 2014; Bryce, 2018b; D. Higgins, 2004; Li et al., 2014; MacKenzie et al., 2011)

While research has identified that children may be able to 'overcome or grow from' single episodic maltreatment instances despite them being devastating, cumulative harm research has identified that as episodes accumulate, the child's ability to endure and maintain resilience diminishes, and with it, the accumulation of multiple developmental insults increases (Bath, 2014; Bryce, 2018b; Kinniburgh et al., 2005; Newman & Blackburn, 2002). This means that as a child is exposed to ongoing 'little risks' or as the child's adversity accumulates, the more harm the child experiences, which correlates with an increased risk of lifelong adverse outcomes (Bryce, 2018b; Edwards et al., 2003; Felitti, 2017; Finkelhor et al., 2007). From a legal perspective, the question then becomes: when does this become intolerable and therefore, when do matters of cumulative risk and harm become considerations for an unacceptable risk test?

Research in social science fields highlights that cumulative harm results from the interaction of various factors like family violence, substance abuse, mental health issues, and neglect. It recognises that these factors often co-occur, whereby a child may face ongoing adversity across different areas of their life without relief (Bryce et al., 2023; Miller, 2007; Sheehan, 2019b). While these may seem minor when considered alone, their combined effect can be substantial, sometimes even catastrophic. This is in line with trauma theory, which further elucidates how persistent exposure to such stressors can disrupt early brain development, attachment, and resilience, leading to long-term detrimental effects, with evidence indicating that neglect may be even more damaging than abuse, although it may not be initially observable (Bryce, 2018a; McQueen et al., 2008; Nader, 2008; Sheehan, 2019a). Child welfare research has identified that procedures must reflect the damaging and pervasive nature of cumulative harm. That processes must be able to identify factors of risk, regardless of whether a child is exhibiting indicators of harm, and if risk is identified, these processes must be able to support intervention, or mitigating requirements and strategies (Bryce, 2024).

In family law matters and across social science more generally, harm is typically explored in terms of specific subtypes: neglect, physical, psychological (emotional abuse), sexual abuse and witnessing family violence (Bath, 2014; Bryce, 2018b; Family Law Act, 1975, s 60CC; Herrenkohl & Herrenkohl, 2009; D. Higgins, 2004). Unfortunately, these factors rarely occur in isolation, and their co-occurrence can increase the risk and potential for harm. The Australian Childhood Maltreatment Study found that one in four children has experienced three or more types of abuse in their childhood, and that the prevalence of emotional abuse is considerably more harmful and prevalent than previously understood (Haslam et al., 2023; Mathews et al., 2023). It found that the dominance and pervasiveness of emotional abuse could be considered more harmful than expected, highlighting that traditional views, which considered neglect to have a higher impact, may be incorrect, as the studies found that the impact of emotional abuse may be at a cumulative level causing the most harm to children (Bryce, 2024; Mathews et al., 2023).

As discussed earlier, in Australian family law, recognising cumulative risk presents a unique challenge due to the traditional focus on separate incidents of harm, as reflected in case law and explicitly in unacceptable risk considerations (*Eastley v Eastley*, 2022; *Isles & Nelissen*, 2021; *M v M*, 1988). However, with the most recent amendments in 2024 and the increasing judicial exploration of section 60CC's aim to promote the child's safety, there appears to be a shift in the family court towards treating safety as a holistic requirement (*Melounis v Melounis (No 4)*, 2024); which may provide a more straightforward pathway for cumulative risk considerations. This growing recognition and understanding of safety factors, however, must also account for the cumulative impact of multiple risk factors when assessing the child's best interests. While there appears to be an acknowledgement that section 60CC *of the Family Law Act* is interconnected, it has not yet reached the stage where numerous 'little' risks are actively considered along a continuum; instead, it appears that in many instances risk factors are still treated as unique and standalone subsets within safety considerations. Arguably, this may be due to evidentiary challenges, where demonstrating cumulative risk requires comprehensive documentation and analysis of patterns over time, which can be difficult in legal proceedings that favour evidentiary proof, and may not be available or may not meet standards of proof. Or this may remain as a byproduct of historical drafting of the legislation and the ongoing discord in the law's use of social science in decision-making more generally (Altobelli, 2021; Bryant, 2012; Family Law Council, 2009; *McGregor v McGregor*, 2012; Rathus, 2018).

If this is the case, it then requires different approaches to adequately recognise, address, and account for aspects of 'little risk', assisting in their identification through complex considerations of cumulative risk. Such practices may include recognising patterns of behaviour or outcomes that result from risk or harm factors; ensuring that child-centred assessments are undertaken, focusing on the child's subjective experience and the impact of their circumstances on their overall wellbeing; and understanding that collaboration between the law and social science is essential to facilitate the first two steps. This acknowledges that while family law is a process overseen by the courts, understanding the content of the legal problem requires social science insights to grasp the nuanced nature of family dynamics and the best interests of a child (Bryant, 2012; *McGregor v McGregor*, 2012; Rathus, 2012, 2014).

While the judiciary ultimately bears the responsibility for making factual determinations in legal cases, it is important to acknowledge that understanding the impact of cumulative harm may not fall within the broader skill set of the legal profession. Experts such as psychologists and social workers, particularly those involved in family reports, play a vital role in evaluating cumulative risk as well as other factors more generally, which may not be specifically legal in nature (Cashmore & Parkinson, 2009; Meagher, 2012; Rathus, 2021). It is generally accepted that these individuals may be better positioned to provide the court with insights into the child's experiences, family dynamics, and the potential impact of various risk factors, as they are often better at identifying and highlighting patterns of concern and understanding the interconnected nature of risks and how these may cumulatively affect a child, given their professional background (Federal Circuit and Family Court of Australia, 2021; Tippins & Wittmann, 2005). This is especially true in family law proceedings where evidence is often fragmented and historical, particularly in cases of alleged abuse or neglect. Such evidence might include uncorroborated testimonies, outdated reports, or incidents from many years ago. This fragmentation can make it challenging to assess the current risk to the child, but courts must navigate these complexities to determine whether past behaviours still pose a threat or if there are new issues affecting the child's best interests together with being able to identify whether these pose an unacceptable risk. The involvement of social science professionals helps the court understand the often complex and nuanced nature of family law matters, as they can provide context, refer to relevant theories, and may be best suited to assist with self-disclosure on disputed issues (Attorney-General's Department, 2021; Family Law Council, 2009; Meagher, 2012; Tippins & Wittmann, 2005) while being able to advise on risk factors and the implications of those at a more holistic level.

Unacceptable risk at its core is a test that asks the court to determine, based on known information and in accordance with the *Family Law Act*, whether there are risks present that create circumstances where the chance of injury is one that cannot be ignored and if that risk is to a level where it cannot be allowed (Pierluigi, 2020). Therefore, what both the theory of cumulative risk and the Court's unacceptable risk test do is identify the imperative to protect children from risks or harms that will cause such damage to a child that it is intolerable for that child to be exposed to it or the potential of it. This requires a nuanced and balanced understanding of the risk involved, the potential consequences and the available interventions or mitigations. It is an understanding that while under protection may expose a child to continued harm, this must be balanced with over-protection, which means that the courts must carefully and thoroughly weigh the evidence before them in a manner that prioritises the child's best interests. Further, it requires the court to make determinations not solely based on facts but rather through evidence-based judicial assessments and predictions (Riethmuller, 2023).

III. FROM UNACCEPTABLE RISK TO CUMULATIVE RISK

Unacceptable risk and cumulative risk each identify factors that indicate, based on those factors, a potential threat to a child that might require a courts intervention to serve the child's best interests. As this article identifies, the best interests are a normative and subjective process that requires consideration of multiple factors when determining the optimal outcome for the child's well-being. This requires the courts to explicitly consider a child's safety, a dynamic and context-dependent concept that involves both risk and harm factors. Through the examination of recent decisions that have contemplated the meaning of safety since the May 2024 reforms, it can be seen that safety is a concept whereby, through orders, the court provides the child with the most appropriate protection from hurt, injury, or danger, and mechanisms are designed to attempt to manage any hazards or conditions that could lead to the child's harm (*Denton v Denton (No 3)*, 2024; *Melounis v Melounis (No 4)*, 2024; *Oyama v Oyama*, 2024; *Paige v Muir*, 2025).

While unacceptable risk and cumulative risk relate to the consideration and determination of risk, their individual purposes are quite different. Unacceptable risk refers to the boundary identified by the courts, where, through assessing indicators of harm, the court considers whether a child has been exposed or could be exposed to a risk so severe that it is intolerable, even if the risk has not yet materialised (*Eastley v Eastley*, 2022; *Fitzwater v Fitzwater*, 2019; *Isles v Nelissen*, 2022; *M v M*, 1988; *Melounis v Melounis (No 4)*, 2024). In considering unacceptable risk, the Court must conduct predictive and forward-looking assessments to determine the likelihood of a potential event and its possible impact, based on historical data and concerns. Although some argue that expecting these possibilities to be proven in court is unreasonable, it is understood that this approach is intentionally flexible. It allows risks to be evaluated using known facts and the specific case circumstances, acknowledging concerns even if they are deemed unlikely. Traditionally, such assessments focus on significant harm, such as allegations of sexual abuse or severe psychological damage. Cumulative risk, however, refers to the accepted theory that the aggregation of multiple risks collectively pose a significant threat to a child's wellbeing, and may cause pervasive and catastrophic harm to a child similar to other forms of significant maltreatment (Bromfield et al., 2007; Bromfield & Higgins, 2005; Bryce, 2018b; Miller, 2007, p. 1). Despite this, it appears that limited judicial attention has been given to whether numerous smaller risks might, collectively, create a situation in which a boundary is established identifying a level of cumulative risk that is intolerable, up to and including the level identified as unacceptable risk. Establishing such a boundary, in the context of unacceptable risk, would align family law with social science and child welfare principles, where it is recognised that the accumulation of adverse child experiences may be significantly damaging to a child, if not managed, mitigated, or removed (Bryce, 2018a; Bryce et al., 2023; Bromfield et al., 2007; Edwards et al., 2003; Jonson-Reid et al., 2012).

This is not to say that the court does not consider cumulative risk; rather, it has not been explicitly considered as a factor of unacceptable risk. Suppose a hypothetical situation similar to that identified in *Isles v Nelssen* (2022), where smaller emotional risk factors are identified instead of a significant sexual abuse risk. In that case, it offers an insightful view of a child facing repeated risks that could be considered minor if isolated but could significantly and irreversibly impact their wellbeing, as illustrated in *Durante v Durante* (2024). For example, imagine a child will be cared for by one of three people who will be allocated at random. Assume one of these carers will regularly and repeatedly belittle the child, expose them to instances of high conflict which includes verbally abusing the other two potential carers in the child's presence, will regularly and repeatedly speak poorly of the other two carers and their families to the child and will not allow the child to engage with friends and family of the other carers when they are in that carers care. Together with this, when it came time to transition the child to another carer, the carer withheld the child and continued to expose them to the ongoing emotional conflict and hostility that the child had already experienced while in their care. No sensible adult would consider this an appropriate living environment for a child. While the prospect of the child being subject to this is only possible, not probable, it still represents a very serious risk for the child. If the court considered this situation through the lens of cumulative harm research, especially concerning emotional abuse, it could be argued that repeated and prolonged exposure to such harm might be disastrous for the child and substantially increase the risk of lifelong negative outcomes. The question then becomes: when does this transition to intolerable?

This scenario highlights another important insight from this article: the subjective nature of safety and risk, where safety is not an abstract legal condition; it varies according to a child's vulnerabilities, needs, and environmental factors. That while harms may be, in some instances, tolerable, they may be disproportionately affected by other factors which require those who are assessing risk to ensure that the child's experience is central, not incidental, to the questions being asked and the considerations made. What this article did highlight is the conceptual gaps between how risk is defined in legal reasoning, in that it is often tied to events or incidents, those which are definable and have some basis that can be proven; and how risk is understood in social science, in that it is often tied to outcomes of adversity where it considers the result rather than the event. This is not a deficiency in either discipline, but rather an acknowledgement of different epistemologies: the law is the process of placing control over human behaviour asking, 'what has happened?'; whereas the social sciences seek to understand the impact of events on human behaviour asking, 'what will this mean for the child's trajectory?'. This provides a space for deeper reflection to better engage and understand how the concept of unacceptable risk might continue to evolve.

This article does not offer a definitive solution. However, it aims to present a conceptual invitation, acknowledging that unacceptable risk exists not only at the dramatic edge of significant harm like sexual abuse but also within the quieter, more common accumulation of smaller risks like parental conflict or neglect. These, if overlooked and unaddressed, have the potential to create significant adversities for children. It is evident that judicial reasoning and procedures already possess the flexibility to consider cumulative risk, even when it is not explicitly presented. Yet, for this to occur, the court would need to carefully and thoroughly examine patterns of risk alongside incidents of harm. It would also require the courts not only to understand but to apply relevant research (which is another issue entirely) to the decision-making process to grasp the nature of these risks and where they fall on the continuum when considering safety. It would result in situations where ongoing events of parental conflict or domestic violence should not be viewed as isolated incidents but as risk factors that may have a cumulative nature, which need to be considered.

The real challenge, then, is the conceptual understanding of how risk is perceived and articulated: is it a binary condition or a developing profile, and how should it be articulated within legal frameworks so that it can demonstrate accumulation rather than escalation? This article on reflection raised more questions than it answered, and several questions present themselves for further discussions including:

- If unacceptable risk is identified as a legal threshold of intolerance, what methods can best account for cumulative risks rather than singular significant risk indicators?
- With reference to the legal expectation of expert knowledge and the application of extrinsic research to decision making, to what extent can courts rely on models of cumulative harm without crossing evidentiary requirements, including understanding the difference between legal inference and clinical speculations?
- Should cumulative risk be understood to exist implicitly within the existing doctrine, or does it require explicit judicial recognition as its own subset of harm and risk considerations?
- How can legal practitioners better communicate concepts of risk so that they capture the contextual experience of the child, rather than the isolated behaviour of parents?
- Is cumulative risk best evaluated as a legal question, a factual question or an interdisciplinary question, which then necessitates the engagement of expertise beyond traditional legal reasoning? and
- Should court experts consider issues of cumulative harm when multiple risk factors, adverse events, or harms are identified in the material, more generally in their evaluations, especially as it relates to best interest considerations, or is this something that falls outside the scope and should be directed by the Court?

These questions show that the link between unacceptable risk and cumulative harm remains uncertain, situated at the crossroads of risk, harm, child development, and judicial reasoning. It also recognises that no single discipline can answer these questions, as they are deeply interconnected and require ongoing dialogue to understand how risk is perceived, interpreted, and acted upon to serve the child's best interests. What is clear is that unacceptable risk will continue to be defined and influenced by case law and the lived experiences of children whose families come before the court.

It is not about finding a fixed definition, direction, or application, but about developing frameworks that reflect the complexities of children lived experiences so that where risks accumulate, they can be identified and managed to give children the best chance of avoiding the potential negative and harmful effects of their circumstances.

REFERENCES

AB v CD (2019) 364 ALR 202.

Altobelli, T. (2021). Judge Thomas Altobelli. *Family Court Review*, *59*(4), 755–759. DOI: 10.1111/fcre.12607

Attorney-General's Department. (2021). *Improving the Competency and Accountability of Family Report Writers* - [Consultation Paper]. Commonwealth of Australia.

Australian Law Reform Commission. (1997). *Seen and Heard: Priority for Children in the Legal Process* (Final Report No. 84). Australia Law Reform Commission.

Australian Law Reform Commission. (2019). *Family Law for the Future—An Inquiry into the Family Law System* (Final Report No. 135; Australian Law Reform Commission).

Bant v Clayton (2015) 53 Fam LR 621.

Bath, H. (2014). The Accumulative Evidence For Cumulative Harm. *Developing Practice*, *38*, 6–14.

Bead v Gaffin [2024] FedCFamC1F 779.

Bonney v Boone [2019] FCCA 135.

Bromfield, L., Gillingham, P., & Higgins, D. (2007). Cumulative Harm and Chronic Child Maltreatment. *Developing Practice: The Child. Youth and Family Work Journal*, *19*, 34–42.

Bromfield, L., & Higgins, D. (2005). Chronic and Isolated Maltreatment in a Child Protection Sample. *Family Matters (Melbourne, Vic.)*, *70*, 38–45.

Bryant, D. (2012). *The Use of Extrinsic Material—With Particular Reference to Social Science and Family Law Decision Making. Address to Judicial Conference of Australia Colloquium*. Judical Conference of Australia, Freemantle.

Bryce, I. (2018a). A Review of Cumulative Harm: A Comparison of International Child Protection Practices. *Children Australia*, *43*(1), 23–31. DOI: 10.1017/cha.2018.3

Bryce, I. (2018b). Cumulative Risk and Harm: The Condition of Accumulation in Child Maltreatment. *Communities, Children and Families Australia*, *12*(1), 7–22.

Bryce, I. (2024). Revisiting cumulative harm: Reflecting on new research insights, legislative developments and coronial evidence as a road map for next steps. *Children Australia*, *46*(2), 3025. DOI: 10.61605/cha_3025

Bryce, I., Beccaria, G., McIlveen, P., & Du Preez, J. (2023). When quantity takes on a quality of its own: A retrospective exploration of the lived experience of cumulative harm. *Child Abuse Review, 32*(4), e2800. DOI: 10.1002/car.2800

Bryce, I., Collier, S., Harris, L., Higgins, D., & Toohey, J. (2024). Measuring accumulation: Constructing a tool for evaluating cumulative harm in children engaged with an intensive family support service. *Child Abuse Review, 33*(5), e2897. DOI: 10.1002/car.2897

Cashmore, J., & Parkinson, P. (2009). *The Voice of a Child in Family Law Disputes* (1st ed.). Oxford University Press.

CDJ v VAJ (No 1) (1998) 157 ALR 686.

Chisholm, R. (2010). *Unacceptable Risk—A Comparison of the Family Law and Care Jurisdictions. Children's Court Conference.*

Chisholm, R. (2011). Child abuse allegations in family law cases: A review of the law. *Australian Journal of Family Law, 25*, 1–32.

Conte v Lachner [2024] FedCfamC2F 1220.

Deiter v Deiter [2011] FamCAFC 82.

Demir v Ozden [2025] FedCFamC2F 80.

Denton v Denton (No 3) [2024] FedCFamC1F 476.

Dodd v Ferrell [2022] FedCFamC2F 1763.

Durante v Durante [2024] FedCFamC1F 794.

Eastley v Eastley [2022] FedCFamC1A 101.

Edwards, V. J., Holden, G. W., Felitti, V. J., & Anda, R. F. (2003). Relationship Between Multiple Forms of Childhood Maltreatment and Adult Mental Health in Community Respondents: Results From the Adverse Childhood Experiences Study. *The American Journal of Psychiatry, 160*(8), 1453–1460. DOI: 10.1176/appi.ajp.160.8.1453

Elizabeth, V., Gavey, N., & Tolmie, J. (2012). He's Just Swapped His Fists for the System" the Governance of Gender Through Custody Law. *Gender & Society, 26*(2), 239–260. DOI: 10.1177/0891243211434765

Family Law Act, Cth (1975).

Family Law Council. (2009). *Improving Responses to Family Violence in the Family Law System: An Advice on the Intersection of Family Violence and Family Law Issues* [Report]. Attorney-General's Department.

Federal Circuit and Family Court of Australia. (2021). *Court Children's Service* [Web Page]. Family Law. www.fcfcoa.gov.au/fl/children/ccs

Felitti, V. J. (2017). Future Applications of the Adverse Childhood Experiences Research. *Journal of Child & Adolescent Trauma, 10*(3), 205–206. DOI: 10.1007/s40653-017-0189-1

Felitti, V. J., Anda, R. F., Nordenberg, D., Williamson, D. F., Spitz, A. M., Edwards, V., Koss, M. P., & Marks, J. S. (1998). Relationship of Childhood Abuse and Household Dysfunction to Many of the Leading Causes of Death in Adults. *American Journal of Preventive Medicine, 14*(4), 245–258. DOI: 10.1016/S0749-3797(98)00017-8

Finkelhor, D., Ormrod, R. K., & Turner, H. A. (2007). Re-victimization patterns in a national longitudinal sample of children and youth. *Child Abuse & Neglect, 31*(5), 479–502. DOI: 10.1016/j.chiabu.2006.03.012

Fitzwater v Fitzwater (2019) 60 Fam LR 212.

Fogarty, J. (2006). Unacceptable risk—A return to basics. *Australian Journal of Family Law, 20*, 249.

Gilmor, D. (2010). Chronic child neglect: Building knowledge, fostering hope. *Policy & Practice, 68*(3), 12–13.

Grella v Jamieson [2017] FamCAFC 21.

Hasip v Ruwan [2024] FedCFamC1F 638.

Haslam, D., Mathews, B., Pacella, R., Scott, J. G., Finkelhor, D., Higgins, D., Meinck, F., Erskine, H. E., Thomas, H. J., Lawrence, D. M., & Malacova, E. (2023). *The prevalence and impact of child maltreatment in Australia: Findings from the Australian Child Maltreatment Study: Brief Report*. Queensland University of Technology., DOI: 10.5204/rep.eprints.239397

Heijman v D'Onofrio [2024] FedCFamC1F 551.

Herrenkohl, R. C., & Herrenkohl, T. I. (2009). Assessing a Child's Experience of Multiple Maltreatment Types: Some Unfinished Business. *Journal of Family Violence, 24*(7), 485–496. DOI: 10.1007/s10896-009-9247-2

Hickson v Matthew [2022] FedCFamC1A 161.

Higgins, D. (2004). Differentiating Between Child Maltreatment Experiences. *Family Matters (Melbourne, Vic.), 69*, 50–55.

Higgins, D. J., & Kaspiew, R. (2011). *Child protection and family law: Joining the dots*. Australian Institute of Family Studies.

Higgins, D. J., & McCabe, M. P. (1998). Parent Perceptions of Maltreatment and Adjustment in Children. *Journal of Family Studies, 4*(1), 53–76. DOI: 10.5172/jfs.4.1.53

In the Marriage of B (1993) 112 FLR 45.

Isles & Nelissen (2021) 65 Fam LR 1.

Isles v Nelissen (2022) 65 Fam LR 288.

Jonson-Reid, M., Kohl, P. L., & Drake, B. (2012). Child and Adult Outcomes of Chronic Child Maltreatment. *Pediatrics, 129*(5), 839–845. DOI: 10.1542/peds.2011-2529

Kellerman v Kellerman [2024] FedCFamC1A 126.

Kinniburgh, K. J., Blaustein, M., Spinazzola, J., & Van Der Kolk, B. A. (2005). Attachment, Self-Regulation, and Competency: A comprehensive intervention framework for children with complex trauma. *Psychiatric Annals, 35*(5), 424–430. DOI: 10.3928/00485713-20050501-08

Li, D., Chu, C. M., Ng, W. C., & Leong, W. (2014). Predictors of re-entry into the child protection system in Singapore: A cumulative ecological–transactional risk model. *Child Abuse & Neglect, 38*(11), 1801–1812. DOI: 10.1016/j.chiabu.2014.08.017

M v M (1988)88 ALR 577.

MacKenzie, M. J., Kotch, J. B., & Lee, L.-C. (2011). Toward a cumulative ecological risk model for the etiology of child maltreatment. *Children and Youth Services Review, 33*(9), 1638–1647. DOI: 10.1016/j.childyouth.2011.04.018

Mathews, B., Pacella, R., Scott, J. G., Finkelhor, D., Meinck, F., Higgins, D. J., Erskine, H. E., Thomas, H. J., Lawrence, D. M., Haslam, D. M., Malacova, E., & Dunne, M. P. (2023). The prevalence of child maltreatment in Australia: Findings from a national survey. *The Medical Journal of Australia, 218*(S6). Advance online publication. DOI: 10.5694/mja2.51873

McGregor v McGregor (2012) 47 Fam LR 498.

McQueen, D., Itzin, C., Kennedy, R., Sinason, V., & Maxted, F. (Eds.). (2008). *Psychoanalytic psychotherapy after child abuse: Psychoanalytic psychotherapy in the treatment of adults and children who have experienced sexual abuse, violence, and neglect in childhood.* Karnac.

Meagher, L. (2012). Assessing the Role of Family Consultants When Providing Evidence in Parenting Disputes. *Macquarie Law Journal, 10*, 59–76. DOI: 10.3316/agispt.20131701

Melounis v Melounis (No 4) [2024] FedCFamC1F 778.

Miller, R. (2007). *Cumulative Harm: A Conceptual Overview*. Victorian Government.

Murphy v Murphy [2007] FamCA 795.

Nader, K. (2008). *Understanding and assessing trauma in children and adolescents: Measures, methods, and youth in context.* Routledge.

Napier v Hepburn (2006) 36 Fam LR 395.

Newman, T., & Blackburn, S. (2002). *Transitions in the lives of children and young people: Resilience factors* (No. 78; Interchange).

Oyama v Oyama [2024] FedCFamC1F 738.

Paige v Muir [2025] FedCFamC2F 470.

Parkinson, P. (2015). Possibilities, Probabilities and the Standard of Proof in Determining an Unacceptable Risk of Sexual Abuse. *Australian Journal of Family Law*, *29*(1), 1–23.

Parkinson, P. (2021). Findings of Unacceptable Risk – A Comment on Webb et al.'s Analysis of Child Sexual Abuse Allegations in the Family Court of Australia. *The Australian Journal of Social Issues*, *56*, 334.

Pierluigi, R. (2020). Accepting the unacceptable risk: A critical appraisal of the unacceptable risk test in contemporary Australian family law and finding a way forward. *Australian Bar Review*, *49*, 479.

Prout, A. (2005). *The Future of Childhood Towards the Interdisciplinary Study of Children* (1st ed.). Routledge Falmer.

Rasheed v Galliano (No 2) [2024] FedCFamC2F 1236.

Rathus, Z. (2012). A Call for Clarity in the Use of Social Science Research in Family Law Decision-Making. *Australian Journal of Family Law*, *26*(2), 81–115.

Rathus, Z. (2014). The Role of Social Science in Australian Family Law: Collaborator, Usurper or Infiltrator? *Family Court Review*, *52*(1), 69–89. DOI: 10.1111/fcre.12071

Rathus, Z. (2018). The Research Says.': Perceptions on the Use of Social Science Research in the Family Law System. *Federal Law Review*, *46*(1), 85.

Rathus, Z. (2021). Social Scientists Operating in the Law: A Case Study of Family Assessment Experts in the Australian Family Law System. *International Journal of Law, Policy and the Family*, *35*(1), 1–24. DOI: 10.1093/lawfam/ebab051

Rathus, Z., Jeffries, S., Menih, H., & Field, R. (2019). "It's Like Standing on a Beach, Holding Your Children's Hands, and Having a Tsunami Just Coming Towards You": Intimate Partner Violence and "Expert" Assessments in Australian Family Law. *Victims & Offenders*, *14*(4), 408–440. DOI: 10.1080/15564886.2019.1580646

Reynolds v Reynolds [2025] FedCFamC2F 85.

Riethmuller, G. (2023). Evidence and Unacceptable Risk. *The Australian Law Journal*, *97*(11), 802–804.

Roberts v Short [2024] FedCFamC2F 1557.

Selwood v Selwood (No 2) [2024] FedCFamC1F 700.

Sheehan, R. (2019a). Cumulative Harm in Child Protection: The Hidden Concern. *Australian Social Work*, *72*(4), 434–446. DOI: 10.1080/0312407X.2019.1603316

Sheehan, R. (2019b). Cumulative harm in the child protection system: T he A ustralian context. *Child & Family Social Work*, *24*(4), 421–429. DOI: 10.1111/cfs.12621

Tippins, T. M., & Wittmann, J. P. (2005). Empirical and Ethical Problems with Custody Recommendations: A Call for Clinical Humility and Judicial Vigilance. *Family Court Review*, *43*(2), 193–222. DOI: 10.1111/j.1744-1617.2005.00019.x

W v W (Abuse Allegations: Unacceptable Risk) (2005) 34 Fam LR 129.

Young v Young [2010] FMCAfam 931.

ENDNOTES

1 Interestingly, and as a side note, this concept of intertwinement is the same position held by the United Nations Committee on the Rights of the Child (UNCROC), when considering the implementation of the UNCROC. The Committee's opinion is that no one individual right can be adopted or imple-

mented without or to the exclusion of the others. They argue the four pillar articles (the basic rights of non-discrimination (Article 2), best interests (Article 3), right to survival and development (Article 6) and respect for the child's views (Article 12)) are necessary for the implementation of each of the other Articles.

2 Deputy Chief Justice McClelland in the matter of *Hickson v Matthew at [39],* opined that the ability to have confidence in one's predictive ability is, in part, a reflection upon the confidence that one has in their factual findings that allow the formation of the predictions.

3 *'a discretionary judgement concerning parenting orders necessarily involves, because of the focus upon the future, significant elements of value judgments, assumptions, necessarily uncertain prediction and intuition'*

4 The only reference to unacceptable risk is found within section 60CG which relates to ensuring that when considering the best interests of a child the court must not expose the child to unacceptable risks of family violence.

Compilation of References

Aamodt, M. G., Leary, T., & Girimurugan, S. (2023). *Radford/FGCU Annual Report on Serial Killer Statistics: 2023*. Radford University.

AB v CD (2019) 364 ALR 202.

Addis, S. (2021). What Works to Prevent Adverse Childhood Experiences (ACEs) at the Community Level? An Evidence Review and Mapping Exercise – Executive Summary. *Public Health Wales* https://phwwhocc.co.uk/wp-content/uploads/2022/02/What-Works-to-Prevent-ACEs-at-the-Community-Level.-An-Evidence-Review-Mapping-Exercise-Executive-Summary.pdf

Advanced Trauma Solutions Professionals. (n.d.). *TARGET curricula*. Retrieved from http://www.advancedtrauma.com/

Afifi, T. D., Mazur, A., Otmar, C., Wagner, A. C., Papernow, P. L., Methikalam, B., & Peightal, B. M. (2022). Coparenting: A focus on divorced families, stepfamilies, intergenerational families, and families with a child on the autism spectrum.

Afifi, T. O., Stewart-Tufescu, A., Taillieu, T., Salmon, S., Fortier, J., & Roos, L. E. (2022). Adverse childhood experiences. In Asmundson, G. J. G., & Noel, M. (Eds.), *Comprehensive clinical psychology* (2nd ed., Vol. 11, pp. 1–16). Elsevier., DOI: 10.1016/B978-0-12-818697-8.00038-8

Agerschou, T. (2014). Preventing radicalization and discrimination in Aarhus. *Journal for Deradicalization*, (1), 5–22.

Agnew, R. (2015). General strain theory and delinquency. The handbook of juvenile delinquency and juvenile justice, 2, 239-256.

Akin Ojelabi, L., & Gutman, J. (2020). Family dispute resolution and access to justice in Australia. *International Journal of Law in Context*, *16*(2), 197–215. DOI: 10.1017/S1744552320000142

Alina Georgeta, S., Mona, V., Luca, T., Adelina Mihaela, ., Otilia Ioana, T., Beatrice, M., & Roxana Andreea, T. (2021). Parental Alienation-Development and Validation of a Behavioral Anchor Scale. *Sustainability (Basel, Switzerland), 13*(316), 316. DOI: 10.3390/su13010316

Allen, M., & Donkin, A. (2015). *The impact of adverse experiences in the home on the health of children and young people, and inequalities in prevalence and effects.* University College London Institute of Health Equity. Retrieved 1 March from www.instituteofhealthequity.org

Almeida, T. C., Cardoso, J., Matos, A. F., Murça, A., & Cunha, O. (2024). Adverse childhood experiences and aggression in adulthood: The moderating role of positive childhood experiences. *Child Abuse & Neglect, 154*, 106929.

Almeida, T. C., Silva, C. C., & Gouveia-Pereira, M. (2024). Adverse childhood experiences and aggression in adulthood. *Children and Youth Services Review, 157*, 107530. DOI: 10.1016/j.childyouth.2024.107530sciencedirect

Altobelli, T. (2021). Judge Thomas Altobelli. *Family Court Review, 59*(4), 755–759. DOI: 10.1111/fcre.12607

Amarante, J. (2024). *Adverse Childhood Experiences and Adolescent Substance Use: The Roles of Emotion Regulation and Attachment Security.* FORDHAM UNIVERSITY.

Amene, E. W., Tao, G., Okello, F., Finlay, J. E., Babalola, S., & Vandevanter, N. (2024). Prevalence of Adverse Childhood Experiences in sub-Saharan Africa: A multicountry analysis of the Violence Against Children and Youth Surveys. *Child Abuse & Neglect, 155*, 106778. DOI: 10.1016/j.chiabu.2023.106778

American Psychiatric Association. (2013). *Diagnostic and Statistical Manual 5 - Posttraumatic Stress Disorder* (5th ed.). American Psychiatric Publishing.

Anda, RF, Dong M, Brown DW, Felitti VJ, Giles WH, Perry GS, Valerie EJ, Dube SR. (2009). The relationship of adverse childhood experiences to a history of premature death of family members. BMC Public Health. Apr 16; 9:106. doi: . PMID: 19371414; PMCID: PMC2674602.DOI: 10.1186/1471-2458-9-106

Anda, R. F., Butchart, A., Felitti, V. J., & Brown, D. W. (2010). Building a framework for global surveillance of the public health implications of adverse childhood experiences. *American Journal of Preventive Medicine, 39*(1), 93–98. DOI: 10.1016/j.amepre.2010.03.015

Anda, R. F., Felitti, V. J., Bremner, J. D., Walker, J. D., Whitfield, C., Perry, B. D., Dube, S. R., & Giles, W. H. (2006). The enduring effects of abuse and related adverse experiences in childhood: A convergence of evidence from neurobiology and epidemiology. *European Archives of Psychiatry and Clinical Neuroscience*, *256*(3), 174–186. DOI: 10.1007/s00406-005-0624-4

Anda, R. F., Porter, L. E., & Brown, D. W. (2020). Inside the Adverse Childhood Experience Score: Strengths, Limitations, and Misapplications. *American Journal of Preventive Medicine*, *59*(2), 293–295. DOI: 10.1016/j.amepre.2020.01.009

Anderson, K. B. (2022). *Determining The Antecedents That Lead To High Conflict Domestic Disputes In Couples With Children.* Oakland University, AustLii. (1998 - 2025). AustLii (Research infrastructure facility). Retrieved from https://www.austlii.edu.au. from Faculties of Law, UTS & UNSW https://www.austlii.edu.au

Andresen, M. A. (2024). (Near-) Repeat Victimization. In: M. A. Andresen, *Environmental Criminology: Evolution, Theory, and Practice* (3rd Ed., pp. 294-314). Routledge.

Andrews, D. A., & Bonta, J. (2010). *The psychology of criminal conduct* (5th ed.). LexisNexis Matthew Bender.

Andrews, D. A., Bonta, J., & Wormith, J. S. (2011). The Risk-Need-Responsivity (RNR) Model. *Criminal Justice and Behavior*, *38*(7), 735–755. DOI: 10.1177/0093854811406356

Anti-Defamation league. (2024). Addressing extremism in online games through platform policies. https://www.adl.org/resources/report/addressing-extremism-online-games-through-plaform-policies

Antolak-Saper, N. (2020). The Adultification of the Youth Justice System: The Victorian Experience. *Law in Context. A Socio-legal Journal, 37*(1), 99-113. https://doi.org/DOI: 10.26826/law-in-context.v37i1.118

Armytage, P., & Ogloff, J. (2017). *Youth Justice Review and Strategy: Meeting needs and reducing offending - Executive Summary July 2017.* Melbourne, Australia: Victoria State Government Retrieved from www.justice.vic.gov.au

Arndt, W. B., Hietpas, T., & Kim, J. (2004). Critical characteristics of male serial murderers. *American Journal of Criminal Justice*, *29*(1), 117–131. DOI: 10.1007/BF02885707

Arrigo, B. A., & Purcell, C. E. (2001). Explaining paraphilias and lust murder: Toward an integrated model. *International Journal of Offender Therapy and Comparative Criminology*, *45*(1), 6–31.

Astridge, B., Li, W. W., McDermott, B., & Longhitano, C. (2023). A systematic review and meta-analysis on adverse childhood experiences: Prevalence in youth offenders and their effects on youth recidivism. *Child Abuse & Neglect, 140*, 1–14. DOI: 10.1016/j.chiabu.2023.106055

Atkinson, R. (2022). *Youth Justice Reforms Review - Final Report.* Brisbane, Australia: Queensland Government Retrieved from www.youthjustice.qld.gov.au/_Australian media/documents

Atkinson, J., Nelson, J., Brooks, R., Atkinson, C., & Ryan, K. (2014). Addressing Individual and Community Transgenerational Trauma. In Dudgeon, P., Milroy, H., & Walker, R. (Eds.), *Working together: Aboriginal and Torres Strait Islander mental health and wellbeing principles and practice*. Kulunga Research Network.

Atran, S. (2015). Role of youth: Countering violent extremism, promoting peace, addressing the UN Security Council. *Psychology Today.*

Attorney-General's Department. (2021). *Improving the Competency and Accountability of Family Report Writers* - [Consultation Paper]. Commonwealth of Australia.

Australian Bureau of Statistics. (2017). *4519.0 - Recorded Crime - Offenders, 2014-15.* https://www.abs.gov.au/ausstats/abs@.nsf/Lookup/by%20Subject/4519.0~2014-15~Main%20Features~Youth%20Offenders~4

Australian Bureau of Statistics. (2021-22). *Childhood abuse.* ABS. https://www.abs.gov.au/statistics/people/crime-and-justice/childhood-abuse/2021-22

Australian Bureau of Statistics. (2024). *Prisoners in Australia.* https://www.abs.gov.au/statistics/people/crime-and-justice/prisoners-australia/latest-release

Australian Bureau of Statistics. (2025). *Recorded Crime - Offenders*. www.abs.gov.au/statistics/people/crime-and-justice/recorded-crime-offenders/latest-release#

Australian Childhood Foundation. (2015). *9 Plain English Principles of Trauma Informed Care*. Retrieved 23 April from https://childhoodtrauma.org.au/2015/april/trauma-informed-care

Australian Human Rights Commission. (2021). *Guidelines for Working With a Trauma-informed Approach.* www.humanrights.gov.au/sites/default/files/ahrc_sr_2021_8_trauma-informed_approach_a4_r2_0.pdf

Australian Human Rights Commission. (2024). *'Help way earlier!': How Australia can transform child justice to improve safety and wellbeing*. www.humanrights.gov.au/our-work/childrens-rights/publications/help-way-earlier

Australian Institute of Family Studies. (2012). *Addressing women's victimisation histories in custodial settings.* (no. 13). Canberra: Australian Government. https://aifs.gov.au/publications/addressing-womens-victimisation-histories-custodial-settings/profile-women-prison

Australian Institute of Family Studies. (2016). *Principles of Trauma-informed approaches to child sexual abuse: A discussion paper.* https://aifs.gov.au/cfca/publications/trauma-informed-care-child-family-welfare-services/introduction

Australian Institute of Health & Welfare. (2023). *Profile of Australia's population.* Retrieved 20 August from www.aihw.gov.au/reports/australias-health/profile-of-australias-population#

Australian Institute of Health & Welfare. (2023a). *The Health of People in Australian Prisons 2022.* https://www.aihw.gov.au/reports/prisoners/the-health-of-people-in-australias-prisons-2022/

Australian Institute of Health and Welfare. (2016). *Youth Justice in Australia 2014–15.* https://www.aihw.gov.au/reports/youth-justice/youth-justice-in-australia-2014-15/data

Australian Institute of Health and Welfare. (2020). *The health and welfare of women in Australia's prisons.*

Australian Institute of Health and Welfare. (2023b). *Community Safety for First Nations People.*

Australian Institute of Health and Welfare. (2024). Youth justice in Australia 2022–23. https://www.aihw.gov.au/reports/youth-justice/youth-justice-in-australia-annual-report-2022-23/contents/numbers-and-rates-of-young-people-under-supervisio

Australian Institute of Health and Welfare. (2025). *Youth justice in Australia 2023-24.* www.aihw.gov.au/reports/youth-justice/youth-justice-in-australia-2023-24/contents/about

Australian Law Reform Commission. (1997). *Seen and Heard: Priority for Children in the Legal Process* (Final Report No. 84). Australia Law Reform Commission.

Australian Law Reform Commission. (2005). *Sentencing of Federal Offenders, Discussion Paper No 70.*

Australian Law Reform Commission. (2019). *Family Law for the Future—An Inquiry into the Family Law System* (Final Report No. 135; Australian Law Reform Commission).

Australian Public Service Academy. (2024). *Delivering Great Policy*. www.apsacademy.gov.au/aps-craft/strategy-policy-evaluation/delivering-great-policy

Auty, K. M., Farrington, D. P., & Coid, J. W. (2017). The Intergenerational transmission of criminal offending: Exploring Gender-Specific Mechanisms. *British Journal of Criminology*, *57*, 215–237. DOI: 10.1093/bjc/azv115

AYJA. (2023). *National Standards for Youth Justice in Australia 2023*. www.ayja.org.au

Baetz, C. L., Surko, M., Moaveni, M., McNair, F., Bart, A., Workman, S., Tedeschi, F., Havens, J., Guo, F., Quinlan, C., & Horwitz, S. M. (2019). Impact of a trauma-informed intervention for youth and staff on rates of violence in juvenile detention settings. *Journal of Interpersonal Violence*, *36*(17–18). Advance online publication. DOI: 10.1177/0886260519857163

Baglivio, M. T., Wolff, K. T., Piquero, A.R., & Epps, N. (2015) The relationship between Adverse Childhood Experiences (ACE) and juvenile offending trajectories in a juvenile offender sample. *Journal of Criminal Justice, 43*(3), 229-241. https://doi.org/. 2015.04.012.DOI: 10.1016/j.jcrimjus

Baglivio, M. T., & Epps, N. (2016). The interrelatedness of adverse childhood experiences among high-risk juvenile offenders. *Youth Violence and Juvenile Justice*, *14*(3), 179–198.

Baglivio, M. T., Epps, N., Swartz, K., Huq, M. S., Sheer, A., & Hardt, N. S. (2014). The prevalence of adverse childhood experiences (ACE) in the lives of juvenile offenders. *Journal of Juvenile Justice*, *3*(2), 1–23.

Baglivio, M. T., Epps, N., Swartz, K., Sayedul Huq, M., Sheer, A., & Hardt, N. S. (2014). The Prevalence of Adverse Childhood Experiences (ACE) in the Lives of Juvenile Offenders. *OJJDP Journal of Juvenile Justice*, *3*(2), 12–34.

Baglivio, M. T., & Wolff, K. T. (2020). Positive Childhood Experiences (PCE): Cumulative Resiliency in the Face of Adverse Childhood Experiences. *Youth Violence and Juvenile Justice*, *19*(2), 1–24. DOI: 10.1177/1541204020972487

Baglivio, M. T., & Wolff, K. T. (2023). Adverse Childhood Experiences (ACEs) and Violent Offending Among Juveniles with Justice System Involvement: Theory, Research, and Implications for Policy. In Portwood, M. J. L. S. G., & Roberts, M. C. (Eds.), *Handbook of Adverse Childhood Experiences: A Framework for Collaborative Health Promotion* (pp. 123–136).

Baglivio, M. T., Wolff, K. T., DeLisi, M., & Jackowski, K. (2020). The Role of Adverse Childhood Experiences (ACEs) and Psychopathic Features on Juvenile Offending Criminal Careers to Age 18. *Youth Violence and Juvenile Justice, 18*(4), 337–364. DOI: 10.1177/1541204020927075

Baglivio, M. T., Wolff, K. T., & Epps, N. (2021). Violent juveniles' adverse childhood experiences: Differentiating victim groups. *Journal of Criminal Justice, 72*, 101769.

Baglivio, M. T., Wolff, K. T., Epps, N., & Nelson, R. (2016). Predicting Adverse Childhood Experiences. *Crime and Delinquency, 63*(2), 166–188. DOI: 10.1177/0011128715570628

Baidawi, S., Ball, R., Newitt, R., Turnbull, L., Kembhavi-Tam, G., Avery, S., & Sheehan, R. (2023). *Research Report – Care Criminalisation of Children with Disability in Child Protection Systems*. Royal Commission into Violence, Abuse, Neglect and Exploitation of People with Disability.

Baidawi, S., & Sheehan, R. (2019). *Cross-over kids': Effective responses to children and young people in the youth justice and statutory child protection systems. Report to the Criminology Research Advisory Council*. Australian Institute of Criminology.

Baidawi, S., & Sheehan, R. (2019, December). 'Crossover kids': Offending by child protection-involved youth. *Trends and Issues in Crime and Criminal Justice, 582*, 1–23.

Baird, A. (2012). The violent gang and the construction of masculinity amongst socially excluded young men. *Safer Communities, 11*(4), 179–190.

Baker, A. J. L., & Ben-Ami, N. (2011). To Turn a Child Against a Parent Is To Turn a Child Against Himself: The Direct and Indirect Effects of Exposure to Parental Alienation Strategies on Self-Esteem and Well-Being. *Journal of Divorce & Remarriage, 52*(7), 472–489. DOI: 10.1080/10502556.2011.609424

Baker, A. J., & Brassard, M. R. (2013). Adolescents caught in parental loyalty conflicts. *Journal of Divorce & Remarriage, 54*(5), 393–413.

Bandura, A. (1961). *Psychological foundations of thought and action: A social learning analysis*. Prentice-Hall.

Bandura, A. (1977). *Social learning theory*. Prentice-Hall.

Bandura, A. (1978). Social Learning Theory of Aggression. *Journal of Communication, 28*(1), 12–29.

Bant v Clayton (2015) 53 Fam LR 621.

Barboza Solís, C., Kelly-Irving, M., Fantin, R., Darnaudéry, M., Torrisani, J., Lang, T., & Delpierre, C. (2015). Adverse childhood experiences and physiological wear-and-tear in midlife: Findings from the 1958 British birth cohort. *Proceedings of the National Academy of Sciences of the United States of America, 112*(7), E738–E746.

Barnes, G. G. (2020). Parental mental illness and extra difficulties for children when parents divorce. In *Building Children's Resilience in the Face of Parental Mental Illness* (pp. 90–109). Routledge.

Bartol, C. R., & Bartol, A. M. (2021). *Criminal Behavior: A Psychological Approach* (12th ed.). Pearson Education.

Bateman, J., Henderson, C., & Kezelman, C. (2013). *Trauma-Informed Care and Practice: Towards a cultural shift in policy reform across mental health and human services in Australia.* www.mhcc.org.au

Bath, H. (2014). The Accumulative Evidence For Cumulative Harm. *Developing Practice, 38*, 6–14.

Bauer, A., Martins, R. C., Hammerton, G., Hoffmann, M. S., Cardoso, A. S., Colvara, C., Hartmann, C. F., Calegaro, G., Perrone, L. R., Aurélio, N., Menezes, A. M. B., & Murray, J. (2024, April). Adverse childhood experiences and crime outcomes in early adulthood: A multi-method approach in a Brazilian birth cohort. *Psychiatry Research, 334*, 115809. https://pmc.ncbi.nlm.nih.gov/articles/PMC10985840/. DOI: 10.1016/j.psychres.2024.115809

Bead v Gaffin [2024] FedCFamC1F 779.

Beber, B., & Blattman, C. (2013). The logic of child soldiering and coercion. *International Organization, 67*(1), 65–104.

Becker, H. S. (1963). *Outsiders: studies in the sociology of deviance.* The Free Press.

Bellis, M. A., Ashton, K., Hughes, K., Ford, K., Bishop, J., & Paranjothy, S. (2016). Adverse Childhood Experiences (ACEs) in Wales and their Impact on Health in the Adult Population. *European Journal of Public Health, 26*, 111–112.

Bellis, M. A., Hardcastle, K., Ford, K., Hughes, K., Ashton, K., Quigg, Z., & Butler, N. (2017, March 23). Does continuous trusted adult support in childhood impart life-course resilience against adverse childhood experiences - a retrospective study on adult health-harming behaviours and mental well-being. [Erratum in: BMC Psychiatry. 2017 Apr 13;17] [1] [:140. doi: 10.1186/s12888-017-1305-3. PMID: 28335746; PMCID: PMC5364707]. *BMC Psychiatry, 17*(1), 110. DOI: 10.1186/s12888-017-1260-z

Belova-Dalton, O. (2023). The impact of new media and the internet on terrorism. Estonian Academy of Security Sciences. https://doi.org/DOI: 10.15158/0skz-3a87

Benedini, K. M., Fagan, A. A., & Gibson, C. L. (2016). The cycle of victimization: The relationship between childhood maltreatment and adolescent peer victimization. *Child Abuse & Neglect*, *59*, 111–121. DOI: 10.1016/j.chiabu.2016.08.003 PMID: 27568065

Benekos, P. J., & Merlo, A. V. (2016). A Decade of Change: Roper v. Simmons, Defending Childhood, and Juvenile Justice Policy. *Criminal Justice Policy Review*, *30*(1), 102–127. DOI: 10.1177/0887403416648734

Benier, K., Wickes, R., & Moran, C. (2020). 'African gangs' in Australia: Perceptions of race and crime in urban neighbourhoods. *Australian and New Zealand Journal of Criminology*, *54*(2), 220–238. DOI: 10.1177/0004865820965647

Bentley, C., & Matthewson, M. (2020). The Not-Forgotten Child: Alienated Adult Children's Experience of Parental Alienation. *The American Journal of Family Therapy*, *48*(5), 509–529. DOI: 10.1080/01926187.2020.1775531

Bentzin, B. (2024). *A conversation about a trauma-informed court*. City of Austin. Retrieved 8 February from www.beingwellwithbianca.com

Bergström, H., Westberg-Broström, A., & Eidevald, C. (2020). Swedish media discourses about child sexual abuse in preschools: The best interest of the child and continued trust in male teachers. *Early Child Development and Care*, *190*(12), 1878–1886. DOI: 10.1080/03004430.2018.1544128

Berk, L. E. (2003). *Child Development* (6th ed.). Pearson Education.

Berliner, L., & Kolko, D. J. (2016). Trauma Informed Care: A Commentary and Critique. *Child Maltreatment*, *21*(2), 168–172. DOI: 10.1177/1077559516643785

Bernet, W., & Greenhill, L. L. (2022). The Five-Factor Model for the Diagnosis of Parental Alienation. *Journal of the American Academy of Child and Adolescent Psychiatry*, *61*(5), 591–594. DOI: 10.1016/j.jaac.2021.11.026

Berzenski, S. R., & Yates, T. M. (2022). Revisiting a Multidimensional Model of Intergenerational Transmission of Child Maltreatment. In: Krugman, R. D., Korbin, and J. E. (Eds.), *Handbook of Child Maltreatment* (2nd Ed., pp. 351-370) Springer. https://doi.org/DOI: 10.1007/978-3-030-82479-2_17

Besemer, S., Ahmad, S. I., Hinshaw, S. P., & Farrington, D. P. (2017). A systematic review and meta-analysis of the intergenerational transmission of criminal behavior. *Aggression and Violent Behavior*, *37*, 161–178. DOI: 10.1016/j.avb.2017.10.004

Beyene, M. (2024). Secular Interpretation of the Best Interest of the Child: CCI's Decision on Child Custody in the Context of Divorced Parents (Case Comment). *Mizan law review, 18*(2), 447-456. doi:DOI: 10.4314/mlr.v18i2.8

Birnbaum, R., & Lach, L. M. (2016). Children With Neurodevelopmental Disorders in Parental Separation. *Parenting plan evaluations: Applied research for the family court*, 205.

Birnbaum, R., & Bala, N. (2024). A Retrospective Study of Outcomes of Custody Reversal in Parental Alienation Cases. *University of New Brunswick Law Journal, 75*, 62.

Bjur, K. (2023). *The Donald Mackay Churchill Fellowship to investigate effective responses to youth gangs for use in youth detention centres.* www.churchilltrust.com.au/fellow/kate-bjur-qld-2022/

Blair, A., Marryat, L., & Frank, J. (2019). How community resources mitigate the association between household poverty and the incidence of adverse childhood experiences. *International Journal of Public Health, 64*(7), 1059–1068. DOI: 10.1007/s00038-019-01258-5

Bloom, B., Owen, B., & Covington, S. (2003). *Gender-responsive strategies: Research practice and guiding principles for women offenders.* Department of Justice, National Institute of Corrections.

Boduszek, D., Hyland, P., & Bourke, A. (2012). An investigation of the role of personality, familial, and peer-related characteristics in homicidal offending using retrospective data. *Journal of Criminal Psychology, 2*(2), 96–106. DOI: 10.1108/20093821211264468

Bonach, K. (2005). Factors contributing to quality coparenting: Implications for family policy. *Journal of Divorce & Remarriage, 43*(3-4), 79–103.

Bonney v Boone [2019] FCCA 135.

Bonta, J., & Andrews, D. A. (2017). *The Psychology of Criminal Conduct* (6th ed.). Routledge.

Borja, K., & Ostrosky, F. (2013). Early traumatic events in psychopaths. *Journal of Forensic Sciences, 58*(4), 927–931. DOI: 10.1111/1556-4029.12104

Bowlby, J. (1969). Attachment and Loss Volume 1: Attachment. Hogarth Press.

Boxall, H. (2025). From Home to Heart: Adolescent Violence in the Home as a Turning Point in Intimate Partner Violence Trajectories. In Cortes-Perez, O. I. (Ed.), *Ecologies of Violence: A Comparative Perspective in Contemporary Victimology and Criminology* (pp. 121–138). Springer., DOI: 10.1007/978-3-031-91957-2_7

Brantley, A. C., & Kosky, R. H. (2005). Serial murder in the Netherlands: A look at motivation, behavior, and characteristics. *FBI Law Enforcement Bulletin, 74*(1), 26–32. DOI: 10.1037/e559082006-004

Brew-Bevan, E. (2023). *Parental Needs of Incarcerated Mothers – Hidden figures in need of a voice.* [Honours thesis, Flinders University].

Briere, J., Scott, C., & Sage, p. (2025). *Principles of trauma therapy: a guide to symptoms, evaluation, and treatment* (Third edition. ed.). Thousand Oaks, California: SAGE.

Bromfield, L. M., Gillingham, P., & Higgins, D. J. (2007). Cumulative harm and chronic child maltreatment. Developing practice: the child youth and family work journal, 19, 34-42.

Bromfield, L., Gillingham, P., & Higgins, D. (2007). Cumulative Harm and Chronic Child Maltreatment. *Developing Practice: The Child. Youth and Family Work Journal, 19*, 34–42.

Bromfield, L., & Higgins, D. (2005). Chronic and Isolated Maltreatment in a Child Protection Sample. *Family Matters (Melbourne, Vic.), 70*, 38–45.

Bromfield, L., & Miller, R. (2012). *Cumulative harm: Best interests case practice model.* Victorian Government Department of Human Services.

Brown, D. W., Anda, R. F., Tiemeier, H., Felitti, V. J., Edwards, V., Croft, J. B., & Giles, W. H. (2009). Adverse childhood experiences and the risk of premature mortality. *American Journal of Preventive Medicine, 37*(5), 389–396. DOI: 10.1016/j.amepre.2009.06.021library.csp+1

Brummer, J., & Thorsborne, M. (2024). *Becoming a Trauma-Informed Restorative Educator: Practical skills to change culture and behavior.* Jessica Kingsley Publishers.

Bryant, D. (2012). *The Use of Extrinsic Material—With Particular Reference to Social Science and Family Law Decision Making. Address to Judicial Conference of Australia Colloquium.* Judical Conference of Australia, Freemantle.

Bryce, I. (2019). Cumulative harm: Chronicity, revictimisation, and developmental victimology. In: I. Bryce, Y. Robinson, & W. Petherick (Eds.), *Child abuse and neglect forensic issues in evidence, impact and management* (pp. 151–173). Academic Press. https://doi.org/DOI: 10.1016/B978-0-12-815344-4.00009-X

Bryce, I., Collier, S., Harris, L., Higgins, D., & Toohey, J. (2024). Measuring accumulation: Constructing a tool for evaluating cumulative harm in children engaged with an intensive family support service. *Child abuse review (Chichester, England: 1992), 33*(5), n/a. doi:DOI: 10.1002/car.2897

Bryce, I. (2018). Cumulative risk and harm: The condition of accumulation in child maltreatment. *Communities, Children and Families Australia, 12*(1), 7–22.

Bryce, I. (2018a). A Review of Cumulative Harm: A Comparison of International Child Protection Practices. *Children Australia, 43*(1), 23–31. DOI: 10.1017/cha.2018.3

Bryce, I. (2018b). Cumulative Risk and Harm: The Condition of Accumulation in Child Maltreatment. *Communities, Children and Families Australia, 12*(1), 7–22.

Bryce, I. (2024). Revisiting cumulative harm: Reflecting on new research insights, legislative developments and coronial evidence as a road map for next steps. *Children Australia, 46*(2), 3025. DOI: 10.61605/cha_3025

Bryce, I., Beccaria, G., McIlveen, P., & Du Preez, J. (2023). When quantity takes on a quality of its own: A retrospective exploration of the lived experience of cumulative harm. *Child Abuse Review, 32*(4), e2800.

Bryce, I., & Schaffer, K. (2024). Motivations for Juvenile Offending Behaviour and Femicide. In *Forensic Victimology and Femi (ni) cide: A Transdisciplinary Approach on Forensic Evidence and its Contexts* (Vol. II, pp. 165–188). Springer Nature Switzerland.

Bryce, I., & Schaffer, K. (2024a). Child Femicide. In Cortes-Perez, O. I. (Ed.), *Forensic Victimology and Femi(ni)cide: A Transdisciplinary Approach on Forensic Evidence and its Contexts* (Vol. I, pp. 99–116). Springer., DOI: 10.1007/978-3-031-72512-8_3

Burgess, A. W., Hartman, C. R., Ressler, R. K., Douglas, J. E., & McCormack, A. (1986). Sexual homicide: A motivational model. *Journal of Interpersonal Violence, 1*(3), 251–272.

Burke, C., Conn, B. M., Sutter, M., Willmott, J. A., & Chandler, J. (2022). Adverse childhood experiences and pathways to violent reoffending. *Criminal Justice and Behavior, 49*(8), 1157–1177.

Burke, C., Ellis, J. D., Peltier, M. R., Roberts, W., Verplaetse, T. L., Phillips, S., Moore, K. E., Marotta, P. L., & McKee, S. A. (2023). Adverse childhood experiences and pathways to violent behaviour for women and men. *Journal of Interpersonal Violence*, *38*(3-4), 4034–4060. DOI: 10.1177/08862605221113012

Calleja, N. G. (2022). Developmentally informed treatment for adolescent sex offenders: An effectiveness evaluation of the Forward-Focused Model. *Journal of Offender Rehabilitation*, *61*(2), 106–120.

Campbell, E., Fernando, T., Gassner, L., Hill, J., Seidler, Z., & Summers, A. O. (2024). *Unlocking the prevention potential: Accelerating action to end domestic, family and sexual violence. Report of the Rapid Review of Prevention Approaches*. Department of the Prime Minister and Cabinet. https://www.pmc.gov.au/sites/default/files/resource/download/unlocking-prevention-potential.pdf

Campbell, J. A., Walker, R. J., & Egede, L. E. (2016). Associations between adverse childhood experiences, high-risk behaviors, and morbidity in adulthood. *American Journal of Preventive Medicine*, *50*(3), 344–352. 022guides.library.uq+1DOI: 10.1016/j.amepre.2015.07.

Carlsson, C., Rostami, A., Mondani, H., Sturup, J., Sarnecki, J., & Edling, C. (2020). A Life-Course Analysis of Engagement in Violent Extremist Groups. *British Journal of Criminology*, *60*(1), 74–92.

Carmen, E. H., Rieker, P. P., & Mills, T. (1984). Victims of violence and psychiatric illness. *The American Journal of Psychiatry*, *141*(3), 378–383. DOI: 10.1176/ajp.141.3.378

Case, S., Lorenzo-Dus, N., & Morton, R. (2021). YOT Talk: Examining the communicative influences on children's engagement with youth justice assessment processes. *European Journal of Criminology*, •••, 1–20. DOI: 10.1177/1477370821996850

Cashmore, J. (2011). Children's participation in family law decision-making: Theoretical approaches to understanding children's views. *Children and Youth Services Review*, *33*(4), 515–520.

Cashmore, J., & Parkinson, P. (2009). *The Voice of a Child in Family Law Disputes* (1st ed.). Oxford University Press.

Cavadino, M., & Dignan, J. (2006). *Penal Systems: A Comparative Approach*. Sage Publications Ltd.

CDJ v VAJ (No 1) (1998) 157 ALR 686.

Centers for Disease Control and Prevention. (2024). *About Adverse Childhood Experiences*. www.cdc.gov/aces/about/index.html

Centers for Disease Control and Prevention. (2024). *About the CDC-Kaiser ACE Study*. U.S. Department of Health & Human Services. https://www.cdc.gov/violenceprevention/aces/about.html

Charak, R., Ford, J. D., Modrowski, C. A., & Kerig, P. K. (2019). Polyvictimization, Emotion Dysregulation, Symptoms of Posttraumatic Stress Disorder, and Behavioral Health Problems among Justice-Involved Youth: A Latent Class Analysis. *Journal of Abnormal Child Psychology*, *47*(2), 287–298. DOI: 10.1007/s10802-018-0431-9

Chein, J. M., Albert, D., O'Brien, L., Uckert, K., & Steinberg, L. (2011). Peers increase adolescent risk taking by enhancing activity in the brain's reward circuitry. *Developmental Science*, *14*(2), F1–F10. DOI: 10.1111/j.1467-7687.2010.01035.x

Chen, J. (2016). Maltreatment Onset and Subtypes Predict Internalising and Externalising Symptomatology in Maltreated Children. (Unpublished master's thesis), James Cook University.

Chesney-Lind, M., & Shelden, R. G. (2004). *Girls, delinquency, and juvenile justice* (3rd ed.). Thompson Wadsworth.

Cheung, R. Y. M., & Chung, K. K. H. (2023). Interparental conflict and mindful parenting practices: Transactional effects between mothers and fathers. *Journal of Marriage and Family*, *85*(1), 280–292. DOI: 10.1111/jomf.12868

Chisholm, R. (2007). 'Less adversarial' proceedings in children's cases. *Family Matters (Melbourne, Vic.)*, (77), 28–32.

Chisholm, R. (2010). *Unacceptable Risk—A Comparison of the Family Law and Care Jurisdictions. Children's Court Conference.*

Chisholm, R. (2011). Child abuse allegations in family law cases: A review of the law. *Australian Journal of Family Law*, *25*, 1–32.

Chng, G. S., Chu, C. M., Zeng, G., Li, D., & Ting, M. H. (2016). A Latent Class Analysis of Family Characteristics Linked to Youth Offending Outcomes. *Journal of Research in Crime and Delinquency*, *53*(6), 765–787. DOI: 10.1177/0022427816644947

Chong, F. P., Samion, S., Teo, L. P., Goh, E. K., Basir, S. K., & Won, T. L. (2004). *A study on the programming needs of women offenders in Changi Women's Prison*. Singapore Prison Service.

Chopin, J., & Beauregard, E. (2021). Patterns of overkill in sexual homicides. *Journal of Criminal Psychology*, *11*(1), 44–58. DOI: 10.1108/JCP-10-2020-0045

Chopin, J., DeLisi, M., & Beauregard, E. (2023). Developmental sequela for sexual homicide: Testing an integrated multi-theoretical model. *Journal of Interpersonal Violence, 38*(7-8), 5721–5747. DOI: 10.1177/08862605221127199

Chung, K. M., Chung, E., & Lee, H. (2024). Behavioral Interventions for Autism Spectrum Disorder: A Brief Review and Guidelines With a Specific Focus on Applied Behavior Analysis. *Soa--ch'ŏngsonyŏn chŏngsin ŭihak = Journal of child & adolescent psychiatry, 35*(1), 29-38. doi:DOI: 10.5765/jkacap.230019

Chung, E. O., LeMasters, K., Nisar, Y. B., Kim, H., & Ji, Y. (2023). Maternal adverse childhood experiences on child growth and development in rural Pakistan. *PLOS Global Public Health, 3*(10), e0001669. DOI: 10.1371/journal.pgph.0001669

Clawar, S. S. (2020). *Parent-Child Reunification: A Guide to Legal and Forensic Strategies*. ABA Book Publishing.

Clemmow, C., Fowler, N., Seaward, A., & Gill, P. (2025). Risk of What and Why? Disaggregating Pathways to Extremist Behaviours in Individuals Susceptible to Violent Extremism. *Behavioral Sciences & the Law, 43*(2), 228–247. PMID: 39645658

Cockbain, E., & Olver, K. (2019). Child trafficking: characteristics, complexities, and challenges. In *Child abuse and neglect* (pp. 95–116). Academic Press.

Cohen, J. A., Mannarino, A. P., Jankowski, K., Rosenberg, S., Kodya, S., & Wolford, G. L. (2016). A Randomized Implementation Study of Trauma-Focused Cognitive Behavioural Therapy for Adjudicated Teens in Residential Treatment Facilities. *Child Maltreatment, 21*(2), 156–167. DOI: 10.1177/1077559515624775

Cohen, L. E., & Felson, M. (1979). Social change and crime rate trends: A routine activity approach. *American Sociological Review, 44*(4), 588–608. DOI: 10.2307/2094589

Cohen, S. (1972). *Folk Devils and Moral Panics: The Creation of the Mods and Rockers*. Granada Publishing.

Colton, K. C., Cao, V. T., & Davies, P. T. (2025). The Impact of Parental Conflict and Emotional Abuse on Children and Families. *Partner Abuse, 16*(1), 173–202. DOI: 10.1891/PA-2024-0042

Commerford, J., & Hunter, C. (2015). Children's Contact Services. *Key issues (Report no 35 2015). Australia, Melbourne: Australian Institute of Family Studies.*

Condry, R., & Smith, P. S. (2018). The Sociology of Punishment and the Effects of Imprisonment on Families. In Condry, R., & Smith, P. S. (Eds.), *Prisons, Punishment and Family: Towards a New Sociology of Punishment* (pp. 1–24). Oxford University Press.

Connolly, H. (2022). *Join the Dots: considering the impact of parental incarceration on children and young people*. Commissioner for Children and Young People.

Conte v Lachner [2024] FedCfamC2F 1220.

Contreras-Taibo, L., Huepe-Artigas, D. & Navarrete-García, G. (2019). Magnitude and characteristics of revictimization through child sexual abuse in Chile. *Legal and Criminological Psychology*. 01-14 https://doi.org/DOI: 10.1111/lcrp.12158

Contreras-Taibo, L. (2024). Victimización Reiterada. In Contreras-Taibo, L., & García-López, E. (Eds.), *Victimología Forense. Perspectivas Iberoamericanas* (pp. 101–116). Manual Moderno.

Contreras-Taibo, L., Navarrete, G., Pereda, N., & Pinto-Cortez, C. (2025). Transformación tras la adversidad: Crecimiento postraumático en sobrevivientes de violencia sexual infantil. *Anuario de Psicología Jurídica, 35*(1), 79–87. DOI: 10.5093/apj2025a10

Costello, B. J., & Laub, J. H. (2020). Social Control Theory: The Legacy of Travis Hirschi's Causes of Delinquency. *Annual Review of Criminology, 3*(1), 21–41. DOI: 10.1146/annurev-criminol-011419-041527

Covington, S. S. (2001). *A Woman's journey home: Challenges for female offenders and their children [Commissioned paper]*. From Prisons to Home: The Effect of Incarceration and Reentry on Children, Families, and Communities Conference. https://aspe.hhs.gov/reports/womans-journey-home-challenges-female-offenders-their-children

Covington, S. (1998). The relational theory of women's psychological development: Implications for the criminal justice system. In Zaplin, R. T. (Ed.), *Female offenders: Critical perspectives and effective interventions* (pp. 113–128). Aspen Publishing.

Covington, S. S. (1998). Women in prison: Approaches in the treatment of our most invisible population. *Women & Therapy, 21*(1), 141–155.

Covington, S. S. (2008). Women and addiction: A trauma-informed approach. *Journal of Psychoactive Drugs*, (Suppl 5), 377–385. DOI: 10.1080/02791072.2008.10400665

Cprek, S. E., Fisher, B. S., McDonald, M. J., McDaniel, H. M., Williamson, L., & Williams, C. M. (2021). Adverse childhood experiences and interpersonal violence among college students: Does a relationship exist? *Journal of American College Health*, *69*(8), 913–920. DOI: 10.1080/07448481.2020.1715413

Craig, J. M., Malvaso, C., & Farrington, D.P. (2023). The Association Between Adverse Childhood Experiences and Different Types of Offending Behavior: An Examination Across Two Generations of British Males. *International Journal of Offender Therapy and Comparative Criminology*, 306624X231198808. https://doi.org/DOI: 10.1177/0306624X231198808

Craig, J. M. (2019). The Potential Australian mediating Impact of Future Orientation on the ACE–Crime Relationship. *Youth Violence and Juvenile Justice*, *17*(2), 111–128. DOI: 10.1177/1541204018756470

Craig, J. M., Malvaso, C., & Farrington, D. P. (2021). All in the Family? Exploring the Intergenerational Transmission of Exposure to Adverse Childhood Experiences and Their Effect on Offending Behavior. *Youth Violence and Juvenile Justice*, *19*(3), 292–307. DOI: 10.1177/15412040211003648

Craig, J. M., Zettler, H., & Trulson, C. R. (2023). Trauma and Violent Misconduct Among Incarcerated Juveniles: The Australian mediating Role of Mental Health. *Journal of Developmental and Life-Course Criminology*, *9*(1), 121–140. DOI: 10.1007/s40865-022-00220-z

Creeden, K. (2009). How trauma and attachment can impact neurodevelopment: Informing our understanding and treatment of sexual behaviour problems. *Journal of Sexual Aggression*, *15*(3), 261–273. DOI: 10.1080/13552600903335844

Cronin Favazza, P., & Munson, L. J. (2010). Loss and grief in young children. *Young Exceptional Children*, *13*(2), 86–99.

Cummings, E. M., & Davies, P. T. (2011). *Marital conflict and children: An emotional security perspective*. Guilford Press.

Cunneen, C. (2006). Racism, Discrimination and the Over-Representation of Indigenous People in the Criminal Justice System: Some Conceptual and Explanatory Issues. *Current Issues in Criminal Justice*, *17*(3), 329–346. DOI: 10.1080/10345329.2006.12036363

Cunneen, C. (2008). Changing the Neo-Colonial Impacts of Juvenile Justice. *Current Issues in Criminal Justice*, *20*(1), 43–58.

Cunneen, C., & White, R. D. (2011). *Juvenile Justice: Youth and Crime in Australia* (4th ed.). Oxford University Press.

Cunningham, T. (2025). *Criminalised young people and the worlds we create for them: An exploration of discourse, power and subjectivity.* [PhD thesis, Flinders University].

D'Onofrio, B., & Emery, R. (2019). Parental divorce or separation and children's mental health. *World Psychiatry; Official Journal of the World Psychiatric Association (WPA), 18*(1), 100–101. DOI: 10.1002/wps.20590

Daigle, L. (2021). Recurring Victimization. In: L. Daigle (Eds.), *Victimology. The Essentials* (3° Ed., pp. 58-72). SAGE.

Daklallah, M. (2022). *Attachment style, self-esteem, and locus of control in adult children of divorce.*

Daly, A. (2018). *Children, autonomy and the courts: beyond the right to be heard.* Brill Nijhoff.

Davies, P. T., Thompson, M. J., Hentges, R. F., Coe, J. L., & Sturge-Apple, M. L. (2020). Children's Attentional Biases to Emotions as Sources of Variability in Their Vulnerability to Interparental Conflict. *Developmental Psychology, 56*(7), 1343–1359. DOI: 10.1037/dev0000994

Davoren, H. (2023, 5 October). False Witness. *Background Briefing.* Retrieved from https://www.abc.net.au/news/2023-06-19/family-court-report-writer-recording-expert-witness-ahpra/102185414

Day, A., & Malvaso, C. (2024). 'Back to Basics': A Practice Approach to Reforming Youth Justice. *Child and Youth Services,* •••, 1–25. Advance online publication. DOI: 10.1080/0145935x.2024.2372790

Day, A., Malvaso, C., Boyd, C., Hawkins, K., & Pilkington, R. (2023). The effectiveness of trauma-informed youth justice: A discussion and review. *Frontiers in Psychology, 14,* 1157695. DOI: 10.3389/fpsyg.2023.1157695

Day, D. M., Hart, T. A., Wanklyn, S. G., McCay, E., Macpherson, A., & Burnier, N. (2013). Potential mediators between child abuse and both violence and victimization in juvenile offenders. *Psychological Services, 10*(1), 1–11. DOI: 10.1037/a0028057

Deepak, S. A., & Ramdoss, S. (2021). The life-course theory of serial killing: A motivation model. *International Journal of Offender Therapy and Comparative Criminology, 65*(13-14), 1446–1472. DOI: 10.1177/0306624X20981030

DeFronzo, J., Ditta, A., Hannon, L., & Prochnow, J. (2007). Male serial homicide: The influence of cultural and structural variables. *Homicide Studies, 11*(1), 3–14. DOI: 10.1177/1088767906297434

DeFronzo, J., & Prochnow, J. (2004). Violent cultural factors and serial homicide by males. *Psychological Reports*, *94*, 104–108. DOI: 10.2466/pr0.94.1.104-108

Deiter v Deiter [2011] FamCAFC 82.

DeLisi, M., & Beauregard, E. (2018). Adverse childhood experiences and criminal extremity: New evidence for sexual homicide. *Journal of Forensic Sciences*, *63*(2), 484–489. DOI: 10.1111/1556-4029.13584

DeLisi, M., Drury, A. J., & Elbert, M. J. (2021). Frequency, chronicity, and severity: New specification of adverse childhood experiences among federal sexual offenders. *Forensic Science International. Mind and Law*, *2*(202111), 1–7. DOI: 10.1016/j.fsiml.2021.100051

Demir v Ozden [2025] FedCFamC2F 80.

Dennison, S., Stewart, A., & Freiberg, K. (2013). A prevalence study of children with imprisoned fathers: Annual and lifetime estimates. *The Australian Journal of Social Issues*, *48*(3), 339–362. DOI: 10.1002/j.1839-4655.2013.tb00286.x

Denton v Denton (No 3) [2024] FedCFamC1F 476.

Department of Child Safety Youth and Women. (2018). *Working Together Changing the Story: Youth Justice Strategy 2019–2023*. www.youthjustice.qld.gov.au/_Australian media/documents/our-department/strategies-and-reform/changing-the-youth-justice-story/strategy.pdf

Department of the Premier and Cabinet. (2024). *Community Safety Plan for Queensland*. Retrieved 1 May from www.qld.gov.au/communitysafety

Department of Youth Justice and Victim Support. (2024a). *About Youth Justice*. www.youthjustice.qld.gov.au/our-department/who-we-are/about

Department of Youth Justice and Victim Support. (2024b). *Early Action Groups*. www.youthjustice.qld.gov.au

Department of Youth Justice Employment Small Business and Training. (2023). *Youth justice: key information*. https://desbt.qld.gov.au/youth-justice/about

Department of Youth Justice. (2020). *Youth Justice Framework for Practice Foundations: Our way of working*. Queensland Government. https://www.youthjustice.qld.gov.au/search?num_ranks=10&collection=qld-gov&query=major&profile=youth-justice

Department of Youth Justice. (2024). *Youth Justice Pocket Stats March 2024*. Retrieved from www.desbt.qld.gov.au/youth-justice/data

Đerlek, M. (2024). DEPRIVATION OF PARENTAL RIGHTS AND "THE BEST INTEREST OF THE CHILD". *Pravo, teorija i praksa, 41*(1), 151-163. doi:DOI: 10.5937/ptp2401151D

Dierkhising, C. B., & Branson, C. E. (2016). Looking Forward: A Research and Policy Agenda for Creating Trauma-Informed Juvenile Justice Systems. *Journal of Juvenile Justice*, *5*(5), 14–30.

Dimopoulos, G., Hew, E., Vosz, M., & Walsh, H. (2025). 'Talk to Us, Not About Us': Children's Understandings and Experiences of Participation in Australian Family Law. *Child & Family Social Work*. Advance online publication. DOI: 10.1111/cfs.13275

Dodd v Ferrell [2022] FedCFamC2F 1763.

Dodds, L., Creamer, C., Powell, Z., & Davis, C. (2023). "Stay in Your Own Lane" the Inherent Flaws Undermining Children's Rights Within Australia's Family Law System: A Perspective from the Field. *Journal of Human Rights and Social Work*, *8*(4), 370–375.

Doel-Mackaway, H., & Williamson, B. (2023). *'Just ask us, come and see us'. Aboriginal young people in the Northern Territory must be listened to, not punished.* https://theconversation.com/just-ask-us-come-and-see-us-aboriginal-young-people-in-the-northernterritory-must-be-listened-to-not-punished-199297

Doelman, E. H., Luijk, M. P., Haen Marshall, I., Jongerling, J., Enzmann, D., & Steketee, M. J. (2023). The association between child maltreatment and juvenile delinquency in the context of Situational Action Theory: Crime propensity and criminogenic exposure as mediators in a sample of European youth? *European Journal of Criminology*, *20*(2), 528–547.

Donaldson, W., Jury, A., & Poole, S. (2018). *Trauma-Informed Care: Literature Scan*. www.tepou.co.nz

Dong, M., Anda, R. F., Dube, S. R., Giles, W. H., & Felitti, V. J. (2003). The relationship of exposure to childhood sexual abuse to other forms of abuse, neglect, and household dysfunction during childhood. *Child Abuse & Neglect*, *27*(6), 625–639. DOI: 10.1016/S0145-2134(03)00105-4

Douglas, K. R., Chan, G., Gelernter, J., Arias, A. J., Anton, R. F., Weiss, R. D., & Kranzler, H. R. (2010). Adverse childhood events as risk factors for substance dependence: Partial mediation by mood and anxiety disorders. *Addictive Behaviors*, *35*(1), 7–13.

Dowdell, E. B., Freitas, E., Owens, A., & Greenle, M. M. (2022). School shooters: Patterns of adverse childhood experiences, bullying, and social media. *Journal of Pediatric Health Care*, *36*(4), 339–346. DOI: 10.1016/j.pedhc.2021.12.004

Dowell, C. M., Preen, D. B., & Segal, L. (2017). Quantifying maternal incarceration: A whole-population linked data study of Western Australian children born 1985–2011. *Australian and New Zealand Journal of Public Health*, *41*(2), 151–157. DOI: 10.1111/1753-6405.12613

Drake, D. H., & Henley, A. J. (2014). 'Victims' Versus 'Offenders' in British Political Discourse: The Construction of a False Dichotomy. *Howard Journal of Criminal Justice*, *53*(2), 141–157. DOI: 10.1111/hojo.12057

Duke, N. N., Pettingell, S. L., McMorris, B. J., & Borowsky, I. W. (2010). Adolescent violence perpetration: Associations with multiple types of adverse childhood experiences. *Pediatrics*, *125*(4), e778–e786. DOI: 10.1542/peds.2009-0597

Durante v Durante [2024] FedCFamC1F 794.

Duron, J. F., Williams-Butler, A., Liu, F. Y., Nesi, D., Pirozzolo Fay, K., & Kim, B. E. (2021). The Influence of Adverse Childhood Experiences (ACEs) on the Functional Impairment of Justice-Involved Adolescents: A Comparison of Baseline to Follow-Up Reports of Adversity. *Youth Violence and Juvenile Justice*, •••, 1–18. DOI: 10.1177/15412040211016035

Dutton, D. G., & Hart, S. D. (1992). Evidence for long-term, specific effects of childhood abuse and neglect on criminal behaviour in men. *International Journal of Offender Therapy and Comparative Criminology*, *36*(2), 129–137. DOI: 10.1177/0306624X9203600205

Dyer, F., Gibson, R., Morrison, P., & Murphy, C. (2024). *Youth Justice in Scotland: Still fit for the future?* www.cycj.org.uk

Eastley v Eastley [2022] FedCFamC1A 101.

Echeburúa-Odriozola, E. (2021). De la macrovictimización a la microvictimización. Vulnerabilidad, resiliencia, y estrategias de afrontamiento en las víctimas de sucesos traumáticos. En: G. Varona-Martínez, *Macrovictimización, Abuso de Poder y Victimología: impactos intergeneracionales* (pp. 551-567). Aranzadi.

Eck, K. (2014). Coercion in rebel recruitment. *Security Studies, 23*(2), 364-398.
Evans-Campbell, T. (2008). Historical trauma in American Indian/Native Alaska communities: A multilevel framework for exploring impacts on individuals, families, and communities. *Journal of Interpersonal Violence*, *23*(3), 316–338.

Edalati, H., & Nicholls, T. L. (2017). The effects of adverse childhood experiences on risk of criminal justice involvement and victimization among homeless adults with mental illness. *Child Abuse & Neglect, 72*, 20–29. DOI: 10.1016/j.chiabu.2017.07.020 5

Eddy, B. (2012). *High conflict people in legal disputes*. Unhooked Books.

Edwards, V. J., Holden, G. W., Felitti, V. J., & Anda, R. F. (2003). Relationship Between Multiple Forms of Childhood Maltreatment and Adult Mental Health in Community Respondents: Results From the Adverse Childhood Experiences Study. *The American Journal of Psychiatry, 160*(8), 1453–1460. DOI: 10.1176/appi.ajp.160.8.1453

Egede, L. E. (2023). Addressing structural inequalities, structural racism, and health disparities: A perspective for moving toward health equity. *Ethnicity & Disease, 33*(3), 302–308. DOI: 10.18865/ed.33.3.302

Egger, S. A. (2002). *The killers among us: An examination of serial murder and its investigation*. Prentice Hall.

Eisner, M., Averdijk, M., Kaiser, D., Murray, A. L., Nivette, A., Shanahan, L., van Gelder, J., & Ribeaud, D. (2021). The association of polyvictimization with violent ideations in late adolescence and early adulthood: A longitudinal study. *Aggressive Behavior, 47*, 472–482. DOI: 10.1002/ab.21965 PMID: 33908056

Elizabeth, V., Gavey, N., & Tolmie, J. (2012). He's Just Swapped His Fists for the System" the Governance of Gender Through Custody Law. *Gender & Society, 26*(2), 239–260. DOI: 10.1177/0891243211434765

Elwyn, L. J., Esaki, N., & Smith, C. A. (2015). Safety at a girls secure juvenile justice facility. *Therapeutic Communities, 36*(4), 209–218. DOI: 10.1108/tc-11-2014-0038

Engel, GL., (1977). The need for a new medical model: a challenge for biomedicine. Science. Apr 8;196(4286):129-36. doi: 10.1126/science.847460. PMID: 847460.

Epstein, R. (2014). *Mothers in prison: The sentencing of mothers and the rights of the child. Howard League What is Justice? Working Papers 3/2014.* The Howard League for Penal Reform.

Esmaeili, N. S., & Yaacob, S. N. (2012). Correlates of self-esteem among adolescents of divorced families. *Archives des Sciences, 65*(8), 52–59.

Evans, C., Graves, K., & Antonopoulos, G. (2018). Trauma among children and legal implications. *CogentSocialSciences, 4*(1), 1–9. DOI: 10.1080/23311886.2018.1546791

Evans, J. A., Krumrei-Mancuso, E. J., & Rouse, S. V. (2024). What you are hiding could be hurting you: Autistic masking in relation to mental health, interpersonal trauma, authenticity, and self-esteem. *Autism in Adulthood: Challenges and Management*, *6*(2), 229–240.

Everhart Newman, J. L., Falligant, J. M., Thompson, K. R., Gomez, M. D., & Burkhart, B. R. (2018). Trauma-focused cognitive behavioural therapy with adolescents with illegal sexual behaviour in a secure residential treatment facility. *Children and Youth Services Review*, *91*, 431–438. DOI: 10.1016/j.childyouth.2018.06.028

Fabio, A., Tu, X., Loeber, R., & Cohen, J. (2011). Neighborhood socioeconomic disadvantage and the shape of the age–crime curve. *American Journal of Public Health, 101*(s1), S325–S332. DOI: 10.2105/AJPH.2011.300238

Family Law Act 1975, (Cth).

Family Law Act, Cth (1975).

Family Law Council. (2009). *Improving Responses to Family Violence in the Family Law System: An Advice on the Intersection of Family Violence and Family Law Issues* [Report]. Attorney-General's Department.

Fares, R., Najem, R., Hallit, S., Pelissolo, A., Haddad, G., & Naja, W. J. (2023). Parental alienation in Lebanon: A case report. *Journal of Medical Case Reports*, *17*(1), 164–167. DOI: 10.1186/s13256-023-03911-3

Farrington, D. P., & Malvaso, C. G. (2019). Physical Punishment and Offending in Two Successive Generations of Males. In I. Bryce, Y. Robinson, W. Petherick (Eds.), *Child Abuse and Neglect: Forensic Issues in Evidence, Impact and Management* (pp. 203–224). Academic Press. https://doi.org/DOI: 10.1016/B978-0-12-815344-4.00011-8

Farrington, D. P. (2003). Developmental and Life Course Criminology: Key Theoretical and Empirical Issues – *The 2002 Sutherland Award Address. Criminology*, *41*, 221–225. https://doi.rog/10.1111/j.1745-9125.2003.tb00987.x

Farrington, D. P., Barnes, G., & Lambert, S. (1996). The concentration of offending in families. *Legal and Criminological Psychology*, *1*(1), 47–63.

Farrington, D. P., Ttofi, M. M., Crago, R. V., & Coid, J. W. (2015). Intergenerational similarities in risk factors for offending. *Journal of Developmental and Life-Course Criminology*, *1*(1), 48–62. DOI: 10.1007/s40865-015-0005-2

Fattah, E. A. (2019). *Victimology: A Discipline in Transition.* Canadian Scholar Press.

Faust, J. (2017). *Reunification family therapy: A treatment manual.* Hogrefe Publishing.

Federal Circuit and Family Court of Australia. (2021). *Court Children's Service* [Web Page]. Family Law. www.fcfcoa.gov.au/fl/children/ccs

Felitti, V. J. (2017). Future Applications of the Adverse Childhood Experiences Research. *Journal of Child & Adolescent Trauma, 10*(3), 205–206. DOI: 10.1007/s40653-017-0189-1

Felitti, V. J., Anda, R. F., Nordenberg, D., Williamson, D. F., Spitz, A. M., Edwards, V., Koss, M. P., & Marks, J. S. (1998). Relationship of Childhood Abuse and Household Dysfunction to Many of the Leading Causes of Death in Adults: The Adverse Childhood Experiences (ACE) Study. *American Journal of Preventive Medicine, 14*(4), 245–258. DOI: 10.1016/s0749-3797(98)00017-8

Felitti, V. J., Anda, R. F., Nordenberg, D., Williamson, D. F., Spitz, A. M., Edwards, V., Koss, M. P., & Marks, J. S. (1998). Relationship of childhood abuse and household dysfunction to many of the leading causes of death in adults: The Adverse Childhood Experiences (ACE) Study. *American Journal of Preventive Medicine, 14*(4), 245–258. DOI: 10.1016/S0749-3797(98)00017-8

Fernando, M. (2013). Children's direct participation and the views of Australian judges. *Family Matters (Melbourne, Vic.)*, (92), 41–47.

Festinger, L., Schachter, S., & Back, K. (1950). Social pressures in informal groups: A study of human factors in housing (pp. x, 240). Harper.

Fidler, B. J., & Bala, N. (2020). Concepts, controversies and conundrums of "alienation:" Lessons learned in a decade and reflections on challenges ahead. *Family Court Review, 58*(2), 576–603.

Finkelhor, D. (2008b). Developmental Victimology. In D. Finkelhor, Childhood Victimization. Violence, Crime, and Abuse in the Lives of Young People, (pp. 22–46). Oxford University Press.

Finkelhor, D., & Kendall-Tackett, K. (2008). Developmental Impact. In: D. Finkelhor, Childhood Victimization: Violence, Crime, and Abuse in the Lives of Young People (pp. 65–91). Oxford University Press.

Finkelhor, D. (2008a). Child Victims: An Introduction. In Finkelhor, D. (Ed.), *Childhood Victimization. Violence, Crime, and Abuse in the Lives of Young People, (pp. 03–21).* Oxford University Press.

Finkelhor, D. (2018). Screening for adverse childhood experiences (ACEs): Cautions and suggestions. *Child Abuse & Neglect*, *85*, 174–179. DOI: 10.1016/j.chiabu.2017.07.016

Finkelhor, D., Ormrod, R. K., & Turner, H. A. (2007b). Re-victimization patterns in a national longitudinal sample of children and youth. *Child Abuse & Neglect*, *31*(5), 479–50. PMID: 17537508

Finkelhor, D., Shattuck, A., Turner, H., & Hamby, S. (2013). Improving the Adverse Childhood Experiences Study scale. *JAMA Pediatrics*, *167*(1), 70–75. DOI: 10.1001/jamapediatrics.2013.420

Fiorini, J. J., & Mullen, J. A. (2006). Understanding grief and loss in children. *Vistas Online*, 31-33.

Fischer, L., Wilson, M., Schofield, P. W., Jones, J., Kariminia, A., Barrett, E., Dean, K., Sullivan, E., Covington, S., & Butler, T. (2024). Exposure to childhood adversity and intimate partner violence in a sample of incarcerated women in Australia. *International Journal of Offender Therapy and Comparative Criminology*, •••, 1–18. DOI: 10.1177/0306624X241270577

Fitzwater v Fitzwater (2019) 60 Fam LR 212.

Flynn, C., Bartlett, T., Arias, P. F., Evans, P., & Burgess, A. (2015). Responding to children when their parents are incarcerated: Exploring the responses in Victoria and New South Wales, Australia. *Law in Context (Bundoora, Vic.)*, *32*, 4–27. DOI: 10.3316/informit.040884869356222

Foell, A., Pitzer, K. A., Nebbitt, V., Lombe, M., Yu, M., Villodas, M. L., & Newransky, C. (2021). Exposure to community violence and depressive symptoms: Examining community, family, and peer effects among public housing youth. *Health & Place*, *69*, 102579. DOI: 10.1016/j.healthplace.2021.102579

Fogarty, J. (2006). Unacceptable risk—A return to basics. *Australian Journal of Family Law*, *20*, 249.

Folk, J. B., Ramaiya, M., Holloway, E., Ramos, L., Marshall, B. D. L., Kemp, K., Li, Y., Bath, E., Mitchell, D. K., & Tolou-Shams, M. (2023). The Association Between Expanded ACEs and Behavioral Health Outcomes Among Youth at First Time Legal System Contact. *Research on Child and Adolescent Psychopathology*, *51*(12), 1857–1870. DOI: 10.1007/s10802-022-01009-w

Ford, J. D., & Blaustein, M. E. (2013). Systemic Self-Regulation: A Framework for Trauma-Informed Services in Residential Juvenile Justice Programs. *Journal of Family Violence*, *28*(7), 665–677. DOI: 10.1007/s10896-013-9538-5

Ford, J. D., Chapman, J. F., Hawke, J., & Albert, D. (2007). *Trauma among youth in the juvenile justice system: Critical issues and new directions*. National Center for Mental Health and Juvenile Justice Research.

Ford, J. D., & Russo, E. (2006). Trauma-focused, present-centered, emotional self-regulation approach to integrated treatment for posttraumatic stress and addiction: Trauma adaptive recovery group education and therapy (TARGET). *American Journal of Psychotherapy*, *60*(4), 335–355.

Ford, K., Bellis, M. A., Hughes, K., Barton, E. R., & Newbury, A. (2020). Adverse childhood experiences: A retrospective study to understand their associations with lifetime mental health diagnosis, self-harm or suicide attempt, and current low mental wellbeing in a male Welsh prison population. *Health & Justice*, *8*(1), 13. DOI: 10.1186/s40352-020-00115-5

Ford, K., Bellis, M. A., Hughes, K., Judd, N., & Barton, E. R. (2024). Exploring the intergenerational continuity of ACEs amongst a sample of Welsh male prisoners: A retrospective cross-sectional study. *Child Protection and Practice*, *3*, 100053. DOI: 10.1016/j.chipro.2024.100053

Forster, M., Gower, A. L., McMorris, B. J., & Borowsky, I. W. (2020). Adverse childhood experiences and school-based victimization and perpetration. *Journal of Interpersonal Violence*, *35*(3-4), 662–681. DOI: 10.1177/0886260517689885

Fox, B. H., Perez, N., Cass, E., Baglivio, M. T., & Epps, N. (2015). Trauma changes everything: Examining the relationship between adverse childhood experiences and serious, violent and chronic juvenile offenders. *Child Abuse & Neglect*, *46*(1), 163–173. DOI: 10.1016/j.chiabu.2015.01.011

Fox, B. H., Perez, N., Cass, E., Baglivio, M. T., & Epps, N. (2015). Trauma changes everything: Examining the relationship between adverse childhood experiences and serious, violent, and chronic juvenile offenders. *Child Abuse & Neglect*, *46*, 163–173. DOI: 10.1016/j.chiabu.2015.01.011library.csp+1

Freeze, C. (9 April 2019). Adverse Childhood Experiences and Crime FBI Law Enforcement Bulletin. https://leb.fbi.gov/articles/featured-articles/adverse-childhood-experiences-and-crime

Friestad, C., Rustad, A. B., & Kjelsberg, E. (2012). Adverse childhood experiences among women prisoners: Relationships to suicide attempts and drug abuse. *The International Journal of Social Psychiatry*, *60*(1), 40–46. DOI: 10.1177/0020764012461235

Fulu, E., Miedema, S., Roselli, T., McCook, S., Chan, K. L., Haardörfer, R., Jewkes, R., Warner, X., Lang, J., Naved, R. T., Huque, H., Farah, S., Shuvra, M. M. R., Erken, A., Wang, X., Gang, F., Li, H., Mudrovcic, Z., & Hua, W. UN Multi-Country Study on Men and Violence study team. (2017). Pathways between childhood trauma, intimate partner violence, and harsh parenting: Findings from the UN Multi-country Study on Men and Violence in Asia and the Pacific. *The Lancet. Global Health*, *5*(5), e512–e522. DOI: 10.1016/S2214-109X(17)30103-1

Gardner, M., & Steinberg, L. (2005). Peer influence on risk taking, risk preference, and risky decision making in adolescence and adulthood: An experimental study. *Developmental Psychology*, *41*(4), 625–635. DOI: 10.1037/0012-1649.41.4.625

GBD US Health Disparities Collaborators, Strassle, P. D., Kendrick, P., Baumann, M. M., Kelly, Y. O., Li, Z., Schmidt, C., Sylte, D. O., Compton, K., Bertolacci, G. J., La Motte-Kerr, W., Daoud, F., Naghavi, M., Rodriquez, E. J., Mensah, G. A., Murray, C. J. L., Mokdad, A. H., Dwyer-Lindgren, L., & Pérez-Stable, E. J. (2025). Homicide rates across county, race, ethnicity, age, and sex in the US: A Global Burden of Disease Study. *JAMA Network Open*, *8*(2), e2462069. DOI: 10.1001/jamanetworkopen.2024.62069

Gerard, F. J., & Khachatryan, N. (2024). Youth homicide offenders: A review of recent literature. In Burgason, K. A., & DeLisi, M. (Eds.), *Routledge Handbook of Homicide Studies* (pp. 188–213). Routledge., DOI: 10.4324/9781003399476-12

Gerritsen, R., McDonald, T., Anthony, T., & Napaltjari, V. (2023). *Beneath the Alice Springs 'crime wave' are complex issues – and a lot of politics*. The Conversation. Retrieved 29 January from https://theconversation.com/beneath-the-alice-springs-crime-wave-are-complex-issues-and-a-lotof-politics

Giedd, J. N., Blumenthal, J., Jeffries, N. O., Castellanos, F. X., Liu, H., Zijdenbos, A., Paus, T., Evans, A. C., & Rapoport, J. L. (1999). Brain development during childhood and adolescence: A longitudinal MRI study. *Nature Neuroscience*, *2*(10), 861–863. DOI: 10.1038/13158

Gill, P., Horgan, J., & Deckert, P. (2014). Bombing Alone: Tracing the Motivations and Antecedent Behaviors of Lone-Actor Terrorists. *Journal of Forensic Sciences*, *59*, 425–435. PMID: 24313297

Gilmor, D. (2010). Chronic child neglect: Building knowledge, fostering hope. *Policy & Practice*, *68*(3), 12–13.

Gjelsvik, A., Zierler, S., Blume, J., & Nie, N. (2004). Homicide risk across race and class: A small-area analysis in Massachusetts and Rhode Island. *Journal of Urban Health*, *81*(3), 372–382. DOI: 10.1093/jurban/jth130

Goddard, A. (2021). Adverse Childhood Experiences and Trauma-Informed Care. *Journal of Pediatric Health Care, 35*(2), 145–155. DOI: 10.1016/j.pedhc.2020.09.001

Goldstein, S., & Brooks, R. B. (2005). Resilience in children. *New York: Springer. Gooding, HC, Milliren, CE, Austin, SB, Sheridan, MA, & McLaughlin, KA (2016). Child abuse, resting blood pressure, and blood pressure reactivity to psychological stress. Journal of Pediatric Psychology, 41*, 5–12.

Goodfellow, P. (2024). *An Exploration of Factors Influencing the Recent Levels of Incarceration of Girls in England and Wales*. University of Bedfordshire.

Gottfredson, M. R., & Hirschi, T. (1990). *A general theory of crime*. Stanford University Press.

Gottlieb, L. (2017). Turning points for families: A therapeutic vacation. *Retrieved from End Parental Alienation:* http://endparentalalienation. weebly. com

Gottlieb, L. J. (2012). *The parental alienation syndrome: A family therapy and collaborative systems approach to amelioration*. Charles C Thomas Publisher.

Graf, G. H. J., Simoes, C., & Koerting, J. (2021). Adverse Childhood Experiences and Justice System Contact: A Systematic Review. *Pediatrics, 147*(1), e2020021030. DOI: 10.1542/peds.2020-021030 3

Grape, L., Skoglund, J., Haugen, G. M. D., & Thørnblad, R. (2024). Adolescents' Negotiations of Loyalty and Fairness in Relation to Parents' Separation Process. *Child & Family Social Work*.

Greenberg, L. R., & Schnider, R. A. (2020). We're still taking x-rays but the patient is dying: What keeps us from intervening more quickly in resist-refuse cases? *Family Court Review, 58*(2), 488–506. DOI: 10.1111/fcre.12484

Grella v Jamieson [2017] FamCAFC 21.

Grella, C. E., Lovinger, K., & Warda, U. S. (2013). Relationships among trauma exposure, familial characteristics, and PTSD: A case-control study of women in prison and in the general population. *Women & Criminal Justice, 23*(1), 63–79. DOI: 10.1080/08974454.2013.743376

Gustafsson, L., & Ranstorp, M. (2017). Swedish foreign fighters in Syria and Iraq: An analysis of open-source intelligence and statistical data.

Hagan, J. (1996). The Next Generation: Children of Prisoners. In: *The Unintended Consequences of Incarceration: Papers from a conference organized by the Vera Institute of Justice* (pp. 21 – 40). Vera Institute of Justice.

Haines, J., Matthewson, M., & Turnbull, M. (2019). *Understanding and managing parental alienation: A guide to assessment and intervention*. Routledge.

Hales, G., Debowska, A., Rowe, R., Boduszek, D., & Levita, L. (2023). Comparison of person-centered and cumulative risk approaches in explaining the relationship between adverse childhood experiences and behavioral and emotional problems. *Journal of Interpersonal Violence*, *38*(13-14), 8065–8087. DOI: 10.1177/08862605231153877

Hales, T., Kusmaul, N., & Nochajski, T. (2016). Exploring the Dimensionality of Trauma-Informed Care: Implications for Theory and Practice. *Human Service Organizations, Management, Leadership & Governance*, *41*(3), 317–325. DOI: 10.1080/23303131.2016.1268988

Halsey, M., & De Vel-Palumbo, M. (2020). *Generations through prison: Experiences of intergenerational incarceration*. Routledge.

Hannis, C. K. (2015). *Understanding the victim-offender overlap: An exploratory study* (Master's thesis, Missouri State University). MSU Graduate Theses, 2840. https://bearworks.missouristate.edu/theses/2840

Hanson, R. F., & Lang, J. (2016). A Critical Look At Trauma-Informed Care Among Agencies and Systems Serving Maltreated Youth and Their Families. *Child Maltreatment*, *21*(2), 95–100. DOI: 10.1177/1077559516635274

Hardyman, P. L., & Van Voorhis, P. (2004). *Developing gender-specific classification systems for women offenders*. U.S. Department of Justice, National Institute of Corrections.

Harman, J. J., Bernet, W., & Harman, J. (2019). Parental Alienation: The Blossoming of a Field of Study. *Current directions in psychological science: a journal of the American Psychological Society*, *28*(2), 212-217. doi:DOI: 10.1177/0963721419827271

Harman, J. J., Warshak, R. A., Lorandos, D., & Florian, M. J. (2022). Developmental psychology and the scientific status of parental alienation. *Developmental Psychology*, *58*(10), 1887–1911. DOI: 10.1037/dev0001404

Harman, Matthewson, M. L., & Baker, A. J. (2022). Losses experienced by children alienated from a parent. *Current Opinion in Psychology*, *43*, 7–12.

Harold, G. T., & Sellers, R. (2018). Annual research review: Interparental conflict and youth psychopathology: An evidence review and practice focused update. *Journal of Child Psychology and Psychiatry, and Allied Disciplines*, *59*(4), 374–402.

Harrison, M. (2007). Finding a better way: A bold departure from the traditional common law approach to the conduct of legal proceedings.

Harrison, M. A., Murphy, E. A., Ho, L. Y., Bowers, T. G., & Flaherty, C. V. (2015). Female serial killers in the United States: Means, motives, and makings. *Journal of Forensic Psychiatry & Psychology, 26*(3), 383–406. DOI: 10.1080/14789949.2015.1007516

Hart, R. (2015). *An analysis of global homicide patterns* (Undergraduate honors thesis, University of California, Berkeley). https://econ.berkeley.edu/sites/default/files/HART-Honors%20Thesis.pdf

Harwin, J. P., Madge, N. P., & Heath, S. (2010). Children affected by parental alcohol problems (ChAPAPs).

Hashemi, L., Fanslow, J., Gulliver, P., & McIntosh, T. (2022). Intergenerational impact of violence exposure: Emotional-behavioural and school difficulties in children aged 5–17. *Frontiers in Psychiatry, 12*, 771834. DOI: 10.3389/fpsyt.2021.771834

Hashweh, N., Johnson, F., Chrusciel, T., & Barnes, A. (2024). Effect of trauma-informed supervision in youth detention center: A retrospective study. *Journal of Family Trauma, Child Custody & Child Development, 21*(1), 96–109. DOI: 10.1080/26904586.2023.2218856

Hasip v Ruwan [2024] FedCFamC1F 638.

Haslam, D., Mathews, B., Pacella, R., Scott, J. G., Finkelhor, D., Higgins, D. J., Meinck, F., Erskine, H. E., Thomas, H. J., Lawrence, D., & Malacova, E. (2023). *The prevalence and impact of child maltreatment in Australia: Findings from the Australian Child Maltreatment Study: Brief Report.* Australian Maltreatment Study. http://doi.org/DOI: 10.5204/rep.eprints.239397

Hay, C., Hargrove, E., Davidson, K. M., & Cobb, A. (2024). Knowing and Caring About the Impact of Crime on Victims: Results From an Intervention for Justice-Involved Youth. *Youth Violence and Juvenile Justice.* Advance online publication. DOI: 10.1177/15412040241305327

Heberle, A. E., Obus, E. A., & Gray, S. A. (2020). An intersectional perspective on the intergenerational transmission of trauma and state-perpetrated violence. *The Journal of Social Issues, 76*(4), 814–834.

Heide, K. M. (1999). Youth homicide. In Smith, M. D., & Zahn, M. A. (Eds.), *Studying and preventing homicide: Issues and challenges* (pp. 175–196). Sage Publications.

Heide, K. M., & Solomon, E. P. (2006). Biology, childhood trauma, and murder: Rethinking justice. *International Journal of Law and Psychiatry, 29*, 220–233. DOI: 10.1016/j.ijlp.2005.10.001

Heijman v D'Onofrio [2024] FedCFamC1F 551.

He, J., Yan, X., Wang, R., Zhao, J., Liu, J., Zhou, C., & Zeng, Y. (2022). Does childhood adversity lead to drug addiction in adulthood? A study of serial mediators based on resilience and depression. *Frontiers in Psychiatry*, *13*, 871459.

Hentges, R. F., Davies, P. T., & Cicchetti, D. (2015). Temperament and Interparental Conflict: The Role of Negative Emotionality in Predicting Child Behavioral Problems. *Child Development*, *86*(5), 1333–1350. DOI: 10.1111/cdev.12389

Herman, J. L. (1992). *Trauma and recovery: The aftermath of violence—from domestic abuse to political terror*. Basic Books.

Herrenkohl, R. C., & Herrenkohl, T. I. (2009). Assessing a Child's Experience of Multiple Maltreatment Types: Some Unfinished Business. *Journal of Family Violence*, *24*(7), 485–496. DOI: 10.1007/s10896-009-9247-2

Herzog, J. I., & Schmahl, C. (2018). Adverse childhood experiences and the consequences on neurobiological, psychosocial, and somatic conditions across the lifespan. *Frontiers in Psychiatry*, *9*, 420. DOI: 10.3389/fpsyt.2018.00420

Hickey, A., & Wallis, R. (2023). *Why the Australian media aren't helping to solve the 'youth crime crisis' they're reporting*. Retrieved 19 November from https://theconversation.com/why-the-Australian media-arent-helping-to-solve-the-youth-crime-crisis-theyrereporting-208947

Hickey, E. (1997). *Serial murderers and their victims* (2nd ed.). Wadsworth.

Hickson v Matthew [2022] FedCFamC1A 161.

Higgins, D. (2004). Differentiating Between Child Maltreatment Experiences. *Family Matters (Melbourne, Vic.)*, *69*, 50–55.

Higgins, D. J., & Kaspiew, R. (2011). *Child protection and family law: Joining the dots*. Australian Institute of Family Studies.

Higgins, D. J., & McCabe, M. P. (1998). Parent Perceptions of Maltreatment and Adjustment in Children. *Journal of Family Studies*, *4*(1), 53–76. DOI: 10.5172/jfs.4.1.53

Higgins, D. J., & McCabe, M. P. (2001). Multiple forms of child abuse and neglect: Adult retrospective reports. *Aggression and Violent Behavior*, *6*, 547–578. DOI: 10.1016/S1359-1789(00)00030-6

Higginson, A., Eggins, E., & Mazerolle, L. (2017). *Investigating Serious Violent Crime: What works, what doesn't and for what crime types?* www.aic.gov.au/about-us/governance/criminology-research-advisory-council

Hindelang, M. J., Gottfredson, M. R., & Garofalo, J. (1978). *Victims of personal crime: An empirical foundation for a theory of personal victimization*. Ballinger Publishing Co.

Hine, B. A. (2024). Parental Alienation-What Do We Know, and What Do We (Urgently) Need to Know? A Narrative Review. *Partner Abuse, 15*(3), 362–396. DOI: 10.1891/PA-2023-0015

Hoehn, E., & De Young, A. (2024). *QMHC Trauma Strategy - Infant and Early Childhood*. Retrieved 7 March from https://www.qmhc.qld.gov.au/

Hoeve, M., Semon-Dubas, J., Eichelsheim, V. I., van der Laan, P. H., Smeenk, W., & Gerris, J. R. M. (2009). The relationship between Parenting and Delinquency: A Meta-analysis. *Journal of Abnormal Child Psychology, 37*(1), 749–775.

Hoge, R. D., & Andrews, D. A. (2021). *YLS/CMI 2.0 User Manual*. www.EPIC-21-11-05-DC-DYRS-FOIA-20211130-YLS-CMI-User-Manual

Holt, S., Buckley, H., & Whelan, S. (2008). The impact of exposure to domestic violence on children and young people: A review of the literature. *Child Abuse & Neglect, 32*(8), 797–810. DOI: 10.1016/j.chiabu.2008.02.004

Homant, R. J., & Kennedy, D. B. (2009). Understanding serial sexual murder: A biopsychosocial approach. In Petherick, W. (Ed.), *Profiling and Serial crime: Theoretical and practical issues* (pp. 341–372). Elsevier.

Homel, R., & Thomsen, L. (Eds.). (2017). *Developmental Crime Prevention* (2nd ed.). Routledge.

Honnavalli, V., Neo, L. S., Gan, R., Tee, S. H., Khader, M., & Chin, J. (2019). Understanding violent extremism and child abuse: A psychological analysis. In *Child Abuse and Neglect* (pp. 79–94). Academic Press.

Hopper, E. K., Bassuk, E. L., & Olivet, J. (2009). Shelter from the Storm: Trauma-Informed Care in Homelessness Services Settings. *The Open Health Services and Policy Journal, 3*(1), 131–151.

Hoskins, Z. (2022). Public Reason and the Justification of Punishment. *Criminal Justice Ethics*, •••, 1–21. DOI: 10.1080/0731129x.2022.2102838

Hosokawa, R., & Katsura, T. (2019). Exposure to marital conflict: Gender differences in internalizing and externalizing problems among children. *PLoS One, 14*(9), e0222021.

Huang, H., Sim, Y., & Draper, R. (2019). Adverse Childhood Experiences and Trauma-Informed Care in Rehabilitation Counseling. *Rehabilitation Research, Policy, and Education, 33*(2), 103–118. DOI: 10.1891/2168-6653.33.2.103

Huebner, B. M. (2013). *Appendix B: The Missouri Model: A Critical State of Knowledge*. Department of Criminology and Criminal Justice, University of Missouri Retrieved 16 October from https://www.nap.edu/read/14685/chapter/16

Hughes, K., Bellis, M. A., Hardcastle, K. A., Sethi, D., Butchart, A., Mikton, C., Jones, L., & Dunne, M. P. (2017). The effect of multiple adverse childhood experiences on health: A systematic review and meta-analysis. *The Lancet. Public Health, 2*(8), e356–e366. DOI: 10.1016/S2468-2667(17)30118-4

In the Marriage of B (1993) 112 FLR 45.

Isles & Nelissen (2021) 65 Fam LR 1.

Isles v Nelissen (2022) 65 Fam LR 288.

Jackson, R. D., Kethineni, S., & Cao, Y. (2023). Hopes for healing: An exploratory study of trauma-informed care training and the juvenile justice system. *Children and Youth Services Review, 148*, 1–9. DOI: 10.1016/j.childyouth.2023.106877re

Jacobson, N. S., & Truax, P. (1991). Clinical significance: A statistical approach to defining meaningful changes in psychotherapy research. *Journal of Consulting and Clinical Psychology, 59*(1), 12–19. DOI: 10.1037//0022-006x.59.1.12

Jaffe, P., Wolfe, D., Wilson, S., & Zak, L. (1986). Similarities in behavioural and social maladjustment among child victims and witnesses to family violence. *The American Journal of Orthopsychiatry, 56*(1), 142–146. DOI: 10.1111/j.1939-0025.1986.tb01551.x

Jahic, I., Trulson, C. R., Caudill, J. W., Bonner, T., Slemaker, A., & DeLisi, M. (2021). Adverse childhood experiences and forensic typologies: Getting specific about trauma among institutionalized youth. *International Journal of Environmental Research and Public Health, 18*(21), 11307. DOI: 10.3390/ijerph182111307

Jankowski, M. K., Schifferdecker, K. E., Butcher, R. L., Foster-Johnson, L., & Barnett, E. R. (2019). Effectiveness of a Trauma-Informed Care Initiative in a State Child Welfare System: A Randomized Study. *Child Maltreatment, 24*(1), 86–97. DOI: 10.1177/1077559518796336

Jekielek, S. M. (1998). Parental conflict, marital disruption and children's emotional well-being. *Social Forces, 76*(3), 905–936.

Jenkins, P. (1994). *Using murder: The social construction of serial homicide*. Aldine de Gruyter.

Jennings, S. (2005). AUTISM IN CHILDREN AND PARENTS. Unique Considerations for Family Court Professionals. *Family Court Review*, *43*(4), 582–595. DOI: 10.1111/j.1744-1617.2005.00057.x

Jiang, F. Y., Wijayaratne, D. C., Choo, J., Lin, A. L., & Tay, A. (2025). From adversity to desistance: An exploratory study of adverse childhood experiences, agency, and social support among justice-involved youths. *Advancing Corrections*, *19*, 81–94.

Jobe-Shields, L., Williams, J., & Hardt, M. (2017). Predictors of emotional security in survivors of interpersonal violence. *Journal of Child and Family Studies*, *26*(10), 2834–2842.

Johnson, E. I., & Arditti, J. A. (2022). Adolescents with Incarcerated Parents: Toward Developmentally Informed Research and Practice. In Krysik, J., & Rodriguez, N. (Eds.), *Children of Incarcerated Parents: From Understanding to Impact* (pp. 23–40). Springer Nature., DOI: 10.1007/978-3-030-84713-5_2

Johnson, H. (2013). The gendered nature of violence: An international focus. In *Routledge international handbook of crime and gender studies* (pp. 91–119). Routledge.

Johnson, S. M. (2003). Introduction to Attachment. In Johnson, S. M., & Whiffen, V. E. (Eds.), *Attachment processes in couple fna family therapy*. Guildford Press.

Johnston, J. R. (1994). High-conflict divorce. *The Future of Children*, •••, 165–182.

Johnston, J., Roseby, V., & Kuehnle, K. (2009). *In the Name of the Child: A Developmental Approach to Understanding and Helping Children of Conflicted and Violent Divorce* (2nd ed.). Springer Publishing Company, Incorporated.

Jollife, D., & Auty, K. M. (2023). Developmental and Life-Course Criminology: An Overview. In A. Liebling, S. Maruna & L. McAra, The Oxford Handbook of Criminology (7th Ed., pp. 121-145). Oxford University Press.

Jones, M. S., & Hoffman, J. P. (2024). Adverse childhood experiences and homicide. In Burgason, K. A., & DeLisi, M. (Eds.), *Routledge handbook of homicide* (pp. 349–368). Routledge., DOI: 10.4324/9781003399476-19

Jonson-Reid, M., Kohl, P. L., & Drake, B. (2012). Child and Adult Outcomes of Chronic Child Maltreatment. *Pediatrics*, *129*(5), 839–845. DOI: 10.1542/peds.2011-2529

Joshi, A., & Truong, M. (2024). *The role of adverse childhood experiences (ACEs) in adolescent use of violence.* Australian Institute of Family Studies. www.aifs.gov.au/resources/policy-and-practice-papers/role-adverse-childhood-experiences-aces-adolescent-use

Joshi, A., & Truong, M. (2025). The role of adverse childhood experiences (ACEs) in adolescent use of violence. Child Family Community Australia (CFCA) Australian Institute of Family Studies (AIFS).https://aifs.gov.au/resources/policy-and-practice-papers/role-adverse-childhood-experiences-aces-adolescent-use

Joshi, A. (2021). Parental Alienation Is Real: Exposing the Myth of the Woozle. *Litigation*, *47*(3), 8–9.

Joyce, A. N. (2016). High-Conflict Divorce: A form of Child Neglect. *Family Court Review*, *54*(4), 642–656. DOI: 10.1111/fcre.12249

Justice Reform Initiative. (2023). *Alternatives to incarceration in Queensland* www.justicereforminitiative.org.au

Kahn, R. E., Jackson, K., Keiser, K., Ambroziak, G., & Levenson, J. S. (2020). Adverse Childhood Experiences Among Sexual Offenders: Associations With Sexual Recidivism Risk and Psychopathology. *Sexual Abuse*, *33*(7), 839–866. DOI: 10.1177/1079063220970031

Kaspiew. (2016). Separated parents and the family law system: what does the evidence say? Kaspiew, & Carson, R. (2019). *Parenting arrangments after separation: Evidence Summary.* Southbank: Commonwealth of Australia Retrieved from https://aifs.gov.au/sites/default/files/2022-06/1910_parenting_arrangements_after_separation.pdf

Kaspiew, R., Carson, R., Qu, L., Horsfall, B., Tayton, S., Moore, S., & Dunstan, J. (2015). *Court outcomes project.* Australian Institute of Family Studies.

Kazemian, L., Farrington, D. P., & Piquero, A. R. (2019). Developmental and Life-Course Criminology. In Farrington, D. P., Kazemian, L., & Piquero, A. R. (Eds.), *The Oxford Handbook of Developmental and Life-Course Criminology (pp. 03-10).* Oxford University Press., DOI: 10.1093/oxfordhb/9780190201371.013.1

Keeney, B. T., & Heide, K. M. (1994). Gender differences in serial murderers: A preliminary analysis. *Journal of Interpersonal Violence*, *9*(3), 383–398. DOI: 10.1177/088626094009003007

Kellerman v Kellerman [2024] FedCFamC1A 126.

Kelley, T. M., Pransky, J., & Sedgeman, J. A. (2014). Realizing Resilience in Trauma Exposed Juvenile Offenders: A Promising New Intervention for Juvenile Justice and Prevention Professionals. *Journal of Child & Adolescent Trauma*, *7*(3), 143–151. DOI: 10.1007/s40653-014-0018-8

Kelly, J. B., & Johnston, J. R. (2001). THE ALIENATED CHILD:A Reformulation of Parental Alienation Syndrome. *Family Court Review*, *39*(3), 249–266. DOI: 10.1111/j.174-1617.2001.tb00609.x

Kempf, J. P., & Outlaw, B. D. (2023). Reunification therapy: A mechanism for managing the chaos. *Oklahoma Bar Journal, 94(9)*, 12 - 17. Retrieved from https://www.okbar.org/barjournal/november-2023/reunification-therapy-a-mechanism-for-managing-the-chaos/

Keppel, R. D., & Birnes, W. J. (2003). *The psychology of serial killer investigations: The grisly business unit*. Academic Press.

Kerr-Davis, A., Hillman, S., Anderson, K., & Cross, R. (2023). Introducing Routine Assessment of Adverse Childhood Experiences For Looked-After Children: The Use and Properties of the Trauma and Adverse Life Events (TALE) Screening Tool. *Journal of Child & Adolescent Trauma*, *16*(4), 981–994. DOI: 10.1007/s40653-023-00559-5

Keynejad, R. C., & Howard, L. M. (2025). Intergenerational "transmission" of intimate partner violence and abuse: Interpretations and implications. *The Lancet Regional Health. Europe*, *53*, 101299. DOI: 10.1016/j.lanepe.2025.101299

Khan, M. M. R. (1963). The concept of cumulative trauma. *The Psychoanalytic Study of the Child*, *18*(1), 286–306.

Khoury, L., Tang, Y. L., Bradley, B., Cubells, J. F., & Ressler, K. J. (2010). Substance use, childhood traumatic experience, and posttraumatic stress disorder in an urban civilian population. *Depression and Anxiety*, *27*, 1077–1086. DOI: 10.1002/da.20751

Kimmel, M. S. (2018). *Healing from Hate: How Young Men Get Into—and Out Of—violent Extremism*. University of California Press.

King, A. R. (2020). The ACE Questionnaire and Lifetime Physical Aggression. *Journal of Aggression, Maltreatment & Trauma*, •••, 1–18. DOI: 10.1080/10926771.2020.1796875

King, S. (2019). Sentencing Parents – Sentencing their Children? *EuroVista*, *1*(3), 137–146.

Kinniburgh, K. J., Blaustein, M., Spinazzola, J., & van der Kolk, B. A. (2005). Attachment, Self-Regulation, and Competency: A comprehensive intervention framework for children with complex trauma. *Psychiatric Annals*, *35*(5), 424–430. DOI: 10.3928/00485713-20050501-08

Kistin, C., & Brotanek, J. (2022). Screening for Adverse Childhood Experiences in Children. *JAMA Pediatrics*, *176*(2), e220121. DOI: 10.1001/jamapediatrics.2022.0121

Knight, B. (2024). *Victorian government cops criticism over youth crime as crucial debate over justice bill approaches*. https://www.abc.net.au/news/2024-08-13/victoria-youth-crime-age-of-criminal-responsibility-inspotlight/104215232

Knight, Z. G. (2006). Some thoughts on the psychological roots of the behaviour of serial killers as narcissists: An object-relations perspective. *Social Behaviour and Personality: An International Journal*, *34*(10), 1189–1206. DOI: 10.2224/sbp.2006.34.10.1189

Konecky, E. M., & Lynch, S. M. (2019). Cumulative trauma exposure, emotion regulation, and posttraumatic stress disorder among incarcerated women. *Journal of Traumatic Stress*, *32*(5), 806–811. DOI: 10.1002/jts.22443

Krieg, S. M., Murphy, L., & Elliott, J. C. (2022). Adverse childhood experiences and pathways to violent behavior in adults: A latent class analysis. *Frontiers in Psychology*, *13*, 9852029. DOI: 10.3389/fpsyg.2022.9852029pmc.ncbi.nlm.nih

Krischer, M. K., Sevecke, K., & Lehmkuhl, G. (2021). Family upbringing: Family factors as predictors for the development of antisocial behaviour and psychopathy dimensions. In A. R. Felthous & H. Sab (Eds.), *The Wiley International Handbook on Psychopathic Disorders and the Law: Volume 1 Diagnosis and Treatment* (2nd ed., pp. 389-402). John Wiley and Sons Ltd.

Krushas, A. E., Kulig, T. C., & Goslar, M. (2025). Advancing the Study of Adverse Childhood Experiences: An Examination of Measurement and Latent Classes. *Justice Quarterly*, •••, 1–37. DOI: 10.1080/07418825.2025.2451311

Kruttschnitt, C., & Kang, T. (2021). Theoretical Perspectives on the Victimization of Women. In Pratt, T. C., & Turanovic, J. J. (Eds.), *Revitalizing Victimization Theory: Revisions, Applications, and New Directions* (pp. 163–184). Routledge.

Kubiak, S. P., Kasiborski, N., & Schmittel, E. (2017). Assessing long-term outcomes of an intervention designed to reduce child maltreatment among parents involved in the child welfare system. *Journal of Public Child Welfare*, *11*(2), 131–149.

Kurlychek, M. C., & Johnson, B. D. (2019). Cumulative Disadvantage in the American Criminal Justice System. *Annual Review of Criminology*, *2*(1), 291–319. DOI: 10.1146/annurev-criminol-011518-024815

Laajasalo, T., Pajunen, T., Martikainen, P., & Kivivuori, J. (2025). Adverse childhood experiences (ACEs) and juvenile violent delinquency in multiple successive birth cohorts. *Nordic Journal of Criminology*, *26*(2), 1–14. DOI: 10.18261/njc.26.2.3

LaBrode, R. T. (2007). Etiology of the psychopathic serial killer: An analysis of antisocial personality disorder, psychopathy, and serial killer personality and crime scene characteristics. *Brief Treatment and Crisis Intervention*, *7*(2), 151–160. DOI: 10.1093/brief-treatment/mhm004

Lacey, R. E., Howe, L. D., Kelly-Irving, M., Bartley, M., & Kelly, Y. (2020). The Clustering of Adverse Childhood Experiences in the Avon Longitudinal Study of Parents and Children: Are Gender and Poverty Important? *Journal of Interpersonal Violence*, •••, 1–24. DOI: 10.1177/0886260520935096

LaFree, G. (2018). *Losing legitimacy: Street crime and the decline of social institutions in America*. Routledge.

Laletas, S., & Khasin, M. (2021). Children of high conflict divorce: Exploring the experiences of primary school teachers. *Children and Youth Services Review*, *127*, 106072.

Lange, A. M. C., Visser, M. M., Scholte, R. H. J., & Finkenauer, C. (2022). Parental Conflicts and Posttraumatic Stress of Children in High-Conflict Divorce Families. *Journal of Child & Adolescent Trauma*, *15*(3), 615–625. DOI: 10.1007/s40653-021-00410-9

LaNoue, M. D., George, B. J., Helitzer, D. L., & Keith, S. W. (2020). Contrasting cumulative risk and multiple individual risk models of the relationship between Adverse Childhood Experiences (ACEs) and adult health outcomes. *BMC Medical Research Methodology*, *20*(1), 239. DOI: 10.1186/s12874-020-01120-w

Lauritzen, C., Reedtz, C., Van Doesum, K. T. M., & Martinussen, M. (2014). Implementing new routines in adult mental health care to identify and support children of mentally ill parents. *BMC Health Services Research*, *14*(1), 58–58. DOI: 10.1186/1472-6963-14-58

Leary, T., Southard, L., Hill, J., & Ashman, J. (2017). The Macdonald triad revisited: An empirical assessment of relationships between triadic elements and parental abuse in serial killers. *North American Journal of Psychology*, *19*(3), 627–640.

Legislative Council Legal and Social Issues Committee. (2022). *Inquiry into children affected by parental incarceration*. Parliament of Victoria.

Leitch, L. (2017). Action steps using ACEs and trauma-informed care: A resilience model. *Health & Justice*, *5*, 1–5. DOI: 10.1186/s40352-017-0050-5

Leiting, M., Beck, K., Bürgin, D., Fegert, J. M., Jenkel, N., Boonmann, C., Schmeck, K., Grob, A., & Schmid, M. (2024). Adverse Childhood Experiences, Quality of Life and the Australian mediating Roles of Self-Efficacy and Self-Directedness in Youth Residential Care Leavers. *Applied Research in Quality of Life*, *19*(6), 3479–3499. DOI: 10.1007/s11482-024-10392-z

Leung, C. C., Goh, J. H., & Chionh, Y. J. S. (2015). *Drug motives study: Comparing the profiles and drug motives of drug offenders and penal offenders with concurrent drug consumption record* [PowerPoint slides]. Singapore Prison Service.

Leung, S., Goh, E., & Chionh, Y. (2015). *Motivations for drug use among female inmates*. Singapore Prison Service. *Research Bulletin (International Commission for the Northwest Atlantic Fisheries)*.

Levenson, J. S., Willis, G. M., & Prescott, D. S. (2015). Adverse childhood experiences in the lives of female sex offenders. *Sexual Abuse*, *27*(3), 258–283. DOI: 10.1177/1079063214544332

Levin, J., & Fox, J. A. (2017). Multiple homicide: Understanding serial and mass murder. In F. Brookman., E. R. Maguire & M. Maguire. (Eds.), *The handbook of homicide*, (pp. 249-267). John Wiley & Sons, Incorporated.

Lewis, J., & Marsden, S. (2021). Trauma, adversity, and violent extremism. *Centre for Research and Evidence on Security Threats, 9*.

Leyton, E. (1986). *Compulsive killers: The story of modern multiple murder*. New York University Press.

Li, D., Chu, C. M., Goh, J. T. L., Ng, I. Y., & Zeng, G. (2015). Impact of childhood maltreatment on recidivism in youth offenders: A matched-control study. *Criminal Justice and Behavior*, *42*(10), 990–1007.

Li, D., Chu, C. M., Ng, W. C., & Leong, W. (2014). Predictors of re-entry into the child protection system in Singapore: A cumulative ecological–transactional risk model. *Child Abuse & Neglect*, *38*(11), 1801–1812. DOI: 10.1016/j.chiabu.2014.08.017

Lim, R. W. (2017). *Adverse Childhood Experiences and Aggression in Juvenile Offenders in Singapore: Exploring the Moderating Influence of Prosocial Peers and Social Support*. Singapore Prison Service.

Li, N., Shelton, M., & Grigorenko, E. L. (2025). Adverse childhood experiences, anger, and violence among justice-involved youth: A network analysis. *Child Abuse & Neglect*, *161*, 107301. DOI: 10.1016/j.chiabu.2025.107301

Littman, R. (2017). Children and Extreme Violence: Insights from Social Science on Child Trajectories Into and Out Of Non-State Armed Groups.

Liu, D., Chu, C. M., Neo, L. H., Ang, R. P., Tan, M. Y., & Chu, J. (2016). Multiple trauma exposure and psychosocial functioning in Singaporean children in out -of-home care. *Psychological Trauma: Theory, Research, Practice, and Policy*, *8*(4), 431–438. DOI: 10.1037/tra0000098

Lopez-Tamayo, R., Suarez, L., Simpson, D., & Volpe, K. (2022). The impact of adverse childhood experiences and community violence exposure on a sample of anxious, treatment-seeking children. *Journal of Child & Adolescent Trauma*, *15*(4), 1081–1093. DOI: 10.1007/s40653-022-00447-4

Lovell, B., Steen, M., Esterman, A., & Brown, A. (2020). The Parenting Education Needs of Women Experiencing Incarceration in South Australia: Proposal for a Mixed Methods Study. *JMIR Research Protocols*, *9*(8), e18992. DOI: 10.2196/18992

Luby, J. L., Baram, T. Z., Rogers, C. E., & Barch, D. M. (2021). Adverse Childhood Experiences in a low-income Black cohort: Prevalence, sex differences, and links to violent crime exposure. *Child and Adolescent Psychiatry and Mental Health*, *15*, 35. Advance online publication. DOI: 10.1186/s13034-021-00390-y

Lujan, M. J. W. M., & Fanniff, A. M. (2018). Justice for All: Trauma and the Need for Safety and Fairness Within Juvenile Justice Facilities. *Criminal Justice and Behavior*, *46*(1), 63–81. DOI: 10.1177/0093854818796060

Lu, Mueser, Rosenberg, & Jankowski. (2023). Variety of ACEs and risk of anxiety-depression: Females demonstrated higher rates and more complex trauma profiles. *Frontiers in Psychiatry*, *14*, 1233981.

Lux, U., Christ, S. L., & Walper, S. (2021). Coparenting problems and parenting behavior as mediating links between interparental conflict and toddlers' adjustment difficulties in Germany. *Zeitschrift für Kinder- und Jugendpsychiatrie und Psychotherapie*.

Lynch, N., van den Brink, Y., & Forde, L. (2022). Introduction. In *Responses to Serious Offending by Children* (pp. 1–8). Routledge., DOI: 10.4324/9781032107707-1

Lyon, D. R., & Welsh, A. (2017). *The psychology of criminal and violent behaviour*. Oxford University Press.

M v M (1988)88 ALR 577.

MacKenzie, M. J., Kotch, J. B., & Lee, L.-C. (2011). Toward a cumulative ecological risk model for the etiology of child maltreatment. *Children and Youth Services Review, 33*(9), 1638–1647. DOI: 10.1016/j.childyouth.2011.04.018

Malvaso, C., Day, A., Delfabbro, P., Cale, J., Hackett, L., & Ross, S. (2022). *Adverse childhood experiences and trauma among young people in the youth justice system* (Report to the Criminology Research Advisory Council, Grant: CRG 12/18–19). Australian Institute of Criminology. https://www.aic.gov.au/sites/default/files/2022-06/crg_1218_19_adverse_childhood_experiences_v8.pdf

Malvaso, C. G., Cale, J., Whitten, T., Day, A., Singh, S., Hackett, L., Delfabbro, P. H., & Ross, S. (2021). Associations Between Adverse Childhood Experiences and Trauma Among Young People Who Offend: A Systematic Literature Review. *Trauma, Violence & Abuse, 23*(5), 1677–1694. DOI: 10.1177/15248380211013132

Malvaso, C. G., Day, A., & Boyd, C. M. (2024). The Outcomes of Trauma-Informed Practice in Youth Justice: An Umbrella Review. *Journal of Child & Adolescent Trauma, 17*(3), 939–955. DOI: 10.1007/s40653-024-00634-5

Malvaso, C. G., Delfabbro, P. H., & Day, A. (2019). Adverse childhood experiences in a South Australian sample of young people in detention. *Australian and New Zealand Journal of Criminology, 52*(3), 411–431. DOI: 10.1177/0004865818810069

Malvaso, C., Day, A., Cale, J., Hackett, L., Delfabbro, P., & Ross, S. (2022a). Adverse Childhood Experiences and Trauma among Young People in the Youth Justice System. *Trends and Issues in Crime and Criminal Justice, 651*(202206), 1–19.

Malvaso, C., Day, A., Cale, J., Hackett, L., Delfabbro, P., & Ross, S. (2022b). Adverse childhood experiences and trauma among young people in the youth justice system. *Trends and Issues in Crime and Criminal Justice, 651*(June), 1–19.

Malvaso, C., Harris, D., McGee, T. R., & Craig, J. (2023). The Implications of Adverse Childhood Experiences (ACEs) Research in the Treatment and Prevention of Offending Behaviour. In *Frontiers in Developmental and Life-Course Criminology* (pp. 102–114). Routledge., DOI: 10.4324/9781003294740-10

Mannarino, A. P., & Cohen, J. A. (2011). Traumatic loss in children and adolescents. *Journal of Child & Adolescent Trauma, 4*(1), 22–33.

Marchment, Z., Clemmow, C., & Gill, P. (2025). Adverse Childhood Experiences and Susceptibility to Violent Extremism. *Terrorism and Political Violence, •••*, 1–15.

Marono, A. J., Reid, S., Yaksic, E., & Keatley, D. A. (2020). A behavior sequence analysis of serial killers' lives: From childhood abuse to methods of murder. *Psychiatry, Psychology, and Law : an Interdisciplinary Journal of the Australian and New Zealand Association of Psychiatry, Psychology and Law*, *27*(1), 126–137. DOI: 10.1080/13218719.2019.1695517

Marrow, M. T., Knudsen, K. J., Olafson, E., & Bucher, S. E. (2014). The Value of Implementing TARGET within a Trauma-Informed Juvenile Justice Setting. *Journal of Child & Adolescent Trauma*, *5*(3), 257–270. DOI: 10.1080/19361521.2012.697105

Marzano, L., Hawton, K., Rivline, A., & Fazel, S. (2011). Psychosocial influences on prisoner suicide: A case-control study of near-lethal self-harm in women prisoners. *Social Science & Medicine*, *72*, 874–883. DOI: 10.1016/j.socscimed.2010.12.028

Massachusetts Association for Mental Health. (n.d.). *CDC-Kaiser ACEs Study*. https://www.mamh.org/advocacy/prevention/impact-of-traumatic-experiences/cdc-kaiser-aces-study

Masten, A. S., & Cicchetti, D. (2010). Developmental Cascades. *Development and Psychopathology*, *22*(3), 491–495. DOI: 10.1017/S0954579410000222 PMID: 20576173

Mathews, B., Pacella, R., Dunne, M., & Higgins, D. (2023). The Australian Child Maltreatment Study: Prevalence, outcomes and implications. *The Medical Journal of Australia*, *218*(9), 420–424. DOI: 10.5694/mja2.51971acms+1

Mathews, B., Pacella, R., Scott, J. G., Finkelhor, D., Meinck, F., Higgins, D. J., Erskine, H. E., Thomas, H. J., Lawrence, D. M., Haslam, D. M., Malacova, E., & Dunne, M. P. (2023). The prevalence of child maltreatment in Australia: Findings from a national survey. *The Medical Journal of Australia*, *218*(S6). Advance online publication. DOI: 10.5694/mja2.51873

Matthewson, M. (2023). A qualitative exploration of reunification post alienation from the perspective of adult alienated children and targeted parents. *Frontiers in Psychology, 14 - 2023*. doi: https://doi.org/DOI: 10.3389/fpsyg.2023.1189840

Matza, D. (1990). *Delinquency & Drift*. Transactions Publishers.

McAra, L., & McVie, S. (2023). Raising the minimum age of criminal responsibility: Lessons from the Scottish experience. *Current Issues in Criminal Justice*, *36*(4), 386–407. DOI: 10.1080/10345329.2023.2272362

McDermott, B. M. (2004). Child and youth emotional trauma: An explanatory model of adverse outcomes. *Psychiatry, Psychology, and Law : an Interdisciplinary Journal of the Australian and New Zealand Association of Psychiatry, Psychology and Law, 11*(2), 269–279. DOI: 10.1375/pplt.2004.11.2.269

McGregor v McGregor (2012) 47 Fam LR 498.

McGuire, D. R. (2019). *A Blueprint for Change: Adapting the lessons of the Spanish Youth Justice System to the Northern Territory - Report of Diagrama visit.* https://www.diagramafoundation.org.uk/

McGuire, A., Singh, M., & Jackson, Y. (2024). Let it go, let it go: Stop measuring child maltreatment as a binary yes/no. *Child Abuse & Neglect, 155*, 106994. DOI: 10.1016/j.chiabu.2024.106994

McIntosh, J. E., Bryant, H. D., & Murray, K. (2008). Evidence of a different nature: The child-responsive and less adversarial initiatives of the Family Court of Australia. *Family Court Review, 46*(1), 125–136.

McKinley, A. (2020). Vulnerability to fatal violence: Child sexual abuse victims as homicide participants in Australia. In Bryce, I., & Petherick, W. (Eds.), *Child Sexual Abuse: Forensic Issues in Evidence* (pp. 351–372). Impact, and Management., DOI: 10.1016/B978-0-12-819434-8.00017-9

McKinley, A. (2024). Homicide Solvability. In Perez, O. (Ed.), *Ciencias Forenses y Femicidio/Feminicidio: Evidencia y Contextos "Forensic Sciences & Femicide/ Feminicide: Evidence & Contexts".*

McLachlan, K. J. (2024). *Trauma-Informed Criminal Justice: Towards a More Compassionate Criminal Justice System.* Palgrave Macmillan/Springer Nature. https://link.springer.com/book/10.1007/978-3-031-59290-4

McLachlan, K.J. (2022). *'I cannot dismiss from my mind your traumatic and tragic upbringing': Trauma-informed sentencing in South Australia* [PhD Thesis, University of South Australia].

McLachlan, K. J. (2023). Trauma-informed sentencing of adults who are life-course persistent offenders. In Malvaso, C., McGee, T. R., & Homel, R. (Eds.), *Frontiers in Developmental and Life-Course Criminology: Methodological Innovation and Social Benefit* (pp. 115–124). Routledge., DOI: 10.4324/9781003294740-11

McLachlan, K. J. (2024a). *Trauma-informed Criminal Justice Towards a More Compassionate Criminal Justice System.* Springer Nature., DOI: 10.1007/978-3-031-59290-4

McLachlan, K. J. (2024b). *Trauma-Informed Criminal Justice: Towards a More Compassionate Criminal Justice System*. Palgrave MacMillan.

McLennan, J. D., Gonzalez, A., MacMillan, H. L., & Afifi, T. O. (2024). Routine screening for adverse childhood experiences (ACEs) still doesn't make sense. *Child Abuse & Neglect*, (106708), 1–7. Advance online publication. DOI: 10.1016/j.chiabu.2024.106708

McQueen, D., Itzin, C., Kennedy, R., Sinason, V., & Maxted, F. (Eds.). (2008). *Psychoanalytic psychotherapy after child abuse: Psychoanalytic psychotherapy in the treatment of adults and children who have experienced sexual abuse, violence, and neglect in childhood*. Karnac.

McSweeney, B. (2021). Fooling ourselves and others: Confirmation bias and the trustworthiness of qualitative research – Part 1 (the threats). *Journal of Organizational Change Management*, *34*(5), 1063–1075. DOI: 10.1108/JOCM-04-2021-0117

Meagher, L. (2012). Assessing the Role of Family Consultants When Providing Evidence in Parenting Disputes. *Macquarie Law Journal*, *10*, 59–76. DOI: 10.3316/agispt.20131701

Meier, J. S., & Sankaran, V. (2021). Breaking down the silos that harm children: A call to child welfare, domestic violence and family court professionals. *Va. J. Soc. Pol'y & L.*, *28*, 275.

Meland, E., Furuholmen, D., & Jahanlu, D. (2024). Parental alienation–a valid experience? *Scandinavian Journal of Public Health*, *52*(5), 598–606.

Melounis v Melounis (No 4) [2024] FedCFamC1F 778.

Meloy, J. R. (2000). The nature and dynamics of sexual homicide: An integrative review. *Aggression and Violent Behavior*, *5*(1), 1–22. DOI: 10.1016/S1359-1789(99)00006-3

Mercer, J., & Drew, M. (2021). *Challenging Parental Alienation*. Routledge.

Merlo, A. V. (2024). Progress and Persistent Challenges in the Juvenile Justice System. *Justice Evaluation Journal, Advance online publication*, 1-19. https://doi.org/DOI: 10.1080/24751979.2024.2444923

Messina, N., Burdon, W., Hagopian, G., & Prendergast, M. (2010). A randomized experimental study of gender-responsive substance abuse treatment for women in prison. *Journal of Substance Abuse Treatment*, *38*(2), 97–107. https://pubmed.ncbi.nlm.nih.gov/20015605/

Messina, N., & Grella, C. E. (2006). Childhood trauma and women's health outcomes in a California prison population. *American Journal of Public Health, 96*(10), 1842–1848. DOI: 10.2105/AJPH.2005.082016

Miedema, S. S., Le, V. D., Chiang, L., Ngann, T., & Shortt, J. W. (2023). Adverse childhood experiences and intimate partner violence among youth in Cambodia: A latent class analysis. *Journal of Interpersonal Violence*, *38*(3-4), NP1446–NP1472. DOI: 10.1177/08862605221090573

Miller, L. (2000). The predator's brain: Neuropsychodynamics of serial killing. In Schlesinger, L. B. (Ed.), *Serial Offenders: Current though, recent findings* (pp. 135–166). CRC Press.

Miller, L. (2014). Serial killers: II. Development, dynamics, and forensics. *Aggression and Violent Behavior, 19*(1), 1–11. DOI: 10.1016/j.avb.2013.11.002

Miller, N. A., & Najavits, L. M. (2012). Creating trauma-informed correctional care: A balance of goals and environment. *European Journal of Psychotraumatology*, *3*, 17246. Advance online publication. DOI: 10.3402/ejpt.v3i0.17246

Miller, R. (2007). *Cumulative Harm: A Conceptual Overview*. Victorian Government.

Minds, E. (n.d.). Adverse childhood experiences (ACEs): Summary of evidence and impacts. Emerging Minds. https://emergingminds.com.au/resources/adverse-childhood-experiences-aces-summary-of-evidence-and-impacts/

Miralles, P., Godoy, C., & Hidalgo, M. D. (2023). Long-term emotional consequences of parental alienation exposure in children of divorced parents: A systematic review. *Current Psychology (New Brunswick, N.J.)*, *42*(14), 12055–12069. DOI: 10.1007/s12144-021-02537-2

Mitchell, H., & Aamodt, M. G. (2005). The incidence of child abuse in serial killers. *Journal of Police and Criminal Psychology*, *20*(1), 40–47. DOI: 10.1007/BF02806705

Modrowski, C. A., Sheerin, K., Grant, M., Collibee, C., & Kemp, K. A. (2023). Applying the Exploration, Preparation, Implementation, and Sustainment Framework to Trauma-Focused Screening in the Juvenile Legal System: Considerations and Recommendations for Future Research. *Psychological Injury and Law*, *17*(3), 245–258. DOI: 10.1007/s12207-023-09482-4

Moffitt, T. E. (1993). Adolescence-Limited and Life-Course Persistent Antisocial Behavior: A Developmental Taxonomy. *Psychological Review*, *100*(4), 674–701.

Mohammadi, A., & Ceccato, V. (2022). Homicide rates are spatially associated with built environment, socioeconomic and demographic conditions in Toronto neighbourhoods. *Scientific Reports, 12*, 13398. DOI: 10.1038/s41598-022-17718-5

Moloney, L. (2013). From Helping Court to Community-Based Services: The 30-Year Evolution of Australia's Family Relationship Centres. *Family Court Review, 51*(2), 214–223. DOI: 10.1111/fcre.12021

Mongan, D., Millar, S. R., Brennan, M. M., Doyle, A., Galvin, B., & McCarthy, N. (2025). Associations and mediating factors between adverse childhood experiences and substance use behaviours in early adulthood: A population-based longitudinal study. *Addictive Behaviors, 161*, 108194. DOI: 10.1016/j.addbeh.2024.107869

Moore, M. D., & Tatman, A. W. (2016). Adverse Childhood Experiences and Offender Risk to Re-offend in the United States: A quantitative examination. *International Journal of Criminal Justice Sciences, 11*(2), 148–158.

Morgan, N. (2017). *Behaviour management practices at Banksia Hill Detention Centre*. www.oics.wa.gov.au

Morris, A. (2009). Gendered dynamics of abuse and violence in families: considering the abusive household gender regime. *Child abuse review (Chichester, England: 1992), 18*(6), 414-427. doi:DOI: 10.1002/car.1098

Morton, R. J., & Hilts, M. A. (Eds.). (2008). *Serial murder: Multi-disciplinary perspectives for investigators*. Federal Bureau of Investigation; Behavioral Analysis Unit-2; National Center for the Analysis of Violent Crimes.

Moss, D., & Klapdor, C. (2022). *Working with children to prevent self-blame after disclosures of child sexual abuse*. www.emergingminds.com.au

Muller, W. (2019). The relation between adverse childhood experiences and types of offending: A literature review (Bachelor thesis, Tilburg University). Retrieved from http://arno.uvt.nl/show.cgi?fid=150029

Muncie, J. (2015). *Youth & Crime* (4th ed.). Sage Publications Ltd.

Murphy v Murphy [2007] FamCA 795.

Murray, J., Farrington, D. P., & Sekol, I. (2012). Children's Antisocial Behavior, Mental Health, Drug Use, and Educational Performance After Parental Incarceration: A Systematic Review and Meta-Analysis. *Psychological Bulletin, 138*(2), 175–210. DOI: 10.1037/a0026407

Myers, W. C. (2004). Serial murder by children and adolescents. *Behavioral Sciences & the Law, 22*(3), 357–374. DOI: 10.1002/bsl.590

Nader, K. (2008). *Understanding and assessing trauma in children and adolescents: Measures, methods, and youth in context*. Routledge.

Napier v Hepburn (2006) 36 Fam LR 395.

Nation, A., Pacella, R., Monks, C., Mathews, B., & Meinck, F. (2023). Prevalence of violence against children in the United Kingdom: A systematic review and meta-analysis. *Child Abuse & Neglect*, *146*, 106518. DOI: 10.1016/j.chiabu.2023.106518

National Center for Juvenile Justice. (2010). *Finding your ACE score*. https://www.ncjfcj.org/publications/finding-your-ace-score/

National Child Traumatic Stress Network. (2016). *Structured Psychotherapy for Adolescents Responding to Chronic Stress (SPARCS)*. National Child Traumatic Stress Network. Retrieved 11 March 2016 from www.NCTSN.org

National University. (n.d.). *A Guide to Trauma Informed Care Principles*. https://www.nu.edu/blog/trauma-informed-care-principles/

Negriff, S. (2019). ACEs are not equal: Examining the relative impact of adversity type and multiple adversities on adolescent health and violence outcomes. *Child Abuse & Neglect*, *98*, 104208. DOI: 10.1016/j.chiabu.2019.104208

Neil, R., & Sampson, R. J. (2021). The Birth Lottery of History: Arrest over the Life Course of Multiple Cohorts Coming of Age, 1995-2018. *American Journal of Sociology*, *126*, 1127–1178. DOI: 10.1086/714062

Newell, S., & Moss, A. (2011). *Supporting children and young people through change, loss and grief: An evaluation of the Seasons for Growth program*. Good Grief.

Newman, T., & Blackburn, S. (2002). *Transitions in the lives of children and young people: Resilience factors* (No. 78; Interchange).

Noel, M. E., Gatewood, B. J., Turner, S. M., & Muhammad, B. (2024). "We Have Unique Experiences": Familial Socialization of Children of Incarcerated Parents. *Criminal Justice and Behavior*, *51*(7), 1012–1031. DOI: 10.1177/00938548241240063

Noonan, L. P. (1985). *Effects of long-term parental conflict on personality functioning of children of divorce*. The Wright Institute.

Novak, A. (2022). The Association Between Adverse Childhood Experiences, Neuropsychological Deficits, and Experiences of Exclusionary Discipline in Early Childhood. *Journal of Developmental and Life-Course Criminology*, •••, 1–31. DOI: 10.1007/s40865-022-00192-0

Novero, C. M., Booker Loper, A., & Warren, J. I. (2011). Second-Generation Prisoners. *Criminal Justice and Behavior, 38*(8), 761–778. DOI: 10.1177/0093854811406637

O'Driscoll, D. (2017). Links between childhood experience of violence and violent extremism. *Helpdesk report. Available online:* https://assets. publishing. service. gov. *uk/media/5c1903f740f0b60c2c1c798a/248_Childhood_Experience_of_Violence_and _Violent_Extremism. pdf (accessed on 15 December 2024).*

O'Hear, M., & Wheelock, D. (2025). The sentencing advantage of female defendants in homicide cases. *Drake Law Review, 72*(1), 37–72.

Oberg, G., Adams, B., & Stahl, G. (2023). The role of trauma and mental health in violent extremism: The perceptions of countering violent extremism (CVE) practitioners and why we can't get it wrong. *Journal of Aggression, Maltreatment & Trauma, 32*(12), 1744–1762.

Office for National Statistics. (2020). *Child abuse in England and Wales: March 2020*. ONS. https://www.ons.gov.uk/peoplepopulationandcommunity/crimeandjustice/bulletins/childabuseinenglandandwales/march2020

Ogilvie, J., Thomsen, L., Barton, J., Harris, D. A., Rynne, J., & O'Leary, P. (2022). Adverse childhood experiences among youth who offend: Examining exposure to domestic and family violence for male youth who perpetrate sexual harm and violence. www.anrows.org.au/publication/adverse-childhood-experiences-among-youth-who-offend-examining-exposure-to-domestic-and-family-violence-for-male-youth-who-perpetrate-sexual-harm-and-violence/

Ogilvie, J. M., Stewart, A. L., Chan, M., & Shinkfield, A. J. (2022). The relationship between adverse childhood experiences and adolescent violence: An Australian study. *Children and Youth Services Review, 134*, 106352. DOI: 10.1016/j.childyouth.2021.106352 2

Oldrup, H., & Frederiksen, S. (2018). Are the Children of Prisoners Socially Excluded? A Child- Centred Perspective. In Condry, R., & Smith, P. S. (Eds.), *Prisons, Punishment and Family: Towards a New Sociology of Punishment?* (pp. 102–116). Oxford University Press.

Olomi, J., Wright, N., & DePrince, A. (2020). Revictimisation of sexually abused children. In I. Bryce & W. Petherick, Child Sexual Abuse: Forensic Issues in Evidence, Impact, and Management, (pp. 267-291). Academic Press. https://doi.org/DOI: 10.1016/B978-0-12-819434-8.00013-1

Oostermeijer, S., & Dwyer, M. (2019). *Design Guide for Small-scale Local Facilities*. https://localtime264843868.wordpress.com/wp-content/uploads/2019/11/localtime_designguide_v1-2.pdf

Oren, L. (2018). No-Fault Divorce Reform in the 1950s: The Lost History of the "Greatest Project" of the National Association of Women Lawyers. *Law and History Review*, *36*(4), 847–890. DOI: 10.1017/S0738248018000172

Oyama v Oyama [2024] FedCFamC1F 738.

Paige v Muir [2025] FedCFamC2F 470.

Papalia, N., Luebbers, S., & Ogloff, J. (2020). A developmental life course approach to the study of offending and victimisation following child sexual abuse. In Bryce, I., & Petherick, W. (Eds.), *Child sexual abuse: Forensic issues in evidence, impact and management* (pp. 293–323). Academic Press., DOI: 10.1016/B978-0-12-819434-8.00014-3

Paquette, S., Chopin, J., & Fortin, F. (2025). *Online sexual crimes, offenders, and victims: Theory, research, and practice*. Routledge., DOI: 10.4324/9781003512653-8

Parkinson, P. (2023). *Australian family law in context: commentary and materials* (8th edition. ed.). Sydney: Thomson Reuters Australia, Limited.

Parkinson, P. (2015). Possibilities, Probabilities and the Standard of Proof in Determining an Unacceptable Risk of Sexual Abuse. *Australian Journal of Family Law*, *29*(1), 1–23.

Parkinson, P. (2021). Findings of Unacceptable Risk – A Comment on Webb et al.'s Analysis of Child Sexual Abuse Allegations in the Family Court of Australia. *The Australian Journal of Social Issues*, *56*, 334.

Patterson, G. R. (2016). Coercion theory: The study of change. In Dishion, T. J., & Snyder, J. J. (Eds.), *The Oxford handbook of coercive relationship dynamics (pp. 07–22)*. Oxford University Press.

Paynter, M., Heggie, C., Matheson, L., Rillie, C., Beals, D., & Bray, M. (2022). Maternal incarceration in a provincial prison in Canada: A qualitative study. *Journal of Advanced Nursing*, *78*(7), 2123–2138. DOI: 10.1111/jan.15154

Pellón, I., Martínez-Pampliega, A., & Cormenzana, S. (2024). Post-divorce adjustment, coparenting and somatisation: Mediating role of anxiety and depression in high-conflict divorces. *Journal of Affective Disorders Reports*, *16*, 100697.

Peltonen, K., Tammilehto, J., Flykt, M., Vanska, M., Kuppens, P., Bosmans, G., & Lindblom, J. (2024). Adverse childhood experiences and emotion dynamics in daily life: A two sample study. *Cognition and Emotion*, •••, 1–21. Advance online publication. DOI: 10.1080/02699931.2024.2434153

Pennsylvania Coalition Against Domestic Violence. (n.d.). *About the ACE study* [PDF]. https://www.pcadv.org/wp-content/uploads/ACE-Handount.pdf

Pereda, N., & Guerra, C. (2025). Exploring the Intersection of Self-Reported Victimization and Offending: Risk Profiles Among a Representative Sample of Spanish Adolescents. *Victims & Offenders*, •••, 1–20. DOI: 10.1080/15564886.2025.2515091

Perez, N. M., Jennings, W. G., & Baglivio, M. T. (2018). A Path to Serious, Violent, Chronic Delinquency: The Harmful Aftermath of Adverse Childhood Experiences. *Crime and Delinquency*, *64*(1), 3–25. DOI: 10.1177/0011128716684806

Perry, B. D. (2008). Child Maltreatment: A Neurodevelopmental Perspective on the Role of Trauma and Neglect in Psychopathology. In Hinshaw, T. B. S. P. (Ed.), *Child and Adolescent Psychopathology* (pp. 93–129). John Wiley & Sons.

Perry, B. D., Griffin, E., Davis, G., Perry, J. A., & Perry, R. D. (Eds.). (2018). *The Impact of Neglect, Trauma and Maltreatment on Neurodevelopment: Implications for Juvenile Justice Practice, Programs and Policy*. John Wiley & Sons, Ltd., https://doi.org/https://doi.org/10.1002/9781118650868.ch31

Pessoa, T. M. G., & Almeida, T. C. (2024). The Link Between Adverse Childhood Experiences and Mental Health in Offenders: A Systematic Review. *Crime and Delinquency*, *0*(0). Advance online publication. DOI: 10.1177/00111287241242478

Peters, M. A., & Mika, C. T. (2017). Aborigine, Indian, indigenous or first nations? *Educational Philosophy and Theory*, *49*(13), 1229–1234. DOI: 10.1080/00131857.2017.1279879

Petherick, W. (2015). Motivations. In Petherick, W. (Ed.), *Applied Crime Analysis: A Social Science Approach to Understanding Crime, Criminals, and Victims* (pp. 148–171). Academic Press., DOI: 10.1016/B978-0-323-29460-7.00008-9

Petherick, W., & Sinnamon, G. (2013). *Motivations: Offender and victim perspectives*. Elsevier.

Petherick, W., & Sinnamon, G. (2014). Motivations: Offender and Victim Perspectives. In Petherick, W. (Ed.), *Profiling and Serial Crime: Theoretical and Practical Issues* (3rd ed., pp. 393–430). Academic Press., DOI: 10.1016/B978-1-4557-3174-9.00018-5

Pettus, C. A. (2023). Trauma and Prospects for Reentry. *Annual Review of Criminology*, *6*(1), 423–446. DOI: 10.1146/annurev-criminol-041122-111300

Pfeifer, J. H., Masten, C. L., Moore, W. E., Oswald, T. M., Mazziotta, J. C., Iacoboni, M., & Dapretto, M. (2011). Entering adolescence: Resistance to peer influence, risky behaviour, and neural changes in emotion reactivity. *Neuron*, *69*(5), 1029–1036. DOI: 10.1016/j.neuron.2011.02.019

Phoenix, J. (2016). Against Youth Justice and Youth Governance, for Youth Penalty. *British Journal of Criminology*, *56*(1), 123–140. DOI: 10.1093/bjc/azv031

Pickens, I. (2016). Laying the Groundwork: Conceptualizing a Trauma-Informed System of Care in Juvenile Detention. *Journal of Infant, Child, and Adolescent Psychotherapy; JICAP*, *15*(3), 220–230. DOI: 10.1080/15289168.2016.1214452

Pierluigi, R. (2020). Accepting the unacceptable risk: A critical appraisal of the unacceptable risk test in contemporary Australian family law and finding a way forward. *Australian Bar Review*, *49*, 479.

Polak, S. (2020). Mental health professionals' practice of reintegration therapy for parent–child contact problems post-separation: A phenomenological study. *Journal of Divorce & Remarriage*, *61*(3), 225–248.

Polak, S., Altobelli, T., & Popielarczyk, L. (2020). Responding to severe parent-child rejection cases without a parentectomy: A blended sequential intervention model and the role of the courts. *Family Court Review*, *58*(2), 507–524. DOI: 10.1111/fcre.12496

Pollack, W. S. (2000). *Real boys: Rescuing our sons from the myths of boyhood.* Owl Books.

Poole, N., & Greaves, L. (2012). *Becoming Trauma Informed.* Centre for Addiction and Mental Health.

Poortman, A.-R., & Voorpostel, M. (2009). Parental divorce and sibling relationships: A research note. *Journal of Family Issues*, *30*(1), 74–91.

Porges, S. W. (2020). *Polyvagal Theory and Protective Responses.* Retrieved 21 April from https://www.presence.academy/porges-poly-vagal/

Powers, P., & Act, R. (2000). https://www.legislation.qld.gov.au/view/html/inforce/current/act-2000-005

Prentky, R. A., Burgess, A. W., Hartman, C. R., Lee, A., Rokous, F., Douglas, J. E., & Ressler, R. (1989). The presumptive role of fantasy in serial sexual homicide. *The American Journal of Psychiatry*, *146*(7), 887–891. DOI: 10.1176/AJP.146.7.887

Productivity Commission. (2024). *Report on Government Services 2024*. www.pc.gov.au/ongoing/report-on-government-services/2024/community-services

Prout, A. (2005). *The Future of Childhood Towards the Interdisciplinary Study of Children* (1st ed.). Routledge Falmer.

Psychology Training and Supervision. (2023). *Trauma-Focused Cognitive-Behavioral Therapy*. www.tfcbtaustralia.com.au/resources

Public Sector Ethics Act, 1994. https://www.legislation.qld.gov.au/view/html/inforce/current/act-1994-067

Purcell, C., & Arrigo, B. A. (2006). *The psychology of lust murder: Paraphilia, sexual killing, and serial homicide*. Elsevier.

QFCC. (2024). *Crossover Cohort: Young people under youth justice supervision and their interaction with the child protection system* www.qfcc.qld.gov.au

Queensland Government Statistician's Office. (2021). *Youth offending: Research brief*. https://www.qgso.qld.gov.au › crime-justice-research

Queensland Government. (2023). *Code of Conduct For the Queensland Public Service*. www.forgov.qld.gov.au/pay-benefits-and-policy/public-service-values-and-conduct/public-service-code-of-conduct

Quigley, C., & Cyr, F. (2018). The Voice of the Child in Parenting Coordination: Views of Children, Parents, and Parenting Coordinators. *Journal of Divorce & Remarriage*, *59*(6), 501–527. DOI: 10.1080/10502556.2017.1403823

Quilty, S. (2005). The magnitude of experience of parental incarceration in Australia. *Psychiatry, Psychology, and Law : an Interdisciplinary Journal of the Australian and New Zealand Association of Psychiatry, Psychology and Law*, *12*(1), 256–257.

Quinn, K., Pacella, M. L., Dickson-Gomez, J., & Nydegger, L. A. (2017). Childhood Adversity and the Continued Exposure to Trauma and Violence Among Adolescent Gang Members. *American Journal of Community Psychology*, *59*(1-2), 36–49. DOI: 10.1002/ajcp.12123

R v ABP (District Court of SA, Judge E, 25 March 2025)

R v AJM (District Court of SA, Judge M, 31 March 2025)

R v AKG (District Court of SA, Judge B, 16 May 2025)

R v BKL (District Court of SA, Judge B, 28 March 2025)

R v CVK (District Court of SA, Judge S, 15 April 2025)

R v DJV (District Court of SA, Judge U, 14 April 2025)

R v DTW (District Court of SA, Judge K, 16 April 2025)

R v FMP (District Court of SA, Judge M, 24 April 2025)

R v JAP (District Court of SA, Judge D, 27 March 2025)

R v JRG (District Court of SA, Judge T, 17 March 2025)

R v JRS (District Court of SA, Judge H, 30 April 2025)

R v KVH (District Court of SA, Judge B, 6 May 2025)

R v LSK (District Court of SA, Judge A, 28 March 2025)

R v MIL (District Court of SA, Judge S, 26 March 2025)

R v NJK (District Court of SA, Judge M, 31 March 2025)

R v NSF (District Court of SA, Judge B, 11 April 2025)

R v RCD (District Court of SA, Judge P, 14 May 2025)

R v SAM (District Court of SA, Judge B, 13 March 2025)

R v SKR (District Court of SA, Judge W, 23 April 2025)

R v SRH (District Court of SA, Judge A, 5 March 2025)

R v WCD (District Court of SA, Judge W, 24 April 2025)

Rasheed v Galliano (No 2) [2024] FedCFamC2F 1236.

Rathus, Z. (2012). A Call for Clarity in the Use of Social Science Research in Family Law Decision-Making. *Australian Journal of Family Law*, *26*(2), 81–115.

Rathus, Z. (2014). The Role of Social Science in Australian Family Law: Collaborator, Usurper or Infiltrator? *Family Court Review*, *52*(1), 69–89. DOI: 10.1111/fcre.12071

Rathus, Z. (2018). The Research Says.': Perceptions on the Use of Social Science Research in the Family Law System. *Federal Law Review*, *46*(1), 85.

Rathus, Z. (2021). Social Scientists Operating in the Law: A Case Study of Family Assessment Experts in the Australian Family Law System. *International Journal of Law, Policy and the Family*, *35*(1), ebab051.

Rathus, Z., Jeffries, S., Menih, H., & Field, R. (2019). "It's Like Standing on a Beach, Holding Your Children's Hands, and Having a Tsunami Just Coming Towards You": Intimate Partner Violence and "Expert" Assessments in Australian Family Law. *Victims & Offenders*, *14*(4), 408–440. DOI: 10.1080/15564886.2019.1580646

Reay, K. M. (2015). Family reflections: A promising therapeutic program designed to treat severely alienated children and their family system. *The American Journal of Family Therapy*, *43*(2), 197–207.

Reese, E. M., Chang, D., Zauszniewski, J. A., & Brown, H. L. (2022). Intergenerational transmission of trauma: The mediating role of family health. *BMC Public Health*, *22*, 976. Advance online publication. DOI: 10.1186/s12889-022-13431-9

Reid, S., Katan, A., Ellithy, A., Della Stua, R., & Denisov, E. V. (2019). The perfect storm: Mapping the life course trajectories of serial killers. *International Journal of Offender Therapy and Comparative Criminology*, *63*(9), 1621–1662. 10.1177%2F0306624X19838683

Reiniger, B., & Zemp, M. (2021). When problems only get bigger: The impact of adverse childhood experiences related to maltreatment and violence in adulthood. *Frontiers in Psychology*, *12*, 693420. DOI: 10.3389/fpsyg.2021.693420frontiersin

Rémond, M., Zeki, R., Austin, K., Bowman, J., Galouzis, J., Stewart, K., & Sullivan, E. (2023). *Intergenerational incarceration in New South Wales: Characteristics of people in prison experiencing parental imprisonment. Trends & issues in crime and criminal justice no. 663*. Australian Institute of Criminology., DOI: 10.52922/ti78863

Ressler, R. K., Burgess, A. W., & Douglas, J. (1988). *Sexual homicide: Patterns and motives*. Free Press.

Ressler, R. K., Burgess, A. W., Douglas, J. E., Hartman, C. R., & D'Agostino, R. B. (1986). Sexual killers and their victims: Identifying patterns through crime scene analysis. *Journal of Interpersonal Violence*, *1*(3), 288–308. DOI: 10.1177/088626086001003003

Ressler, R. K., & Shachtman, T. (2002). *Whoever fights monsters*. St. Martins.

Reupert, A., Cuff, R., & Maybery, D. (2015). *Helping children understand their parent's mental illness*. Cambridge University Press.

Reupert, J., Maybery, D., & Kowalenko, N. M. (2013). Children whose parents have a mental illness: Prevalence, need and treatment. *The Medical Journal of Australia*, *199*(3), S7–S9. DOI: 10.5694/mja11.11200

Reynolds v Reynolds [2025] FedCFamC2F 85.

Riddle, S., Hickey, A., Pocock, C., McKee, A., Skye, D., & Wallis, R. (2024). Moving beyond deficit Australian media figurations of young people: Troubling the contemporary 'youth crime crisis'. *Continuum, 37*(6), 756–769. DOI: 10.1080/10304312.2024.2313565

Riethmuller, G. (2023). Evidence and Unacceptable Risk. *The Australian Law Journal, 97*(11), 802–804.

Roberts v Short [2024] FedCFamC2F 1557.

Robinson, M. (2016). *To examine trauma-informed models of youth detention and bring back findings.* www.churchilltrust.com.au/fellow/murray-robinson-vic-2015/

Rohner, R. P., Khaleque, A., & Cournoyer, D. E. (2005). Parental acceptance-rejection: Theory, methods, cross-cultural evidence, and implications. *Ethos (Berkeley, Calif.), 33*(3), 299–334. DOI: 10.1525/eth.2005.33.3.299

Roma, P., Marchetti, D., Mazza, C., Ricci, E., Fontanesi, L., & Verrocchio, M. C. (2022). A Comparison of MMPI-2 Profiles Between Parental Alienation Cases and Custody Cases. *Journal of Child and Family Studies, 31*(5), 1196–1206. DOI: 10.1007/s10826-021-02076-1

Rose, B., Kuiper, M. E., Reinders Folmer, C., & van Rooij, B. (2024). Can criminology sway the public? How empirical findings about deterrence affect public punishment preferences. *Crime Science, 13*(1), 43. DOI: 10.1186/s40163-024-00240-8

Rostami, A., Sturup, J., Mondani, H., Thevselius, P., Sarnecki, J. and Edling, C. (2018), 'The Swedish Mujahideen: An Exploratory Study of 41 Swedish Foreign Fighters Deceased in Iraq and Syria', Studies in Conflict and Terrorism, 1–14. Published Online, doi: .DOI: 10.1080/1057610X.2018.1463615

Rowlands, G. A., Warshak, R. A., & Harman, J. J. (2022). Abused and Rejected: The Link Between Intimate Partner Violence and Parental Alienation. *Partner Abuse, 14*(1), 37–58.

Royal Commission into Institutional Responses to Child Sexual Abuse. (2017). *Final Report: Impacts* (Vol. 3). Commonwealth of Australia. https://www.childabuseroyal commission.gov.au/final-report

Roy, C., Castonguay, A., Fortin, M., Drolet, C., Franche-Choquette, G., Dumais, A., Lafortune, D., Bernard, P., & Geoffrion, S. (2019). The Use of Restraint and Seclusion in Residential Treatment Care for Youth: A Systematic Review of Related Factors and Interventions. *Trauma, Violence & Abuse*, *22*(2), 318–338. DOI: 10.1177/1524838019843196

Saini, M., & Birnbaum, R. (2007). Unraveling the label of" high conflict": What factors really count in divorce and separated families.

Salisbury, E. J., & Van Voorhis, P. (2009). Gendered pathways: An empirical investigation of women probationers' paths to incarceration. *Criminal Justice and Behavior*, *36*, 541–566.

Sampson, R. J., & Neil, R. (2024). The social foundations of racial inequalities in arrest overthe life course and in changing times. *Criminology*, *62*(2), 177–204. DOI: 10.1111/1745-9125.12374

Sasaki, A., Mochizuki, A., & Yoshihara, D. (2023). Gender Differences in Abusive Parenting among Incarcerated Parents in Japan. *The Prison Journal*, *103*(1), 45–67. DOI: 10.1177/00328855221139865

Saxena, P., & Messina, N. (2021). Adverse Childhood Experiences and Pathways to Violent Behavior: Examining Gender Differences Among Justice-Involved Adults. *Journal of Interpersonal Violence*, *36*(7–8), 4042–4066. DOI: 10.1177/0886260518777551

Schimmenti, A., Carabellese, F. F., & Caretti, V. (2021). Child maltreatment and psychopathy. In A. R. Felthous & H. Sab (Eds.), *The Wiley International Handbook on Psychopathic Disorders and the Law: Volume 1 Diagnosis and Treatment* (2nd ed., pp. 403-419). John Wiley and Sons Ltd.

Schindeler, E. (2019). Family law court orders for supervised contact in custodial disputes - unanswered questions. *Children Australia*, *44*(4), 194–201. DOI: 10.1017/cha.2019.42

Schiraldi, V., Hayes, D., & McGuire, D. R. (2021). *Youth Justice in The Netherlands & Spain*. https://justicelab.columbia.edu/content/netherlands-experience-emerging-adult-justice

Schmidt, A. T., Duron, J., Bergquist, B. K., Bammel, A. C., Maloney, K. A., Williams-Butler, A., & Hanten, G. R. (2023). Prosocial attributes relate to lower recidivism in justice-involved youth: Preliminary evidence using a novel measure of prosocial functioning. *Journal of Public Mental Health*, *22*(4), 202–215. DOI: 10.1108/jpmh-02-2023-0012

Schmidt, C. D., & Grigg, J. (2023). Counseling High Conflict: Navigating the Complexities of High Conflict Divorce. *The Family Journal (Alexandria, Va.)*, •••, 10664807231173689.

Schmucker, M., & Lösel, F. (2015). The effects of sexual offender treatment on recidivism: An international meta-analysis of sound quality evaluations. *Journal of Experimental Criminology, 11*(4), 597–630. DOI: 10.1007/s11292-015-9241-z

Schonbrun, Y. C., Johnson, J. E., Anderson, B. J., Caviness, C., & Stein, M. D. (2016). Hazardously Drinking Jailed Women: Post-Release Perceived Needs and Risk of Reincarceration. *International Journal of Offender Therapy and Comparative Criminology, 61*(16), 1819–1832. https://doi.org/ (Original work published 2017). DOI: 10.1177/0306624X16634702

Schreck, C. J. (1999). Criminal victimization and low self-control: An extension and test of a general theory of crime. *Justice Quarterly, 16*(3), 633–654. DOI: 10.1080/07418829900094291

Scottish Government. (2018). *Understanding childhood adversity, resilience and crime*. Justice Analytical Services. https://www.gov.scot/binaries/content/documents/govscot/publications/research-and-analysis/2018/05/understanding-childhood-adversity-resilience-crime/documents/00535550-pdf/00535550-pdf/govscot:document1

Secretariat of the Pacific Community. (n.d.). *Thematic brief: Ending violence against women in the Pacific*. https://pacificdata.org/data/dataset/acf42df5-54c0-43e2-98c4-e2afefb1bce0/resource/4cf275c7-ea06-419f-845e-7b49cff21e96/download/spc-pwl_thematicbrief_evawg.pdf

Selwood v Selwood (No 2) [2024] FedCFamC1F 700.

Semenza, D. C., Testa, A., & Jackson, D. B. (2022). Intersectional differences in serious violent victimization trajectories across the life course. *Preventive Medicine Reports, 26*, 101732. Advance online publication. DOI: 10.1016/j.pmedr.2022.101732

Sheehan, R. (2019). Cumulative Harm in Child Protection: The Hidden Concern. *Australian Social Work, 72*(4), 434–446. DOI: 10.1080/0312407X.2019.1603316

Sheehan, R. (2019b). Cumulative harm in the child protection system: T he A ustralian context. *Child & Family Social Work, 24*(4), 421–429. DOI: 10.1111/cfs.12621

Sheehan, R., & Levine, G. (2006). *Parents as Prisoners: Maintaining the Parent-Child Relationship. Report for the Criminology Research Council Project Grant CRC 39/05-06*. Australian Institute of Criminology.

Sherman, A. (2005). Children of Prisoners: Background Briefing Report. The Center for Research on Children in the U.S. (CROCUS) & Georgetown Public Policy Institute.

Shine for Kids. (2024). *Case Worker & Foster Carer Guidebook*. https://shineforkids.org.au/wp-content/uploads/2024/08/Case-Worker-and-Foster-Carer-guidebook-FINAL.pdf

Shumaker, D., & Kelsey, C. (2020). The existential impact of high-conflict divorce on children. *Person-Centered and Experiential Psychotherapies*, *19*(1), 22–37. DOI: 10.1080/14779757.2020.1717985

Sicilia, L. (2024). El crecimiento postraumático en sobrevivientes de abuso sexual infantil. En L. Contreras-Taibo y E. García-López, Victimología Forense. Perspectivas Iberoamericanas (pp. 117-147). Manual Moderno.

Siegel, L. J. (2017). *Criminology: Theories, patterns, and typologies* (13th ed.). Cengage Learning.

Silke, A. (2008). Holy Warriors: Exploring the Psychological Processes of Jihadi Radicalization. *European Journal of Criminology*, *5*, 99–123.

Silva, C., Moreira, P., Sá Moreira, D., Rafael, F., Rodrigues, A., Leite, Â., & Lopes, S. (2024). Impact of adverse childhood experiences in young adults and adults: A systematic literature review. *Pediatric Reports*, *16*(2), 461–481. DOI: 10.3390/pediatric16020040

Simi, P., Sporer, K., & Bubolz, B. F. (2016). Narratives of Childhood Adversity and Adolescent Misconduct as Precursors to Violent Extremism: A Life-Course Criminological Approach. *Journal of Research in Crime and Delinquency*, *53*(4), 536–563. DOI: 10.1177/0022427815627312

Simi, P., Windisch, S., & Sporer, K. (2016). *Recruitment and Radicalization among US Far Right Terrorists*. START.

Sinnamon, G. (2017). Psychopathology as a Mediator of Antisocial and Criminal Behavior. In Petherick, W., & Sinnamon, G. (Eds.), *The Psychology of Criminal and Antisocial Behavior: Victim and Offender Perspectives* (pp. 1–50). Academic Press., DOI: 10.1016/B978-0-12-809287-3.00001-8

Sirhan, N., Mufarreh, A., Lee, Y., Mishreky, C., Hunt, B., Anderson, T., & Bailey, B. A. (2024). Adverse Childhood Experiences in the Post-COVID Era. *Journal of Aggression, Maltreatment & Trauma*, •••, 1–13. DOI: 10.1080/10926771.2024.2404002

Smart, P., & Neale, B. (2000). It's my life too'-Children's perspectives on post-divorce parenting. *FAMILY LAW-BRISTOL*, *30*, 163–169.

Smith, C., & Thornberry, T. P. (1995). The relationship between childhood maltreatment and adolescent involvement in delinquency. *Criminology*, *33*(4), 451–481.

Smith, V. C., Wilson, C. R., & Use, C. o. S., Prevention, Ryan, S. A., Gonzalez, P. K., . . . Walker, L. R. (2016). Families affected by parental substance use. *Pediatrics, 138*(2), e20161575.

Smyth, B. M., & Moloney, L. J. (2019). Post-separation parenting disputes and the many faces of high conflict: Theory and research. *Australian and New Zealand Journal of Family Therapy, 40*(1), 74–84.

Sowell, E. R., Thompson, P. M., Holmes, C. J., Jernigan, T. L., & Toga, A. W. (1999). In vivo evidence for post-adolescent brain maturation in frontal and striatal regions. *Nature Neuroscience, 2*(10), 859–861. DOI: 10.1038/13154

Sowell, E. R., Thompson, P. M., Tessner, K. D., & Toga, A. W. (2001). Mapping continued brain growth and gray matter density reduction in dorsal frontal cortex: Inverse relationships during postadolescent brain maturation. *The Journal of Neuroscience : The Official Journal of the Society for Neuroscience, 21*(22), 8819–8829. DOI: 10.1523/JNEUROSCI.21-22-08819.2001

Sowter, D. M. (2018). Advocacy in non-adversarial family law: A recommendation for revision to the model code. *Windsor Yearbook of Access to Justice, 35*, 401–432. DOI: 10.22329/wyaj.v35i0.5788

Sparks, B. (2021). Attitudes toward the Punishment of Juvenile and Adult Sexual Offenders in Canada: The Roles of Sentencing Goals and Criminal Justice Motivations. *Journal of Child Sexual Abuse, 30*(2), 125–145. DOI: 10.1080/10538712.2020.1862947

Sroufe, L. A., Carlson, E. A., Levy, A. K., & Egeland, B. (1999). Implications of attachment theory for developmental psychopathology. *Development and Psychopathology, 11*, 1–13.

Stark, R. (1987). Deviant Places: A Theory of the Ecology of Crime. *Criminology, 25*(4), 893–910. DOI: 10.1111/j.1745-9125.1987.tb00824.x

Stathis, S. L., Letters, P., Doolan, I., Fleming, R., Heath, K., Arnett, A., & Cory, S. (2008). Use of the Massachusetts Youth Screening Instrument to assess mental health problems in young people within an Australian youth detention centre. *Journal of Paediatrics and Child Health, 44*(7-8), 438–443. DOI: 10.1111/j.1440-1754.2008.01324.x

Stein, A. (2009). From their cradle to your grave: How child abuse and dissociation drive violent crime. *The Journal of Psychohistory, 36*(4), 320–327.

Steinberg, L. (2005). Cognitive and affective development in adolescence. *Trends in Cognitive Sciences, 9*(2), 69–74.

Stern, N., & Oehme, K. (2002). The troubling admission of supervised visitation records in custody proceedings. *Temple Law Review*, *75*(2), 271–311.

Stevens, J. E. (n.d.). Got your ACE score? ACEs Too High. Retrieved July 6, 2025, from Suh, B. C., Gallaway, M. S., & Celaya, M. F. (2024). Supportive relationships mitigate the effect of cumulative exposure to adverse childhood experiences on depression, anxiety, stress, and suicide considerations: The Arizona Youth Risk Behavior Survey. *Children, 11*(2), 161. https://doi.org/ /DOI: 10.3390/children11020161https://acestoohigh.com/got-your-ace-score

Stewart, A. L., Livingston, M., & Dennison, S. (2008). Transitions and turning points: Examining the links between child maltreatment and juvenile offending. *Child Abuse & Neglect*, *32*(1), 51–66. DOI: 10.1016/j.chiabu.2007.04.011

Straus, M. A. (1979). Measuring intrafamily conflict and violence: The conflict tactics (CT) scales. *Journal of Marriage and Family*, *41*(1), 75–88. DOI: 10.2307/351733

Strickland, S. M. (2008). Female sex offenders: Exploring issues of personality, trauma, and cognitive distortions. *Journal of Interpersonal Violence*, *23*(4), 474–489. DOI: 10.1177/0886260507312944

Subramaniam, M., Abdin, E., Seow, E., Vaingankar, J. A., Shafie, S., Shahwan, S., Lim, M., Fung, D., James, L., Verma, S., & Chong, S. A. (2020). Prevalence, socio-demographic correlates and associations of adverse childhood experiences with mental illnesses: Results from the Singapore Mental Health Study. *Child Abuse & Neglect*, *103*, 104447. Advance online publication. DOI: 10.1016/j.chiabu.2020.104447

Substance Abuse and Mental Health Services Administration. (2014). *SAMHSA's Concept of Trauma and Guidance for a Trauma-Informed Approach*. US Department of Health and Human Services.

Suh, B. C., Gallaway, M. S., & Celaya, M. F. (2024). Supportive relationships mitigate the effect of cumulative exposure to adverse childhood experiences on depression, anxiety, stress, and suicide considerations: The Arizona Youth Risk Behavior Survey. *Children (Basel, Switzerland)*, *11*(2), 161. DOI: 10.3390/children11020161

Su, W. M., & Stone, L. (2020). Adult survivors of childhood trauma: Complex trauma, complex needs. *Australian Journal of General Practice*, *49*(7), 423–430.

Swedo, E. A., Holditch Niolon, P., Anderson, K. N., Li, J., Brener, N., Mpofu, J., Aslam, M. V., & Underwood, J. M. (2024). Prevalence of Adverse Childhood Experiences Among Adolescents. *Pediatrics*. Advance online publication. DOI: 10.1542/peds.2024-066633

Szirom, T., Jaffe, R., McIntosh, J., Holmes, L. (1998). Contact Services in Australia - Research and Evaluation Project.

Teicher, M. H., & Samson, J. A. (2016). Annual research review: Enduring neurobiological effects of childhood abuse and neglect. *Journal of Child Psychology and Psychiatry, and Allied Disciplines*, *57*(3), 241–266. DOI: 10.1111/jcpp.12507

Ter Beek, E., Spruit, A., Kuiper, C. H. Z., van der Rijken, R. E. A., Hendriks, J., & Stams, G. J. J. M. (2018). Treatment effect on recidivism for juveniles who have sexually offended: A multilevel meta-analysis. *Journal of Abnormal Child Psychology*, *46*(3), 543–556. DOI: 10.1007/s10802-017-0308-3

Thomas, J. L., Keenan-Miller, D., Sumner, J. A., & Hammen, C. (2021). Early Life Adversity and Clinical Intimate Partner Violence in Adulthood: The Australian mediating Role of Interpersonal Conflict in Adolescence. *Journal of Interpersonal Violence*, *8862605211057267*. Advance online publication. DOI: 10.1177/08862605211057267

Thompson, M. P., Kingree, J. B., & Desai, S. (2004). Gender differences in long-term health consequences of childhood physical abuse. *American Journal of Public Health*, *94*(4), 660–665. DOI: 10.2105/ajph.94.4.660

Thomsen, L., & Homel, R. (2024). Cumulative Sociodemographic Risk as a Predictor of Adolescent Antisocial Behaviour. *Child Indicators Research*, *17*(5), 2123–2148. DOI: 10.1007/s12187-024-10157-y

Tippins, T. M., & Wittmann, J. P. (2005). Empirical and Ethical Problems with Custody Recommendations: A Call for Clinical Humility and Judicial Vigilance. *Family Court Review*, *43*(2), 193–222. DOI: 10.1111/j.1744-1617.2005.00019.x

Tonry, M., & Farrington, D. (1995). Strategic Approaches to Crime Prevention. *Crime and Justice*, *19*(1).

Trejo, B. G., Mendoza, F., & Lamas, H. (2024). Characterising the killing of girls and women in urban settings in Latin America, 2000–2019: An analysis of variability and time trends using mortality data from vital registration systems. *BMJ Public Health*, *2*(1), e000985. DOI: 10.1136/bmjph-2023-000985

Trentham, C. E., Hensley, C., & Policastro, C. (2018). Recurrent childhood animal cruelty and its link to recurrent adult interpersonal violence. *International Journal of Offender Therapy and Comparative Criminology*, *62*(8), 2345–2356. DOI: 10.1177/0306624X17720175

Trinder, L. (1997). Competing constructions of childhood: Children's rights and children's wishes in divorce. *Journal of Social Welfare and Family Law*, *19*(3), 291–305. DOI: 10.1080/09649069708415674

Turanovic, J. J. (2018). Towards a Life Course Theory of Victimization. In Decker, S. H., & Wright, K. A. (Eds.), *Criminology and Public Policy: Putting Theory to Work* (2nd ed., pp. 85–103). Temple University Press.

Turanovic, J. J. (2023). Victimization and its consequences over the life course. *Crime and Justice*, *52*(1), 265–342. DOI: 10.1086/727029

Turanovic, J. J., & Ogle, M. R. (2018). State Dependence and Population Heterogeneity in Theories of Victimization. In Huebner, B. M. (Ed.), *Oxford Bibliographies*. Oxford University Press., DOI: 10.1093/obo/9780195396607-0232

Turanovic, J. J., & Pratt, T. C. (2024). *Thinking About Victimization. Context and Consequences* (2nd ed.). Routledge., DOI: 10.4324/9781003269557

Turoy-smith, K. M., & Powell, M. B. (2017). Interviewing of Children for Family Law Matters: A Review. *Australian Psychologist*, *52*(3), 165–173. DOI: 10.1111/ap.12193

Tustin, D., & Tustin, D. (2024a). *Common Co-Parenting Mistakes and Associated Orders*. Springer.

Tustin, D., & Tustin, D. (2024b). *Risk of Cumulative Harm for Children*. Springer.

Ullman, C., Amin, A., Bourassa, A., Chandarana, S., Dutra, F., & Ellsberg, M. (2025). Interventions to prevent violence against women and girls globally: A global systematic review of reviews to update the RESPECT women framework. *BMJ Public Health*, *3*(1).

United Nations Committee on the Rights of the Child (UNCRC). (2011, September 30) Report and Recommendations of the Day of General Discussion on 'Children of Incarcerated Parents'. https://www.ohchr.org/sites/default/files/Documents/HRBodies/CRC/Discussions/2011/DGD2011ReportAndRecommendations.pdf

United Nations Interregional Crime and Justice Research Institute. (2025). Children and Counter-Terrorism. https://unicri.org/sites/default/files/2019-10/Children_counter_terrorism.pdf

United Nations Office on Drugs and Crime. (2023). *Global Study on Homicide 2023*. United Nations. https://www.unodc.org/unodc/en/data-and-analysis/global-study-on-homicide.html

United Nations. (1989, November 20) *Convention on the Rights of the Child*. General Assembly resolution 44/25. https://www.ohchr.org/sites/default/files/crc.pdf

Upton, F. (2023). Addressing Challenges and Opportunities in Juvenile Justice: Meeting the Needs of Incarcerated Adolescent Populations. *Psychological Science in the Public Interest, 24*(3), 127–132. DOI: 10.1177/15291006231218669

Urquhart, C., & Jasiura, F. (2013). *Trauma Informed Practice Guide*. www.cewh.ca/wp-content/uploads/2012/05/2013_TIP-Guide.pdf

Usher, K., Jackson, D., Walker, R., Durkin, J., Smallwood, R., Robinson, M., Sampson, U. N., Adams, I., Porter, C., & Marriott, R. (2021). Indigenous Resilience in Australia: A Scoping Review Using a Reflective Decolonizing Collective Dialogue. *Frontiers in Public Health, 9*, 1–17. DOI: 10.3389/fpubh.2021.630601

Vaismoradi, M., Turunen, H., & Bondas, T. (2013). Content analysis and thematic analysis: Implications for conducting a qualitative descriptive study. *Nursing & Health Sciences, 15*, 398–405. https://doi.org/doi:10.1111/nhs.12048

Van der Kolk, B. A. (Ed.). (2007). *Developmental impact of Childhood Trauma*. Cambridge University Press.

Van Der Kolk, B. A., McFarlane, A. C., & Weisaeth, L. (1996). Background Issues and History. In Van Der Kolk, B. A., & McFarlane, A. C. (Eds.), *Traumatic Stress: The Effects of Overwhelming Experience on Mind, Body, and Society*. Guilford Publications.

Van Wyk, J. A. (2023). ACEs and Angst: Adverse Childhood Experiences, General Strain Theory, and Adolescent Male Suicidal and Violent Behaviors. *SAGE Open, 13*(2), 1–19. DOI: 10.1177/21582440231176710

VanDaalen, R. A., Vallefuoco, A. A., Fernandez, M. L., Liu, S. Y., & Lemaire, C. J. (2025). Public Perceptions of the Neurodiversity Movement: A Thematic Analysis. *Neurodiversity, 3*, 27546330251325973.

Vandana, N. (2023). Crisis of Parental Conflict: Impact on Children and Families. *Horyzonty Wychowania, 22*(64). Advance online publication. DOI: 10.35765/hw.2023.2264.08

Vander Ven, T., & Colvin, M. (2012). Coercion and Crime. In Cullen, F., & Wilcox, P. (Eds.), *The Oxford Handbook of Criminological Theory* (pp. 607–624). Oxford University Press., DOI: 10.1093/oxfordhb/9780199747238.013.0031

Vardon, C. (2021). *Changing the Sentence: Overseeing Queensland's youth justice reforms*. https://www.qfcc.qld.gov.au/

Velleman, R., & Templeton, L. J. (2016). Impact of parents' substance misuse on children: An update. *BJPsych Advances, 22*(2), 108–117.

Verhaar, S., Matthewson, M. L., & Bentley, C. (2022). The Impact of Parental Alienating Behaviours on the Mental Health of Adults Alienated in Childhood. *Children (Basel, Switzerland)*, *9*(4), 475. DOI: 10.3390/children9040475

Vidal, S., Connell, C. M., Prince, D. M., & Tebes, J. K. (2019). Multisystem-Involved Youth: A Developmental Framework and Implications for Research, Policy, and Practice. *Adolescent Research Review*, *4*(1), 15–29. DOI: 10.1007/s40894-018-0088-1

Vincent, G. M., Drawbridge, D. C., Lawson, S. G., Todorovic, K., & Perrault, R. T. (2024). Sustainability of Evidence-Based Practices: Risk-Need-Responsivity in Probation 7 Years Later. *Criminal Justice and Behavior*, *51*(5), 643–666. DOI: 10.1177/00938548241229193

W v W (Abuse Allegations: Unacceptable Risk) (2005) 34 Fam LR 129.

Walker, J. S., & Matarese, M. (2011). Family Voice with Informed Choice: Coordinating Wraparound with Research-Based Treatment for Children and Youth with Complex Needs. *Journal of Child and Family Studies*, *22*(1), 6–18. DOI: 10.1007/s10826-011-9456-2

Walker, L. E. (1979). *The battered woman*. Harper & Row.

Walsh, A. (2019). Section Three: Victimology. In Introduction to Criminology (4th ed., pp. 76–90). SAGE Publications.https://us.sagepub.com/sites/default/files/upm-binaries/90401_Section_Three_Victimology_Exploring_the_Experience_of_Victimization.pdf

Walsh, T., & Douglas, H. (2016). Sentencing Parents: The Consideration of Dependent Children. *Adelaide Law Review*, *37*, 135–161.

Warshak. (2003). Payoffs and Pitfalls of Listening to Children. *Family relations, 52*(4), 373-384. doi:DOI: 10.1111/j.1741-3729.2003.00373.x

Warshak. (2018). Night shifts: Revisiting blanket restrictions on children's overnights with separated parents. *Journal of divorce & remarriage, 59*(4), 282-323.

Weatherby, G. A., Buller, D. M., & McGinnis, K. (2009). The Buller-McGinnis model of serial homicidal behavior: An integrated approach. *Journal of Criminology and Criminal Justice Research & Education*, *3*(1), 1–21.

Weber, S., & Lynch, S. (2021). Understanding the relations among adverse childhood experiences (ACE), substance use, and reoffending among detained youth. *Child Abuse & Neglect, 120*. Advance online publication. DOI: 10.1016/j.chiabu.2021.105211

Webster-Stratton, C. (1985). Comparison of abusive and non-abusive families with conduct-disordered children. *The American Journal of Orthopsychiatry, 55*(1), 59–69. DOI: 10.1111/j.1939-0025.1985.tb03421.x

Westrupp, E. M., Brown, S., Woolhouse, H., Gartland, D., & Nicholson, J. M. (2018). Repeated early-life exposure to inter-parental conflict increases risk of preadolescent mental health problems. *European Journal of Pediatrics, 177*(3), 419–427. DOI: 10.1007/s00431-017-3071-0

White, M., & Gooda, M. (2017). *Royal Commission and Board of Inquiry into the Protection and Detention of Children in the Northern Territory: Final Report*. Darwin, Australia Retrieved from https://www.royalcommission.gov.au/royal-commission-detention-and-protection-children-northern-territory

Whitten, T., McGee, T. R., Homel, R., Farrington, D. P., & Ttofi, M. M. (2018). Comparing the criminal careers and childhood risk factors of persistent, chronic, and persistent–chronic offenders. *Australian and New Zealand Journal of Criminology, 52*(2), 151–173. DOI: 10.1177/0004865818781203

Widom, C. S., & Maxfield, M. G. (2001). *An update on the "cycle of violence"*. National Institute of Justice. https://nij.ojp.gov/library/publications/update-cycle-violence

Widom, C. S. (1989). The cycle of violence. *Science, 244*(4901), 160–166.

Widom, C. S. (2017). Long-term impact of childhood abuse and neglect on crime and violence. *Clinical Psychology : a Publication of the Division of Clinical Psychology of the American Psychological Association, 24*(2), 186–202. DOI: 10.1037/h0101743

Widom, C. S. (2022). Long-term Consequences of Childhood Maltreatment. In Krugman, R. D., & Korbin, J. E. (Eds.), *Handbook of Child Maltreatment* (2nd ed., pp. 371–395). Springer., DOI: 10.1007/978-3-030-82479-2_18

Widom, C. S., & Osborn, M. (2021). The cycle of violence: Abused and neglected girls to adult female offenders. *Feminist Criminology, 16*(3), 266–285. DOI: 10.1177/1557085120987628

Widom, C. S., & Wilson, H. W. (2015). Intergenerational Transmission of Violence. In Lindert, J., & Levav, I. (Eds.), *Violence and Mental Health*. Springer., DOI: 10.1007/978-94-017-8999-8_2

Wiens, K., Gillis, J., Nicolau, I., & Wade, T. J. (2020). Capturing risk associated with childhood adversity: Independent, cumulative, and multiplicative effects of physical abuse, sexual abuse, and family violence on mental disorders and suicidality. The Permanente Journal, 24, 19.079. https://doi.org/DOI: 10.7812/TPP/19.079

Wikström, P. H. Treiber, k., & Roman, G. (2024). *Character, Circumstances, and Criminal Careers: Towards a Dynamic Developmental and Life-Course Criminology*. Oxford University Press.

Wildeman, C., & Andersen, S. H. (2017). Paternal incarceration and children's risk of being charged by early adulthood: Evidence from a Danish policy shock. *Criminology*, *55*(1), 32–58. DOI: 10.1111/1745-9125.12124

Wildeman, C., Sampson, R. J., & Baker, G. (2024). Adult Children of the Prison Boom: Family Troubles and the Intergenerational Transmission of Criminal Justice Contact. *Demography*, *61*(1), 141–164. DOI: 10.1215/00703370-11153107

Williams, B. T. (2023). *Effectiveness of staff training on Trauma-Informed Care*. The University of Southern Mississippi., https://aquila.usm.edu/cgi/viewcontent.cgi?article=1272&context=dnp_capstone

Wilson, L. C., Fauci, J. E., & Goodman, L. A. (2015). Bringing trauma-informed practice to domestic violence programs: A Qualitative Analysis of Current Approaches. *The American Journal of Orthopsychiatry*, *86*(6), 586–599. DOI: 10.1037/ort0000098

Wolff, K. T., Baglivio, M. T., & Intravia, J. (2022). Adverse childhood experiences (ACEs), psychotropic medication prescription, and continued offending among youth with serious offending histories in juvenile justice residential placement. *Journal of Criminal Justice*, *83*(November-December), 1–13. DOI: 10.1016/j.jcrimjus.2022.101922

Wolff, K. T., Craig, J. M., Baglivio, M. T., & Papalia, N. (2025). Are More ACEs Always Worse? Exploring Nonlinear Associations with Youth Behavior. *Journal of Youth and Adolescence*. Advance online publication. DOI: 10.1007/s10964-025-02225-5

Wolff, K. T., Cuevas, C., Intravia, J., Baglivio, M. T., & Epps, N. (2018). The Effects of Neighborhood Context on Exposure to Adverse Childhood Experiences (ACE) Among Adolescents Involved in the Juvenile Justice System: Latent Classes and Contextual Effects. *Journal of Youth and Adolescence*, *47*(11), 2279–2300. DOI: 10.1007/s10964-018-0887-5

Wolff, N., & Shi, J. (2012). Childhood and adult trauma experiences of incarcerated persons and their relationship to adult behavioural health problems and treatment. *International Journal of Environmental Research and Public Health*, *9*, 1908–1926.

Wolfgang, M. E. (1957). Victim Precipitated Criminal Homicide. The Journal of Criminal Law, Criminology, and Police Science, 48(1), 1–11. https://doi.org/ ACEs Aware. (2021). *Your ACE Screening & Clinical Response Approach*. California Department of Health Care Services. https://www.acesaware.org/wp-content/uploads/2021/09/Stage-2-Workbook.pdfDOI: 10.2307/1140160

Women in Prison Project. (2006). *Fact sheet: Why focus on women in prison*. Correctional Association of New York. http://www.correctionalassociation.org

Wood, S., Janssen, H., Hughes, K., Passmore, J., & Bellis, M. A. (2023). *A practical handbook on Adverse Childhood Experiences (ACEs) Delivering prevention, building resilience and developing trauma-informed systems*. Retrieved 26 December from https://phwwhocc.co.uk

Yaksic, E. (2022). *Killer data: Modern perspectives on serial murder*. Routledge.

Yaksic, E., Simkin, M., & Roychowdhury, V. (2021). A statistical study of the time intervals between serial homicides. *Journal of Criminal Justice*, *73*, 101751.

Yannon, M. G., Decrop, R., Le, M., Beery, S., & Tompsett, C. J. (2024). Cumulative Adverse Childhood Experiences (ACEs) and Recidivism: A Meta-Analysis. *Criminal Justice and Behavior*, *51*(11), 1696–1714. DOI: 10.1177/00938548241267230

Yao, X., Zhang, H., & Zhao, R. (2022). Does Trauma Exacerbate Criminal Behavior? An Exploratory Study of Child Maltreatment and Chronic Offending in a Sample of Chinese Juvenile Offenders. *International Journal of Environmental Research and Public Health*, *19*(18), 11197. DOI: 10.3390/ijerph191811197

Yoder, J. R., Hodge, A. I., Ruch, D., & Dillard, R. (2018). Effects of Childhood Polyvictimization on Victimization in Juvenile Correctional Facilities: The Australian mediating Role of Trauma Symptomatology. *Youth Violence and Juvenile Justice*, *17*(2), 129–153. DOI: 10.1177/1541204018757038

Yohros, A. (2023, July). Examining the relationship between Adverse Childhood Experiences and Juvenile Recidivism: A systematic review and meta-analysis. *Trauma, Violence & Abuse*, *24*(3), 1640–1655. DOI: 10.1177/15248380211073846

Younas, F., & Gutman, L. M. (2023). Parental risk and protective factors in child maltreatment: A systematic review of the evidence. *Trauma, Violence & Abuse*, *24*(5), 3697–3714.

Young v Young [2010] FMCAfam 931.

yourtown. (2023, January). *Adverse childhood experiences: What works papers.* https://www.yourtown.com.au/sites/default/files/document/Adverse%20Childhood%20Experiences%20-%20What%20Works%20Papers,%20January%202023.pdf

Yusof, Z. M. (2024, August 7). Rehabilitation programmes for women offenders help drive down two-year recidivism rate. *The Straits Times.* https://www.straitstimes.com/singapore/rehabilitation-programmes-for-women-offenders-see-two-year-recidivism-rate-drop-for-5-straight-years

Yu, Z., Noll, J. G., & Putnam, F. W. (2022). Adverse childhood experiences and homicide victimization: A population-based study. *Child Abuse & Neglect, 127,* 105607. . 105607guides.library.uq+1DOI: 10.1016/j.chiabu.2022

Zettler, H. R., & Craig, J. M. (2022). Residentially-Placed Youth and the Adverse Childhood Experiences-Recidivism Relationship: Considering Racial/Ethnic and Sex Differences. *American Journal of Criminal Justice, 48*(2), 530–544. DOI: 10.1007/s12103-021-09667-0

Zettler, H. R., & Craig, J. M. (2024). The Prevalence of Trauma Among Participants in a Juvenile Mental Health Court. *Criminal Justice and Behavior, 51*(3), 401–419. DOI: 10.1177/00938548231222619

Zettler, H. R., Wolff, K. T., Baglivio, M., Craig, J. M., & Epps, N. (2017). The Racial and Gender Differences in the Impact of Adverse Childhood Experiences on Juvenile Residential Placement. *Youth Violence and Juvenile Justice, 16*(3), 319–337. DOI: 10.1177/1541204017698213

Zhu, J., Exner-Cortens, D., Dobson, K., Wells, L., Noel, M., & Madigan, S. (2024). Adverse childhood experiences and intimate partner violence: A meta-analysis. *Development and Psychopathology, 36*(2), 929–943.

Zlotnick, C., & Najavits, L. M. (2009). Randomized controlled pilot study of cognitive-behavioral therapy in a sample of incarcerated women with substance use disorder and PTSD. *Behavior Therapy, 40*(3), 325–336. https://pubmed.ncbi.nlm.nih.gov/19892078/

Zlotnick, C., Najavits, L. M., Rohsenow, D. J., & Johnson, D. M. (2003). A cognitive-behavioral treatment for incarcerated women with substance abuse disorder and posttraumatic stress disorder: Findings from a pilot study. *Journal of Substance Abuse Treatment, 25*(2), 99–105.

Zuo, X., Lou, C., Gao, E., Lyu, S., Guida, J., Hallman, K., & Li, S. (2021). Childhood adversity subtypes and violence victimization and perpetration among early adolescents in Shanghai, China. *PLoS One, 16*(9), e0256800.

About the Contributors

India Bryce is highly regarded Academic and Researcher with an international reputation in the field of trauma and cumulative adversity and trauma informed practice and her work traverses child protection, family law, criminal justice and education contexts. India is also Co- Director of Unique Minds Consultancy (UMC), a child and family social care service specialising in addressing cumulative adversity in underserved regional, rural and remote communities. India is an experienced forensic social worker, and Associate Professor at the University of Southern Queensland. India holds a Bachelor of Education, a Master of Guidance and Counselling, Master of Social Work (Forensic Studies), Master of Social Work (Qualifying) and a Doctor of Philosophy. She also holds Postgraduate qualifications in Community Services Practice (Client Assessment and Case Management; Statutory Child Protection) and is a Fellow of the Higher Education Academy. India is also appointed by the Federal Court and Family Court of Australia as Regulation 40 Family Consultant. India is also trained in advanced assessment frameworks including Attachment Style Interviews (ASI), Parenting Role Interviews (PRI) and Static-99R (Sex Offender Risk Assessment) and is trained in ICARE forensic interviewing, Parenting Coordination and Child Inclusive Mediation. India's 20-year career spans includes roles in education, school counselling, statutory child protection, emergency departments, non-government agencies and higher education. Her practice is informed by her experience across these diverse but interconnected systems and her firsthand experience working with survivors of childhood trauma, and cumulative adversity. At UMC, India specialises in the assessment of children and families for child protection and family law contexts, providing expert family and social reports, sexual offender risk assessments, parenting and attachment assessments and personal injury expert reports. India's research profile is extensive, with over 40 publications including high quality journal articles, book chapters and edited books in the field of child abuse, trauma and as it relates to welfare, crime, law, education, protection and intervention. India's current research explores cumulative adversity across the lifespan, trauma informed practice and pedagogy, and trauma narratives as they intersect with career, vocational behaviour, health and systemic marginalisation. India has co-edited several reference books; *Child Abuse and Neglect: Forensic Issues in Evidence, Impact and Management, Child Sexual Abuse: Forensic Issues in Evidence, Impact and Management*, as well as this publication with Dr Simone Collier. India has led national research in her role as Associate Professor at UniSQ, in partnership with the Australian Catholic University and Act for Kids, successfully developing and validating an evaluative tool to measure cumulative harm in children and young people. India is a clinical member of the Psychotherapy and Counselling Federation of Australia (PACFA), a Level 4 Member of Australian Counselling Association, a member of the Australian Association of Social Workers. India is an affiliate of the Society for the Advancement of Actuarial Risk Need Assessment (SAARNA), and serves on the steering committee for the Southwest Region Family Law Pathways Network. India is also a member of the Therapeutic Family Law Professionals Network, Parenting Coordination Australia, Child Protection Practitioners Assoc Queensland, Family Law Practitioners Association and Family Report Writers Network. She is deeply committed to evidence and research-based, trauma-informed practice and works to ensure children and their families are empowered and supported as they navigate challenging systems.

Simone Collier is a Co- Director of Unique Minds Consultancy and a highly regarded specialist in childhood trauma, family reunification and complex Behaviour Support. She brings a rare depth of expertise across education, child protection, mental health and the NDIS, with a career spanning frontline practice, statutory systems and senior leadership roles. Simone holds a Bachelor of Education (Special Education), a Master of Special Education, a Master in Child Play Therapy and a Doctor of Professional Studies. She also holds a Postgraduate Diploma in Alcohol and Other Drugs and Mental Health and is trained in advanced assessment frameworks including Attachment Style Interviews (ASI), Parenting Role Interviews (PRI), Step-by-Step Assessment, Static 99R (Sex -Offender Assessment) and ODARA (DV Recidivism Risk Assessment). She is an accredited Animal Assisted Therapist, a Play Therapist using Theraplay principles, and an assessor in cumulative harm and risk and a trained Parenting Co-ordinator. Simone's professional background includes extensive experience in statutory child protection, out-of-home care, residential care and complex family systems. She has worked as a Special Education teacher, Deputy Principal, Guidance Officer and in senior child protection leadership roles including Team Leader, Program Coordinator and Program Manager. Her practice is grounded in a deep understanding of neurodivergence, developmental trauma, FASD, prenatal alcohol exposure and the long-term impacts of cumulative harm. Simone is the developer of a specialist reunification framework for children involved in the child protection system, due for publication in 2026. Her work in this area has been selected for international presentation in Edinburgh, Scotland and Dublin, Ireland in 2026. She has also contributed to research in partnership with the University of Southern Queensland, trialling an evaluative tool to measure cumulative harm in children and young people. Simone has numerous publications, both books and research articles. In addition to her clinical and systems work, Simone is the author of *Jeremy's Changing Family*, a children's book amplifying the voice of a child growing up in a foster care family. She has also developed a specialist program supporting families experiencing child-to-adult violence, where parents are impacted by violence from their adolescent child. Simone is a member of the Psychotherapy and Counselling Federation of Australia (PACFA), a Registered Teacher in Queensland and an affiliate of the Society for the Advancement of Actuarial Risk Need Assessment (SAARNA). She is deeply committed to ethical, trauma-informed practice and works tirelessly to ensure children, young people and families are heard, supported and empowered to achieve safety, stability and improved quality of life.

***

Oscar Ivan Cortes-Perez is a (Forensic) Victimologist and tertiary education professor. He holds a degree in Psychology (Honorific Mention) from the Autonomous University of San Luis Potosí and a master's in Forensic Sciences and Victimology from the Autonomous University of Durango Campus Zacatecas (Mexico). He has carried out forensic victimological investigation in collaboration with the Specialized Prosecutor's Office for the Attention of Women, Family, and Sexual Crimes in San Luis Potosí in cases involving (Institutional) Child Sexual Abuse and Intimate Partner Violence (including Coercive Control and Coercive Reproduction), as well as cases of Stalking. Since 2017, he has been teaching at the Autonomous University of San Luis Potosí. Additionally, between 2023 and mid-2024, he was part of the Child and Adolescent Agenda of the Autonomous University of Yucatan (Mexico) and the Government of the State of Yucatán (Mexico) as an expert collaborator in the strategic line of work "Best Practices in Justice". He is the author of the collection "Forensic Victimology and Femi(ni)cide A Transdisciplinary Approach on Forensic Evidence and its Contexts" (Volume I & II) and "Ecologies of Violence: A Comparative Perspective in Contemporary Victimology and Criminology". His research areas of interest are those related to Gendered Violence (Feminicide), Developmental and Life-Course perspectives in Criminology and Victimology, Psychosocial Criminology, Narrative Victimology, Forensic Victimology, Context Analysis and Psychosocial Forensic Assessments, Psychosocial Harm and Trauma in victims, Victimological Theory, Repeat Victimization and Polyvictimization, Investigative and Forensic Interview, Social Justice for Victims, Critical Victimology and Epistemic Injustice, and the impact of symbolic reparations in contexts of massive/lethal violence. He is a current member of the Mexican Society of Criminology (SOMECRIM) and the World Society of Victimology (WSV).

Fann Jiang is a Lead Psychologist with the Singapore Prison Service (SPS), currently serving as Assistant Director (AD) of the Correctional Research Branch, where she leads on the team's evaluation portfolio. In her 12 years of service, Fann has been involved in a variety of correctional work which includes developing and evaluating Psychology-based Correctional Programmes for a range of offenders such as those who have committed violent, sexually violent, and drug abuse offences. In the last five years, Fann was leading the research team on studies that examined desistance in different incarcerated populations as well as studies that investigated family-related issues which are topics that she is passionate about as well. Fann holds a Masters of Forensic Psychology degree from University of York, United Kingdom.

Hannah Lewis holds a Bachelor of Criminology and Criminal Justice (Hons) from the University of New South Wales, and a Graduate Diploma of Criminal Intelligence from CSU's Australian Graduate School of Policing and Security. She is a current PhD student at Charles Sturt University. Her doctoral thesis is looking at the temporal aspects of serial homicide. Her research interests include serial homicide and serial killers.

Liangyu Lin is a Principal Psychologist with the Singapore Prison Service (SPS), currently serving as Senior Assistant Director (SAD) of the Correctional Research Branch, where she oversees the organisation's research activities. In her previous role as SAD of the Programme Design and Evaluation Branch, she was instrumental in developing Psychology-based Correctional Programmes and evaluating rehabilitation programmes, regimes and policies. With over 16 years of experience in correctional research and practice, April is a strong proponent of the scientist-practitioner model. She remains committed to enhancing service delivery for the offender population through evidence-based approaches. April holds a Master's degree in Applied Psychology from the Nanyang Technological University, Singapore. Her research interest encompasses positive psychology interventions, desistance from crime, substance addiction, and the neurocognitive functioning of offenders with drug abuse issues.

Camelia Liow is currently working as a Senior Correctional Rehabilitation Specialist at Singapore Prison Service, conducting counselling and Psychological Correctional Rehabilitation Programmes for both female and male offenders. Her past working experience was with families and children affected by family violence and abuse. She holds a Master degree in Social Work (Crisis and Trauma Studies) and a degree in Psychology. Her research interest focuses around trauma and the rehabilitation field. She co-authored a research article published in the Women & Criminal Justice Journal - An Exploration of Human and Social Capital Factors of Desistance for Female Offenders in Singapore. She also co-authored two books, 'A Woman's Journey Home' and 'When Love Hurts' (published by Straits Times Press).

Amber McKinley (BA LibStud., MCJ, PhD) is a Clinical and Forensic Victimologist. Her research spans critical areas such as victim vulnerabilities, human exploitation, interpersonal violence, sudden death and death rituals. In addition to her academic achievements, she collaborates with key agencies, including the Australian Border Force, Australian Defence Force, Australian Federal Police, state coroners, and law enforcement organisations. Her most recent research include under-representation of minorities in research, determinants and effects of gender-based violence, forms of hostility, and global homicide. Her dedication to addressing vulnerable people underscores her impact on both academic research and practical applications in criminal justice and victimology.

Katherine McLachlan (ORCID id: 0000-0001-7171-2089) is an Associate Professor and Teaching Program Director of Criminology at Flinders University. She has extensive experience working across criminal justice and social welfare agencies focused on child protection and child exploitation, youth justice, police intelligence, crime policy and research, victim support, and corrections. She is currently a member of the Parole Board of South Australia and has interviewed hundreds of people who have offended. She is an award-winning teacher and Senior Fellow, Advance HE, with a professional interest in victimology, trauma-informed practice, sentencing, and violence against women and children.

Ace Ong is a Senior Correctional Rehabilitation Specialist with the Singapore Prison Service (SPS), where they have played a pivotal role in rehabilitating and reintegrating justice-involved individuals. Ace has conducted assessments, developed intervention plans, and delivered psychology-based counselling programs for youth, drug, and sexual offenders. Ace holds an MSc with Distinction in Forensic Psychology and Mental Health from Coventry University and completed her BSocSci (Hons) in Psychology from the National University of Singapore. Ace's research interests lie in offender rehabilitation and cognitive processes among justice-involved individuals. Passionate about evidence-based rehabilitation, she contributes to the field through program development and frontline engagement with justice-involved populations.

Index

G

H

J

L

M

O

P

R

S

T

U

V

W

Y

www.ingramcontent.com/pod-product-compliance
Lightning Source LLC
LaVergne TN
LVHW080902300926
849162LV00003B/519